Travel Discount Coupon

This coupon entitles you to special discounts when you book your trip through the

TRAVEL NETWORK®
RESERVATION SERVICE

Hotels ♦ Airlines ♦ Car Rentals ♦ Cruises
All Your Travel Needs

Here's what you get: *

♦ A discount of $50 USD on a booking of $1,000** or more for two or more people!

♦ A discount of $25 USD on a booking of $500** or more for one person!

♦ Free membership for three years, and 1,000 free miles on enrollment in the unique Miles-to-Go™ frequent-traveler program. Earn one mile for every dollar spent through the program. Earn free hotel stays starting at 5,000 miles. Earn free roundtrip airline tickets starting at 25,000 miles.

♦ Personal help in planning your own, customized trip.

♦ Fast, confirmed reservations at any property recommended in this guide, subject to availability.***

♦ Special discounts on bookings in the U.S. and around the world.

♦ Low-cost visa and passport service.

♦ Reduced-rate cruise packages.

Visit our website at http://www.travnet.com/Frommer or call us globally at 201-567-8500, ext. 55. In the U.S., call toll-free at 1-888-940-5000, or fax 201-567-1838. In Canada, call toll-free at 1-800-883-9959, or fax 416-922-6053. In Asia, call 60-3-7191044, or fax 60-3-7185415.

* To qualify for these travel discounts, at least a portion of your trip must include destinations covered in this guide. No more than one coupon discount may be used in any 12-month period, for destinations covered in this guide. Cannot be combined with any other discount or p...

**These are U.S. dollars spent ...

***A $10 USD fee, plus fax and ... bookings at each hotel not ... must approve these fees in ...

Valid until December 31, 199...
Go™ program are available o...

D1512211

WHEREVER YOU TRAVEL, *H*ELP IS NEVER FAR AWAY.

From planning your trip to providing travel assistance along the way, American Express® Travel Service Offices are always there to help.

Barcelona

D1364463

American Express Travel Service
Paseo de Gracia 101
Barcelona
3/415-2371

Travel

http://www.americanexpress.com/travel

American Express Travel Service Offices are found in central locations throughout Spain.

Frommer's ®

1st Edition

Barcelona, Madrid & Seville

by Darwin Porter
& Danforth Prince

Macmillan • USA

ABOUT THE AUTHORS

North Carolina–born **Darwin Porter** and **Danforth Prince,** a native of Ohio, are the coauthors of several bestselling Frommer guides—notably to the Caribbean, England, France, Italy, and Germany. Porter, who worked in television advertising and was a former bureau chief for the *Miami Herald,* wrote the first-ever Frommer guide to Spain while still a student. Prince, who began his association with Porter in 1982, worked for the Paris bureau of the *New York Times.* Both of these writers know their destination well, and have made countless annual trips through the cities of Barcelona, Madrid, and Seville and through the countryside of Spain to share their discoveries with you.

MACMILLAN TRAVEL

A Simon & Schuster Macmillan Company
1633 Broadway
New York, NY 10019

Find us online at **http://www.mgr.com/travel** or
on America Online at Keyword: **Frommer's**.

ISBN 0-02-861159-4
ISSN 1090-5499

Editor: Kelly Regan
Production Editor: Carol Sheehan
Design by Michele Laseau
Page Creation by: Heather Pope, Candi McCreary, Tammy Ahrens, Stephanie Mohler, Michelle Croninger, David Faust, Trudy Coler, John Ley, Linda Quigley and Karen Teo.
Digital Cartography by Ortelius Design and Roberta Stockwell

SPECIAL SALES

Bulk purchases (10+ copies) of Frommer's and selected Macmillan travel guides are available to corporations, organizations, mail-order catalogs, institutions, and charities at special discounts, and can be customized to suit individual needs. For more information write to: Special Sales, Macmillan General Reference, 1633 Broadway, New York, NY 10019.

Manufactured in the United States of America

Contents

Appendix 280

Index 283

List of Maps

AN INVITATION TO THE READER

In researching this book, we discovered many wonderful places—hotels, restaurants, shops, and more. We're sure you'll find others. Please tell us about them, so we can share the information with your fellow travelers in upcoming editions. If you were disappointed with a recommendation, we'd love to know that, too. Please write to:

Darwin Porter/Danforth Prince
Frommer's Barcelona, Madrid & Seville, 1st Edition
Macmillan Travel
1633 Broadway
New York, NY 10019

AN ADDITIONAL NOTE

Please be advised that travel information is subject to change at any time—and this is especially true of prices. We therefore suggest that you write or call ahead for confirmation when making your travel plans. The authors, editors, and publisher cannot be held responsible for the experiences of readers while traveling. Your safety is important to us, however, so we encourage you to stay alert and be aware of your surroundings. Keep a close eye on cameras, purses, and wallets, all favorite targets of thieves and pickpockets.

WHAT THE SYMBOLS MEAN

✪ Frommer's Favorites

Hotels, restaurants, attractions, and entertainment you should not miss.

Ⓢ Super-Special Values

Hotels and restaurants that offer great value for your money.

The following abbreviations are used for credit cards:

AE	American Express	MC	MasterCard
DC	Diners Club	V	Visa

Previewing Barcelona, Madrid & Seville

1

Though these three cities are remarkably different in texture and attractions, each is evocative of the region it presides over: Barcelona, capital of Catalonia; Madrid, capital of Castile (and the entire country); and Seville, capital of Andalusia. To walk their streets, to sample their cuisine, to view the monuments, to taste and observe their daily life is reason enough to go to Spain. If you do miss the rest of the country, it would be a pity; but if you manage the cities covered in this guide you'll have found a window on the three different worlds that best exemplify Spain—Catalonia, Castile, and Andalusia.

Barcelona, progressive and industrial, is the most European of Spanish cities, yet also Mediterranean in both climate and atmosphere. Cataláns often speak of their "schizophrenia"—that is, a dichotomy caused between a desire to maintain what is traditional and to embrace what is new.

The palm trees lining the streets may seem languid, but there's dynamism in the air as Barcelona races to keep up with other major cities in Europe. There is commercial vigor—one-fourth of the country's goods are manufactured here—but post-Franco Barcelona is also a place to go to have fun and relax. Never before have there been so many good restaurants, hotels, nightclubs, and new attractions.

In the post-Olympics years, the city has undergone a virtual renaissance, sprucing up its buildings and improving its tourist facilities at a rate equaled by no other city in Spain, including Madrid.

Speaking of the capital city: once staid, almost seedy in its decay, Madrid has burst upon the European scene with enthusiasm for the modern world. It's now lively day and night. Madrid appears to be recovering from a long and dreary sleep and is determined to stay up every minute of the day or night not to miss out on anything.

It's true that the city doesn't match the great attractions and architectural piles of London, Paris, or Rome, but it does have the Prado and its stellar companion art galleries. It does offer a fascinating nightlife, great restaurants, and deluxe hotels, and is within striking distance of some of the country's best day trips, including Toledo, Segovia, El Escorial, and Ávila. Neither Barcelona nor Seville can be used as a base for such a diverse array of attractions.

Moving south, the temperature rises and the pace gets slower as we reach Seville, center of world attention during the 1992 Expo. It doesn't have the great art museums of Barcelona or Madrid, but it does possess a stunning cathedral, along with truly incomparable Moorish architecture. Orange and palm trees line its streets, and lovely vistas await at every turn. Chances are you won't be singing in the rain, as Seville is dry, dusty, and hot—in fact, the hottest city in Iberia.

Fabled for its Easter festivities when hooded and robed penitents march through the streets, Seville follows those events with its April Fair, a week of celebrations. *Sevillanos* ride on horseback looking like stage extras from *Carmen,* and the entire city celebrates with food, wine, and bullfights, followed by nightly flamenco dancing and their own special dance, the *Sevillano.* Almost any time of the year is ideal for a visit to Andalusia's capital, although we prefer the spring or fall. Its cathedral is among the finest in Spain. The Alcazar evokes memories of a great Moorish civilization. The Museo de Bellas Artes has one of the country's best art collections. But go to Seville to capture the sensory pleasures of Andalusia itself.

1 Frommer's Favorite Barcelona Experiences

- **A Walk Through the Barri Goòtic:** Follow in the footsteps of Dalí and Picasso and wander for hours in the Gothic Quarter. The neighborhood's twisted, maze-like layout is sure to get you lost—but that's part of the amusement. Whether it's truly Gothic is the subject of endless debate, but the La Ciutat Vella, or old city, is one of the most evocative sites in Spain. There's more here than a great cathedral; gurgling fountains, vintage stores, wall-to-wall cobblestones and old literary cafés like Els Quatre Gats make it all worthwhile. Get acquainted with the birthplace of Joan Miró, who was born in this *barrio.* Stop in at Sala Parés, Spain's oldest art gallery at Carrer Petritxol 5 (☎ 93/318-70-20)—it was one of the birthplaces of Catalán Modernism. See Chapter 4.

- **Watching the Sardana:** The national dance of Catalonia is performed at noon at the Plaça de San Jaume, in front of the cathedral. Nothing is more folkloric than this true street dance played out against the backdrop of a *cobla,* or brass band. The roots of this dance may have originated in one of the Greek islands and it was brought to Barcelona by sailors. It may even have come from Sardinia (hence the name). But regardless of its point of origin, the Sardana remains uniquely Catalán.

- **Strolling Along Les Rambles:** Les Rambles cuts through the heart of Barcelona'a oldest district beginning at the Plaça de Catalunya and running toward the sea. A tree-lined boulevard, it's the most famous street in Spain—and a lot more intriguing than Madrid's dull Gran Vía. The street is democratic, bringing together the buskers, the shopowners, the tourists, the newsstands, the drag queens, the drug dealers—mixed in with hotels, cafés, porno houses, and flower stalls. It's composed of five different Ramblas or Rambles (either term is correct). It's Spain's most charismatic street; late at night, the scene evokes the writings about Barcelona by Jean Genet.

- **Drinking Cava in a Xampanyería:** Enjoy a glass of bubbly, Barcelona style. Cataláns swear that their *cavas* taste better than French champagne. After the staid Franco years *xampanyerías* (champagne bars) literally burst onto the Barcelona nightlife scene; many stay open until the wee hours of the morning. You can select *brut* or *brut nature* (brut is slightly sweeter). Try any of these popular brands (they're also the best): Mestres, Parxet, Torello, Recaredo, Gramona, or Mont-Marçal. See Chapter 4.

- **Exploring the Museu Picasso:** Examine the evolution of a genius from the age of 14. Barcelona's most popular attraction—housed in three Gothic mansions—

spans Picasso's long, multifaceted career, taking in the blue period, cubism, and beyond. Of special interest are the paintings in the Barcelona section from the years 1895–97, when he lived in the Catalán capital. See works by Picasso-as-copyist (he re-created Velázquez's famous portrait of Philip IV) and admire the portraits, especially the one he painted of his aunt, *Retrato de la Tía Pepa* (Portrait of Aunt Pepa). In the *Caballo Corneado* (Gored Horse) charcoal drawing, you can see the beginnings of cubism. See Chapter 4.

- **Going Gaga over Gaudí:** No architect in Europe was as fantastical as Antoni Gaudí y Cornet. The city of Barcelona is studded with the Modernist architectural works of this extraordinary artist of building materials—in fact, UNESCO now lists all his creations among the World Trust Properties. No two buildings of this eccentric genius are alike—he conceived buildings as "visions." A recluse and a celibate bachelor, he lived out his own fantasy. Nothing is more stunning than his Templo Expiatorio de la Sagrada Familia, Barcelona's best known landmark, a cathedral on which Gaudí labored for the last 43 years of his life before he was run over by a tram in 1926. It was never completed. In Barcelona, the question is not "to be or not to be" but "to finish or not to finish." If it's ever finished, "The Sacred Family" will be Europe's largest cathedral. See Chapter 4.

- **A Night at the Bodega Bohemia:** This Barcelona institution, just off the Rambles, is a *cabaret extraordinaire.* A talent showcase for theatrical personalities of yesteryear, this bodega has been going strong since 1893. The performers are past their prime—indeed, many of the showgirls look old enough to have entertained troops in the Spanish-American war—but they've mastered the theatrical tricks of the trade and still know how to deliver a great show. The raucous audience is consistently filled with people who boo, catcall, cheer, and scream with laughter. At Bodega Bohemia, it's still a hot night in the old town. See Chapter 4.

- **Walking the Waterfront:** A major port of call for international cruise ships, Spain's largest port boasts a pedestrian promenade with benches, contemporary bridges, palm trees, and some of the city's finest (and priciest) restaurants. Begin at the Moll de la Fusta or "Wooden Wharf" where the Barri Gòtic meets the harbor. Continue along the beach of Barceloneta to the Port Vell, or Olympic port. This is the site of Platja Barcelona, a beach constructed for the 1992 Olympic games. If you're hungry, head for one of the several excellent restaurants at the yacht basin. Panoramic views of the sea unfold. Modest cafés serving Spanish *tapas* are also in the area. It's a great way to spend an afternoon or early evening. See the accompanying walking tour in Chapter 4.

2 Frommer's Favorite Madrid Experiences

- **An Afternoon at the Bullfights:** Based on origins as old as pagan Spain, the art of bullfighting is more closely associated with the Iberian temperament and passions than any other pastime. Detractors cite the sport as cruel, bloody, violent, hot, and savage. Aficionados view bullfighting as a microcosm of death, catharsis, and rebirth, and defend it as one of the most evocative and memorable events in Spain. Head for the *plaza de toros* (bullring) in Madrid. Amid feverish crowds, observe the ballet of the *bandilleros,* the thundering fury of the bull, the arrogance of the matador—all leading to "death in the afternoon."

- **Visiting the Prado:** It's one of the world's supreme art museums, ranking up there with the Louvre. The Prado is home to some 4,000 masterpieces, many of them acquired by Spanish kings. The wealth of Spanish art is staggering—everything from Goya's *Naked Maja* to the celebrated *Las Meninas* or "The Maids of Honor" by Velázquez (our favorite). Masterpiece after masterpiece unfolds before your eyes:

you can wander in Hieronymus Bosch's *The Garden of Earthly Delights,* or thrill to the horror of Goya's "Disasters of War" etchings. When the Spanish artistic soul gets too dark, escape to the Italian salons and view canvases by "the divine" Caravaggio, even Fra Angelico and Botticelli. It would take a lifetime to savor the Prado's wonders. See Chapter 6.

- **Feasting on Tapas in the Tascas:** It's reason enough to go to Madrid! Spanish tapas are so good that their once-secret recipes have been broadcast around the world—but they always taste better on home turf. The *tapeo* is the equivalent of the pub crawl in London—that is, going from one tapas bar to another. Each has a different specialty. Tapas bars (called *tascas*) are the quintessential Spanish experience, be it in Galicia, Andalusia, Catalonia, or Castile. Originally tapas consisted of cured ham or *chorizo* (spicy sausage). Today they're likely to include everything: *gambas* (deep-fried shrimp), anchovies marinated in vinegar, stuffed peppers, a cooling gazpacho, or hake salad. To go really native, try lamb sweetbreads or bull's testicles. These dazzling spreads will fortify you until the 10pm fashionable dining hour. The best streets for your tasca crawl include Ventura de la Vega, the area around Plaza de Santa Ana or Plaza de Santa Bárbara, Cava Baja, or Calle de Cuchilleros.

- **Lounging in an Outdoor Café:** In sultry summertime, Madrileños come alive on their *terrazas.* The drinking and good times can go on until dawn. In glamorous hangouts or on lowly street corners, the café scene takes place mainly along an axis shaped by the Paseo de la Castllana, Paseo del Prado, and Paseo de Recoletos. Wander up and down the boulevards and select a spot that appeals to you. For traditional atmosphere, the terrazas at Playa Mayor win out.

- **Shopping the Rastro:** Madrid's flea market represents a tradition that dates back 500 years. Savvy shoppers arrive before 7am every Sunday to beat the rush and claim the best merchandise. The teeming place doesn't really get going until about 9am, and then it's shoulder-to-shoulder stretching down Calle Riberia de Curtidores. Real or fake antiques, secondhand clothing, porno films, Franco-era furniture, paintings (endless copies of Velázquez), bullfight posters, old books, religious relics, and plenty of just plain junk, including motorcycles from World War II, are on sale. These streets also contain some of the finest permanent antiques shops in Madrid. But beware: Pickpockets are out in full force. More than a few mugging victims have later found their purses here for resale—thoroughly emptied, of course.

- **A Sunday Stroll in the Retiro:** Spread across 350 cool acres in sweltering Madrid, Retiro Park was originally designed as the gardens of Buen Retiro palace, occupied by Philip IV in the 1630s. In 1767 Charles III opened part of the gardens to the general public. Only after the collapse of Isabella II's monarchy in 1868 did the park become available for all Madrileños. Statues fill the park, including a towering 1902 monument to Alfonso XII which presides over the lake. Sunday morning before lunch is the best time for a stroll. Vendors hawk their wares, magicians perform their acts, and fortune tellers read tarot cards. You can even rent a boat and float on the lake. For sightseers, there are some 15,000 trees, a rose garden, and a few art galleries.

- **A Drink at Chicote:** The 1930s interior at Madrid's most famous bar looks the same as it did when Hemingway sat here drinking during the Civil War. Shells might have been flying along the Gran Vía but the international press corps covering the war drank on. After the war the crowd of regulars included such screen goddesses as Ava Gardner (always with a bullfighter or two in tow), as well as major writers and artists. By the late 1960s it had degenerated into a pickup bar frequented by prostitutes. But today it has regained the joie de vivre of yore and is one of the smart, sophisticated spots to rendezvous in Madrid. See Chapter 6.

- **Experiencing the Movida:** We can't tell you exactly how to go about this. Just go to Madrid—the *Movida* will seek you out. Meaning in very rough translation the "shift" or the "movement," *Movida* characterizes post-Franco life in Madrid, as Madrileños threw off the yoke of dictatorship and repression. In a larger context, the Movida is a cultural renaissance affecting all aspects of local life, encompassing a wide range of social projects and progressive causes. Movida is best experienced around midnight, when the town just starts to wake up; the action centers around hipper-than-thou places with names like Bar Cock. Madrileños hop from club to club as if they're afraid they'll miss out on something if they stay in one place too long. To truly catch a whiff of Movida, head for the lively nightlife areas of Chueca, Huertas, and Malasaña, and the big clubs around Calle Arenal. See Chapter 6.

3 Frommer's Favorite Seville Experiences

- **Listening to the Sound of Flamenco:** It's best heard in some old tavern, in a ghetto like the Barrio de Triana in Seville. But from the lowliest *taberna* to the poshest nightclub, you can hear the heel clicking, foot stamping, castanet rattling, hand clapping, and the sound of sultry guitar and tambourine—this is flamenco. Its origins lie deep in Asia, but the Spanish Gypsy has given it an original and unique style, a dance to dramatize inner conflict and pain. Performed by a great artist, flamenco can tear your heart out with its soulful and throaty singing.

- **Celebrating Semana Santa (Holy Week):** Since the 16th century, the city's processions and celebrations at Easter have been the biggest and most elaborate in Spain. Solemn evening processions take place each day of the week before Easter, organized by *codafrías,* or religious brotherhoods. Members of various codafrías dress as penitents in hoods, capes, and masks—a little spooky. Huge platforms, or *pasos,* are carried on their shoulders, and religious statues are paraded through the streets. But it's not all solemn; Sevillanos indulge in almost pagan celebrations of singing, eating, and drinking. With hardly enough time for a breather, Semana Santa segues into Feria de Abril, a 6-day festival of bullfights, street dancing, parades, fireworks, and flamenco performances.

- **Strolling Through Barrio Santa Cruz:** Wandering this area of whitewashed houses, winding streets, and artisans' shops is one of the scenic adventures of a trip to Seville. In the Middle Ages the *barrio* was the home of Seville's Jewish community. Enter at Calle de Mateus Gago, which intersects with the monumental realm of Plaza de la Virgen de los Reyes, and plunge right in. The neighborhood is filled with restaurants and tascas so you can take a break whenever you choose. Most historic figures of Seville have passed through this barrio, although few traces of its former Jewish heritage remain. All the former synagogues have been turned into churches, including Santa Maris la Blanca, with Murillo's *Last Supper.* Go during the day—the risk of mugging is high at night.

- **Discovering the Mysteries of Casa de Pilatos:** This palace for the marqués de Tarifa, completed in 1540, was partially modeled on the House of Pontius Pilate which the Marqués had visited in Jerusalem. It's a riot of Mudéjar design: textured wood ceilings, carved stucco filigree, brightly patterned tiles, a Plateresque portal, a central patio with Moorish arches and a Gothic balustrade, a bubbling fountain.

There's nothing quite like it in Seville. It's still the home of the duque de Medinaceli, who sequesters himself in a private wing when visitors come to call. See Chapter 8.

- **Climbing La Giralda:** All that remains of the former Almohad mosque is La Giralda, a 20-story bell tower which you can climb on a clear day to see olive groves in a 360° view around Seville. It was once the minaret of a great Moorish mosque; so intrigued were conquering Christians with its ingenious *sebka* rhomboid brick pattern that they spared the tower and incorporated it into the design of the cathedral they built on the site. The golden spheres, called "Apples of Yanmur," with which the Almohads crowned the tower in the 1100s are long gone. Today the 308-foot tower is crowned with a belfry, lantern, and a revolving statue dedicated to the Christian religion. It's quite a climb to the top, but the view once there and the experience of this remarkable monument are worth the effort. See Chapter 8.

- **Shopping Along Calle Sierpes:** A narrow pedestrian street in the heart of Seville, Calle Sierpes is lined with everything from chic boutiques to innumerable pricey fan shops. The bevy of sidewalk cafés are on hand if you want to take a break and watch the action. Back in Franco-era Spain, a popular saying of Sevillanos (male, of course) was: "The three finest pleasures a man can know are to be young, to be in Sevilla, and to stand in Sierpes at dusk when the girls are passing." The saying might still be true, though in today's Spain it could be said by ladies admiring the young men. Cervantes reputedly began work on *Don Quixote* in a royal prison that once stood on this street. All that's left is a plaque commemorating the poet.

- **A Visit to El Arenal and Triana:** El Arenal and Triana were Seville's 17th-century seafaring quarters, immortalized by such writers as Cervantes, Lope de Vega, and Quevedo. As the site of the 12-sided Torre del Oro, a "gold tower" constructed by the Almohads in 1220, El Arenal draws the most visitors. (The tower was once covered in gold tiles.) Stroll along Marqués de Contadero which stretches from the banks of the Guadalquivir River to the base of the Torre del Oro. From here you can take a tiled boardwalk to the Plaza de Toros, one of the most famous bullrings in Spain, home to the great school of *tauromaquia*. Seville's most important museum, the Museo Provincial de Bellas Artes, is also here, with a impressive collection of works by Seville painters, including Murillo. Across the river, Triana was once Seville's Gypsy quarter, home to potters and tilemakers. But gentrification has jacked up real-estate values. Head for Calle Betis, a terraced riverside promenade, and enjoy a panoramic view of the city skyline.

- **Attending the Opera in Seville:** Seville has been the setting for some of the world's best-loved operas—Bizet's *Carmen,* Donizetti's *La Favorita,* Beethoven's *Fidelio,* Verdi's *La Forza del Destino,* Mozart's *The Marriage of Figaro,* and Rossini's *The Barber of Seville.* Ironically, it wasn't until 1991 that Seville got its own opera house—the Teatro de la Maestranza at Núñez de Balboa, which quickly became one of the world's premier venues for operatic performances. Although you may hear *The Barber of Seville* performed everywhere from Milan to New York, it always sounds better in its hometown.

4 The Cities Today

BARCELONA

Hardworking Barcelona enjoys the most diversified and prosperous economy of any region in the country (it claims 6% of Spain's land mass, but produces 20% of its GNP). Among the roster of natives and long-time residents are Antoni Gaudí, Pablo

Picasso, Salvador Dalí, Joan Miró, and opera star Montserrat Caballé, whose work has helped redefine their respective art forms.

Unlike many cities that have struggled through post-Olympic slumps, Barcelona has reaped residual benefits from the games: a roster of impressive new hotels, top-notch sporting facilities now available for public use, and a glittering airport that funnels 18 million visitors into Catalonia and the rest of Spain every year.

In Barcelona the "new" is actually a return to the "old." Miles of grimy industrial waterfronts have been returned to clean and sandy beaches. Flower stalls, bird cages, and decorative pavements along Les Rambles have been rejuvenated, and a state-of-the-art transportation network carries visitors past discreetly restored Gothic and Romanesque buildings and city monuments that just might look better than when they were first erected 800 years ago. And unlike either of its landlocked competitors, Seville and Madrid, Barcelona can (and does) welcome a growing tourist phenomenon, the cruise-ship industry. And despite the city's burgeoning population, and its regrettable growth in both drug addiction and street crime, access to the city is easier than ever since the construction in the early 1990s of ring roads that have alleviated downtown traffic and lowered pollution.

In the last decades of the 20th century the defiant artistic hegemony of Barcelona has begrudgingly given way to the rise of Madrid as superstar of Spain's large cities. The change has exacerbated the traditional cultural and economic rivalry between the cities, and added a greater sense of passion to the football (soccer) games that lock all of Spain into an obsessional grip whenever a match between the country's two biggest cities is broadcast across Europe. But despite the success of Madrid at groping its way toward a redefinition of its allure in recent years, visitors who favor Barcelona prefer it with a passion deeper than simple nostalgia. Barcelona—grander, older, more poignant, and more evocative than brasher and more bureaucratic Madrid—says it best in its civic motto, *Barcelona Es Teva* (Barcelona Belongs to You).

If you decide you love Barcelona, you won't be alone in your perceptions. Nearly 40% of visitors to Spain go to Catalonia. The fact that about 90% of those visitors have trod on Catalonian soil at least twice before speaks well of the region's depth and allure, and of Barcelona's continuing to attract them.

MADRID

The city of Madrid lies landlocked on a windswept and often arid plain, beneath a sky that has been described as "Velázquez blue." Certain poets have even labeled Madrid the "gateway to the skies." It's populated by adopted sons and daughters from virtually every region of Spain, a demographic fact that adds to its cosmopolitan gloss. Despite its influence as the cultural beacon of the Spanish-speaking world and its quintessentially Spanish nature, the city lacks such all-important Iberian features as a beach, an ancient castle and cathedral, and an archbishop. To compensate for the lack of these amenities, the always-practical Madrileños long ago learned to substitute long strolls through the city's verdant parks and along its paseos. They built an airy and elegant palace (which the Spanish king and queen use mainly for ceremonial purposes) and erected countless churches, many glistening with baroque ornamentation and gilt. As for an archbishop, Madrileños are content with falling under the jurisdiction of the archbishop in nearby Toledo.

Known as a melting pot for individualists, which Spain seems to produce in profusion, Madrid is without question a world-class capital as it moves toward the millennium. Gone are the censorship, the fears, the armed guards, and the priggish morality of the years of Franco, whose influence often impelled Spain's artists, such as Picasso, to ply their crafts in neighboring countries.

Today, artists and writers gravitate to the newly revitalized Madrid, whose allures, freedoms, and promises of acclaim and fiscal recognition pull them into one of the most fertile artistic climates in the world. Whether or not you agree with its expression—artists and art movements, like discos, come and go—Madrid is alive, passionate, and richly able to spearhead the *Movida* ("action") of a newly liberated Spanish culture. The legendary propensity of Spaniards to celebrate their nightlife is observed with something approaching passion in Madrid, as Madrileños stay awake till the wee hours, perhaps congregating in the very early morning over hot chocolate and *churros* (fried fingerlike doughnuts). Standing at the same countertop with them might be representatives of the hundreds of businesspeople and bankers whose zeal and imagination have revitalized the business landscape, transforming hypermodern office towers into well-respected and often feared entrepreneurial forces. For despite Madrid's many pleasures, Madrileños recognize that their city is a place for work as well as for play, as evidenced by the spate of emerging industries, services, and products.

Its inhabitants are enormously proud of their well-endowed city. If you approach it with indulgence, affection, and a sense of humor, you'll be richly rewarded. The capital of the Spanish-speaking world and the object of travel fantasies for thousands of residents of Central and South America, Madrid is at the same time a monolithic big city and a tapestry of small villages that have developed individual identities throughout the various expansions of the capital. Each neighborhood offers countless subcultures that thrive within its precincts. The result is an almost inexhaustible supply of diversions and distractions, some potent enough to justify spending almost all your Spanish holiday in Madrid.

SEVILLE

Seville has more folktales and pithy phrases associated with it than virtually any other city in Spain, and to many visitors it encapsulates all the clichés anyone ever imagined about Iberia. Its sights are more colorful, its *ferias* more uninhibited and garish, its bejeweled wooden Virgins that are carried through the streets during Holy Week more surreal, its bullfights more emotional, and its equestrian grandeur more haughty and aristocratic than anywhere else in Spain.

If you persevere through the blistering heat (the Spaniards refer to it as "La Manzanilla de Espana"-the Frying Pan of Spain), the corrosive sense of poverty and petty crime, and the traffic generated by a city of 800,000 inhabitants, Seville will present wonders to you. Jean Cocteau referred to Seville, along with Venice and Beijing, as the world's most magical city. Composers such as Bizet and Mozart used it as the setting for *Carmen* and *Don Giovanni,* and few tourists can remain immune to the sweltering charms of its winning combinations of Moorish and Christian architecture, and its endless emphasis on palm trees and orange blossoms.

In the 14th century, shortly after the city was ripped away from its domination by the Moors, a Castilian folk saying entered the mainstream of Iberian usage, *"Qui non ha visto Sevilla non ha visto maravilla"* (He who hasn't seen Seville has missed something marvelous).

Set around a medieval Moorish core, a sweltering 70 miles inland from the sea, on the banks of the Guadalquivir, Seville is graced with an architecture whose style was fueled both by the zeal of the Catholic monarchs to strengthen their grip on Andalusia and by floods of gold pouring into its port from the New World.

Today its prominence as a seaport has declined immeasurably, thanks to the deeper drafts of oceangoing vessels, and the fact that the Guadalquivir contains more silt, and is a lot less mighty, than when the Castilians selected the city as the capital of

Catholic Andalusia. Dredging efforts have opened the river somewhat to barge traffic, although its volume will never be comparable to that of the burgeoning seaport of Barcelona or even its prime Andalusian competitor, Cádiz.

Seville has compensated in other ways, however. Few cities have reinvented themselves as aggressively as Seville during the 1990s. Although the city's distinctive traditions were retained with something approaching religious fervor, far-reaching changes were initiated as part of the 1992 Expo festival that celebrated the 500th anniversary of Columbus's departure from Seville for the colonization of the New World. Thanks partly to the fact that Spain's once-powerful prime minister, Felipe González Márquez, was born and reared in Seville, funds poured into the city for the development of the Expo site on an island in the Guadalquivir, Isla de La Cartuja. Seven new bridges were built across the Guadalquivir, and miles of riverfront esplanade, new rail and bus stations, renovated or rebuilt terminals at the local airport, refurbished museums, more than 20 new hotels, a new opera house (Teatro de la Maestranza), and a new convention center were all created in anticipation of the event.

The question on everyone's mind involves how gracefully Seville will fare now that the thrill of the Expo events has long ended and life has returned to a (much-improved) normal train of events.

Although the Movida that has transformed the ambience of Madrid is less intense in Seville than in the Spanish capital, there's a renewed sense of vigor to the syncopated clapping of the flamenco, the crowds milling around the city's legendary tapas bars, and the teenaged Carmen clones appearing during ferias in polka-dot dresses rattling their castanets. Crime—which takes on particularly annoying overtones because of the heat and the exhaust fumes—puts a damper on all aspects of tourism to the city. Despite those ills, Seville continues to arouse passion in its visitors, a pale reflection of the violence that drove the jealous protagonist of *Carmen* to plunge a knife into her heart.

5 A Look at the Past

ANCIENT TIMES   Ancestors of the Basques may have been the first settlers in Spain 10,000 to 30,000 years ago, followed, it is believed, by Iberians from North Africa. They, in turn, were followed by Celts, who crossed the Pyrenees around 600 B.C. These groups melded into a Celtic-Iberian people who inhabited central Spain.

Others coming to the Iberian Peninsula in ancient times were the Phoenicians, who took over coastal areas on the Atlantic beginning in the 11th century B.C. Cádiz, originally the Phoenician settlement of Gades, is perhaps the oldest town in Spain. The Greeks came roughly 500 years after the Phoenicians, lured by the peninsula's wealth of gold and silver. The Greeks established colonies before they were conquered by Carthaginians from North Africa.

Around 200 B.C. the Romans vanquished the Carthaginians and laid the foundations of the present Latin culture. Traces of Roman civilization

Dateline

- **11th c. B.C.** Phoenicians settle Spain's coasts.
- **650 B.C.** Greeks colonize the east.
- **600 B.C.** Celts cross the Pyrenees and settle in Spain.
- **6th–3rd c. B.C.** Carthaginians make Cartagena their colonial capital, driving out the Greeks.
- **2nd c. B.C.–A.D. 2nd c.** Rome controls most of Iberia. Christianity spreads.
- **218–201 B.C.** Second Punic War: Rome defeats Carthage.
- **5th c.** Vandals, then Visigoths, invade Spain.
- **8th c.** Moors conquer most of Spain.

continues

- **1214** More than half of Iberia is regained by Catholics.
- **1469** Ferdinand of Aragón marries Isabella of Castile.
- **1492** Catholic monarchs seize Granada, the last Moorish stronghold. Columbus lands in the New World.
- **1519** Cortés conquers Mexico. Charles I is crowned Holy Roman Emperor, as Charles V.
- **1556** Philip II inherits throne and launches the Counter-Reformation.
- **1588** England defeats Spanish Armada.
- **1700** Philip V becomes king. War of Spanish Succession follows.
- **1713** Treaty of Utrecht ends war. Spain's colonies reduced.
- **1759** Charles III ascends throne.
- **1808** Napoleon places brother Joseph on the Spanish throne.
- **1813** Wellington drives French out of Spain; the monarchy is restored.
- **1876** Spain becomes a constitutional monarchy.
- **1898** Spanish-American War leads to Spain's loss of Puerto Rico, Cuba, and the Philippines.
- **1923** Primo de Rivera forms military directorate.
- **1930** Right-wing dictatorship ends; Primo de Rivera exiled.
- **1931** King Alfonso XIII abdicates; Second Republic is born.
- **1933–35** Falange party formed.
- **1936–39** Civil War between the governing Popular Front and the Nationalists led by Franco.
- **1939** Franco establishes dictatorship, which will last 36 years.

continues

can still be seen today. By the time of Julius Caesar, Spain (Hispania) was under Roman law and began a long period of peace and prosperity.

BARBARIAN INVASIONS, THE MOORISH KINGDOM & THE RECONQUEST   When Rome fell in the 5th century, Spain was overrun, first by the Vandals and then by the Visigoths from eastern Europe. The chaotic rule of the Visigothic kings lasted about 300 years, but the barbarian invaders did adopt the language of their new country and tolerated Christianity as well.

In A.D. 711 Moorish warriors led by Tarik crossed over into Spain and conquered the disunited country. By 714 they controlled most of it, except for a few mountain regions around Asturias. For eight centuries the Moors occupied their new land, which they called *al-Andalus,* or Andalusia, with Córdoba as the capital. A great intellectual center, Córdoba became the scientific capital of Europe; notable advances were made in agriculture, industry, literature, philosophy, and medicine. The Jews were welcomed by the Moors, often serving as administrators, ambassadors, and financial officers. But the Moors quarreled with one another, and soon the few Christian strongholds in the north began to advance south.

The Reconquest, the name given to the Christian efforts to rid the peninsula of the Moors, slowly reduced the size of the Muslim holdings, with Catholic monarchies forming in northern areas. The three powerful kingdoms of Aragón, Castile, and León were joined in 1469, when Ferdinand of Aragón married Isabella of Castile. Catholic kings, as they were called, launched the final attack on the Moors and completed the Reconquest in 1492 by capturing Granada.

That same year Columbus, the Genoese sailor, landed on the West Indies, laying the foundations for a far-flung empire that brought wealth and power to Spain during the 16th and 17th centuries.

The Spanish Inquisition, begun under Ferdinand and Isabella, sought to eradicate all heresy and secure the primacy of Catholicism. Non-Catholics, Jews, and Moors were mercilessly persecuted, and many were driven out of the country.

THE GOLDEN AGE & LATER DECLINE
Columbus's voyage to America and the conquistadors' subsequent exploration of that land ushered Spain into its golden age.

In the first half of the 16th century, Balboa discovered the Pacific Ocean, Cortés seized Mexico for

Spain, Pizarro took Peru, and a Spanish ship (initially commanded by the Portuguese Magellan, who was killed during the voyage) circumnavigated the globe. The conquistadors took Catholicism to the New World and shipped cargoes of gold back to Spain. The Spanish Empire extended all the way to the Philippines. Charles V, grandson of Ferdinand and Isabella, was the most powerful prince in Europe—King of Spain and Naples, Holy Roman Emperor and lord of Germany, Duke of Burgundy and the Netherlands, and ruler of the New World territories.

But much of Spain's wealth and human resources was wasted in religious and secular conflicts. First Jews, then Muslims, and finally Moriscos (Catholicized Moors) were driven out—and with them much of the country's prosperity. When Philip II ascended the throne in 1556, Spain could indeed boast vast possessions: the New World colonies; Naples, Milan, Genoa, Sicily, and other portions of Italy; the Spanish Netherlands (modern Belgium and the Netherlands); and portions of Austria and Germany. But the seeds of decline had already been planted.

- **1941** Spain technically stays neutral in World War II, but Franco favors Germany.
- **1955** Spain joins the United Nations.
- **1969** Franco names Juan Carlos as his successor.
- **1975** Juan Carlos becomes king.
- **1978** New, democratic constitution initiates reforms.
- **1981** Coup attempt by right-wing officers fails.
- **1982** Socialists gain power after 43 years of right-wing rule.
- **1986** Spain joins the European Community (now the European Union).
- **1992** Barcelona hosts the Summer Olympics; Seville hosts Expo '92.
- **1996** A conservative party defeats Socialist party, ending 13-year rule. José Maria Aznar chosen prime minister.

Philip, a fanatic Catholic, devoted his energies to subduing the Protestant revolt in the Netherlands and to becoming the standard bearer for the Counter-Reformation. He tried to return England to Catholicism, first by marrying Mary I ("Bloody Mary") and later by wooing her half sister, Elizabeth I, who rebuffed him. When, in 1588, he resorted to sending the Armada, it was ignominiously defeated; and that defeat symbolized the decline of Spanish power.

In 1700 a Bourbon prince, Philip V, became king, and the country fell under the influence of France. Philip V's right to the throne was challenged by a Hapsburg archduke of Austria, thus giving rise to the War of the Spanish Succession. When it ended, Spain had lost Flanders, its Italian possessions, and Gibraltar (still held by the British today).

During the 18th century, Spain's direction changed with each sovereign. Charles III (1759–88) developed the country economically and culturally. Charles IV became embroiled in wars with France, and the weakness of the Spanish monarchy allowed Napoleon to place his brother Joseph Bonaparte on the throne in 1808.

THE 19TH & 20TH CENTURIES Although Britain and France had joined forces to restore the Spanish monarchy, the European conflicts encouraged Spanish colonists to rebel. Ultimately, this led the United States to free the Philippines, Puerto Rico, and Cuba from Spain in 1898.

In 1876 Spain became a constitutional monarchy. But labor unrest, disputes with the Catholic Church, and war in Morocco combined to create political chaos. Conditions eventually became so bad that the Cortés, or parliament, was dissolved in 1923, and Gen. Miguel Primo de Rivera formed a military directorate. Early in 1930 Primo de Rivera resigned, but unrest continued.

On April 14, 1931, a revolution occurred, a republic was proclaimed, and King Alfonso XIII and his family were forced to flee. Initially the liberal constitutionalists ruled, but soon they were pushed aside by the socialists and anarchists, who adopted a constitution separating church and state, secularizing education, and containing several other radical provisions (for example, agrarian reform and the expulsion of the Jesuits).

The extreme nature of these reforms fostered the growth of the conservative Falange party (*Falange española,* Spanish Phalanx), modeled after Italy's and Germany's fascist parties. By the 1936 elections, the country was divided equally between left and right, and political violence was common. On July 18, 1936, the army, supported by Mussolini and Hitler, tried to seize power, igniting the Spanish Civil War. Gen. Francisco Franco, coming from Morocco to Spain, led the Nationalist (rightist) forces in the two years of fighting that ravaged the country. Towns were bombed and many atrocities were committed. Early in 1939, Franco entered Barcelona and went on to Madrid; thousands of republicans were executed. Franco became chief of state, remaining so until his death in 1975.

Although Franco adopted a neutral position during World War II, his sympathies obviously lay with Germany and Italy, and Spain gave aid to the Axis powers as a nonbelligerent. This action intensified the diplomatic isolation into which the country was forced after the war's end—in fact, it was excluded from the United Nations until 1955.

Before his death, General Franco selected as his successor Juan Carlos de Borbón y Borbón, son of the pretender to the Spanish throne. After the 1977 elections, a new constitution was approved by the electorate and the king; it guaranteed human and civil rights, as well as free enterprise, and canceled the status of the Roman Catholic Church as the church of Spain. It also granted limited autonomy to several regions, including Catalonia and the Basque provinces, both of which, however, are still clamoring for complete autonomy.

In 1981 a group of right-wing military officers seized the Cortés and called upon Juan Carlos to establish a Francoist state. The king, however, refused, and the conspirators were arrested. The fledgling democracy overcame its first test. Its second major accomplishment—under the Socialist administration of Prime Minister Felipe González, the country's first leftist government since 1939—was to gain Spain's entry into the European Community (now Union) in 1986.

Further proof that the new Spain was now fully accepted by the international community came in 1992. In that *annus mirabilis,* as many Spaniards regarded it, Spain was designated by the EU as the Cultural Capital of Europe for the year; but more significant, the Summer Olympics were held successfully in Barcelona and a world's fair, Expo '92, was mounted in Seville, in Andalusia.

In March of 1996, more than 78% of Spain's 32 million registered voters cast ballots, ending the 13-year rule of the scandal-plagued Socialist party of Prime Minister Felipe González, even though he is credited with ushering Spain into the modern world. A conservative party with roots in the Franco dictatorship was swept into power, lead by José Maria Aznar, leader of the Popular party, who pledged to represent "all Spain." González, although congratulating the Popular party, took the

Impressions

I thought that I should never return to the country I love more than any other, except for my own.

—Ernest Hemingway

Three Spaniards, four opinions.

—Old Spanish Proverb

The Spectacle of Death

Many consider bullfighting cruel and shocking. But as Ernest Hemingway pointed out in Death in the Afternoon: "The bullfight is not a sport in the Anglo-Saxon sense of the word, that is, it is not an equal contest or an attempt at an equal contest between a bull and a man. Rather it is a tragedy: the death of the bull, which is played, more or less well, by the bull and the man involved and in which there is danger for the man but certain death for the bull." Hemingway, of course, was an aficionado.

When the symbolic drama of the bullfight is acted out, some think it reaches a higher plane. Some people argue that it is not a public exhibition of cruelty at all, but rather a highly skilled art requiring great qualities of survival, courage, showmanship, and gallantry.

Regardless of how you view it, this spectacle is an authentically Spanish experience and, as such, has much to reveal about the character of the land and its people. The season of the *corridas* (bullfights) lasts from early spring until around mid-October. Fights are held in a *plaza de toros* (bullring), ranging in location from the oldest ring in remote Ronda to the big-time Plaza de Toros in Madrid. Sunday is corrida day in most major Spanish cities, although Madrid and Barcelona may also have fights on Thursday.

Tickets fall into three classifications: *sol* (sun), the cheapest; *sombra* (shade), the most expensive; and *sol y sombra* (a mixture of sun and shade), the medium-price range.

The corrida begins with a parade. For many viewers, this may be the high point of the afternoon's festivities, as all the bullfighters are clad in their *trajes de luce,* or "suits of light."

Bullfights are divided into *tercios* (thirds). The first is the tercio de *capa* (cape), during which the matador tests the bull with various passes and gets acquainted with him. The second portion, the tercio de *varas* (sticks), begins with the lance-carrying picadores on horseback, who weaken, or "punish," the bull by jabbing him in the shoulder area. The horses are sometimes gored, even though they wear protective padding, or the horse and rider may be tossed into the air by the now-infuriated bull. The picadores are followed by the banderilleros, whose job it is to puncture the bull with pairs of boldly colored darts.

In the final tercio de muleta the action narrows down to the lone fighter and the bull. Gone are the fancy capes. Instead, the matador uses a small red cloth known as a *muleta,* which, to be effective, requires a bull with lowered head. (The picadores and banderilleros have worked to achieve this.) Using the muleta as a lure, the matador wraps the bull around himself in various passes, the most dangerous of which is the natural; here, the matador holds the muleta in his left hand, the sword in his right. Right-hand passes pose less of a threat, since the sword can be used to spread out the muleta, making a larger target for the bull. After a number of passes, the time comes for the kill, the "moment of truth." A truly skilled fighter may dispatch the bull in one thrust.

After the bull dies, the highest official at the ring may award the matador an ear from the dead bull, or perhaps both ears, or ears and tail. For a truly extraordinary performance, the hoof is sometimes added. The bullfighter may be carried away as a hero, or if he has displeased the crowd, he may be chased out of the ring by an angry mob. At a major fight, usually six bulls are killed by three matadors in one afternoon.

defeat bitterly, alleging that the vote "was a step back to the fascist dictatorship of Franco."

6 Architecture 101

FROM THE ROMANS TO THE MOORISH INVASION The roots of architecture in Spain began with the Romans, who built aqueducts and more than 12,000 miles of roads and bridges as a means of linking their assorted Iberian holdings. The greatest of these, the Via Augusta, followed the Costa Brava, Costa Blanca, and Costa del Sol to carry armies and supplies between Cádiz and the Pyrenees.

This Hispano-Roman style involves prolific use of the vault and the arch—obvious in such marvels as the aqueduct at Segovia, the triumphal arch at Tarragona, and the rectilinear, carefully planned community at Mérida (whose Roman monuments are among the best preserved in Europe).

Historians mark A.D. 409 as the end of the Roman age in Iberia, the beginning of political anarchy, and the migration into Spain of thousands of immigrants (Vandals, Alans, Suevians, and Visigothic tribespeople) from central Europe. The newcomers, recent converts to some kind of Christianity, built crude chapels and fortresses based on a mishmash of aesthetic ideals from northern Europe and Byzantium, using engineering principles copied from the ancient Romans.

Spain's Romanesque style began to develop around A.D. 800 from the legacy of these crude Visigothic buildings (see below). Meanwhile, a major new aesthetic was forcibly imposed upon Spain from the south.

HISPANO-MOORISH ARCHITECTURE (711–1492) The Moors gained control of the Iberian Peninsula in the 8th century, and their 600-year rule left an architectural legacy that is among the most exotic and colorful in Europe. Regrettably, only a handful of *alcazars* (palaces), *alcazabas* (fortresses), and converted mosques remain intact today. Moorish buildings tended to be relatively flimsy and heavily accented with decorations. Many have collapsed (or were deliberately destroyed) in the Catholic zeal to "re-Christianize" Iberia.

The most visible traits of the Saracenic style included the use of forests of (sometimes mismatched) columns within mosques, each of which was used to support a network of horseshoe-shaped arches. These interconnected to support low, flat roofs. Some arches were scalloped, then decorated with geometric designs or calligraphic inscriptions from the Koran.

MOZARABIC ARCHITECTURE Mozárabes were Christian Spaniards who retained their religion under the Muslim rule. They successfully blended Gothic and Moorish styles in their art and architecture. The few structures that remain intact from this period can be found in Toledo and include the Monastery of El Cristo de la Luz, originally built in the 900s as a mosque; a 12th-century synagogue, now the church of Santa María de la Blanca; and the churches of Santiago del Arrabal and San Román. A secular example of the style in Toledo is the Puerto del Sol, an ornate gate built into the walls that surround the old city. Constructed around 1200, about 150 years after Toledo's reconquest by Christian forces, it combines the distinctive Moorish horseshoe arch with feudal battlements and Christian iconography.

MUDÉJAR ARCHITECTURE Equivalent in some ways to the above-mentioned Mozárabe style (with which it is frequently confused), Mudéjar refers to the architectural and decorative style developed by Spanish Muslims living in Christian territories after the Réconquista. A mix of Gothic and Moorish influences, it reached its peak between 1275 and 1350, made frequent use of brick instead of stone, and specialized in elaborate woodcarvings that merged the Moorish emphasis on geometrics and symmetry with Christian themes. Regrettably, after the final Moorish stronghold fell to the Christians in 1492, Spanish monarchs did everything they could to purge any artistic legacy left by the Moors. Mudéjar influences, however, still cropped up in rural pockets of Spain until the middle of the 18th century, and, in some cases, even merged subtly with ornate features of the baroque.

PRE-ROMANESQUE & ROMANESQUE ARCHITECTURE (700–1290)   Ensconced in Asturias, feudal rulers of the Christian Visigothic tribes refined their architectural tastes. Stonework became better crafted than the crude models of the previous two centuries, and arches became more graceful. Under the rule of Alfonso the Chaste (791–842), dozens of pre-Romanesque churches were built in Oviedo, and a body believed to be that of Saint James was "discovered" in a field in Galicia. Thus was born Santiago de Compostela ("St. James of the Field"), the eventual site of a great cathedral and one of the most famous pilgrimage sites in the Christian world.

From these beginnings, and based on money and cultural influences from the floods of pilgrims pouring in from Italy, France, and other parts of Europe, a trail of Romanesque churches, shelters, monasteries, and convents sprang up across northern Spain, especially in Catalonia, Aragón, and northern Castile. The style is known for semicircular arches, small windows, crude but evocative carvings, and thick walls. It is best represented in the church of San Gil in Zaragoza and the cloisters of San Pedro, near Pamplona in the town of Estella.

SPANISH GOTHIC   This style surged across provinces adjacent to the French border (Catalonia and Navarre) beginning around 1250. By the late 1200s, churches that had been initiated in the Romanesque style (such as the cathedral at Burgos) were completed as sometimes flamboyant Gothic monuments. During the 1300s and 1400s, bishops in León, Toledo, and Burgos even imported architects and masons from Gothic strongholds in other parts of Europe to design their cathedrals. In Spain, the Gothic style included widespread use of the *ogive* (high-pointed) arches and vaults, clustered pilasters, an opening up of walls to incorporate large, usually stained-glass, windows.

THE RENAISSANCE   After the expulsion of the Moors from Iberia, and Columbus's first landings in the New World in 1492, Spain found itself caught up in a vivid, emphatic sense of its own manifest destiny. Searching for a national style of architecture, the Spanish monarchs adapted the aesthetic trends of Renaissance Italy into a "Hispanicized" style. Foremost among these was the 16th-century plateresque, which emulated in stone the finely worked forms that a silversmith might have hammered into silver plate. The style is best viewed in the exterior of the University of Salamanca and the Chapel of the New Kings inside the cathedral at Toledo.

CLASSICAL SPANISH ARCHITECTURE   The austere regime of Philip II welcomed (and demanded) a less ornate national style from the country's architects. Fervently religious and obsessively ambitious for the advancement of Spanish interests, he embraced the austere ancient Roman forms that had been revived during Italy's late Renaissance. The style's most megalomaniacal manifestation within Spain came with Juan de Herrera's gargantuan, brooding, and military-looking monastery and palace at El Escorial (1563–84) on an isolated and windswept plateau outside Madrid. Philip II considered the style an appropriate manifestation of the stern principles of the Counter-Reformation and the new Inquisition that followed.

Later during the Renaissance, Herrera's rectilinear gridirons were replaced with the curved lines of the baroque. This style was avidly embraced by the Jesuits, one of the most powerful religious orders in Spain at the time, whose austere religious bent stood in marked contrast to their flamboyant architectural tastes. The baroque style appears at its most ornate in Andalusia, a region enjoying a building boom at the time thanks to the wealth that poured into its ports from the gold mines of Mexico and Peru.

Ironically, baroque was the style most enthusiastically embraced by the Spanish colonies in South America. Spain's interpretation of Italian baroque architecture is sometimes referred to as Churrigueresque, after José Churriguera (1665–1725), designer to the kings of Spain and architect of Salamanca's New Cathedral. The style is characterized by its dense concentrations of busy ornamentation that often completely disguised the basic form of the building itself. An example of baroque style in Spain is the wedding-cake facade of the cathedral at Murcia.

FROM BAROQUE TOWARD MODERN   Under the Spanish Bourbon rulers of the 18th century, the favored style embraced the baroque and neoclassical influences of aristocratic France. El Pardo, Riofrio, and Aranjuez were all built as Europeanized hideaways. Even the design of the Royal Palace in Madrid was modeled after Versailles.

In the 19th century the Romantic age encouraged a revolt against the ideals of balance and reason that had defined upscale European architecture during the late 1700s. Spanish architecture throughout the 19th century was torn between the value of the individual architect's eclectic, personalized, and sometimes flamboyant vision, and the inevitable reactions that swung the pendulums of public taste back toward greater restraint and symmetry. There developed a new respect for the Gothic, as many 500-year-old Gothic cathedrals were adapted or altered with neo-Gothic alterations that modern art historians sometimes view with horror.

Out of this tension emerged one of Spain's most widely recognized architectural giants, Antonio Gaudí (1852–1926). His idiosyncratic, organic style coincided neatly with the most intense building boom ever experienced within his hometown of Barcelona. His curiously curved and sinuous buildings are genius-quality precursors of 20th-century modernism. One of the best examples of his ideas can be seen in Barcelona's Casa Milá.

ARCHITECTURE TODAY   Other than occasional models of genuine inspiration, such as the whimsical and surrealist buildings devised by Salvador Dalí, much of modern Spain's architecture is derived from the older, tried-and-true sources that span the country's distinguished range of architectural traditions. When it comes to recycling the feudal or Renaissance monuments of yesteryear, Spain has no equal, as evidenced by the country's network of historic paradors. Regrettably, some areas of modern Spain, including many neighborhoods of Madrid and long stretches of the Costa del Sol, have bristled with high-rise, concrete-and-glass apartment houses. Few boast any distinguishing features, provoking laments from traditionalists.

7 Art 101

EARLY ROOTS   Spain's art has always been characterized by a curious mixture of passion and austerity that makes it one of the most unusual and riveting contributions from Europe.

Some of the best examples of prehistoric art were discovered in Spanish caves, including the hunting scenes within the caves of Altamira and Puente Viesgo, and the mysterious dolmens that stand like Celtic sentinels at Antequera, near Málaga. Equivalent dolmens (known locally as *talayots* and *navetas*) were erected on the Balearics between around 2500 and 1000 B.C.

By 1000 B.C. Spain became a crossroads of civilizations, a role it would play for the next 3,000 years. Many of the most prized artifacts in Spanish museums date from this era; the statue *The Lady of Elche,* the lions of Córdoba, and the bulls (*toros*) of Guisando all reflect the influence of ancient Greeks and Phoenicians, who used Spain's coast as a port of call on their trade routes. In such port cities as Cádiz, for example, rows of Phoenician sarcophagi have been unearthed.

ANCIENT & EARLY MEDIEVAL SPAIN   The Romans, who took an uncharacteristically long 200 years to subdue the natives of Iberia, were noted more for their architectural legacy (see "Architecture 101," above) than for their paintings and sculpture. Their buildings incorporated elaborate mosaics that depicted heroic or mythic themes, often entwined with leaves, flowers, vines, and symbols of the natural world, which later Visigothic and Romanesque artists adapted for their own use.

HISPANO-MOORISH ART   Beginning in A.D. 711, when the first Moorish armies poured into Andalusia, the preconceptions of Spanish art changed forever. Forbidden by religious law to portray human or animal forms, Muslim artists restricted themselves to geometric patterns, ornate depictions of plant life, and calligraphic renderings of verses from the Koran. Their works influenced the Mozárabes, who brought these themes within a Christian context. The Moors also excelled at landscape architecture—the symmetrical placement of fountains, plants, and statues in some of the greatest gardens and pleasure pavilions ever built (see "Architecture 101," above).

ROMANESQUE ART   Other than its architecture, the greatest artistic legacy of the Romanesque age, which began around A.D. 1000, was its sculpture. A vast number of churches and abbeys sprang up along the medieval world's most famous pilgrimage route (St. James's way across Asturias and Galicia), and each house of worship required sculpture to adorn the columns and altars. San Juan de la Peña was a master of the carved form, and his students branched out across the pilgrimage route, carving crude but symbolic references to apocryphal tales.

In Catalonia, aggressive merchants appropriated aesthetic ideals from Italy and France and had paintings executed on fresh plaster. Several of the most memorable of these Romanesque frescoes that remain today are credited to a mysterious painter, the Master of Tahull, who may have trained as far away as Byzantium. By 1300, Catalonia had been home to more than 1,000 artists, many of whom were inspired by this mysterious master.

GOTHIC ART   Beginning around 1250, as the Gothic aesthetic trickled from France into Spain, the production of painting and sculpture accelerated. Works followed religious themes, often rendered in the form of polychrome triptychs and altarpieces that stretched toward the soaring heights of a cathedral's ceiling. Many painters took their inspiration from such contemporary pre-Renaissance Italians as Giotto; others looked to France and Flanders, and the attention their painters paid to naturalistic, and sometimes stylized, detail. Eventually, the slumbering figures atop funerary sarcophagi came to resemble, in sometimes ghoulish detail, the living body of the person buried within, and decorative adornments became almost obsessive.

RENAISSANCE, BAROQUE & BEYOND   The defeat of the Muslims in 1492, and the colonialization the same year of the New World, marked the debut of the Renaissance in Spain. Choir stalls, altarpieces, funerary sarcophagi, and historical statues became commonplace throughout the newly united Spain. The popularity of gilding was a direct result of the precious metals flooding into the country from the mines of the New World. The cathedrals of Burgos and Barcelona and some of the chapels within the cathedral at Granada are fine examples of the heights to which Renaissance sculpture rose. A new technique, *estofado,* was introduced, whereby multiple colors were applied over a base of gold leaf, then rubbed or scratched to expose subtly gilded highlights in a way that prefigured the eventual rise of the baroque.

The greatest Spanish painter of the Renaissance was El Greco (Domenico Theotocopoulos, born in Crete in 1541), whose interpretation of Iberian mysticism reached deeper into the Spanish soul than any painter before or since. He was well versed in classical references and trained in all the methods popular in both Italy (especially Venice) and Byzantium. His was an intensely personal vision—amplified emotion, elongated limbs, and characters that were lifted bodily, and ecstatically, toward heaven. His style, known today as mannerism, met with violent criticism and lawsuits from disgruntled patrons.

After El Greco, the leading Spanish painter was Diego de Silva y Velázquez (1599–1660). Appointed court painter to the vain and self-indulgent monarch Philip IV, he painted 40 portraits of Philip, and dozens of other members of the royal family. Influenced by Rubens, who urged him to travel to Italy, his craftsmanship improved to the point where he has been hailed as the single greatest painter in the lexicon of Spanish art. Other important painters of this baroque period included José Ribera (1591–1652) and Francisco de Zurbarán (1598–1664). Bartolomé Murillo (1617–82) produced religious paintings that appealed, 200 years after his death, to the sentimentalism of the English Victorians.

The mantle of greatness was next passed to Francisco de Goya y Lucientes (1746–1828), an artist whose skill as a draftsman produced everything from tapestries to portraits of noble ladies. Rendered deaf in 1792 after a serious illness, Goya adopted a style of dark and brooding realism that many critics view as at least a century ahead of his contemporaries. In his work are vivid precursors of such future trends as romanticism and the psychological intricacies of expressionism. Victim of the political incompetencies of the Spanish regime, he was forced to flee in 1824 to Bordeaux, where he died, dejected, embittered, and broken.

MODERNISM & SURREALISM   Around the turn of the 20th century, artists of note were so frustrated by the official repression of the Spanish establishment, that they emigrated, almost en masse to Paris. Such outstanding innovators as Joan Miró, Salvador Dalí, and Juan Gris were among this group, whose names later became as closely associated with France as with Spain.

The most influential of these expatriates was Pablo Picasso, born in Málaga in 1881. Before the end of his extraordinary career, he would become the most famous artist of the 20th century, mastering a variety of styles and in defining such major schools of art as cubism.

A divergent school, surrealism, was developed by Catalonia-born Dalí. His sometimes authentic, sometimes fraudulent commercial endeavors explored the subconscious levels of the human mind, using dream sequences whose content might have appealed to Jung and Freud.

Among the important Spanish abstract painters are Antoni Tàpies, a pioneer in the use of texture and geometric placement of shapes and forms, and Juan José Tharrats. Major sculptors include Jorge Otieza, Eduardo Chillida (whose abstract works bear almost no resemblance to the human form), and Andréu Alfaro, whose works hang in influential galleries in such cities as Barcelona and Madrid.

8   The Cuisine: From Tapas to Paella & Sangría

Barcelona, Madrid, and to a much lesser extent, Seville manage to incorporate inside their borders a gastronomic sampling of each of the country's best-loved dishes. The cities' highly varied cuisines seems to hold one thing in common: The portions are immense. Regrettably, prices in the 1990s have skyrocketed, and dining out in such cities as Barcelona and Madrid, and to some extent Seville, is like dining out in Paris or London. Whenever possible, try to sample some of Spain's regional specialties, abundantly offered at restaurants throughout the city. Many of these, such as Andalusian gazpacho and Valencian paella, have transcended their region and are now considered great dishes of the world.

MEALS   Breakfast   In Spain, the day starts with a continental breakfast of hot coffee, hot chocolate, or tea, with assorted rolls, butter, and jam. A typical Spanish breakfast often includes *churros* (fried fingerlike doughnuts) and a hot chocolate that's very sweet and thick. The coffee is usually strong and black, served with hot milk. Some people consider it too strong and bitter for their tastes and therefore ask for instant coffee instead.

Lunch   An important meal in Spain, lunch here is comparable to the farm-style noonday "dinner" in America. It usually includes three or four courses, beginning with a choice of soup or several dishes of hors d'oeuvres called *entremeses.* Often a fish or egg dish is served after this, then a meat course with vegetables. Wine is always on the table. Dessert usually consists of pastry, custard, or assorted fruit; this is followed by coffee. Lunch is served from 1 to 3:30pm, with "rush hour" at 2pm.

Tapas   After an early-evening promenade, many Spaniards head for their favorite *tascas,* or bars, where they drink wine and sample assorted *tapas* such as bits of fish, eggs in mayonnaise, or olives.

Dinner   Another extravaganza. A typical meal starts with a bowl of soup, followed by a second course, often a fish dish, and by another main course, usually veal, beef, or pork, which is accompanied by vegetables. Again, desserts tend to be fruit, custard, or pastries.

Wine is always available. Afterward, you might have a demitasse and a fragrant Spanish brandy. The chic dining hour, even in one-donkey towns, is 10 or 10:30pm. In Madrid's popular tourist districts, as well as in hardworking Barcelona, you can usually dine by 8pm. In most middle-class establishments, people dine no later than 9:30pm. Your choice. Dining is usually later in the south—perhaps 10pm in Seville.

THE CUISINE   Soups & Appetizers   Soups are usually served in big bowls. Cream soups, such as asparagus and potato, can be fine; sadly, however, they are too often made from powdered ingredients in foil packets from such companies as Knorr and Liebig. The chilled gazpacho, on the other hand, is tasty and usually made fresh. Served year round, it's particularly refreshing during the hot months. The combination of ingredients is pleasant: olive oil, garlic, ground cucumbers, and raw tomatoes with a sprinkling of croutons. Madrid and Barcelona also offer a sampling of the many varieties of fish soup (*sopa de pescado*) that seem to derive from each of Spain's many provinces, and many of these are superb.

In top restaurants in all three cities, as many as 15 tempting hors d'oeuvres might be offered, often among the best of their kind anywhere. In lesser-known places, including restaurants without an active turnover of clients or inventories, avoid these *entremeses,* which often consist of last year's sardines and shards of sausage left over from the Moorish conquest.

Eggs   These are served in countless ways. A Spanish omelet, *tortilla española,* is made with potatoes. A simple omelet is called a *tortilla francesa.* A *tortilla portuguesa* is similar to the American version of a Spanish omelet.

Fish   Restaurants in both Madrid and Barcelona seek out the raw ingredients and the regional recipes for some of the finest fish dishes in Spain. One of the most common varieties is hake (*merluza*), sweet and white. *Langosta,* a variety of small-clawed lobster, is seen everywhere, particularly on ice or in refrigerated display cases. Although it's a treat, it's also terribly expensive. The Portuguese in particular, but some Spaniards, too, go into raptures at the mention of barnacles (*percebes*). Gourmets relish their seawater taste; others find them tasteless. *Rape* is the Spanish name for monkfish, a sweet, wide-boned ocean fish with a scalloplike texture. Also try a few dozen half-inch baby eels. They rely heavily on olive oil and garlic for their flavor, but they're great tasting. Squid cooked in its own ink is suggested only to those who want to go native. The cities' frequent offerings of charcoal-broiled sardines, a particular treat in the Basque provinces but occasionally available in Madrid or Barcelona, however, are a culinary delight. Trout Navarre is one of Spain's most popular fish dishes, carefully deboned and usually stuffed with bacon or ham.

Paella   You can't go to Spain without sampling what might be the most famous dish to ever emerge from the country. Originally a specialty of the seacoast city of Valencia and now considered the property of Spaniards around the world, it's an aromatic rice-and-saffron dish usually topped with shellfish, chicken, sausage, peppers, and local spices. Served authentically, it comes steaming hot from the kitchen in a metal pan called a *paellera.* (Incidentally, what's known in America as Spanish rice isn't Spanish at all. If you ask an English-speaking waiter for your Spanish rice, he'll probably serve you paella.)

Meats   Don't expect Kansas City steak, but do try the spit-roasted suckling pig, so sweet and tender it can often be cut with a fork. The veal is also good, and the Spanish *lomo de cerdo* (loin of pork) is unmatched anywhere. As for chicken, it will sometimes qualify for the Olympics because it's stringy and muscular. Spit-roasted chicken, however, can often be flavorful.

Vegetables & Salads   Such treats as vine-ripened tomatoes—available in summer—are excellent, but in winter some of the cheaper restaurants often serve canned vegetables instead of fresh. String beans, peas, and artichokes are among the most popular vegetables in Spain, and potatoes are a staple. Salads in the 1990s have more variety in choice of lettuce and appear more frequently on menus than in days of yore.

Desserts   The Spanish don't emphasize dessert. Flan, a home-cooked egg custard, appears on all menus—sometimes with a burnt-caramel sauce. Ice cream appears on nearly all menus as well. The best bet is to ask for a basket of fresh fruit, which you can wash at your table in the bowl of water that's usually provided. Homemade pastries are usually moist and not too sweet. As a dining oddity, many restaurants serve fresh orange juice for dessert. Madrileños love it!

Olive Oil & Garlic   Olive oil is used lavishly throughout Spain. Despite its well-documented health effects, you may not want it in all dishes. If, for example, you prefer your fish fried in butter, the word for butter is *mantequilla* (in some instances you'll be charged extra for the butter). Garlic is also an integral part of the Spanish diet, and even if you love it, you may find the Spaniard loves it more than you do and uses it in the oddest dishes.

BEVERAGES   Water   Tap water is usually considered safe to drink in Barcelona, Madrid, and Seville. Despite that, many frequent travelers opt to drink bottled

From Vineyards to the Bodegas

Wines were first cultivated in Spain more than 2,000 years ago by the ancient Greeks and Romans, and during the early years of the Christian church great emphasis was placed on the export from Spain of wines used both during the orgies of the latter days of the Roman Empire and during the celebration of Catholic communion.

Some of the country's vintages have been acknowledged as superb since the turn of the century, when vinters from Bordeaux, fleeing the phyloxxera epidemic that had devastated many of the vineyards of France, carried their expertise to such regions as La Rioja, Navarre, and Catalonia. Beginning about a century earlier, others, most notably the vintners of such Andalusian regions as Jerez, grew rich on exporting sherries to the dinner tables of faraway Britain.

Today Spain devotes more acreage to the cultivation of wine grapes than any other nation in the world, but regrettably, because of trade restrictions and economic stagnation during the Franco years, the output of many of those acres was not considered the equivalent of wines from the best of such competing regions as France, Italy, Chile, and California. Consequently, modern connoisseurs, when faced with a Spanish wine list, tend to focus rather narrowly on the wines of Jerez, La Rioja, and the Penedés region of Catalonia.

Thanks to some of the most aggressive and enlightened marketing in Europe, however, all that is changing. Beginning in the 1990s, based partly on subsidies and incentives from the European Union, Spanish vintners scrapped most of the country's obsolete winemaking equipment, hired new talent, and poured time and money into the improvement and promotion of wines derived even from high-altitude and arid regions that were never previously suitable for the drink's production. Thanks to irrigation, improved varieties of grape, technological developments, and the expenditure of billions of pesetas, bodegas and vineyards are sprouting up throughout the country, opening their doors to visitors interested in how the stuff is grown, fermented, and bottled. These same wines are now earning awards at wine competitions around the world for their quality and bouquet.

Interested in impressing a new-found Spanish friend over a wine list? Consider bypassing the usual array of Riojas, sherries, and sparkling Catalonian *cavas* in favor of, say, a Galician white from Rias Baixas that some connoisseurs consider the perfect accompaniment for seafood. Among reds, make a beeline for vintages from the fastest-developing wine region of Europe, the arid, high-altitude district of Ribero del Duero, midway between Madrid and Santander, near Burgos, whose alkaline soil, cold nights, and sunny days have earned unexpected praise (and encouraged massive investments) in the past 5 years.

For more information about these and others of the 10 wine-producing regions of Spain (and the 39 officially recognized wine-producing Denominatións de Origen scattered across those regions), contact **Wines from Spain,** ℅ the Commercial Office of Spain, 405 Lexington Ave., 44th Floor, New York, NY 10174-0331 (☎ **212/661-4818**).

water instead, simply because it usually tastes better. If you'd like your water with a little kick, then ask for *agua mineral con gas.*

Soft Drinks   In general, avoid the carbonated citrus drinks on sale everywhere—most of them never saw an orange, much less a lemon. If you want a citrus drink, order old, reliable Schweppes. An excellent noncarbonated drink for the summer is

Tri-Naranjus, which comes in lemon and orange flavors. Your cheapest bet is a liter bottle of *gaseosa,* which comes in various flavors. In summer you should also try a drink we've never seen outside Spain, *horchata,* a nutty, sweet milklike beverage made of tubers called *chufas.* Its flavor is vaguely reminiscent of liquefied almonds.

Coffee Even if you're a dedicated coffee drinker, you may find the *café con leche* (coffee with milk) a little too strong. We suggest *leche manchada,* a little bit of strong, freshly brewed coffee in a glass, filled with lots of frothy hot milk.

Milk Even though some old-time aficionados in rural districts claim that some of milk's flavor is lost during the pasteurization process, always avoid untreated milk and milk by-products. Most of the milk sold in Spain, fortunately, is bottled and properly sterilized. One of Spain's popular brands of fresh and pasteurized milk is Lauki, sold in food stores throughout the country.

Beer Although not native to Spain, beer (*cerveza*) is now drunk everywhere. Domestic brands include San Miguel, Mahou, Aguila, and Cruz Blanca.

Wine Sherry (*vino de Jerez*) has been called the "wine with a hundred souls." Drink it before dinner (try the topaz-colored *finos,* a very pale sherry) or whenever you drop in at some old inn or bodega for refreshment; many of them have rows of brimming kegs with spigots. Manzanilla, a golden-colored, medium-dry sherry, is extremely popular. The sweet cream sherries (Harvey's Bristol Cream, for example) are favorite after-dinner wines (called *olorosos*). While the French may be disdainful of Spanish table wines, they can be truly noble, especially two leading varieties, Valdepeñas and Rioja, both from Castile. If you're fairly adventurous and not too demanding in your tastes, you can always ask for the *vino de la casa* (wine of the house) wherever you dine. The Ampurdan of Catalonia is a heavy and somewhat coarse, but flavorful wine. From Andalusia comes the fruity Montilla. There are also some good Spain-derived champagnes (*cavas*) widely available in Barcelona, and also Madrid. A favorite is Freixenet. One brand, Benjamin, also comes in individual-size bottles.

Sangría This is the all-time favorite refreshing drink in Spain, especially in Madrid and Seville. It's red-wine punch that combines wine with oranges, lemons, seltzer, and sugar.

Whisky & Brandy Imported whiskies are available at most bars, but at a high price. If you're a drinker, switch to brandies and cognacs, where the Spanish reign supreme. Try Fundador, made by the Pedro Domecq family in Jerez de la Frontera near Seville. If you're seeking a smooth cognac, ask for "103" white label.

Planning a Trip to Barcelona, Madrid & Seville

2

This chapter is devoted to the where, when, and how of your trip—the advance planning required to get it together and take it on the road.

After deciding where to go, most people have two fundamental questions: What will it cost? and How do I get there? This chapter will address these and such other important issues as when to go, what entry requirements there are, what pretrip preparations are needed, and where to obtain more information about these three cities.

1 Visitor Information & Entry Requirements

VISITOR INFORMATION

IN THE U.S. For information before you go, contact the **Tourist Office of Spain,** 666 Fifth Ave., 5th Floor, New York, NY 10103 (☎ **212/265-8822**). It can provide sightseeing information, calendars of events, train and ferry schedules, and more. Other information offices are the Spanish Tourist Office, 8383 Wilshire Blvd., Suite 960, Beverly Hills, CA 90211 (☎ **213/658-7188**); Tourist Office of Spain, Water Tower Place, Suite 915 East, 845 N. Michigan Ave., Chicago, IL 60611 (☎ **312/642-1992**); and Tourist Office of Spain, 1221 Brickell Ave., Miami, FL 33131 (☎ **305/358-1992**).

OUTSIDE THE U.S. In **Australia,** contact the Spanish Tourist Information, 203 Castlereagh St., Suite 21A (P.O. Box 675), NSW 2000 Sydney, South Australia (☎ **612/264-7966**); in **Canada,** the Tourist Office of Spain, 102 Bloor St. West, 14th Floor, Toronto, ON M5S 1M9 (☎ **416/961-3131**); and in the **United Kingdom,** the Spanish Tourist Office, 57–58 St. James's St., London SW1 (☎ **0171/499-0901**).

ENTRY REQUIREMENTS

PASSPORTS A valid passport is all American, Canadian, or New Zealand citizens and British subjects need to enter Spain. (Australians need a visa—see below.) You don't need an international driver's license if you're renting a car; your local license from back home should suffice.

VISAS For visits to Spain of less than 3 months, visas are not required for citizens of the United States, Canada, and New Zealand, and for British subjects. Australians, however, need a visa and should apply in advance at the Spanish Consulate in their home country.

SPANISH CUSTOMS Spain permits you to bring in most personal effects and the following items duty free: two still cameras with 10 rolls of film per camera, one movie or video camera, tobacco for personal use, one bottle of wine and one bottle of liquor per person, a portable radio, a tape recorder, a typewriter, a bicycle, sports equipment, fishing gear, and two hunting weapons with 100 cartridges each.

RETURNING TO YOUR HOME COUNTRY Citizens and permanent residents returning to the **United States** from Spain may bring in $400 worth of merchandise duty free, provided they have not made a similar claim within the past 30 days. Remember to keep receipts for purchases made in Spain. For more specific guidance, request the free pamphlet "Know Before You Go" by writing to the U.S. Customs Service, P.O. Box 7407, Washington, DC 20044.

For total clarification citizens of **Canada** can write for the booklet "I Declare," issued by Revenue Canada, Communications Branch, 875 Heron Rd., Ottawa, ON K1A 0L8. Canada allows its citizens a $500 exemption after an absence of 7 days or more. They can bring back, duty free, 200 cigarettes, 400 grams of manufactured tobacco, 50 cigars or cigarillos, and 30 ounces of liquor. In addition, they're allowed to mail unsolicited gifts (except alcohol or tobacco) to Canada from abroad at the rate of CAN$60 or less. On the package, mark "Unsolicited Gift, Under $60 Value." All valuables you own and take with you should be declared before you depart from Canada on Form Y-38, including serial numbers.

Residents in the **United Kingdom,** as with citizens of European Union (formerly European Community) countries, do not necessarily have to go through Customs when returning home, providing all their travel was within EU countries. Of course, Customs agents reserve the right to search if they are suspicious. However, there are certain EU guidelines for returning passengers, who can bring in 400 cigarillos, 200 cigars, 800 cigarettes, and 1 kilogram of smoking tobacco. They can also bring in 10 liters of spirits, 20 liters of fortified wine, 90 liters of wine, and 110 liters of beer. Persons exceeding these limits may be asked to prove that the excess is either for their personal use or gifts for friends. For further details, contact HM Customs and Excise, Advice Centre, Dorset House, Stamford St., London SE1 9NG (☎ 0171/202-4227).

The duty-free allowance in **Australia** is A$400, or A$200 for those under 18. Personal property mailed back from Spain should be marked "Australian Goods Returned" to avoid payment of duty. Upon returning to Australia, citizens can bring in 200 cigarettes or 250 grams of loose tobacco and 1 liter of alcohol. If you're returning with valuable goods you already own, such as foreign-made cameras, you should file Form B263. A helpful brochure, available from Australian consulates or Customs offices, is "Customs Information for All Travellers." For more information, contact the Australian Customs Service, 5 Constitution Ave., Canberra, ACT 2601 (☎ 6/275-62-55).

The duty-free allowance in **New Zealand** is NZ$700. Citizens over age 16 can bring in 200 cigarettes or 250 grams of loose tobacco or 50 cigars; and 4.5 liters of wine or beer, or 1.125 liters of liquor. New Zealand currency does not carry restrictions regarding import or export. A Certificate of Export listing valuables taken out of the country allows you to bring them back without paying duty. Most questions are answered in a free pamphlet "New Zealand Customs Guide for Travellers," available at New Zealand Consulates and Customs offices. For more information, contact New Zealand Customs, 50 Anzac Ave. (P.O. Box 29), Auckland (☎ 9/377-35-20).

2 Money

CASH/CURRENCY   The basic unit of Spanish currency is the **peseta** (abbreviated **pta.**), currently worth about 8¢ in U.S. currency ($1 U.S. is worth about 125 pesetas). Coins come in denominations of 1, 5, 25, 50, 100, 200, and 500 pesetas. Paper notes come in 500, 1,000, 5,000 and 10,000 pesetas.

All world currencies fluctuate, so you should be aware that the amounts appearing in this book are not exact. Currency conversions are presented only to give you a rough idea of the price you'll pay in U.S. dollars. There's no way to predict exactly what the rate of exchange will be when you visit Spain. Check the newspaper or ask at your bank for last-minute quotations.

Be advised that rates of exchange vary, depending on where you convert your money. In general, you'll get the best exchange rate by using a credit or charge card or by withdrawing cash from an ATM. Banks also offer competitive rates, but keep in mind that they charge a commission for cashing traveler's checks. You'll get the worst rates of exchange at your hotel, as well as at point-of-entry sites like the airport or train station.

ATM NETWORKS   PLUS, Cirrus, and other networks connecting automated-teller machines operate in Spain. If your bank card has been programmed with a PIN (Personal Identification Number), it's likely that you can use your card at ATMs abroad to withdraw money directly from your home bank account. Check with your bank to see if your PIN code must be reprogrammed for usage in Spain. Before leaving, always determine the frequency limits for withdrawals, and what fees—if any—your bank will assess. For Cirrus locations abroad, call 800/424-7787; also, Cirrus ATM locations in selected cities are available on MasterCard's Internet site (http://www.mastercard.com). For PLUS usage abroad, contact your local bank or check Visa's page on the World Wide Web (http://www.visa.com).

TRAVELER'S CHECKS   Though ATM usage is becoming increasingly commonplace, many people prefer the security of traveler's checks. Purchase them before leaving home and arrange to carry some ready cash (usually about $250, depending on your needs). In the event of theft, if the checks are properly documented, the value of your checks will be refunded. Most large banks sell traveler's checks, charging fees that average between 1% and 2% of the value of the checks you buy, although some out-of-the-way banks, in rare instances, have charged as much as 7%. If your bank wants more than a 2% commission, call the traveler's check issuers directly for the address of outlets where this commission will be less.

Issuers sometimes have agreements with groups to sell checks commission free. For example, American Automobile Association (AAA) clubs sell American Express checks in several currencies without commission.

American Express (☎ 800/221-7282 in the U.S. and Canada) is one of the largest and most immediately recognized issuers of traveler's checks. No commission is charged to holders of certain types of American Express cards. The company issues checks denominated in U.S. dollars, Canadian dollars, and British pounds, among other currencies. The vast majority of checks sold in North America are denominated in U.S. dollars. For questions or problems that arise outside the United States or Canada, contact any of the company's many regional representatives.

The Spanish Peseta

For American Readers   At this writing, $1 = approximately 125 ptas. (or 1 pta. = 8¢ U.S.). This was the rate of exchange used to calculate the dollar equivalents given throughout this edition.

For British Readers   At this writing, £1 = approximately 188 ptas. (or l pta. = 5.3p). This was the rate of exchange used to calculate the pound values in the table below.

Pesetas	U.S.$	U.K.£	Pesetas	U.S.$	U.K.£
50	.40	.27	3,000	24.00	15.90
100	.80	.53	4,000	32.00	21.20
200	1.60	1.06	5,000	40.00	26.50
300	2.40	1.59	7,500	60.00	39.75
400	3.20	2.12	10,000	80.00	53.00
500	4.00	2.65	15,000	120.00	79.50
600	4.80	3.18	20,000	160.00	106.00
700	5.60	3.71	25,000	200.00	132.50
800	6.40	4.24	30,000	240.00	159.00
900	7.20	4.77	35,000	280.00	185.50
1,000	8.00	5.30	40,000	320.00	212.00
1,250	9.20	6.63	45,000	360.00	238.50
1,500	12.00	7.95	50,000	400.00	265.00
2,000	16.00	10.60	75,000	600.00	397.50

Citicorp (☎ **800/645-6556** in the U.S. and Canada, or 813/623-1709, collect, from anywhere else in the world), can issue checks in U.S. dollars as well as British pounds.

Thomas Cook (☎ **800/223-7373** in the U.S., or 609/987-7300, collect, from other parts of the world) can issue MasterCard traveler's checks denominated in U.S. dollars, British pounds, Spanish pesetas, and Australian dollars. Depending on individual banking laws in each of the various states, some of the above-mentioned currencies may not be available in every outlet.

Interpayment Services (☎ **800/221-2426** in the U.S. and Canada, or 212/858-8500 from most other parts of the world) sells Visa checks sponsored by a consortium of member banks and the Thomas Cook organization. Traveler's checks can be denominated in U.S. or Canadian dollars or British pounds.

MONEYGRAM   If you find yourself out of money, a new wire service provided by American Express can help you tap willing friends and family for emergency funds. Through MoneyGram, 6200 S. Quebec St. (P.O. Box 5118), Englewood, CO 80155 (☎ **800/926-9400**), money can be sent around the world in less than 10 minutes. Senders should call AmEx to learn the address of the closest outlet that handles MoneyGrams. Cash, credit/charge card, or the occasional personal check (with ID) are acceptable forms of payment. AmEx's fee for the service is $10 for the first $300 with a sliding scale for larger sums. The service includes a short telex message and a

3-minute phone call from sender to recipient. The beneficiary must present a photo ID at the outlet where the money is received.

CREDIT & CHARGE CARDS American Express, Visa, and Diners Club are widely recognized in Spain. If you see the Eurocard or Access sign on an establishment, it means that it accepts MasterCard. Discover cards are accepted only in the United States.

Credit and charge cards can be lifesavers when you're abroad. With American Express and Visa, for example, not only can you charge purchases in shops and restaurants that take the card, but you can also withdraw pesetas (as a cash advance on your card) from ATM machines at many locations in Spain. Check with your card company before leaving home.

Keep in mind that the price of purchases is not converted into your national currency until notification is received in your home country, so the exchange rate may have fluctuated slightly in the interim.

CURRENCY EXCHANGE Many hotels in Spain don't accept dollar or pound denominated checks; those that do will almost certainly charge for the conversion. In some cases they'll accept countersigned traveler's checks or a credit or charge card, but if you're prepaying a deposit on hotel reservations, it's cheaper and easier to pay with a check drawn on a Spanish bank.

This can be arranged by a large commercial bank or by a specialist such as **Ruesch International,** 700 11th St. NW, 4th Floor, Washington, DC, 20001-4507 (☎ **800/424-2923**), which performs a wide variety of conversion-related tasks, usually for only $2 per transaction.

If you need a check payable in pesetas, call Ruesch's toll-free number, describe what you need, and note the transaction number given to you. Mail your dollar-denominated personal check (payable to Ruesch International) to its office in Washington, D.C. Upon receiving this, the company will mail a check denominated in pesetas for the financial equivalent, minus the $2 charge. The company can also help you with many different kinds of wire transfers and conversions of VAT (Value-Added Tax, which is known as IVA in Spain) refund checks and also will mail brochures and information packets on request. Britishers can go to **Ruesch International Ltd.,** 18 Savile Row, London W1X 2AD (☎ **0171/734-2300**).

3 When to Go: Climate, Holidays & Events

CLIMATE

May and October are the best months, weather-wise and crowd-wise—in fact, spring and fall are ideal times to visit any of these cities. In our view, however, the balmy month of May (average temperature: 61°F) is the best time for making your own descent on Barcelona, Madrid, or Seville. In summer it's hot, hot, and hot again; Madrid and Seville stew up the most scalding brew. Madrid has dry heat; the temperature can hover around 84°F in July, 75° in September. Seville has the dubious reputation of being about the hottest part of Spain in July and August, often baking under temperatures that average around 93°. Barcelona is humid. The overcrowded Costa Brava where city residents of Barcelona escape to the beach has temperatures around 81° in July and August.

August remains the major vacation month in Europe. The traffic from France to Spain becomes a veritable migration, and low-cost hotels are almost fully booked

Average Daytime Temperatures (°F)

	Jan	Feb	Mar	Apr	May	June	July	Aug	Sept	Oct	Nov	Dec
Barcelona	49	51	54	59	64	72	76	76	72	64	57	51
Madrid	43	45	49	54	61	68	75	74	68	58	48	43
Seville	51	54	59	63	68	77	77	83	77	68	59	52

along the coastal areas, with top prices in effect. To compound the problem, many restaurants and shops also decide that it's time for a vacation, thereby limiting the visitor's selections for both dining and shopping.

HOLIDAYS

National holidays in Spain include January 1 (New Year's Day), January 6 (Epiphany), March 19 (Feast of St. Joseph), Good Friday, Easter Monday, May 1 (May Day), June 10 (Corpus Christi), June 29 (Feast of St. Peter and St. Paul), July 25 (Feast of St. James), August 15 (Feast of the Assumption), October 12 (Spain's National Day), November 1 (All Saints' Day), December 8 (Immaculate Conception), and December 25 (Christmas). In addition, Madrid celebrates the Feast of Saint Isidro on May 15, and Barcelona observes Catalunya Day on September 11.

CALENDAR OF EVENTS: BARCELONA, MADRID & SEVILLE

The dates given below may not be precise. Sometimes the exact days are not announced until 6 weeks before the actual festival. Check with the National Tourist Office of Spain (see "Visitor Information & Entry Requirements," earlier in this chapter) if you're planning to attend a specific event.

January

- **Three Kings Parade,** Barcelona. Parades are staged throughout the main arteries of old Barcelona in anticipation of the Feast of the Three Kings (January 6). Usually on January 5 or 6.

February

- **ARCO,** at the Crystal Pavilion of the Casa de Campo, Madrid. This International Contemporary Art Fair is one of the biggest draws in Spain's cultural calendar, bringing the best in contemporary art from Europe and America. The exhibition presents both regional and internationally known artists. Dates vary.
- **Madrid Carnival.** The carnival kicks off with a big parade along Paseo de la Castellana, culminating in a masked ball at the Círculo de Belles Artes the following night. Fancy-dress competitions last until Ash Wednesday, when the festivities end with a tear-jerking "burial of a sardine" at the Fuente de los Pajaritos in the Casa de Campo; the evening is topped off with a concert in the Plaza Mayor. Dates vary.
- **Salon de Anticuarios en Barcelona.** This giant antiques fair is held in the Fira de Barcelona. Usually late February to mid-March.

March

- **Marathon Catalunya,** Barcelona. This annual marathon begins in Mataró, winds its way through the city, and ends at the Olympic Stadium in Montjuïc. Usually in mid-March.

April

- ✪ **Semana Santa (Holy Week).** A series of processions with hooded penitents moves to the piercing wail of the *saeta,* a love song to the Virgin or Christ. *Pasos* (heavy floats) bear images of the Virgin or Christ.

Where: Seville. **When:** From Palm Sunday until Easter Sunday. **How:** Make hotel reservations way in advance. Call the Seville Office of Tourism for details (☎ 95/422-14-04).

- **Bullfights,** nationwide. Holy week traditionally kicks off the season all over Spain. Although not as popular in Barcelona as in the rest of Spain, this national pastime affords the visitor an unparalleled insight into the Spanish temperament.

✪ **Feria de Sevilla (Seville Fair).** This is the most celebrated week of revelry in all of Spain, with all-night flamenco dancing, merrymaking in casetas, bullfights, horseback riding, flower-decked coaches, and dancing in the streets.

Where: Seville. **When:** Mid-April. **How:** You'll need to reserve a hotel early for this one. For general information and exact festival dates, contact the Office of Tourism in Seville (☎ 95/422-14-04).

- **Festivat de Sant Jordi and Parades de Libres I Roses,** Barcelona. On the feast day of Catalonia's patron saint, Sant Jordi, citizens of Barcelona shower each other with books and roses. April 23.

May

✪ **Fiestas de San Isidro.** Madrileños run wild with a 10-day celebration honoring their city's patron saint. Food fairs, Castilian folkloric events, street parades, parties, music, dances, bullfights, and other festivities mark the occasion.

Where: Madrid. **When:** May 12–21. **How:** Make hotel reservations early. Expect crowds and traffic (and beware of pickpockets). For information, write to Oficina Municipal de Información y Turismo, Plaza Mayor, 3, 28014 Madrid.

- **Fira del Libre de Barcelona.** This annual book fair is located primarily on the Passeig de Grácia. Late May to early July.

June

- **Corpus Christi,** Seville. This major religious holiday is marked by processions and celebrations centered around the town's towering Gothic cathedral. June 10.
- **Verbena de Sant Joan,** Barcelona. The town literally "lights up"—with fireworks, bonfires, and dances until dawn. It's customary to eat coca, a sweet made of fruit and pine nuts. The highlight of the festival is its culmination at Montjuïc with fireworks. Dates vary.

July

- **Veranos de la Villa,** Madrid. Called "the summer binge" of Madrid, this summer-long program presents folkloric dancing, pop music, classical music, zarzuelas, and flamenco at various venues throughout the city. Open-air cinema is a feature in the Parque del Retiro. Ask at the various tourist offices for complete details (which change every summer). Sometimes admission is charged, but often these events are free. All summer.

August

- **Fiestas of Lavapíes and La Paloma,** Madrid. These two fiestas—the most traditional in Madrid—begin with the Lavapíes on August 1 and continue through the hectic La Paloma celebration on August 15, the day of the Virgen de la Paloma. Tens of thousands of residents and visitors race through the narrow streets. Apartment dwellers above hurl buckets of cold water onto the crowds below to cool them off. Children's games, floats, music, flamenco, and zarzuelas, along with street fairs, mark the occasion. August 1–15.

September

- **Diada,** Barcelona. This is the most significant holiday in all of Catalonia. It celebrates the glory of autonomy from the rest of Spain, following years of repression under the dictator Franco. Demonstrations and other "flag-waving" events take place. The *senyera,* the flag of Catalonia, is much in evidence. Not your typical tourist fare, but interesting nevertheless. September 11.

- **Cádiz Grape Harvest Festival,** Jerez de la Frontera. The major wine festival in Andalusia (of which Seville is the nearby capital) honors the famous sherry of Jerez with 5 days of processions, flamenco dancing, bullfights, livestock on parade, and, of course, sherry drinking. A good day trip from Seville (see Chapter 8). Mid-September (dates vary).

- ✪ **Autumn Festival**   Both Spanish and international artists participate in this cultural program, with a series of operatic, ballet, dance, music, and theatrical performances. From Strasbourg to Tokyo, this event is a premier attraction, yet tickets are reasonable.

  Where: Madrid. **When:** Mid-September to mid-November. **How:** Make hotel reservations early, and write for tickets to Festival de Otoño, Plaza de España 8, 28008 Madrid (☎ 91/580-25-75).

- **Fiesta de la Mercé,** Barcelona. The city abounds with various musical and theatrical performances in honor of one of the city's patron saints, the Virgin de la Mercé. Shows are staged throughout Barcelona. A pageant and fireworks display signal the end of the festival. Week of September 24.

November

- **All Saints' Day,** Seville. This holy day is celebrated all over Spain, but the citizens of Seville show a certain fervor in lamenting the souls of their dead. Family and friends place wreaths and garlands on the graves of the dead. November 1.

- **Festival Internacional de Jazz de Barcelona.** The dates and locations for this jazz festival change yearly. For information call 93/447-12-90.

December

- **Dia de los Santos Inocentes,** Seville. Another country-wide holiday that's celebrated with particular gusto in sunny Seville. On this day the Spanish play many practical jokes and in general do loco things to one another—it's the Spanish equivalent of April Fools' Day. December 28.

4 Health & Insurance

HEALTH   The cities of Barcelona, Madrid, and Seville should not pose any major health hazards. The overly rich cuisine—garlic, olive oil, and wine—may give travelers mild diarrhea, so take along some antidiarrhea medicine, moderate your eating habits, and even though the water is generally considered safe, drink mineral water only. Milk and milk products are pasteurized and generally safe. Fish and shellfish from the horrendously polluted Mediterranean should only be eaten cooked.

If you need a doctor, ask your hotel to locate one for you. You can also obtain a list of English-speaking doctors in Spain from the **International Association for Medical Assistance to Travelers (IAMAT),** in the United States at 417 Center St., Lewiston, NY 14092 (☎ **716/754-4883**), and in Canada at 40 Regal Rd., Guelph, ON N1K 1B5 (☎ 519/836-0102). Getting medical help in Spain is relatively easy compared to many countries, and competent English-speaking doctors are found in Barcelona, Madrid, and Seville.

If you have a chronic medical condition, talk to your doctor before taking an international trip. For such conditions as epilepsy, a heart condition, and diabetes, wear a Medic Alert Identification Tag; it immediately alerts any doctor to your condition and will provide a 24-hour hotline phone number so a foreign doctor can obtain medical records for you. The initial membership costs $35. There's a $15 annual fee. Contact the **Medic Alert Foundation,** P.O. Box 1009, Turlock, CA 95381-1009 (☎ **800/432-5378**).

Take all vital medicines with you in your carry-on luggage, and bring enough to last you during your stay. Also bring copies of each prescription written with the generic name—not the brand name—of the drug you're taking. It's a good idea to bring a sunscreen with a high SPF, since the sun can be intense, especially in Seville.

VACCINATIONS   You aren't required to have any particular inoculations to enter Spain (except for yellow fever, if you're arriving from an infected area).

INSURANCE   Before purchasing any additional insurance, check your home-owner's, automobile, and medical insurance policies, as well as the insurance provided by your credit- and charge-card companies and auto and travel clubs. You may have adequate off-premises theft coverage or your card company may even provide can-cellation coverage if the ticket is paid for with its card.

Remember, Medicare only covers U.S. citizens traveling in Mexico and Canada.

Also note that to submit any claim you must always have thorough documenta-tion, including all receipts, police reports, medical records, and such.

If you're prepaying for your vacation or are taking a charter or any other flight that has cancellation penalties, look into cancellation insurance. Most companies listed below offer insurance packages that include provisions for lost luggage, medical cov-erage, emergency evacuation, accidental death, and trip cancellation. Call for policy specifics.

Among the firms to try are **Travel Guard International,** 1145 Clark St., Stevens Point, WI 54481 (☎ 800/826-1300); **Mutual of Omaha** (Tele-Trip), Mutual of Omaha Plaza, Omaha, NE 68175 (☎ 800/228-9792); **Healthcare Abroad (MEDEX),** C/o Wallach & Co., 107 W. Federal St. (P.O. Box 480), Middleburg, VA 22117-0480 (☎ 800/237-6615 or 540/687-3166); **Access America,** 6600 W. Broad St., Richmond, VA 23230 (☎ 800/284-8300); **Travel Assistance Interna-tional** by Worldwide Assistance Services, Inc., 1133 15th St. NW, Suite 400, Wash-ington, DC 20005 (☎ 800/821-2828 or 202/331-1596); and **Travel Insured International, Inc.,** P.O. Box 280568, East Hartford, CT 06128-0568 (☎ 800/243-3174 in the U.S., or 860/528-7663).

Insurance For British Travelers   Most big travel agents offer their own insurance and will probably try to sell you their package when you book a holiday. Think be-fore you sign. Britain's Consumers' Association recommends that you insist on see-ing the policy and reading the fine print before buying travel insurance.

You should also shop around for better deals. You might contact **Columbus Travel Insurance Ltd.** (☎ 0171/375-0011 in London), or, if you're a student, **Cam-pus Travel** (☎ 171/730-3402 in London).

5 Tips for Travelers with Special Needs

FOR PEOPLE WITH DISABILITIES   Because of Spain's many hills and endless flights of stairs, physically disabled visitors may have difficulty getting around the country. But conditions are slowly improving. Newer hotels are more sensitive to the needs of the disabled; and the more expensive restaurants, in general, are wheelchair-accessible. (In Madrid, the capital, there's even a museum designed for the blind and sight impaired—see the Museo Tiflológico in "Outside the City Center," in Chap-ter 6). However, since most places have limited, if any, facilities for people with disabilities, consider taking an organized tour specifically designed to accommodate travelers with disabilities.

For the names and addresses of tour operators as well as other related information, contact the **Society for the Advancement of Travel for the Handicapped,** 347 Fifth Ave., New York, NY 10016 (☎ 212/447-7248). Annual membership dues are $45, or $25 for senior citizens and students.

FEDCAP Rehabilitation Services (formerly Federation of the Handicapped), 154 W. 14th St., New York, NY 10011 (☎ 212/727-4200), operates summer tours to Europe and elsewhere for its members. Membership costs $4 yearly.

You can also obtain a free copy of **"Air Transportation of Handicapped Persons,"** published by the U.S. Department of Transportation. Write to Free Advisory Circular No. AC12032, Distribution Unit, U.S. Department of Transportation, Publications Division, M-4332, Washington, DC 20590.

For the blind or visually impaired, the best source is the **American Foundation for the Blind,** 15 W. 16th St., New York, NY 10011 (☎ 800/232-5463 to order information kits and supplies, or 212/502-7600). It offers information on travel and various requirements for the transport and border formalities for seeing-eye dogs. It also issues indentification cards to those who are legally blind.

The **Information Center for Individuals with Disabilities,** Fort Point Place, 27–43 Wormwood St., Boston, MA 02210 (☎ 800/462-5015 or 617/727-5540), is another good source. It has lists of travel agents who specialize in tours for persons with disabilities.

One of the best organizations serving the needs of those with disabilities (wheelchairs and walkers) is **Flying Wheels Travel,** 143 W. Bridge (P.O. Box 382), Owatonna, MN 55060 (☎ 800/535-6790 or 507/451-5005), offering various escorted tours and cruises internationally.

For a $25 annual fee, consider joining **Mobility International USA,** P.O. Box 10767, Eugene, OR 97440 (☎ 541/343-1284 voice and TDD). It answers questions on various destinations and also offers discounts on videos, publications, and programs it sponsors.

For British Travelers with Disabilities   Two annual holiday guides for travelers with disabilities are available from the **Royal Association for Disability and Rehabilitation (RADAR),** Unit 12, City Forum, 250 City Rd., London EC1V 8AF (☎ 0171/250-3222). "Holidays and Travel Abroad" costs £5, whereas "Holidays in the British Isles" goes for £7. RADAR (whose patroness is Elizabeth, the Queen Mother), also provides a number of holiday information packets on such subjects as sports and outdoor holidays, insurance, financial arrangements for persons with disabilities, and accommodations in nursing care units for groups or for the elderly. Each of these fact sheets is available for £2. Both the fact sheets and the holiday guides can be mailed outside the U.K. for a nominal mailing fee.

Another good service is the **Holiday Care Service,** Imperial Buildings, 2nd Floor, Victoria Road, Horley, Surrey RH6 7PZ (☎ 01293/774-535; fax 01293/784-647), a national charity that advises on accessible accommodations for elderly people or those with disabilities. Annual membership costs £10 (U.K. residents) and £25 (abroad). Once you're a member, you can receive a newsletter and access to a free reservations network for hotels throughout Britain and—to a lesser degree—Europe and the rest of the world.

If you're flying around Spain, the airline and ground staff will help you on and off planes and reserve seats for you with sufficient leg room, but it's essential to arrange for this assistance *in advance* by contacting your airline.

The **Airport Transport Users Council,** 5/F Kingsway House, 103 Kingsway, London WC2B 6QX (☎ 0171/242-3882), publishes a free pamphlet, "Flight

Plan—A Passenger's Guide to Planning and Using Air Travel," that's packed with information for all travelers.

FOR GAYS & LESBIANS   In 1978 Spain legalized homosexual behaviors among consenting adults. In April 1995 the parliament of Spain banned discrimination based on sexual orientation. Madrid and Barcelona are the major gay centers of the country. The leading gay resort is Sitges, south of Barcelona.

To learn about gay and lesbian travel in Spain, you can obtain publications or join data-dispensing organizations before you go. Men can order *Spartacus,* the international gay guide ($32.95) or *Odysseus 1997, The International Gay Travel Planner,* a guide to international gay accommodations ($25).

Both lesbians and gay men might want to pick up a copy of *Gay Travel A to Z* ($16), which specializes in general information, as well as listings of bars, hotels, restaurants, and places of interest for gay travelers throughout the world. These books and others are available from **Giovanni's Room,** 1145 Pine St., Philadelphia, PA 19107 (☎ **215/923-2960**), and other gay and lesbian bookstores around the country.

Our World, 1104 N. Nova Rd., Suite 251, Daytona Beach, FL 32117 (☎ **904/441-5367**), is a magazine devoted to options and bargains for gay and lesbian travel worldwide. It costs $35 for 10 issues. *Out and About,* 8 W. 19th St., Suite 401, New York, NY 10011 (☎ **800/929-2268**), has been hailed for its "straight" reporting about gay travel. It profiles the best gay or gay-friendly hotels, gyms, clubs, and other places, with coverage of destinations throughout the world. The cost is $49 a year for 10 information-packed issues. It aims for the more upscale gay male traveler, and has been praised by everybody from *Travel & Leisure* to the *New York Times.* Both these publications are also available at most gay and lesbian bookstores.

The **International Gay Travel Association (IGTA),** P.O. Box 4974, Key West, FL 33041 (☎ **800/448-8550** for voice-mail messages, or 305/292-0217), encourages gay and lesbian travel worldwide. With around 1,200 member agencies, it specializes in networking travelers with the appropriate gay-friendly service organization or tour specialist. It offers a quarterly newsletter, marketing mailings, and a membership directory that's updated four times a year. Travel agents who are IGTA members will be tied into this organization's vast information resources.

Madrid is now one of the major gay capitals of Europe. Much of the gay activity centers around the Chueca district, north of the Gran Vía, where bar life begins around 11pm and often lasts until dawn. The **Librería El Galeón,** Calle Sagasta, 7 (☎ **91/445-57-38;** metro: Bilbao), is a gay bookshop where you can purchase the annual version of *Guia Gay Visado,* containing the most complete list of gay and lesbian entertainment in the country. The shop is open Monday to Saturday from 10am to 3pm and 5 to 8:30pm. For women, the best bookshop to patronize is the **Librería de Mujeres,** Calle San Cristóbal, 17 (☎ **91/521-70-43;** metro: Puerta del Sol), near the Plaza Mayor. This feminist bookshop provides much useful data and sponsors poetry readings, concerts, and talks, and boasts a good international bookstore with some English-language editions. Open Monday to Saturday from 10am to 2pm and 5 to 8pm.

For gay men in Barcelona a wide assortment of establishments, ranging from discos to saunas, from restaurants to bars, awaits the visitor. And if you get bored with the gay scene in Barcelona, it's just half an hour by train to the sands of Sitges, the premier gay resort of Europe. For gay men, a source of information is **Front d'Allibrement Gai de Catalunya,** Carrer Villaroel, 63 (☎ **93/454-63-98**), which is found at the corner of Carrer Consell de Cant. For women, inquire about activities at **Grup de Lesbianes Feministes de Barcelona,** Caspe 38 Principal (☎ **93/412-77-01**).

Another source of information about gay life in Barcelona is provided by **Sextienda,** Rauric, 11 (☎ **93/318-86-76**), open Monday to Saturday from 10am to 8:30pm. This is the premier gay pornography shop in Spain, located on a street with some gay bars. The English-speaking staff will give you a free map pinpointing the bars, restaurants, discos, and other places catering to gay men. It's called *Plano Gay de Barcelona y Sitges,* and it's revised every year.

FOR SENIORS   Many discounts are available for seniors, but often you need to be a member of an association to obtain them.

For information before you go, write for the free booklet "101 Tips for the Mature Traveler," available from **Grand Circle Travel,** 347 Congress St., Suite 3A, Boston, MA 02210 (☎ **800/221-2610** or 617/350-7500).

One of the most dynamic travel organizations for seniors is **Elderhostel,** 75 Federal St., Boston, MA (☎ **617/426-7788**). Established in 1975, it operates an array of programs throughout Europe, including Spain. Most courses last around 3 weeks and are a good value, since they include airfare, accommodations in student dormitories or modest inns, all meals, and tuition. Courses involve no homework, are ungraded, and are often liberal arts–oriented. These aren't luxury vacations, but they're fun and fulfilling. Participants must be at least 60 years old. A companion must be at least 50 years old; spouses may participate regardless of age.

SAGA International Holidays, 222 Berkeley St., Boston, MA 02116 (☎ **800/ 343-0273**), runs tours for seniors age 50 and older. Many tours are all-inclusive; all cover air transfers and accommodations. Insurance, including baggage and medical, is included in the net price of the tours.

In the United States, the best organization to belong to is the **American Association of Retired Persons (AARP),** 601 E St. NW, Washington, DC 20049 (☎ **202/ 434-AARP**). Members are offered discounts on car rentals, hotels, and airfares. The association's group travel is provided by the AARP Travel Experience from American Express. Tours may be purchased through any American Express office or travel agent, or by calling 800/927-0111. Flights to the various destinations are handled by the toll-free number as part of land arrangements.

Information is also available from the **National Council of Senior Citizens,** 1331 F St. NW, Washington, DC 20005-1171 (☎ **202/347-8800**), which charges $12 per person or per couple. You receive a monthly newsletter, part of which is devoted to travel tips, and reduced discounts on hotel and auto rentals are available.

For British Seniors   Located opposite Platform 2 in Victoria Station, London SW1V 1J2, **Wasteels** (☎ **0171/834-6744**), currently provides a Rail Europe Senior Card to those over age 60. Its price is £5 to any Britisher with government-issued proof of his or her age and £19 to anyone with a certificate of age not issued by the British government. With this card, discounts are sometimes available on certain trains within Britain and throughout the rest of Europe.

FOR FAMILIES   A newsletter about traveling with children, *Family Travel Times* costs $40 for four issues. Subscribers can also call in with travel questions, but only on Wednesday from 10am to 1pm eastern standard time. Contact **TWYCH** (which stands for **Travel With Your Children**), 40 Fifth Ave., New York, NY 10011 (☎ **212/477-5524**).

For British Families   The best deals for families are often package tours put together by some of the giants of the British travel industry. Foremost among these is Thomsons Tour Operators. Through its subsidiary, **Skytours** (☎ **0171/**

387-9321), Thomsons offers dozens of air/land packages to Spain where a predesignated number of airline seats are reserved for the free use of children under 18 who accompany their parents. To qualify, parents must book airfare and hotel accommodations lasting 2 weeks or more and must do so as far in advance as possible. Savings for families with children can be substantial.

FOR SINGLES   It's no secret the travel industry caters to people who don't travel alone. Double rooms, for example, are usually much more reasonably priced than singles. One company, Travel Companion, has had great success in matching single travelers with like-minded companions. Its founder, Jens Jurgen, charges $99 for a 6-month listing in his well-publicized records. New applicants desiring a travel companion fill out a form stating their preferences and needs. They then receive a list of people who might be suitable. Companions of the same or opposite sex can be requested. A bimonthly newsletter averaging 46 large pages also gives numerous money-saving travel tips of special interest to solo travelers. A sample copy is available for $5. For an application and more information, write to **Jens Jurgen, Travel Companion,** P.O. Box P-833, Amityville, NY 11701 (☎ **516/454-0880**).

Another agency to check is **Grand Circle Travel,** 347 Congress St., Boston, MA 02110 (☎ **800/221-2610** or 617/350-7500), which offers escorted tours and cruises for retired people, including singles.

Since single supplements on tours are usually hefty, a way to get around paying the supplement is to find a tour company that allows you to share a room with a hitherto-unknown fellow traveler. One company offering a "guaranteed-share plan" for its tours in Spain is **Cosmos** (an affiliate of Globus Tours), 5301 S. Federal Circle, Littleton, CO 80123 (☎ **800/221-0090**). Upon your arrival in Spain, a suitable roommate will be assigned to you from among the tour's other participants. Double-occupancy rates are guaranteed; if a roommate is unavailable, you don't pay the single-occupancy supplement. You can obtain information about its tours through any travel agency.

Dedicated independent travelers may want to check out **The Globetrotters Club,** BCM/Roving, London WCIN 3XX, which enables members to exchange information and generally assist each other in traveling as cheaply as possible. Persons in the United States, and elsewhere outside the U.K. and Europe, pay $23 for the first year and then an $18 annual renewal fee. Residents of the United Kingdom or citizens of Europe pay £12 for the first year or £9 for each year's renewal.

For British Singles   Single people sometimes feel comfortable traveling with groups composed mostly of other singles. One tour operator whose groups are usually composed of at least 50% unattached persons is **Explore Worldwide Ltd.,** 1 Frederick St., Aldershot, Hampshire GU11 1LQ (☎ **01252/344-161**), with a well-justified reputation for offering offbeat tours. Groups rarely include more than 16 participants, and children under 14 are not allowed.

FOR STUDENTS   America's largest student, youth, and budget travel group, **Council Travel** has more than 60 offices worldwide, including the main office at 205 E. 42nd St., New York, NY 10017-5706 (☎ **888/COUNCIL;** call this number to find the location nearest you). It also sells a number of publications for young people considering traveling abroad. For a copy of *Student Travels* magazine—which provides information on all of Council Travel's services as well as on programs and publications of the Council on International Educational Exchange—send $1 in postage.

The most commonly accepted form of identification is also an "open sesame" to bargains. The **International Student Identity Card (ISIC)** gets you such benefits as special student airfares to Europe, medical insurance, and many special discounts.

In Spain the card secures you free entrance into state museums, monuments, and archeological sites. Domestic train fares in Spain are also reduced for students. The card, which costs $18, is available at Council Travel offices nationwide, as well as on hundreds of college/university campuses across the country. Proof of student status and a passport-size photograph (2 in. by 2 in.) are necessary. For the ISIC-issuing office nearest you, contact the **Council on International Educational Exchange,** 205 E. 42nd St., New York, NY 10017 (☎ **800/GET-AN-ID**).

The **International Youth Hostel Federation (IYHF)** was designed to provide bare-bones overnight accommodations for budget-conscious travelers. For information, contact HI-AYH (Hostelling International / American Youth Hostels), 733 15th St. NW, No. 840, Washington, DC 20005 (☎ **800/444-6111** or 202/783-6161). Membership costs $25 annually; those under 18 pay $10, and those 54 or more pay $15.

For British Students   One organization, **Campus Travel,** 52 Grosvenor Gardens, London SW1W OAG (☎ **0171/730-3402**), provides a wealth of information and offers for the student traveler, ranging from route planning to flight insurance, including railcards.

The **International Student Identity Card (ISIC)** is an internationally recognized proof of student status that will entitle you to savings on flights, sightseeing, food, and accommodations. It costs only £5 and is well worth the price. Always show your ISIC when booking a trip—you may not get a discount without it.

Youth hostels are the place to stay if you're a student or, in some cases, if you're traveling on an ultra-tight budget. You'll need an International Youth Hostels Association card, which you can purchase from either of London's **youth hostel retail outlets.** Housed near Covent Garden at 14 Southampton St., London WC23 7HY (☎ **0171/836-1036**), and in the same building as the previously recommended Campus Travel, 52 Grosvenor Gardens, London SW1W OAG (☎ **0171/ 823-4739**), they sell rucksacks, hiking boots, maps, and all the paraphernalia a camper, hiker, or shoestring traveler might need. To apply for a membership card, take both your passport and some passport-sized photos of yourself, plus a membership fee of £9.

The Youth Hostel Association puts together a *YHA Budget Accommodations Guide* (Volumes 1 and 2), which lists the address, phone number, and admissions policy for every youth hostel in the world. (Volume 1 covers Europe and the Mediterranean; volume 2 covers the rest of the globe.) Their cost is £6.99 each, and either of them can be purchased at the retail outlets listed above. If ordering by mail, add 61p for postage if either volume is mailed to any point in the U.K.

In summer many youth hostels are full, so be sure to book ahead. In London, you can make advance reservations at the membership department at 14 Southampton St. (see above).

6 Getting There

BY PLANE

Any information about fares or even flights in the highly volatile airline industry is not writ in stone; even travel agencies with banks of computers have a hard time keeping abreast of last-minute discounts and schedule changes. For up-to-the-minute information, including a list of the carriers that fly to Barcelona and Madrid, check with a travel agent or the individual airlines.

FROM NORTH AMERICA

Flights to Barcelona and Madrid from the U.S. East Coast take 6 to 7 hours, depending on the season and prevailing winds. The national carrier of Spain, **Iberia Airlines** (☎ 800/772-4642), offers more routes into and within Spain than any other airline, with daily nonstop service to Madrid from both New York and Miami. From Miami, Iberia takes off for at least eight destinations in Mexico and Central America, and, in cooperation with its air partner, Ladeco (an airline based in Chile), to dozens of destinations throughout South America as well. Iberia also flies from Los Angeles to Madrid, with a brief stop in Miami. Iberia also has service to Madrid from Toronto (through Montréal) two or three times a week, depending on the season. Also available are attractive rates on fly/drive programs within Iberia and Europe which can be substantially cheaper than booking an air ticket and a car rental separately.

Iberia's fares are lowest if you reserve an APEX (advance-purchase excursion) ticket at least 21 days in advance, schedule your return 7 to 30 days after your departure, and leave and return between Monday and Thursday. Iberia does not offer direct flights to Barcelona or Seville; all ongoing passengers must change planes in Madrid. Fares, which are subject to change, are lower off-season. Most transatlantic flights are on carefully maintained 747s and DC-10s, and in-flight services reflect an interpretation of Spanish traditions, values, and cuisine.

A noteworthy cost-cutting option is Iberia's Europass. Available only to passengers who simultaneously arrange for transatlantic passage on Iberia and a minimum of two additional flights, it allows passage on any flight within Iberia's European or Mediterranean dominion for $250 for the first two flights and $125 for each additional flight (prices are subject to change). This is especially attractive for passengers wishing to combine trips to Spain with, for example, visits to such far-flung destinations as Cairo, Tel Aviv, Istanbul, Moscow, and Munich. For details, ask Iberia's phone representative.

Iberia's main Spain-based competitor is **Air Europa** (☎ 888/238-7672), which offers nonstop service from New York's JFK Airport to Madrid, with continuing service to major cities within Spain. Fares are competitive.

Employee-owned **Trans World Airlines** (☎ 800/221-2000) operates separate daily nonstop flights to both Barcelona and Madrid from JFK. TWA's cheapest APEX ticket requires a 21-day advance purchase and a delay of between 7 and 30 days before activating the return portion of your flight. Traveling between Monday and Thursday usually affords the least expensive tickets. Changes are permitted in departure dates, but are subject to a surcharge.

TWA also offers a limited number of youth fares, which must be arranged 3 days or less before any particular flight. They're available only for passengers aged 12 to 24 who insist on a minimum of restrictions. But know that at TWA, as at each of its competitors, youth fares don't represent any noteworthy financial savings over the price of the APEX ticket described above; they do, however, allow a prolonged sojourn in Spain without the penalties sometimes associated with long-term stays abroad and are therefore ideal for anyone studying or traveling without fixed itineraries. Like its competitors, TWA has a trip-planning service (in this case, the Getaway Vacation desk), and can arrange fly/drive holidays, land packages at Spanish hotels, and/or escorted motorcoach tours.

American Airlines (☎ 800/433-7300) offers daily nonstop service to Madrid from its massive hub in Miami, with excellent connections from there to the rest of the airline's impressive North and South American network. Imposing restrictions that are more flexible than in years gone by, American charges a penalty for any changes in itinerary once you've used the outbound portion of your ticket.

Delta (☎ **800/241-4141**) maintains daily nonstop service from Atlanta (centerpiece of its worldwide network) to Madrid, with continuing service (and no change of plane) to Barcelona. (Many travelers use Delta as a cost-conscious means of landing in one city and departing from the other at the end of their trip.) Delta's Dream Vacation department maintains access to fly/drive programs, land packages, and escorted bus tours through the Iberian peninsula.

Since 1991 **United Airlines** (☎ **800/538-2929**) has flown passengers nonstop to Madrid every day from Washington, D.C.'s Dulles Airport. United also offers fly/drive programs and escorted motorcoach tours.

Continental Airlines (☎ **800/231-0856**) offers six or seven nonstop flights per week, depending on the season, to Madrid from Newark, N.J., an airport many New York residents prefer. Continental offers 10% discounts on most of its fares to anyone 62 or older, as well as to a senior citizen's companion, regardless of his or her age. Like the others, Continental offers regularly scheduled sales promotions that come and go with the seasons.

USAir (☎ **800/428-4322**) offers daily nonstop service between Philadelphia and Madrid. USAir also has connecting flights to Philadelphia from more than 50 cities throughout the United States, Canada, and The Bahamas.

Most U.S.-based carriers offer service solely to Madrid; once in Madrid, Spain's airline, Iberia, offers low fares to cities throughout the country.

FROM GREAT BRITAIN

British Airways (☎ **0171/897-4000** in London) and **Iberia** (☎ **0171/437-5622** in London) are the two major carriers flying between the United Kingdom and Spain. In spite of the frequency of their departures, however, we suspect that most vacationing Brits fly charter (see below).

More than a dozen daily flights, on either BA or Iberia, depart from both London's Heathrow and Gatwick Airports. The Midlands is served by flights from Manchester and Birmingham, two major airports that can also be used by Scots flying to Spain. About seven flights a day go between London and Madrid, with at least six to Barcelona (trip time: 2 to $2^1/2$ hours). From either the Madrid airport or the Barcelona airport, you can tap into Iberia's domestic network—flying, for example, to Seville or the Costa del Sol (centered at the Málaga airport). The best air deals on scheduled flights from the United Kingdom are those requiring a Saturday-night stopover.

As mentioned, most vacationing Brits go charter, at least those looking for air-flight bargains. Delays are frequent (some last 2 whole days and nights), and departures are often at inconvenient hours. Booking conditions can also be severe, and you must read the fine print carefully and deal only with a reputable travel agent. Stays rarely last a month, and booking must sometimes be made at least a month ahead of time, although a 2-week advance reservation is sometimes possible.

Charter flights leave from most British regional airports for various destinations (for example, Málaga), bypassing the congestion at the Madrid airports. Figure on saving approximately 10% to 15% off regularly scheduled flight tickets. But check carefully. British Sunday papers are full of charter deals, and a travel agent can always advise what the best values are at the time of your intended departure.

Other Good-Value Choices

Most airlines divide their year roughly into seasonal slots, with the lowest fares between November 1 and March 14. The shoulder season (spring and early fall) is only slightly more expensive—and includes October, which many Western tourists consider the ideal time to visit Spain. Summer, of course, is the most expensive time.

CHARTER FLIGHTS A charter flight is one reserved months in advance for a one-time-only transit to a predetermined destination. For reasons of economy, some travelers choose this option.

Before paying for a charter, check the restrictions on your ticket or contract. You may be asked to purchase a tour package and pay far in advance. You'll pay a stiff penalty (or forfeit the ticket entirely) if you cancel. Charters are sometimes canceled if the tickets don't sell out. In some cases the charter-ticket seller will offer you an insurance policy for your own legitimate cancellation (proving illness with a hospital certificate, or having a death in the family, for example).

There's no way to predict whether a charter flight or a bucket-shop (see below) flight will be cheaper. You'll have to investigate this at the time of your trip. Charter operators and bucket shops used to perform separate functions, but today many perform both functions.

Among charter-flight operators is **Council Charter,** a subsidiary of the Council on International Educational Exchange (CIEE), 205 E. 42nd St., New York, NY 10017 (☎ **212/822-2700**). This outfit can arrange charter seats to most major European cities, including Madrid, on regularly scheduled aircraft.

One of the biggest New York charter operators is **Travac,** 989 Sixth Ave., 16th Floor, New York, NY 10018 (☎ **800/TRAV-800** or 212/563-3303).

Be warned: Some charter companies have proved unreliable in the past.

BUCKET SHOPS Bucket shops, or consolidators, as they're also called, exist in many forms. In their purest sense they act as clearinghouses for blocks of tickets that airlines discount and consign during normally slow periods of air travel. Ticket prices vary, sometimes to as much as 35% off full fare. Terms of payment can be anywhere from 45 days before departure to the last minute.

Bucket shops abound from coast to coast, but just to get you started, here are some recommendations (look also for ads in your local newspaper's travel section):

In New York, try **TFI Tours International,** 34 W. 32nd St., 12th Floor, New York, NY 10001 (☎ **800/745-8000** in the U.S. outside New York State, or 212/736-1140). They offer service to cities worldwide, including Madrid and Barcelona.

In the Midwest, there's **Travel Avenue,** 10 S. Riverside Plaza, Suite 1404, Chicago, IL 60606 (☎ **800/333-3335**), a national agency whose headquarters are here. Its tickets are often cheaper than those sold by most shops, and it charges the customer only $25 on international tickets, rather than taking the usual commission from an airline. Travel Avenue rebates most of that back to its customers—hence, the lower fares.

Another possibility is **TMI (Travel Management International),** 3617 Dupont Ave. South, Minneapolis, MN 55409 (☎ **800/245-3672**). It offers a wide variety of discounts, including youth fares, student fares, and access to other kinds of air-related discounts. Madrid is one of their destinations.

One of the biggest U.S. consolidators is **Travac,** 989 Ave. of the Americas, New York, NY 10018 (☎ **800/TRAV-800** or 212/563-3303), which offers discounted seats throughout the United States to most cities in Europe, including Madrid, on TWA, United, Delta, and other major airlines.

UniTravel, 1177 N. Warson Rd., St. Louis, MO 63132 (☎ **800/325-2222**), offers tickets to Madrid and elsewhere in Europe at prices that may be lower than what airlines charge if you order tickets directly from them. UniTravel is best suited to providing discounts for passengers who want (or need) to get to Europe on short notice.

You can also try **1-800-FLY-4-LESS,** in the RFA Building, 5440 Morehouse Dr., San Diego, CA 92121. Travelers unable to buy their tickets 3 weeks in advance can utilize this service to obtain low discounted fares with no advance-purchase requirements. 1-800-FLY-4-LESS is a nationwide airline reservation and ticketing service that specializes in finding only the lowest fares. For information on available consolidator airline tickets for last-minute travel, call 800/359-4537.

A final option—suitable only for clients with supremely flexible travel plans—is available through **Airhitch,** 2472 Broadway, Suite 20, New York, NY 10025 (☎ **212/864-2000**). If you let Airhitch know which 5 consecutive days you're available to fly to Europe, they will agree to fly you there within those 5 days. Airhitch arranges for departures from any of three U.S. regions (the East Coast, West Coast, and Midwest/Southeast); they try, but cannot guarantee, to fly you from and to the cities of your choice.

TRAVEL CLUBS   Another possibility for low-cost air travel is the travel club, which supplies an unsold inventory of tickets offering discounts in the usual range of 20% to 60%.

After you pay an annual fee, you're given a "hotline number" to call to find out what discounts are available. Many discounts become available several days, or sometimes as much as a month, before departure. So you have to be fairly flexible.

Some of the best of these clubs include **Moment's Notice,** 7301 New Utrecht Ave., New York, NY 11228 (☎ **212/486-0500**), which has a 24-hour members' hotline (regular toll charges) and a yearly fee of $45 per family. **Sears Discount Travel Club,** 3033 S. Parker Rd., Suite 900, Aurora, CO 80014 (☎ **800/ 433-9383**), offers members, for $50, a catalog (issued four times a year), maps, discounts at select hotels, and a 5% cash bonus on purchases. The **Encore Travel Club,** 4501 Forbes Blvd., Lanham, MD 20706 (☎ **800/638-8976**), charges $49.95 per year for membership that offers up to a 50% discount at more than 4,000 hotels, sometimes during off-peak periods. It also offers substantial discounts on airfares, cruises, and car rentals through its volume-purchase plans. Membership includes a travel package outlining the company's many services, plus use of a toll-free number for advice and information.

TIPS FOR BRITISH TRAVELERS

A regular fare from the United Kingdom to Spain is extremely high, so savvy Brits usually call a travel agent for a "deal"—either a charter flight or some special air-travel promotion. These so-called deals are always available, because of the great interest in Spain as a tourist destination. If one's not possible for you, then an APEX (advance-purchase excursion) ticket might be the way to keep costs trimmed. However, a PEX (public excursion fare) ticket offers a discount without the usual booking restrictions. You might also ask the airlines about a Eurobudget ticket, which often has restrictions or length-of-stay requirements.

British newspapers are always full of classified advertisements touting "slashed" fares to Spain. One good source is *Time Out,* a magazine published in London. London's *Evening Standard* has a daily travel section, and the Sunday edition of almost any newspaper will run many ads. Recommended companies include

Trailfinders (☎ **0171/937-5400** in London) and **Avro Tours** (☎ **0181/543-0000** in London), which operate charters.

There are many London bucket shops around Victoria Station and Earl's Court that offer low fares. Make sure the company you deal with is a member of the IATA, ABTA, or ATOL. These umbrella organizations will help you out if anything goes wrong.

CEEFAX, a British TV information service included on many home and hotel TVs, runs details of package holidays and flights to Europe and beyond. Just switch to your CEEFAX channel to find a menu of listings that includes travel information.

Make sure you understand the bottom line on any special deal you purchase—that is, ask if all surcharges, including airport taxes and other hidden costs—are cited before committing yourself to purchase. Upon investigation, some of these "deals" are not as attractive as advertised. Also, make sure you understand what the penalties are if you're forced to cancel at the last minute.

BY TRAIN

If you're already in Europe, you may want to go to Spain by train, especially if you have a Eurailpass. Even without a pass, you'll find that the cost of a train ticket is relatively moderate. Rail passengers who visit from Britain or France should make couchette and sleeper reservations as far in advance as possible, especially during the peak summer season.

Since Spain's rail tracks are of a wider gauge than those used for French trains (except for the TALGO and Trans-Europe Express trains), you'll probably have to change trains at the border unless you're on an express (see below). For long journeys on Spanish rails, seat and sleeper reservations are mandatory.

The most comfortable and the fastest trains in Spain are the TER, TALGO, and Electrotren. However, you pay a supplement to ride on these fast trains. Both first- and second-class are sold on Spanish trains. Tickets can be purchased in the United States or Canada at the nearest office of FrenchRail, Inc., or from any reputable travel agent. Confirmation of your reservation will take about a week.

If you want your car carried, you must travel Auto-Expreso in Spain. This type of auto transport can be booked only through travel agents or rail offices once you arrive in Europe.

To go from London to Spain by rail, you'll need to change not only the train but also the rail terminus in Paris. In Paris, it's worth the extra bucks to purchase a TALGO express or a "Puerta del Sol" express—that way you can avoid having to change trains once again at the Spanish border. Trip time from London to Paris is about 6 hours; from Paris to Madrid, about 15 hours or so, which includes 2 hours spent in Paris changing trains and stations. Many rail passes are available in the United Kingdom for travel in Europe. Stop in at **Wasteels,** opposite Platform 2 in Victoria Station, London SW1V 1JZ (☎ **0171/834-6744**), which can help you find the best option for the trip you're planning.

BY BUS

Bus travel to Spain is possible but not popular—it's quite slow. But coach services do operate regularly from major capitals of Western Europe to Madrid and Barcelona, from which bus connections can be made to Seville. The busiest routes are from London and are run by **Eurolines Limited,** 23 Crawley Rd., Luton LU1 1HX in Bedfordshire (☎ **01582/404511,** or 0171/730-8235 in London). The journey from London's Victoria Station to Madrid is provided by two services: Service 180 is an express from Victoria Station to Madrid, departing London daily at 9pm, arriving in Madrid the following day at 9:30pm. Service 181 leaves London at 9pm on the first day, arriving in Madrid at 12:30am on the third day.

Other bus trips can be arranged from London to Barcelona, Alicante, Benidorm, and Marbella.

Julia Tours of Barcelona (☎ **93/490-40-00** in Barcelona) operates a coach that departs from London's Victoria Station on Monday, Wednesday, and Saturday. It leaves London at 11am and gets into Barcelona the following morning at 10:45. An English-speaking staff in Barcelona can make reservations for you and supply more details.

BY CAR

If you're touring the rest of Europe in a rented car, you might, for an added cost, be allowed to drop off your vehicle in a major city such as Madrid or Barcelona.

Motor approaches from Europe to Spain are across France on expressways. The most popular border crossing into Spain is east of Biarritz. To Madrid, the best route to take is E70 west to Bilbao; then cut south on E804 to the junction with E05, which heads southwest to Burgos. Bypass Burgos and continue south on the route to Madrid, which is also known as N-I.

To get to Barcelona from the north, take A7 or E9 to A18; from the Costa Brava, you'll take A19 heading southwest, and from the south, you'll enter Barcelona on A16.

If you're driving from Madrid to Seville, connect with E90 and head southwest toward Mérida; from there, head south on E803 to Seville. For an alternative route, head south on E5 to Córdoba. After exploring Córdoba, continue southwest on E5 and this highway will take you to Seville.

BY ORGANIZED TOUR

Some people prefer that a tour operator make all their travel arrangements. There are many such companies, each offering transportation to and around Spain, prearranged accommodations, and such extras as bilingual tour guides and lectures. Often these tours to Spain include an excursion to Morocco or Portugal.

American Express Vacations, P.O. Box 1525, Fort Lauderdale, FL 33302 (☎ **800/446-6234** in the U.S. and Canada), offers some of the most comprehensive programs available to Spain, with trips that include Barcelona, Madrid, and Seville as major stopovers.

Sun Holidays, 7280 W. Palmetto Park Rd., Suite 301, Boca Raton, FL 33433 (☎ **800/422-8000** or 407/367-0105), has been specializing in extended vacations for senior citizens since 1980. The company features excursions to the Costa del Sol in Spain and the Algarve and Cascais/Lisbon areas of Portugal. The company also sponsors fully escorted motorcoach tours of Spain and Portugal. They pay special attention to retired Americans.

Settling into Barcelona   3

Blessed with rich and fertile soil, an excellent harbor, and a hard-working population, Barcelona has always prospered. At a time when Madrid was still a dusty and unknown Castilian backwater, Barcelona was a powerful, diverse capital, one influenced more by the Mediterranean empires that conquered it than by the cultures of the arid Iberian plains to the west. Carthage, Rome, Charlemagne-era France—each overran Catalonia, and each left an indelible mark on the region's nascent identity.

The Catalán people have clung fiercely to their unique culture—a culture that, earlier in this century, Franco systematically tried to eradicate. But Catalonia has endured, becoming a semiautonomous region of Spain (with Catalán its official language). And Barcelona, the region's lodestar, has come into its own. The city's most powerful monuments are those that open a window onto its history: from the intricately carved edifices that comprise the medieval Gothic Quarter to the curvilinear *modernismo* that inspired Gaudí's Sagrada Familia, to the seminal surrealist works of Picasso and Miró found in museums that peg Barcelona as a crucial incubator for 20th-century art.

As if the attractions of Barcelona weren't enough, it stands on the doorstep of some of the great playgrounds and vacation retreats of Europe: the Balearic Islands to the east, the Costa Brava (Wild Coast) to the north, the Penedés wine country to the west, the Roman city of Tarragona, the monastery at Montserrat, and such Costa Dorada resort towns as Sitges, to the south.

Despite its allure, Barcelona grapples with problems common to many major cities—the increasing polarization of rich and poor, a rising tide of drug abuse, and an escalating crime rate. But in reaction to a rash of negative publicity, city authorities have, with some degree of success, brought crime under control, at least within the tourist zones.

A revitalized Barcelona eagerly prepared for and welcomed thousands of visitors as part of the 1992 Summer Olympic Games. But the action didn't end when the last medal was handed out. Barcelona turned its multi-million-dollar building projects into permanently expanded facilities for sports and tourism. Its modern $150-million terminal at El Prat de Llobregat airport can accommodate 12 million passengers a year. Barcelona is indeed poised to meet the challenges of the 21st century.

1 Orientation

GETTING THERE

BY PLANE   During the months prior to the 1992 Olympics, airlines scrambled to provide nonstop transatlantic service to Barcelona. In the post-Olympic world, however, most passengers must first change aircraft in Madrid. The only exception is **TWA,** which has maintained its nonstop transatlantic service from New York to Barcelona long after other carriers, including Iberia, discontinued theirs. Passengers originating in such European capitals as London, Paris, and Rome can fly nonstop to Barcelona (usually on their national airlines), but most passengers, for whatever reason, opt for transit through Madrid. For more information on flying into Madrid, refer to "Getting There" in Chapter 2.

Within Spain, the most likely carrier is **Iberia,** which offers peak-hour shuttle flights at 15-minute intervals between Madrid and Barcelona. Service from Madrid to Barcelona at less congested times of the day averages around one flight every 30 to 40 minutes. Iberia also offers flights between Barcelona and Valencia, Granada, Seville, and Bilbao. In Barcelona you can arrange ticketing at one of two Iberia offices. The easiest to find lies a few blocks north of the sprawling Plaça de Catalunya, at Passeig de Gràcia, 30 (☎ **93/412-47-48;** metro: Passeig de Gràcia).

El Prat de Llobregat, 08820 Prat de Llobregat (☎ **93/298-38-38**), the Barcelona airport, lies 7$^{1}/_{2}$ miles (12km) southwest of the city. The route to the center of town is carefully signposted. A train runs daily on the 21-minute trip between the airport and Barcelona's Estació Central de Barcelona-Sants from 6:14am (the first airport departure) to 10:44pm (the last city departure). If your hotel lies near Plaça de Catalunya, you might opt instead for an Aerobús that runs daily every 15 minutes between 5:30am and 10pm. A taxi from the airport into central Barcelona is considerably more expensive.

BY TRAIN   A train called the Barcelona-TALGO provides rail service between Paris and Barcelona in 11$^{1}/_{2}$ hours. For many other connections from the mainland of Europe, it's necessary to change trains at Port Bou, on the French-Spanish border. Most trains issue seat and sleeper reservations.

Trains departing from the **Estació de Franca,** Avenida Marqués de l'Argentera (metro: Barceloneta, L3), cover long distances within Spain as well as international routes, carrying a total of 20,000 passengers daily. There are express night trains to Paris, Zurich, Milan, and Geneva. Every international route served by the state-owned RENFE railway company uses the Estació de Franca, including some of its most luxurious express trains, such as the *Pau Casals* and the *TALGO Catalán.*

This totally modernized 1929 station includes a huge screen with updated information on train departures and arrivals, personalized ticket dispatching, a passenger attention center, a tourism information center, showers, internal baggage control, and a first-aid center, as well as centers for hotel reservations and car rentals. But it's much more than a departure point: The station has an elegant restaurant, a cafeteria, a book-and-record store, a jazz club, and even a disco. The Estació de Franca is just steps away from Ciutadella Park, the zoo, and the port and is near Vila Olímpica.

From this station you can book tickets to the major cities of Spain: Madrid (5 TALGO trains per day, 7 hours; and 3 *rápidos,* 10 hours), Seville (2 trains daily, 10$^{1}/_{2}$ hours), and Valencia (11 daily, 4 hours).

RENFE also has a terminal at **Estació Central de Barcelona-Sants,** Plaça de Països Catalanes (metro: Sants-Estació).

For general **RENFE information,** call **93/490-02-02.**

BY BUS   Bus travel to Barcelona is possible but not popular—it's slow. Coach services do not operate regularly from the major capitals of Western Europe to Barcelona. **Eurolines Limited,** 23 Crawley Rd., Luton LU1 1HX, Bedfordshire, England (☎ **01582/404-511,** or 0171/730-8235 in London), can arrange your trip from London to Barcelona.

Enatcar, Estació del Nord (☎ **93/245-25-28**), operates 5 buses per day to Madrid (trip time: 8 hours) and 10 buses per day to Valencia (trip time: 4¹/₂ hours). For bus travel to one of the beach resorts along the Costa Brava, go to **Sarfa,** Estació del Nord (☎ **93/265-11-58**), which operates buses from Barcelona to such resorts as Tossa de Mar. Trip time is usually 2 hours.

BY CAR   From France (the usual road approach to Barcelona), the major access route is at the eastern end of the Pyrenees. You have a choice of the express highway (E-15) or the more scenic coastal road. But be warned: If you take the scenic coastal road in July and August you'll often encounter bumper-to-bumper traffic. From France, you can also approach Barcelona via Toulouse. Cross the border into Spain at Puigcerdá (frontier stations are there), near the principality of Andorra. From there, take N-152 to Barcelona.

From Madrid, take N-2 to Zaragoza, then A-2 to El Vendrell, followed by the A-7 motorway to Barcelona. From the Costa Blanca or Costa del Sol, take E-15 north from Valencia along the eastern Mediterranean coast.

BY FERRY   **Transmediterránea,** Muelle de Barcelona Estación Maritima (☎ **93/ 443-25-32**), operates daily voyages to the Balearic island of Majorca (trip time: 8 hours) and also to Minorca (trip time: 9 hours). In summer it's important to have a reservation as far in advance as possible, because of overcrowding.

VISITOR INFORMATION

A conveniently located tourist office is the **Patronat de Turisme,** Gran Vía de les Corts Catalanes, 658 (☎ **93/301-74-43;** metro: Urquinaona or Plaça de Catalunya). It's open Monday to Saturday from 9am to 7pm. There's also an office at the airport, El Prat de Llobregat (☎ **93/478-47-04**), which you'll pass as you clear Customs. It's open year round Monday to Saturday from 9:30am to 8pm and Sunday from 9:30am to 2pm.

There's another office at the **Estació Central de Barcelona-Sants,** Plaça Països Catalanes (☎ **93/491-44-31;** metro: Sants-Estació). In summer it's open daily from 8am to 8pm; off-season, Monday to Friday from 8am to 8pm and on Saturday and Sunday from 8am to 2pm. At these offices you can pick up maps and information.

CITY LAYOUT

MAIN SQUARES, STREETS & ARTERIES   **Plaça de Catalunya** (Plaza de Cataluña in Spanish) is the city's heart; the world-famous Les Rambles (Las Ramblas in Spanish) are its arteries. Les Rambles begin at Plaça Portal de la Pau, with its 164-foot-high monument to Columbus and a panoramic view of the port, and stretch north to Plaça de Catalunya, with its fountains and trees. Along this wide promenade you'll find bookshops and newsstands, stalls selling birds and flowers, and benches or café tables and chairs where you can sit and watch the passing parade.

At the end of the Rambles is the **Barri Xinés** (Barrio Chino in Spanish, Chinese Quarter in English), which has enjoyed notoriety as a haven of prostitution and drugs, populated in Jean Genet's *The Thief's Journal* by "whores, thieves, pimps, and beggars." Still a dangerous district, it's best viewed during the day, if at all.

Off the Rambles lies **Plaça Reial** (Plaza Real in Spanish), the most harmoniously proportioned square in Barcelona. Come here on Sunday morning to see the stamp and coin collectors peddle their wares.

The major wide boulevards of Barcelona are **Avinguda** (Avenida in Spanish) **Diagonal** and **Passeig** (Paseo in Spanish) **de Colom,** and an elegant shopping street, **Passeig de Gràcia.**

A short walk from the Rambles will take you to **Passeig del Moll de la Fusta,** a waterfront promenade developed in the 1990s, with some of the finest (but not the cheapest) restaurants in Barcelona. If you can't afford the high prices, come here at least for a drink in the open air and take in a view of the harbor.

To the east is the old port of the city, called **La Barceloneta,** which dates from the 18th century. This strip of land between the port and the sea has traditionally been a good place for seafood.

The **Barri Gòtic** (Barrio Gótico in Spanish, Gothic Quarter in English) lies to the east of the Rambles. This is the site of the city's oldest buildings, including the cathedral.

North of Plaça de Catalunya, the **Eixample** unfolds. An area of wide boulevards, in contrast to the Gothic Quarter, it contains two major roads leading out of Barcelona, the previously mentioned Avinguda Diagonal and Gran Vía de les Corts Catalanes. Another major area, Gràcia, lies north of the Eixample.

Montjuïc, one of the mountains of Barcelona, begins at Plaça d'Espanya, a traffic rotary. This was the setting for the 1992 Summer Olympic Games and is today the site of Vila Olímpica (see below). The other mountain is Tibidabo, in the northwest, which boasts great views of the city and the Mediterranean. It contains an amusement park.

FINDING AN ADDRESS/MAPS   Finding an address in Barcelona can be a problem. The city is characterized by long boulevards and a complicated maze of narrow, twisting streets. Therefore, knowing the street number is all-important. If you see the designation *s/n* it means that the building is without a number (*sin número*). Therefore it's crucial to learn the cross street if you're seeking a specific establishment.

The rule about street numbers is that there is no rule. On most streets, numbering begins on one side and runs up that side until the end, then runs in the opposite direction on the other side. Therefore, no. 40 could be opposite no. 408. But there are many exceptions. Sometimes street numbers on buildings in the older quarters have been obscured by the patina of time.

Arm yourself with a good map before setting out. Those given away free by tourist offices and hotels aren't adequate, since they don't label the little streets. The best map for exploring Barcelona, published by **Falk,** is available at most bookstores and newsstands, such as those found along Les Rambles. This pocket map includes all the streets, with an index of how to find them.

NEIGHBORHOODS IN BRIEF

Barri Gòtic   The Gothic Quarter rises to the north of Passeig de Colom, with its Columbus Monument, and is bordered on its east by a major artery, Vía Laietana, which begins at La Barceloneta at Plaça d'Antoni López and runs north to Plaça d'Urquinaona. Les Rambles are the western border of the Gothic Quarter, and on the northern edge is the Ronda de Sant Pere, which intersects with Plaça de Catalunya and Passeig de Gràcia. The heart of this medieval quarter is Plaça de Sant Jaume, which was a major crossroads in the old Roman city. Many of the structures in the old section are ancient, including the ruins of a Roman temple dedicated to Augustus.

Antiques stores, restaurants, cafés, museums, some hotels, and bookstores fill the place today. It's also the headquarters of the Generalitat, seat of the Catalán government.

Les Rambles   The most famous promenade in Spain, ranking with Madrid's Paseo del Prado, was once a drainage channel. These days, street entertainers, flower vendors, news vendors, café patrons, and strollers flow along its length. Les Rambles is actually composed of five different sections, each a particular *rambla,* with names like Rambla de Canaletes, Rambla dels Estudis, Rambla de Sant Josep, Rambla dels Caputxins, and Rambla de Santa Mònica. The pedestrian esplanade is shaded as it makes its way from Plaça de Catalunya to the port—all the way to the Columbus Monument. Along the way you'll pass the Gran Teatre del Liceu, on Rambla dels Caputxins, one of the most magnificent opera houses in the world until it caught fire in 1994. Miró did a sidewalk mosaic at Plaça de la Boqueria. During the stagnation of the Franco era, this street grew seedier and seedier. But the opening of the Ramada Renaissance hotel and the restoration of many buildings have brought energy and hope for the street.

Barri Xinés   This isn't "Chinatown," as most people assume—in fact, historians are unsure just how the neighborhood got its name. For decades it's had an unsavory reputation, known for its houses of prostitution. Franco outlawed prostitution in 1956, but apparently no one ever told the denizens of this district of narrow, often murky, old streets and dark corners. Petty thieves, drug dealers, and purse snatchers are just some of the neighborhood characters. Nighttime is dangerous, so exercise caution; still, most visitors like to take a quick look to see what all the excitement is about. Just off Les Rambles, the area lies primarily between the waterfront and Carrer de l'Hospital.

Barri de la Ribera   Another *barrio* that stagnated for years but is now well into a renaissance, the Barri de la Ribera is adjacent to the Barri Gòtic, going east to Passeig de Picasso, which borders the Parc de la Ciutadella. The centerpiece of this district is the Museu Picasso, housed in the 15th-century Palau Agüilar, at Montcada, 15. Numerous art galleries have opened around the museum, and the old quarter is fashionable. Many mansions in this area were built at the time of one of the major maritime expansions in Barcelona's history, principally in the 1200s and 1300s. Most of these grand homes still stand along Carrer de Montcada and other nearby streets.

La Barceloneta & the Harborfront   Although Barcelona was founded on seagoing tradition, its waterfront was in decay for years. Today it's bursting with activity along the waterfront promenade, Passeig del Moll de la Fusta. The best way to get a bird's-eye view of the area is to take an elevator to the top of the Columbus Monument in Plaça Portal de la Pau.

In the vicinity of the monument were the Reials Drassanes, or royal shipyards, a booming place of industry during Barcelona's maritime heyday in the Middle Ages. Years before Columbus landed in the New World, ships sailed around the world from here, flying the traditional yellow-and-red flag of Catalonia.

To the east lies a mainly artificial peninsula called La Barceloneta (Little Barcelona), formerly a fishing district, dating mainly from the 18th century. It's now filled with seafood restaurants. The blocks here are long and surprisingly narrow—architects planned them that way so that each room in every building fronted a street. Many bus lines terminate at Passeig Nacional here, site of the Barcelona Aquarium.

Eixample (Ensanche)   To the north of Plaça de Catalunya lies the Eixample, or Ensanche, the section of Barcelona that grew beyond the old medieval walls. This great period of "extension," or enlargement (*eixample* in Catalán), came mainly in the

19th century. Avenues form a grid of perpendicular streets, cut across by a majestic boulevard—Passeig de Gràcia, a posh shopping street ideal for leisurely promenades. The area's main traffic artery is Avinguda Diagonal, which links the expressway and the heart of this congested city.

The Eixample possesses some of the most original buildings any architect ever designed—not just those by Gaudí, but ones by others as well. The area was the center of Barcelona's *modernismo* movement. And of course, Gaudí's Sagrada Familia is one of the major attractions.

Montjuïc & Tibidabo   Montjuïc, called Hill of the Jews after a Jewish necropolis there, gained prominence in 1929 as the site of the World's Fair and again in 1992 as the site of the Summer Olympic Games. Its major attraction is the Poble Espanyol (Spanish Village), a 5-acre site constructed for the World's Fair, where examples of Spanish art and architecture are displayed against the backdrop of a traditional Spanish village. Tibidabo (1,650 feet) is where you should go for your final look at Barcelona. On a clear day you can see the mountains of Majorca (the most famous of the Balearic Islands). Reached by train, tram, and cable car, Tibidabo is the most popular Sunday excursion in Barcelona.

Pedralbes   Pedralbes is where the wealthy people live, some in stylish blocks of apartment houses, others in 19th-century villas behind ornamental fences, and still others in stunning *modernismo* structures. Set in a park, the Palau de Pedralbes (at Avinguda Diagonal, 686) was constructed in the 1920s as a gift from the city to Alfonxo XIII, the grandfather of today's King Juan Carlos. The king abdicated and fled in 1931, never making much use of the palace. Today it has a new life, housing a museum of carriages and a group of European paintings called the Col·lecció Cambó.

Vila Olímpica   This seafront property contains the tallest buildings in the city. The revitalized site, in the post–Olympic Games era, is the setting for numerous showrooms for imported cars, designer clothing stores, restaurants, and business offices. The "village" was the center of the 1992 games. A regular city-in-miniature is taking shape, complete with banks, art galleries, nightclubs, bars, even pastry shops.

2 Getting Around

DISCOUNTS   To save money on public transportation, buy one of two transportation cards, each good for 10 trips; **Tarjeta T-1** is good for the metro, bus, Montjuïc funicular, and Tramvía Blau, which runs from Passeig de Sant Gervasi / Avinguda del Tibidabo to the bottom part of the funicular to Tibidabo. **Tarjeta T-2** is good on everything but the bus.

Passes (*abonos temporales*) are available at the office of **Transports Metropolita de Barcelona,** Plaça de Catalunya, open Monday to Friday from 8am to 7pm and on Saturday from 8am to 1pm.

To save money on sightseeing tours during the summer, take a ride on **Bus Turistic,** which passes by a dozen of the most popular sights. You can get on and off the bus as you please and also ride the Tibidabo funicular and the Montjuïc cable car and funicular for the price of a single ticket. Tickets may be purchased on the bus or at the transportation booth at Plaça de Catalunya.

BY SUBWAY   Barcelona's metro system consists of five main lines; it crisscrosses the city more frequently and with greater efficiency than the bus network. Two commuter trains also service the city, fanning out to the suburbs. Service is Monday to Friday from 5am to 11pm, on Saturday from 5am to 1am, and on Sunday and holidays from 6am to 1am. The entrance to each metro station is marked with a red diamond. The major station for all subway lines is Plaça de Catalunya.

Barcelona Metro

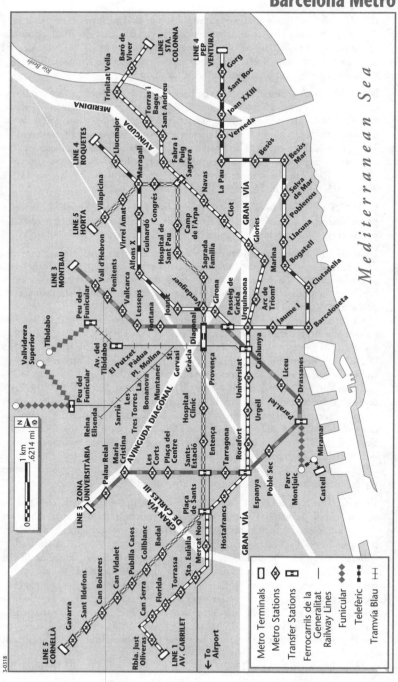

49

BY BUS   Some 50 bus lines traverse the city, and as always, you don't want to ride them at rush hour. The driver issues a ticket as you board at the front. Most buses operate daily from 6:30am to 10pm; some night buses go along the principal arteries from 10pm to 4am. Buses are color-coded—red ones cut through the city center during the day and blue ones do the job at night.

BY TAXI   Each yellow-and-black taxi bears the letters SP (*servicio público*) on both its front and its rear. A lit green light on the roof and a LIBRE sign in the window indicate that the taxi is free to pick up passengers. Check to make sure you're not paying the fare of a previously departed passenger; taxi drivers have been known to "forget" to turn back the meter. There's an additional charge for each kilometer you cover in slow-moving traffic. Supplements might also be added—for a large suitcase, for instance. Rides to the airport carry a supplement as well. For a taxi, call **93/ 330-08-04, 93/300-38-11,** or **93/358-11-11.**

BY BICYCLE   Ever wonder why you see so few people riding bicycles in Barcelona? As in Madrid, the heavy pollution from traffic and the narrow pedestrian-clogged streets of the inner city make riding a bicycle very difficult. It's better to walk.

BY CAR   Driving is next to impossible in congested Barcelona, and it's potentially dangerous. Besides, it's unlikely that you'd ever find a place to park. Try other means of getting around. Save your car rentals for 1-day excursions from the Catalonian capital to such places as Sitges and Tarragona to the south, Montserrat to the west, or the resorts of the Costa Brava to the north.

All three of the major U.S.-based car-rental firms are represented in Barcelona, both at the airport and at downtown offices. The company with the longest hours and some of the most favorable rates is **Budget,** Travesera de Gràcia, 71 (☎ **93/ 201-21-99**), open Monday to Friday (without a midday break) from 8am to 8pm and on Saturday and Sunday from 9am to 1pm.

Other contenders include **Avis,** Carrer de Casanova, 209 (☎ **93/209-95-33**), open Monday to Friday from 9am to 1pm and 4 to 7pm, and on Saturday from 8am to 1pm. **Hertz** maintains its office at Tuset, 10 (☎ **93/217-80-76**); it's open Monday to Friday from 8am to 2pm and 4 to 7pm, and on Saturday from 9am to 1pm. Both Hertz and Avis are closed on Sunday, forcing clients of those companies to trek out to the airport to pick up or return their cars.

Remember that it's usually cheaper and easier to arrange your car rental before leaving North America by calling one of the firms' toll-free numbers.

FUNICULARS & RAIL LINKS   At some point in your journey, you may want to visit both Tibidabo and Montjuïc. There are various links to these mountaintops. A train called the **Tramvía Blau (Blue Streetcar)** goes from Passeig de Sant Gervasi / Avinguda del Tibidabo to the bottom of the funicular to Tibidabo every 3 to 15 minutes. It operates Monday to Saturday from 7am to 10pm and on Sunday and holidays from 7am to 10:30pm. At the end of the run, you can continue the rest of the way by funicular to the top, at 1,600 feet, for a panoramic view of Barcelona. The funicular operates every half hour Monday to Friday from 7:05am to 9:43pm, on Saturday from 7:15am to 9:45pm, and on Sunday and holidays from 7:15 to 10:15am and 8:45 to 9:45pm. During peak visiting hours (10:15am to 8:45pm) service is increased, with a funicular departing every 15 minutes.

Montjuïc, the site of the 1992 Olympics, can be reached by the Montjuïc funicular, linking up with subway line 3 at Parallel. The funicular operates in summer daily from 11am to 8pm; in winter, on Saturday, Sunday, and holidays from 10:45am to 2pm.

A **cable car** linking the upper part of the Montjuïc funicular with Castell de Montjuïc is in service from June through September, daily from noon to 3pm and 4 to 8:30pm; off-season, only on Saturday, Sunday, and holidays from 11am to 2:45pm and 4 to 7:30pm.

To get to these places, you can board the **Montjuïc telèferic,** which runs from La Barceloneta to Montjuïc. Service June through September is daily from 11am to 9pm; off-season, Monday to Friday from noon to 5:45pm and on Saturday and Sunday from noon to 6:15pm.

FAST FACTS: Barcelona

American Express   For your mail or banking needs, the American Express office in Barcelona is at Passeig de Gràcia, 101 (☎ 93/217-00-70; metro: Diagonal), near the corner of Carrer del Rosselló. It's open Monday to Friday from 9:30am to 6pm and on Saturday from 10am to noon.

Area Code   The telephone area code for Barcelona is **93.**

Bookstores   The best selection of English-language books, including travel maps and guides, is LAIE, Pau Claris, 85 (☎ 93/318-17-39; metro: Plaça de Catalunya or Urquinaona), 1 block from the Gran Vía de les Corts Catalanes. It's open Monday to Saturday from 10am to 9pm. The bookshop has an upstairs café with a little terrace, serving breakfast, lunch (salad bar), even dinners. Meals begin at 1,650 ptas. ($13.20). The café is open Monday to Saturday from 9am to 1am. The shop also presents cultural events, including art exhibits and literary presentations.

Climate   See "When to Go," in Chapter 2.

Consulates   The Consulate of the **United States,** at Reina Elisenda, 23 (☎ 93/280-22-27; train: Reina Elisenda), is open Monday to Friday from 9am to 12:30pm and 3 to 5pm. The Consulate of **Canada,** at Travessera de les Corts, 265 (☎ 93/410-66-99; metro: Plaça Molina), is open Monday to Friday from 9am to 2pm and 3 to 5:30pm. The Consulate of the **United Kingdom,** at Avinguda Diagonal, 477 (☎ 93/419-90-44; metro: Hospital Clinic), is open Monday to Friday from 9am to 2pm and 4 to 5pm. The Consulate of **Australia** is at Gran Vía Carlos III, 98, 9th Floor (☎ 93/330-04-96; metro: María Cristina), and is open Monday to Friday from 10am to noon.

Currency Exchange   Most banks will exchange currency Monday to Friday from 8:30am to 2pm and on Saturday from 8:30am to 1pm. A major *oficina de cambio* (exchange office) is operated at the Estació Central de Barcelona-Sants, the principal rail station for Barcelona. It's open Monday to Saturday from 8:30am to 10pm and on Sunday from 8:30am to 2pm and 4:30 to 10pm. Exchange offices are also available at Barcelona's airport, El Prat de Llobregat, open daily from 7am to 11pm.

Dentist   Call Clinica Dental Beonadex, Paseo Bona Nova, 69, 3rd Floor (☎ 93/418-44-33), for an appointment. It's open on Monday from 4 to 9pm and Tuesday to Friday from 8am to 3pm.

Doctors   See "Hospitals," below.

Drugstores   The most central one is Farmacía Manuel Nadal i Casas, Rambla de Canaletes, 121 (☎ 93/317-49-42; metro: Plaça de Catalunya), open Monday to Friday from 9am to 1:30pm and 4:30 to 8pm and on Saturday from 9am to 1:30pm.

Various pharmacies take turns staying open late at night. Pharmacies that aren't open post the names and addresses of the pharmacies in the area that are open.

Emergencies   In case of a **fire,** call 080; for the **police,** 092; and to call an **ambulance,** 061.

Hospitals   Barcelona has many hospitals and clinics, including the Hospital Clínic and the Hospital de la Santa Creu i Sant Pau, at the intersection of Carrer Cartagena and Carrer Sant Antoni Maria Claret (☎ 93/291-90-00; metro: Hospital de Sant Pau).

Launderettes   Ask at your hotel for the one nearest you, or try one of the following: Lavandería Brasilia, Avinguda Meridiana, 322 (☎ 93/352-72-05; metro: Plaça de Catalunya), is open Monday to Friday from 9:30am to 1:30pm and 4 to 8pm. Also centrally located is Lavandería Yolanda, Carrer Carma, 114 (☎ 93/329-43-68; metro: Liceu, at Les Rambles); it's open Monday to Friday from 9am to 1:30pm and 4 to 8pm and on Saturday from 9am to 1:30pm.

Luggage Storage/Lockers   The train station, Estació Central de Barcelona-Sants (☎ 93/491-44-31), has lockers for 400 to 600 ptas. ($3.20 to $4.80) per day. You can obtain locker space daily from 7am to 11pm.

Police   See "Emergencies," above.

Post Office   The main post office is at Plaça d'Antoni López (☎ 93/318-38-31; metro: Jaume I). It's open Monday to Friday from 8am to 10pm and on Saturday from 8am to 8pm.

Rest Rooms   Some public rest rooms are available, including those at popular tourist spots, such as Tibidabo and Montjuïc. You'll also find rest rooms at the major museums of Barcelona, at all train stations and airports, and at metro stations. The major department stores, such as El Corté Ingles, also have good rest rooms. Otherwise, out on the streets you may be a bit hard-pressed. Sanitation is questionable in some of the public facilities. If you use the facilities of a café or tavern, it's customary to make a small purchase at the bar, even if only a glass of mineral water.

Taxes   If you're not a European Union resident and you make purchases in Spain worth more than 86,520 ptas. ($692.15), you can get a tax refund. (The internal tax, known as VAT in most of Europe, is called IVA in Spain.) Depending on the goods, the rate usually ranges from 7% to 12% of the total worth of your merchandise. Luxury items are taxed at 33%.

To get this refund, you must complete three copies of a form that the store will give you, detailing the nature of your purchase and its value. Citizens of non-EU countries show the purchase and the form to the Spanish Customs Office. The shop is supposed to refund the amount due you. Inquire at the time of purchase how they will do so and discuss in what currency your refund will arrive.

Taxis   See "Getting Around," earlier in this chapter.

Telephone   Dial **003** for local operator information within Barcelona. For elsewhere in Spain, dial **009.** Hotels impose various surcharges on phone calls, especially long distance, either in Spain or abroad. It's cheaper to go to the central telephone office at Fontanella, 4, off Plaça de Catalunya (metro: Plaça de Catalunya), open Monday to Saturday from 8:30am to 9pm.

Transit Information   For general RENFE (train) information, dial 93/490-02-02. For details about airport information, call 93/298-38-38.

3 Best Hotel Bets

- **Best Historic Hotel:** The great hotelier, César Ritz, founded the **Hotel Ritz** (☎ **800/223-1230** in the U.S., or 93/318-52-00) in 1919, and it was immediately labeled "the grande dame" of Barcelona hotels. Although that's a dated term to describe hotels, the label still holds true. It's Barcelona's traditional and authentic old-world favorite, ranking along with the Ritz in Madrid for prestige. Thoroughly renovated, it hides its luxuries behind a glamorous facade. Although there's great competition in the luxury five-star hotel market in Barcelona, the rich and famous still show up on the doorstep of the Ritz.
- **Best for Business Travelers:** It's not the grandest hotel in Barcelona, but the 12-story Barcelona Hilton (☎ **800/445-8667** in the U.S. and Canada, or 93/419-22-33), near the main soccer stadium, has a state-of-the-art business center, plus four floors of executive rooms, one reserved exclusively for women. Even the bedrooms are somewhat businesslike, with bedside controls and security locks. Rapid check-out means that you'll get to the airport on time; the highly professional staff is able to connect you with the movers and shakers in Barcelona with whom you'll be doing business.
- **Best for a Romantic Getaway:** Barcelona isn't exactly a summer resort city, but the **Claris** (☎ **800/888-4747** in the U.S., or 93/487-62-62)—which some regard as the best in Barcelona—offers such luxury and comfort that it will suffice. From its Japanese water garden to its rooftop pool, this is a beautifully restored palace from the 1800s. Even its upstairs-downstairs duplex configurations—separating sleeping from living areas—add to its secretive, romantic ambience. The owners' collection of Egyptian and Indian artifacts creates an exotic flavor. The most romantic (also expensive) public area is the Caviar Bar, a pocket of posh, served in cozy, intimate surroundings—followed by an haute cuisine dinner in the continental restaurant.
- **Best Trendy Hotel:** The **Hotel Arts** (☎ **800/241-3333** in the U.S., or 93/221-10-00), the only hotel in Europe commanded by the prestigious Ritz-Carlton group, is the place to stay for the fashionable and those who want to be. The 44-story glass-and-steel tower enjoys a dramatic seafront location. Decorators and architects from the United States worked to create a glamorous and chic rendezvous; the view from the open-air pool to the lush fabrics in the bedrooms is simply splendid.
- **Best Lobby for Pretending You're Rich:** There's the Ritz, of course (see above), but the **Avenida Palace** (☎ **93/301-96-00**) recaptures some of the city's long-ago glamour. In an old stone palace, this longtime favorite has a rich, historic atmosphere. It boasts one of the plushest lobbies in the world, with glittering chandeliers, red carpeting (the only color to use, of course), and a curving marble staircase posh enough to make you feel like a Morgan, Ford, or Getty of yesteryear. Naturally, you enjoy all this fin-de-siècle atmosphere to piano accompaniment.
- **Best for Families:** In the Barri Gòtic opposite the cathedral, the **Hotel Colón** (☎ **800/845-0636** in the U.S., or 93/301-14-04) has long been a favorite because of its choice location near many of the major sights of Barcelona. The setting is traditional, with a Spanish-style lobby and high-ceilinged rooms in a part of town usually known for hotels with small, dark bedrooms. Families should try for one of the nine sixth-floor units boasting spacious terraces. Baby-sitting can be arranged, and families can avail themselves of the relatively speedy laundry service.

- **Best Moderately Priced Hotel:** Cited for its good value, the **Hotel Regencia Colón** (☎ 93/318-98-58) is a sibling of the Colón (see above). It enjoys the same remarkable location in the Barri Gòtic near the cathedral but charges far less for the privilege of staying here. Updated in 1991, it maintains good housekeeping and roomy comfort. Antiques are used here and there to create a warm, welcoming atmosphere, and the accommodations are often rather large, with such amenities as big closets and private safes.

- **Best Budget Hotel:** Long popular with Frommer readers, the **Hotel Continental** (☎ 93/301-25-70) lies on the top two floors of a building opening onto the upper Rambles. A choice location for sightseeing, it also offers modern bedrooms that, although hardly the grandest in town, sometimes open onto half-moon balconies overlooking this most famous boulevard in Spain. The hotel is not only considered good value for Barcelona, but its buffet breakfast is exceedingly generous.

- **Best B&B:** For the price, the **Hostal Levante** (☎ 93/317-95-65) is a rather good-size B&B with a total of 38 decent and well-kept bedrooms. Of course, only seven of them contain a private bath, but the hallway baths are generally kept immaculate. It's a viable alternative for those hoping to keep costs low in a very high-priced city. You'll also save money on sightseeing; the hotel is only a brief stroll from Plaça de Sant Jaume, which is in the exact center of the Barri Gòtic.

- **Best Service:** Many hotels in this price range are better than the **Princesa Sofía** (☎ 93/330-71-11), but the manager at this HUSA chain entry has hired one of the best, most professional, and politest staffs in town. Nearly everyone speaks English, and though the hotel is gargantuan they somehow seem to address personal problems carefully and to fulfill requests quickly and efficiently without ever losing their cool. The Sofía's business service facilities are on par with those of the Barcelona Hilton.

- **Best Location:** There's the Colón and its sibling, the Regencia Colón (see above), but there's also **Le Meridien Barcelona** (☎ 800/543-4300 in the U.S., or 93/318-62-00), the only five-star hotel in the old town. Former guests may remember it as the seedy Hotel Manila, but it was completely renovated in 1988 and is now one of the city's leading hotels. Handsomely furnished and decorated, Le Meridien is just steps from Les Rambles. You can literally walk out your door and be involved in Barcelona street life within a minute. The Colón is still a better location for those who want to be in the heart of the old quarter, but for the Rambles and its dozens of restaurants and attractions, Le Meridien is the stellar choice.

- **Best Hotel Health Club:** Massive but plush, the **Princesa Sofía** (☎ 93/330-71-11) provides an attractive mixture of formal service in a hypermodern format, with a design placing great emphasis on such American-style amenities as a health club. Consequently, what you'll find one level below the lobby manages to incorporate everything you'd find at a well-run California gym, with a Catalán staff that really seems to care about the state of your physical well-being. Views from the exercise bikes and treadmills encompass a verdant garden and a very large outdoor swimming pool measuring about 80 feet in length. This Americanized health club is open only to hotel guests. There's a U.S.-style restaurant that serves cool drinks, light meals, and salads in the hotel's garden, midway between the pool and the health club.

- **Best Hotel Pool:** The 44-story **Hotel Arts** (☎ 800/241-3333 in the U.S., or 93/221-10-00) soars above a position close to the edge of the sea, adjacent to the harbor used for Olympic sailing events. Part of the hotel's allure derives from its azure-colored outdoor pool, the focal point of the second floor, which functions in both utilitarian and ornamental capacities. No one will mind if you aggressively swim several laps, but for side-sitting, there's an alfresco restaurant, the Marina, that serves party-colored drinks and well-flavored food throughout the day and evening. Water buffs appreciate the pool's proximity to the beach, and as such, can alternate between fresh and saltwater swimming venues.

- **Best Views:** The **Rey Juan Carlos I** (☎ **800/448-8355** in the U.S., or 93/ 448-08-08) made its debut in 1993—a 17-story marble-and-glass tower built around the most dramatic atrium in town. The glass-bubble elevators are worth riding for the panoramic view of Barcelona alone. Not only that, but the hotel offers interior balconies as well. Even more vistas unfold from the hotel's big outdoor swimming pool and sundeck, which is set in a large garden.

4 Accommodations

Barcelona hotels have never been better—or as plentiful. In the wake of the 1992 Olympics, old palaces were restored and converted into hotels, and long-seedy and tarnished hotels were completely renovated in time for the games. The final result is an abundance of good hotels in all price ranges. Regrettably, the first-class and deluxe hotels are vastly overpriced, in the view of many visitors from less expensive parts of the world. For top-grade comfort, you'll pay, and pay dearly, in the Barcelona of the 1990s.

Safety is an important factor to consider when choosing a hotel in Barcelona. Some of the least expensive hotels are not in good locations. A popular area for the budget-conscious traveler is the Barri Gòtic, located in the heart of town. You'll live and eat less expensively here than in any other part of Barcelona. But you should be especially careful when returning to your hotel late at night.

More modern, but also more expensive, accommodations can be found north of Les Rambles and the Barri Gòtic in the Eixample district, centered around the metro stops Plaça de Catalunya and Plaça de la Universitat. Many of the buildings are in the *modernismo* style (that is, turn-of-the-century art nouveau), but sometimes the elevators and plumbing tend to be of the same vintage. The Eixample is a desirable and safe neighborhood, especially along its wide boulevards. Noise is the only problem you might encounter.

Farther north still, above Avinguda Diagonal, you'll enter the Gràcia area, where you can enjoy Catalán neighborhood life. You'll be a bit away from the main attractions, but they can be reached by public transportation.

Hotels judged **Very Expensive** charge 28,000 ptas. ($224) and up per day for a double room; those considered **Expensive** ask 17,500 to 30,000 ptas. ($140 to $240) for a double; and those viewed as **Moderate** charge 12,000 to 20,000 ptas. ($96 to $160) for a double. Hotels asking under 12,000 ptas. ($96) for a double are considered **Inexpensive.**

CIUTAT VELLA

"Old City" in Catalán, Ciutat Vella forms the monumental heartland of Barcelona, taking in Les Rambles, Plaça de Sant Jaume, Vía Laietana, Passeig Nacional, and Passeig de Colom. It contains some of the city's best hotel bargains, which exist in older structures. Most of the glamorous—and more expensive—hotels are in Sur Diagonal (see below).

Accommodations in Central Barcelona

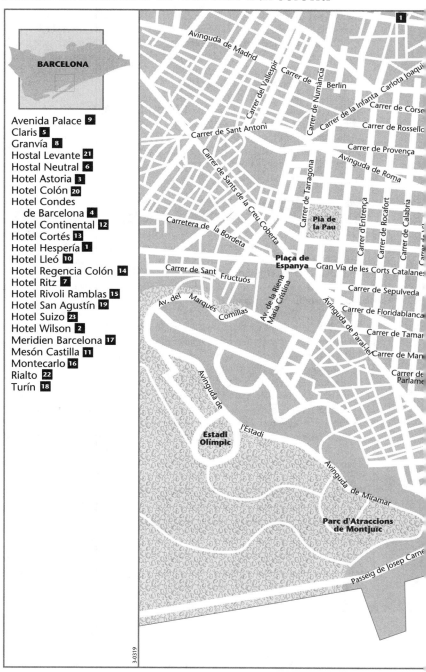

Avenida Palace **9**
Claris **5**
Granvía **8**
Hostal Levante **21**
Hostal Neutral **6**
Hotel Astoria **3**
Hotel Colón **20**
Hotel Condes
  de Barcelona **4**
Hotel Continental **12**
Hotel Cortés **13**
Hotel Hespería **1**
Hotel Lleó **10**
Hotel Regencia Colón **14**
Hotel Ritz **7**
Hotel Rivoli Ramblas **15**
Hotel San Agustín **19**
Hotel Suizo **23**
Hotel Wilson **2**
Meridien Barcelona **17**
Mesón Castilla **11**
Montecarlo **16**
Rialto **22**
Turín **18**

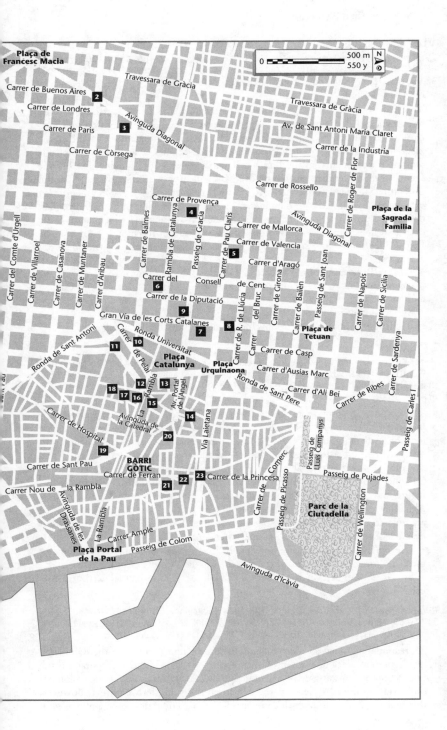

Very Expensive

✪ **Le Meridien Barcelona.** Rambles, 111, 08002 Barcelona. ☎ **800/543-4300** in the U.S., or 93/318-62-00. Fax 93/301-77-76. 200 rms, 8 suites. A/C MINIBAR TV TEL. 29,000–38,000 ptas. ($232–$304) double; from 48,000 ptas. ($384) suite. AE, DC, MC, V. Metro: Liceu or Plaça de Catalunya.

This is the finest hotel in the old town of Barcelona, as Michael Jackson and other former guests will surely agree. It's superior in both amenities and comfort to its two closest rivals in the area: the Colón and the Rivoli Ramblas. Built in the classic *modernismo* style in 1956, it was called the Hotel Manila. Then it was completely renovated and opened as the Ramada Renaissance in 1988. Finally, in 1991 the French-owned Meridien chain took over. It's a medley of artful pastels and tasteful decorating. Its guest rooms are spacious and comfortable, with such amenities as extra-large beds, heated bathroom floors, 18-channel TVs, three in-house videos, hair dryers, and two phones in each room; all rooms have double-glazed windows. However, that doesn't prevent noise from Les Rambles from reaching the rooms. The Renaissance Club—the executive floor popular with businesspeople—provides extra amenities.

Dining/Entertainment: The chic lobby bar, open daily from 7 to 11pm, has live piano music. The main restaurant, Le Patio, serves a fine continental and Catalán cuisine.

Services: Concierge, room service (24 hours), laundry, baby-sitting.

Facilities: Business center, rooms for people with disabilities, small gym.

Expensive

Hotel Colón. Avenida de la Catedral, 7, 08002 Barcelona. ☎ **800/845-0636** in the U.S., or 93/301-14-04. Fax 93/317-29-15. 136 rms, 11 suites. A/C MINIBAR TV TEL. 20,500–32,500 ptas. ($164–$260) double; from 37,000 ptas. ($296) suite. AE, DC, MC, V. Bus: 16, 17, 19, or 45.

The Colón is an appropriate choice if you plan to spend a lot of time exploring the medieval neighborhoods of Barcelona. Blessed with what might be the most dramatic location in the city, immediately opposite the main entrance to the cathedral, this hotel sits behind a dignified neoclassical facade graced with carved pilasters and ornamental wrought-iron balustrades. Inside, you'll find conservative and slightly old-fashioned public rooms, a helpful staff, and guest rooms filled with comfortable furniture and, despite recent renovations, an appealingly dowdy kind of charm. Although not all rooms have views, they all have private baths. The rooms in back are quieter. Sixth-floor rooms with balconies overlooking the square are the most desirable. Some of the lower rooms are rather dark.

Dining/Entertainment: The hotel maintains two well-recommended restaurants, the Grill (for continental specialties) and the Carabela (for Catalán specialties).

Services: Concierge, room service (24 hours), laundry/valet, limousine, baby-sitting.

Rivoli Ramblas. Rambla dels Estudis, 128, 08002 Barcelona. ☎ **93/302-66-43.** Fax 93/317-50-53. 78 rms, 9 suites. A/C MINIBAR TV TEL. 24,000–26,000 ptas. ($192–$208) double; from 36,000 ptas. ($288) suite. AE, DC, MC, V. Metro: Plaça de Catalunya.

Set behind a dignified, art deco town house on the upper section of the Rambles, a block south of Plaça de Catalunya, this recently renovated hotel incorporates many fine examples of avant-garde Catalán design into its stylish interior. The Colón has more tradition and style, and the Meridien more modern comfort; however, this remains choice number three in the old town. The public rooms glisten with polished marble and a pristinely contrived minimalism. The guest rooms are carpeted, soundproof, and elegant, although rather cramped for the prices charged. Along with safety deposit boxes and private baths, the guest rooms boast such electronic amenities as VCRs, radios, and TVs with satellite hookups.

Dining/Entertainment: Le Brut Restaurant serves regional, Spanish, and international dishes. The Blue Moon cocktail bar features piano music and a soothingly high-tech design. A rooftop terrace, decked with flowers and suitable for coffee or drinks, offers a view over the rooftops of one of Barcelona's most architecturally interesting neighborhoods.

Services: Concierge, room service, baby-sitting, laundry/valet.

Facilities: Small health club / fitness center, sauna, solarium, car rentals, shopping boutiques.

MODERATE

Hotel Lleó. Pelal, 22–24, 08001 Barcelona. ☎ **93/318-13-12.** Fax 93/412-26-57. 76 rms. A/C MINIBAR TV TEL. 12,000 ptas. ($96) double. AE, DC, MC, V. Parking 2,000 ptas. ($16) nearby. Metro: Plaça de Catalunya or Plaça de la Universitat.

Solid, well run, and conservative, this hotel occupies the premises of an 1840s building on a busy commercial street in one of the most central neighborhoods in town. Completely renovated in 1992 in time for the Olympics, it offers clean, streamlined, and comfortable bedrooms, each equipped with a lock-box and comfortable, functional furniture. There's a restaurant on one of the upper floors. For the price, this is a good, standard, functional choice, but not a lot more.

☉ Hotel Regencia Colón. Carrer Sagristans, 13–17, 08002 Barcelona. ☎ **93/318-98-58.** Fax 93/317-28-22. 55 rms. A/C MINIBAR TV TEL. 15,500 ptas. ($124) double; 19,000 ptas. ($152) triple. Rates include breakfast. AE, DC, MC, V. Metro: Jaume I or Urquinaona.

This stately stone six-story building stands directly behind the more prestigious, superior, and more expensive Hotel Colón—both lie in the shadow of the cathedral. It's attractive to tour groups. The formal lobby seems a bit dour, but the well-maintained rooms are comfortable and often roomy, albeit worn. Rooms are insulated against sound, and 40 of them have full tub baths (the remainder have showers). All have piped-in music. The hotel's location at the edge of the Barri Gòtic is a plus. Considering the prices charged and what you get, the hotel is a good value for Barcelona.

INEXPENSIVE

Granvía. Gran Vía de les Cortes Catalanes, 642, 08007 Barcelona. ☎ **93/318-19-00.** Fax 93/318-99-97. 50 rms. A/C MINIBAR TV TEL. 11,500 ptas. ($92) double. AE, DC, MC, V. Parking 2,100 ptas. ($16.80). Metro: Plaça de Catalunya.

A grand hotel on one of the most fashionable boulevards in Barcelona, the Granvía has public rooms that reflect the opulence of the 1860s—chandeliers, gilt mirrors, and French provincial furniture—and a grand balustraded staircase. Although the traditional bedrooms contain interesting antique reproductions, they're comfortable rather than luxurious. The courtyard, graced with a fountain and palm trees, is set with tables for alfresco drinks; in the garden room off the courtyard, continental breakfast is served. Centrally heated in the winter, the hotel has one drawback: the noise. Street sounds might disturb the light sleeper.

☉ Hostal Levante. Baïxada de Sant Miguel, 2, 08002 Barcelona. ☎ **93/317-95-65.** 38 rms, 7 with bath. 3,500 ptas. ($28) double without bath, 4,500 ptas. ($36) double with bath. No credit cards. Metro: Liceu or Jaume I.

This is one of the nicest and most reasonably priced places to stay in Barcelona. In a quiet, imposing building more than two centuries old, it stands just a short distance from Plaça de Sant Jaume, in the center of the Barri Gòtic. The units are clean and comfortable, and there's central heating. The staff speaks English. No meals are served.

Ⓢ Hostal Neutral. Rambla de Catalunya, 42, 08007 Barcelona. ☎ **93/487-63-90.** Fax 93/ 487-40-28. 35 rms. TEL. 3,950–4,950 ptas. ($31.60–$39.60) double; 4,725–6,210 ptas. ($37.80–$49.70) triple. MC, V. Metro: Passeig de Gràcia.

An older pension, but very recommendable, this hostal has a reputation for cleanliness and efficiency. As the name suggests, the small rooms here are neutral—but comfortable nevertheless, although furnished with a medley of odds and ends. Colorful antique floor tiling brightens some of the high-ceilinged rooms. Breakfast is served in a salon with a coffered ceiling, and there's a large TV room nearby. English is spoken. The entrance is one flight up.

Hotel Continental. Rambla de Canaletes, 138, 08002 Barcelona. ☎ **93/301-25-70.** Fax 93/ 302-73-60. 36 rms. MINIBAR TV TEL. 8,650–9,900 ptas. ($69.20–$79.20) double; 9,900 ptas. ($79.20) triple; 10,850–12,600 ptas. ($86.80–$100.80) quad. Rates include buffet breakfast. AE, DC, MC, V. Metro: Plaça de Catalunya.

This hotel lies on the upper two floors of a commercial building in a safer section of the upper Rambles. The flowery, slightly faded reception area is clean and accented with 19th-century statues. The rooms are pleasant and modern, and 10 have semicircular balconies overlooking the Rambles. Though the decor in some of the bedrooms seems to shout "Laura Ashley gone mad," everything is clean and comfortable. Amenities include safe-deposit boxes and hair dryers. A buffet breakfast is served daily from 6am to noon.

Hotel Cortés. Santa Anna, 25, 08002 Barcelona. ☎ **93/317-91-12.** Fax 93/302-78-70. 46 rms. TV TEL. 7,970 ptas. ($63.75) double. Rates include breakfast. AE, DC, MC, V. Metro: Plaça de Catalunya.

A short walk from the cathedral, the Cortés was originally built around 1910 and, like many of its competitors in Barcelona, was thoroughly renovated in time for the 1992 Olympics. It competes effectively against the Continental. The bedrooms are scattered over five floors; about half overlook a quiet central courtyard, while the other half open onto the street. The hotel's ground floor contains a simple, unpretentious restaurant and bar, where breakfast is served and where clients can enjoy a beer throughout the day and night.

Hotel San Agustín. Plaça de San Agustín, 3, 08001 Barcelona. ☎ **93/318-16-58.** Fax 93/ 317-29-28. 77 rms. A/C TV TEL. 8,900 ptas. ($71.20) double Mon–Fri, 8,000 ptas. ($64) double Sat–Sun. Rates include breakfast. AE, MC, V. Metro: Plaça de Catalunya.

This tastefully renovated five-story hotel stands in the center of the old city, near the covered produce markets overlooking the brick walls of an unfinished Romanesque church. The bedrooms are comfortable and modern, containing such amenities as piped-in music and safety deposit boxes. Some rooms are specially equipped for individuals with disabilities. The hotel also runs a good restaurant offering reasonably priced meals.

Hotel Suizo. Plaça de l'Angel, 12, 08010 Barcelona. ☎ **93/315-41-11.** Fax 93/315-38-19. 48 rms. A/C MINIBAR TV TEL. 11,550 ptas. ($92.40) double. AE, DC, MC, V. Parking 1,800 ptas. ($14.40) nearby. Metro: Jaume I.

A few blocks from the cathedral in a 19th-century building, the Hotel Suizo has an elaborate belle époque–style bar where drinks and snacks are served. A Gargallo hotel, it's a sibling of the Rialto (see below). The Suizo doesn't have the roomy hall-ways of the Rialto, but its public rooms are more attractively furnished and inviting. The reception area is pleasantly modern. The bedrooms have antique-patterned wall-paper, Spanish furniture, and private baths. The staff is polite and helpful.

✪ **Mesón Castilla.** Valldoncella, 5, 08002 Barcelona. ☎ **93/318-21-82.** Fax 93/412-40-20. 56 rms. A/C TEL. 9,500 ptas. ($76) double. AE, DC, MC, V. Parking 1,500 ptas. ($12). Metro: Plaça de Catalunya or Plaça de la Universitat.

This two-star hotel, a former apartment building, has a Castilian facade with a wealth of art nouveau detailing, and the high-ceilinged lobby is filled with cabriole-legged chairs. Owned and operated by the Spanish hotel chain HUSA, the Castilla is clean, charming, and well maintained. Its nearest rival is the Regencia Colón, to which it is comparable in atmosphere and government ratings. It's far superior to either the Cortés or the Continental. The rooms are comfortable—the beds have ornate Catalán-style headboards—and some open onto large terraces. Breakfast is the only meal served, but it's a fine buffet, with ham, cheese, and eggs. One reader found the location of the hotel "fantastic," right in the center of Barcelona, close to the Rambles.

Montecarlo. Rambla dels Estudis, 124, 08002 Barcelona. ☎ **93/412-04-04.** Fax 93/318-73-23. 76 rms. A/C MINIBAR TV TEL. Mon–Thurs, 12,000 ptas. ($96) double; 15,000 ptas. ($120) triple. Fri–Sun, 10,000 ptas. ($80) double; 12,700 ptas. ($101.60) triple. AE, DC, MC, V. Parking 1,900 ptas. ($15.20). Metro: Plaça de Catalunya.

This hotel, set beside the wide and sloping promenade of the Rambles, was originally built around 200 years ago as an opulent and aristocratic private home, with supe-rior comfort to such previously recommended competitors as the Lleó. In the 1930s it was transformed into the comfortably unpretentious hotel you'll find today. Each of the bedrooms is efficiently decorated and comfortable, most of them renovated around 1989. Double-glazed windows help keep out some of the noise. Public areas include some of the building's original accessories, with carved doors, a baro-nial fireplace, and crystal chandeliers.

Rialto. Ferran, 40–42, 08002 Barcelona. ☎ **93/318-52-12.** Fax 93/315-38-19. 141 rms. A/C MINIBAR TEL. 11,500 ptas. ($92) double. AE, DC, MC, V. Parking 1,800 ptas. ($14.40) nearby. Metro: Jaume I.

One of the best choices in the Barri Gòtic, this hotel is part of the Gargallo chain, which also owns the Hotel Suizo. The three-star Rialto is furnished with Catalán flair and style; completely overhauled in 1985, it offers clean, well-maintained, and com-fortably furnished guest rooms with private baths. There's a cafeteria.

Turín. Carrer Pintor Fortuny, 9–11, 08001 Barcelona. ☎ **93/302-48-12.** Fax 93/302-10-05. 60 rms. A/C TV TEL. 8,000 ptas. ($64) double; 10,000 ptas. ($80) triple. AE, DC, MC, V. Park-ing 1,800 ptas. ($14.40). Metro: Plaça de Catalunya.

This neat and well-run three-star hotel is in a terra-cotta–grillwork building located in a shopping district. It offers small, streamlined accommodations with balconies. An elevator will take you to your room. The Turín also offers a restaurant, special-izing in grilled meats and fresh fish. It's a clean, safe choice, comparable to the Lleó, but in its price range inferior in atmosphere to the Mesón Castilla.

SUR DIAGONAL
VERY EXPENSIVE

Barcelona Hilton. Avinguda Diagonal, 589, 08014 Barcelona. ☎ **800/445-8667** in the U.S. and Canada, or 93/419-22-33. Fax 93/405-25-73. 275 rms, 15 suites. A/C MINIBAR TV TEL. 32,000 ptas. ($256) double; from 40,000 ptas. ($320) suite. AE, DC, MC, V. Parking 2,900 ptas. ($23.20). Metro: María Cristina.

Family-Friendly Hotels

Hotel Colón *(see p. 58)*   Opposite the cathedral in the Gothic Quarter, this hotel has been compared to a country home. Families ask for—and often get—the more spacious rooms.

Hotel Hesperia *(see p. 66)*   At the northern edge of the city, this hotel has gardens and a safe neighborhood setting. The rooms are generous enough in size for an extra bed.

Hotel Princesa Sofía *(see p. 65)*   Although primarily a business-oriented hotel, the Princesa Sofía has excellent baby-sitting services, as well as two pools (one indoor and one outdoor), making it ideal for the business traveler and his or her family.

Opened in 1990 as one of the most publicized hotels in Barcelona, this five-star property lies in a desirable position on one of the city's most famous and elegant boulevards. Opposite the gates to the fairgrounds of Barcelona (beyond that, to the Olympic Stadium), this is a huge seven-floor corner structure, with a massive tower placed on top of it. It hides behind a rather lackluster white marble facade. The lobby is sleek with lots of marble, and the public lounges are furnished with black leather and velvet chairs. The patio is undistinguished and rather minimalist. Most bedrooms are fairly large and finely equipped, although none are set aside for nonsmokers. Furnishings are standard Hilton, but with suitable amenities such as private safes. The bathrooms are also well equipped with such features as large mirrors and hair dryers.

   Dining/Entertainment: The Restaurant Cristal Garden serves well-prepared international and Spanish menus in a relaxed but polished setting. A bar/lounge lies nearby. Night owls head for a popular local disco, Up & Down, a short walk from the hotel.

   Services: Concierge, room service (24 hours), laundry/valet, translation and secretarial services, express check-out, limousine service, baby-sitting.

   Facilities: The hotel maintains a cooperative relationship with a well-equipped health club half a mile away. Tennis courts are a mile away, and the hotel can arrange golf at a course 16 miles away. Shopping boutiques and a news kiosk are on the premises.

✪ **Claris.** Carrer de Pau Claris, 150, 08009 Barcelona. ☎ **800/888-4747** in the U.S., or 93/487-62-62. Fax 93/487-87-36. 121 rms, 38 suites. A/C MINIBAR TV TEL. Mon–Thurs, 31,850 ptas. ($254.80) double; from 35,100 ptas. ($280.80) suite. Fri–Sun (including breakfast), 17,800 ptas. ($142.40) double; from 22,800 ptas. ($182.40) suite. AE, DC, MC, V. Parking 1,750 ptas. ($14). Metro: Passeig de Gràcia.

One of the most unusual hotels built in Barcelona since the 1930s, this postmodern structure is the only five-star grand *luxe* hotel in the city center. It incorporates vast quantities of teak, marble, steel, and glass into the historically important facade of a landmark 19th-century building (the Verdruna Palace). We think the Ritz (see below) is number one, but many hotel critics hail the Claris as the stellar choice. It opened in 1992, in time for the Barcelona Olympics, in a seven-story format that includes a swimming pool and garden on its roof, a mini-museum of Egyptian antiquities on its second floor, and two restaurants, one of which specializes in different brands of caviar. Each of the bedrooms is painted an iconoclastic shade of blue-violet and combines unusual art objects with state-of-the-art electronic accessories.

(Art objects, depending on the inspiration of the decorator, include Turkish kilims, English antiques, Hindu sculptures, Egyptian stone carvings, and engravings inspired by Napoleon's campaigns in Egypt.) Committed to celebrating many facets of Catalán culture, the hotel's owner and developer, art dealer Jordi Clos, named his hotel after the 19th-century Catalán writer Pau Claris.

Dining/Entertainment: On site is the Restaurante Claris, where Catalán meals in the Ampurdan style are served. Also on the premises is a restaurant sponsored by the international caviar emporium, Caviar Caspa, where sturgeon eggs from many different distributors compete for gastronomic attention with an array of smoked meats, smoked fish, and bubbly wines. The restaurant's forte is light but elegant lunches and suppers.

Services: Room service, laundry/valet, baby-sitting.

Facilities: Swimming pool, sauna, currency exchange.

✪ **Hotel Ritz.** Gran Vía de les Corts Catalanes, 668, 08010 Barcelona. ☎ **800/223-1230** in the U.S., or 93/318-52-00. Fax 93/318-01-48. 155 rms, 6 suites. A/C MINIBAR TV TEL. 43,000–52,000 ptas. ($344–$416) double; from 126,000 ptas. ($1,008) suite. AE, DC, MC, V. Parking 3,000 ptas. ($24). Metro: Passeig de Gràcia.

Acknowledged as the finest, most prestigious, and most architecturally distinguished hotel in Barcelona, the Ritz was built in art deco style in 1919. Richly remodeled during the late 1980s, it has welcomed more millionaires, famous people, and aristocrats (with their official and unofficial consorts) than any other hotel in northeastern Spain. One of the finest features is the cream-and-gilt neoclassical lobby, whose marble floors and potted palms are flooded with sunlight from an overhead glass canopy, and where afternoon tea is served to the strains of a string quartet. The bedrooms are as formal, high-ceilinged, and richly furnished as you'd expect, sometimes with Regency furniture and bathrooms accented with mosaics and bathtubs inspired by those in ancient Rome.

Dining/Entertainment: The elegant Restaurante Diana serves French and Catalán cuisine amid soaring ceilings, crystal chandeliers, and formally dressed waiters (see our separate recommendation in "Dining," later in this chapter). Nearby lies the elegantly paneled Bar Parilla, where music from a grand piano will soothe your frazzled nerves while you enjoy the deep leather upholstery and gilded cove moldings.

Services: Concierge, room service (24 hours), laundry, limousine service, baby-sitting.

Facilities: Business center, car rentals, handful of shopping kiosks and boutiques.

✪ **Rey Juan Carlos I.** Avinguda Diagonal, 661, 08028 Barcelona. ☎ **800/448-8355** in the U.S., or 93/448-08-08. Fax 93/448-06-07. 375 rms, 37 suites. A/C MINIBAR TV TEL. Mon–Thurs, 37,000 ptas. ($296) double; 63,000 ptas. ($504) suite. Fri–Sun, 16,200 ptas. ($129.60) double; 44,000 ptas. ($352) suite. AE, DC, MC, V. Free parking for guests; otherwise 2,500 ptas. ($20) per day. Metro: Palau Reial.

Named for the Spanish king, who attended its opening and who has visited it several times since, this is the only five-star choice that competes effectively against the Ritz and Claris. Opened in 1992, in time for the Olympics, it rises 17 stories from a position at the northern end of Avinguda Diagonal in a prestigious neighborhood known for its corporate headquarters and banks. The design includes a soaring inner atrium, at one end of which a bank of glass-sided elevators glide silently up and down. The bedrooms contain many electronic extras, conservatively comfortable furnishings, and in many cases, views out over Barcelona to the sea.

Dining/Entertainment: The hotel's most elegant restaurant is Chez Vous, a glamorous and panoramic locale with impeccable service and French/Catalán meals.

Saturday night a dinner dance offers a live orchestra accompanied by a set menu. There's also a Japanese restaurant (Kokoro) and the Café Polo, which serves an endless series of buffets at lunch and dinner. The gardens surrounding the hotel contain fountains, flowering shrubs, and the Café Terraza.

Services: Concierge staff, room service (24 hours), laundry.

Facilities: Swimming pool, health club, jogging track, men's and women's hairdresser, car-rental facilities, business center.

EXPENSIVE

Avenida Palace. Gran Vía de les Corts Catalanes, 605 (at Passeig de Gràcia), 08007 Barcelona. ☎ **93/301-96-00.** Fax 93/318-12-34. 147 rms, 18 suites. A/C MINIBAR TV TEL. 20,000 ptas. ($160) double; from 35,000 ptas. ($280) suite. AE, DC, MC, V. Parking 2,000 ptas. ($16). Metro: Plaça de Catalunya.

Set in an enviable 19th-century neighborhood filled with elegant shops and apartment buildings, this hotel lies behind a pair of mock-fortified towers that were built (like the hotel) in 1952. Despite its relative modernity, it evokes an old-world sense of charm, partly because of the attentive staff, the scattering of flowers and antiques, and the 1950s-era accessories that fill its well-upholstered public rooms. The bedrooms, all with private baths, are solidly traditional and quiet, and some are set aside for nonsmokers, a rarity in Spain.

Dining/Entertainment: The hotel has an elegantly proportioned dining room, El Restaurante Pinateca, which serves lunch and dinner Monday to Friday. The bar/lounge contains potted palms, a scattering of interesting antiques, and a sense of graciousness.

Services: Concierge, room service, translation and secretarial services, currency exchange, hairdresser/barber, express check-out, baby-sitting.

✪ **Hotel Condes de Barcelona.** Passeig de Gràcia, 73–75, 08008 Barcelona. ☎ **93/488-22-00.** Fax 93/488-06-14. 181 rms, 2 suites. A/C MINIBAR TV TEL. 19,000 ptas. ($152) double; 25,000–40,000 ptas. ($200–$320) suite. AE, DC, MC, V. Metro: Passeig de Gràcia.

Located off the architecturally splendid Passeig de Gràcia, this four-star hotel, originally designed to be a private villa (1895), is one of Barcelona's most glamorous. Business was so good that it opened a 74-room extension, which regrettably lacks the élan of the original core. It boasts a unique neomedieval facade, influenced by Gaudí's *modernismo* movement. During recent renovation, just enough hints of high-tech furnishings were added to make the lobby exciting, but everything else has the original opulence. The curved lobby-level bar and its adjacent restaurant add a touch of art deco. All the comfortable salmon-, green-, or peach-colored guest rooms contain marble baths, reproductions of Spanish paintings, and soundproof windows. Some rooms are beginning to show a post-Olympics wear and tear.

Dining/Entertainment: In times past you might have seen the late conde de Barcelona, father of King Juan Carlos, passing through on the way to a refreshing snack in the Café Condal, featuring regional dishes. Guests also enjoy the piano bar, including, on occasions, the baron von Thyssen and his Catalán-born wife, who sold their fabulous art collection to Madrid.

Services: Room service, laundry, baby-sitting.

Facilities: Outdoor swimming pool.

Hotel Meliá Barcelona Sarrià. Avinguda Sarrià, 50, 08029 Barcelona. ☎ **800/336-3542** in the U.S., or 93/410-60-60. Fax 93/321-51-79. 295 rms, 20 suites. A/C MINIBAR TV TEL. 26,000 ptas. ($208) double; from 40,000 ptas. ($320) suite. AE, DC, MC, V. Parking 2,300 ptas. ($18.40). Metro: Hospital Clínic.

Located just a block away from the junction of Avinguda Sarría and Avinguda Diagonal, right in the modern business heart of Barcelona, this five-star hotel originally opened in 1976. Some of its rooms were renovated as late as 1993, but others are beginning to look a bit worn. It offers comfortably upholstered and carpeted bedrooms in a neutral international modern style. The hotel—a member of the nationwide Spanish chain Meliá—caters to both the business traveler and the vacationer.

Dining/Entertainment: The hotel restaurant serves both Catalán and international dishes, and a cocktail bar provides not only drinks but also piano music six nights a week.

Services: Concierge, room service (24 hours), laundry/valet, executive floor, private parking, baby-sitting on request.

Facilities: Business center, one of the best-equipped health clubs in Barcelona.

Hotel Princesa Sofía. Plaça de Pius XII, 4, 08028 Barcelona. ☎ **93/330-71-11.** Fax 93/ 330-76-21. 481 rms, 24 suites. A/C MINIBAR TV TEL. 20,000 ptas. ($160) double; from 40,000 ptas. ($320) suite. AE, DC, MC, V. Parking 1,800 ptas. ($14.40). Metro: Palau Reial or María Cristina.

Set beside Avinguda Diagonal, about a block east of the Palau Reial and about 2 miles (3km) northwest of Barcelona's historic center, the high-rise Princesa Sofía is perhaps the busiest, most business-oriented, and most international of the large-volume modern hotels in Barcelona. It's much better than the Hilton. Although it was a five-star hotel when it opened, its new government rating of four stars is more in keeping with the reality here. The hotel was built in 1975 and renovated during the early 1990s. Packed with glamorous grace notes (including a branch of Régine's disco in the basement) and named after the wife of the Spanish monarch, the Princesa Sofía is the venue for dozens of daily conferences and social events. The guest rooms contain comfortable traditional furniture, often with a vaguely British feel.

Dining/Entertainment: Le Gourmet restaurant serves continental and Catalán meals, but the fare is lackluster. L'Emporda is slightly less expensive, and an in-house coffee shop, El Snack 2002, is open until midnight. Also on the premises is a bar.

Services: Concierge, room service (24 hours), laundry/valet, in-house branch of Iberia Airlines, baby-sitting.

Facilities: An upscale shopping boutique, barber/hairdresser, car rentals, amply equipped gym and health club, sauna, indoor and outdoor swimming pools, several well-conceived gardens, extensive conference and meeting facilities, unusually well-managed business center offering translation (English and French) and secretarial services.

MODERATE

✪ **Hotel Astoria.** París, 203, 08036 Barcelona. ☎ **93/209-83-11.** Fax 93/202-30-08. 114 rms. A/C MINIBAR TV TEL. 8,000–16,200 ptas. ($64–$129.60) double. AE, DC, MC, V. Metro: Diagonal.

One of our favorite hotels, the Astoria has an art deco facade that makes it appear older than it is. The high ceilings, geometric designs, and brass-studded detailings in the public rooms could be Moorish or Andalusian. Each of the comfortable bedrooms is soundproofed; half have been renovated with slick louvered closets and glistening white paint. The more old-fashioned rooms have warm textures of exposed cedar and elegant, pristine modern accessories.

Hotel Derby / Hotel Gran Derby. Loreto, 21–25, and Loreto, 28, 08029 Barcelona. ☎ **93/ 322-32-15.** Fax 93/410-08-62. 111 rms, 40 suites. A/C MINIBAR TV TEL. 9,000–17,350 ptas.

($72–$138.80) double; 11,500–17,850 ptas. ($92–$142.80) suite. AE, DC, MC, V. Parking 1,800 ptas. ($14.40). Metro: Hospital Clínic.

Divided into two separate buildings, these twin hotels (owned and managed by the same corporation) lie in a tranquil neighborhood about 2 blocks south of the busy intersection of Avinguda Diagonal and Avinguda Sarría. The Derby offers 111 conventional hotel rooms, whereas the Gran Derby (across the street) contains 40 suites, many of which have small balconies overlooking a flowered courtyard. (All drinking, dining, and entertainment facilities are in the larger of the two establishments, the Derby.) A team of English-inspired designers imported a British aesthetic into these hotels, and the pleasing results include well-oiled hardwood panels, soft lighting, and comfortably upholstered armchairs. Less British in feel than the public rooms, the guest rooms and suites are outfitted with simple furniture in a variety of decorative styles, each comfortable and quiet.

Dining/Entertainment: Although the hotel doesn't have a full-fledged restaurant, it contains a dignified but unpretentious coffee shop, The Times, which serves Spanish, British, and international food. The Scotch Bar, an upscale watering hole, has won several Spanish awards for the diversity of its cocktails.

Services: Concierge, laundry, baby-sitting.

NORTE DIAGONAL
MODERATE

Hotel Hesperia. Los Vergós, 20, 08017 Barcelona. ☎ **93/204-55-51.** Fax 93/204-43-92. 139 rms. A/C MINIBAR TV TEL. 14,500 ptas. ($116) double Mon–Thurs, 9,500 ptas. ($76) double Fri–Sun. AE, DC, MC, V. Parking 1,450 ptas. ($11.60). Metro: Tres Torres.

This hotel, on the northern edge of the city, a 12-minute taxi ride from the center, is surrounded by the verdant gardens of one of Barcelona's most pleasant residential neighborhoods. Built in the late 1980s, the hotel was renovated before the 1992 Olympics. You'll pass a Japanese rock garden to reach the stone-floored reception area, with its adjacent bar. Sunlight floods the monochromatic interiors of the bedrooms—all doubles, although singles can be rented at the prices above. The uniformed staff offers fine service. A restaurant on the premises serves a regional cuisine.

INEXPENSIVE

Hotel Wilson. Avinguda Diagonal, 568, 08021 Barcelona. ☎ **93/209-25-11.** Fax 93/200-83-70. 51 rms, 6 suites. A/C MINIBAR TV TEL. 12,000 ptas. ($96) double; from 21,500 ptas. ($172) suite. AE, DC, MC, V. Metro: Diagonal.

Set in a neighborhood rich with architectural curiosities, this comfortable hotel is a member of the nationwide HUSA chain. The small lobby isn't indicative of the rest of the building, which on the second floor opens into a large and sunny coffee shop/bar/TV lounge. The guest rooms are well kept. Laundry services are provided.

VILA OLÍMPICA
EXPENSIVE

Hotel Arts. Carrer de la Marina, 19–21, 08005 Barcelona. ☎ **800/241-3333** in the U.S., or 93/221-10-00. Fax 93/221-10-70. 397 rms, 56 suites. A/C MINIBAR TV TEL. Mon–Thurs, 25,000–26,000 ptas. ($200–$208) double; from 30,000 ptas. ($240) suite. Fri–Sun, 20,000 ptas. ($160) double; from 30,000 ptas. ($240) suite. AE, DC, MC, V. Parking 2,500 ptas. ($20). Metro: Ciutadella–Vila Olímpica.

This is the only hotel in Europe managed by the luxury-conscious Ritz-Carlton chain, the first of what the company hopes will be a string of hotels across the European continent. It occupies 33 floors of one of the tallest buildings in Spain, a 44-story postmodern tower whose upper floors contain the private condominiums of some of

Iberia's most gossiped-about aristocrats and financiers. The location is about 1¹/₂ miles southwest of Barcelona's historic core, adjacent to the sea and the Olympic Village. Although some rooms were occupied by athletes and Olympic administrators in 1992, the hotel didn't become fully operational until 1994. Its decor is contemporary and elegant, including a large lobby sheathed in slabs of soft gray and yellow marble, and bedrooms outfitted in pastel shades of yellow or blue. Views from the bedrooms sweep out over the skyline of Barcelona and the Mediterranean. The staff is youthful, well trained, polite, and hardworking, each the product of months of training by Ritz-Carlton.

Dining/Entertainment: Three in-house restaurants include the Newport Room, which pays homage to new American cuisine and the seafaring pleasures of New England; the Café Veranda, a light and airy indoor/outdoor restaurant; and the Goyesca, which serves Spanish food and shellfish in a Catalán setting.

Services: Concierge staff (who can arrange almost anything), room service (24 hours), laundry.

Facilities: Fitness center, outdoor pool, business center. Adjacent to the hotel is an upscale cluster of many different luxury boutiques operated by the Japanese retailer Sogo.

5 Best Restaurant Bets

- **Best Decor:** Once **Beltxenea** (☎ 93/215-30-24) was a chic and elegant apartment in the Eixample, but in 1987 it was converted to a restaurant. The dining rooms still retain the atmosphere of exclusivity and elegance, and these days, the restaurant serves some of the best Basque cookery in Catalonia.
- **Best View:** Dining by the sea at one of the most fabled ports of the world is worth the trek to Barcelona. **Gambrinus** (☎ 93/221-96-07), a seafood restaurant, has a statue of a giant lobster on top, and outdoor tables set on a pier. Since the sun is often hot, the terrace is shaded with parasols. At night you can dine while enjoying the twinkling lights of the harbor.
- **Best Wine List: Neichel** (☎ 93/203-84-08) enjoys a dedicated loyal following, drawn not only to Jean-Louis Neichel's French and Catalán cuisine, but also to the best wine list in the city—a medley of the finest vintages from both France and Catalonia, as well as throughout Spain. The sommelier is helpful in guiding you to the perfect choice of wine with your meal, which might include filet of sea bass in a sea urchin–cream sauce. He doesn't push the most expensive selections, either.
- **Best Value:** The most celebrated restaurant in La Boquería, the covered food market of Barcelona, is **Garduña** (☎ 93/302-43-23). Originally a hotel, it was converted into a restaurant in the 1970s, today serving artists, writers, actors, and others in a blue-collar atmosphere. The food is super-fresh; you get hearty seafood medleys here at prices far below what most other restaurants charge. It also offers one of the best fixed-price menus in town.
- **Best for Kids:** If such Catalán dishes as whole baby eels cooked simmering in olive oil and garlic frighten your child, take him or her to the familiar fare of **Henry J. Bean's Bar and Grill** (☎ 93/218-29-98), an old favorite on Avinguda Diagonal. It serves one of the best smokehouse burgers in town, and most definitely nachos, baby back ribs, and chili con carne.
- **Best Continental Cuisine:** In a *modernismo* house in a chic part of town, chef Josep Bullick of **La Dama** (☎ 93/202-06-86) turns out a delectable cuisine that rivals many of the top restaurants of Paris. After sampling such dishes as the langoustine salad with orange vinegar, you'll be won over by his bold innovative cuisine. Peerless ingredients and a faultless technique produce such dishes as roast

filet of goat—which may not sound appetizing, but in this chef's hands it becomes a dish of wonder.

- **Best French Cuisine: Jaume de Provença** (☎ 93/430-00-29) boasts modern French cuisine that's often perfumed with the delicate spices and aromas of Provence. Chef Jaume Bargués enjoys a well-earned reputation as one of Barcelona's finest chefs. Haute cuisine is handled here with deft hands, and imagination and vision go into the constantly changing menus that depend on what's the best and the freshest in any given season.

- **Best Seafood:** On the main thoroughfare of Gràcia is **Botafumiero** (☎ 93/218-42-30), where you get the city's best array of seafood. The chief attraction of which is mariscos Botafumiero—that's a myriad selection of the best shellfish in Spain, with one plate arriving right after the other. The fresh fish is flown daily to Barcelona, often from the sea coast of Galicia where the restaurant owner originates.

- **Best Catalán Cuisine: Los Caracoles** (☎ 93/302-31-85), below Plaça Reial, is the old favorite in town; despite the fact that it's a tourist haunt, it serves delectable local cuisine. It has been Barcelona's most colorful and popular restaurant since 1835. Everybody from Richard Nixon to John Wayne has sampled its spit-roasted chicken and the namesake snails. There's nothing else quite like it in town.

- **Best for Late-Night Dining:** The good food at **Els Quatre Gats** (☎ 93/302-41-40) is prepared in an unpretentious style of Catalán cookery called *cuina de mercat* (based on whatever is fresh at the market that day). This is the most legendary café in Barcelona, patronized by the likes of Picasso when he was wandering around the port at the tender age of 18. In the heart of the Barri Gòtic, it becomes particularly animated late at night, serving food and drink until 2am.

- **Best Picnic Fare:** There's no better place for the makings of a picnic than the **Mercat de la Boquería,** in the center of the Rambles. Also known as the Mercat de Sant Josep, it's one of the world's most extensive produce markets, a sight in its own right. Dating from 1914, it offers aisle upon aisle of attractively displayed produce from both sea and land. Many of the ingredients are already cooked and prepared, and can be packed for you to carry along in your picnic basket.

- **Best Local Favorite:** Since 1836, **Siete Puertas** (☎ 93/319-30-33) has been feeding locals its several variations of paella, including ones with rabbit or with sardines. It offers one of the most extensive menus in Barcelona, and is a classic, mellow place with waiters wearing long white aprons.

6 Dining

Finding an economical restaurant in Barcelona is easier than finding an inexpensive, safe hotel. There are sometimes as many as eight places per block, if you include tapas bars as well as restaurants. Reservations are seldom needed, except in the most expensive and popular places.

The Barri Gòtic offers the cheapest meals. There are also many low-cost restaurants in and around Carrer de Montcada, site of the Picasso museum. Dining rooms in the Eixample tend to be more formal and expensive, but less adventurous.

However, if you're not a budget traveler and can afford to dine in first-class and deluxe restaurants, you'll find in Barcelona some of the grandest culinary experiences in Europe. The widely diversified Catalán cuisine reaches its pinnacle in Barcelona, and many of the finest dishes feature fresh seafood. But you don't get just Catalán fare here, as the city is also rich in the cuisines of all the major regions of Spain, including Castile and Andalusia. Because of Barcelona's proximity to France, many of the finer restaurants also serve French or French-inspired dishes, the latter often with a distinctly Catalán flavor.

CIUTAT VELLA
EXPENSIVE

✪ **Agut d'Avignon.** Trinitat, 3. ☎ **93/302-60-34.** Reservations required. Main courses 1,800–4,200 ptas. ($14.40–$33.60). AE, MC, V. Daily 1–3:30pm and 9–11:30pm. Metro: Jaume I or Liceu. CATALÁN.

Founded in 1962, one of our favorite restaurants in Barcelona is located near Plaça Reial, in a tiny alleyway (the cross street is Calle d'Avinyó). The restaurant explosion in Barcelona has toppled Agut d'Avignon from its once stellar position, but it's still going strong, still drawing in habitués. The restaurant attracts the leading politicians, writers, journalists, financiers, industrialists, and artists of Barcelona—even the king and various ministers of the cabinet, along with visiting presidents from other countries. Since 1983 the restaurant has been run by Mercedes Giralt Salinas and her son, Javier Falagán Giralt. A small 19th-century vestibule leads to the multilevel dining area, which has two balconies and a main hall; the whole of it evokes a hunting lodge. You might need help translating the Catalán menu. Specialties—all prepared according to traditional recipes—are likely to include acorn-squash soup served in its shell, fisherman soup with garlic toast, haddock stuffed with shellfish, sole with nyoca (a medley of different nuts), large shrimp with aïoli (a garlicky mayonnaise sauce), duck with figs, chicken with shrimp, and filet steak in a sherry sauce.

Casa Leopoldo. Carrer Sant Rafael, 24. ☎ **93/441-30-14.** Reservations required. Main courses 1,800–8,500 ptas. ($14.40–$68). AE, DC, MC, V. Tues–Sat 1–4pm and 9–11pm, Sun 1–4pm. Closed Aug. Metro: Liceu. SEAFOOD.

An excursion through the seedy streets of the Barri Xinés is part of the experience of coming to this restaurant. At night, though, it's safer to come by taxi. This colorful restaurant (founded in 1939) has some of the freshest seafood in town and caters to a loyal clientele. There's a popular stand-up tapas bar in front, then two dining rooms, one slightly more formal than the other. Specialties include eel with shrimp, barnacles, cuttlefish, seafood soup with shellfish, and deep-fried inch-long eels.

Quo Vadis. Carme, 7. ☎ **93/302-40-72.** Reservations recommended. Main courses 1,650–3,500 ptas. ($13.20–$28); menú del día 3,750 ptas. ($30). AE, DC, MC, V. Mon–Sat 1:15–4pm and 8:30–11:30pm. Metro: Liceu. SPANISH/CONTINENTAL.

Elegant and impeccable, this is one of the finest restaurants in Barcelona. Set in a century-old building near the open stalls of the Bouqería food market, it was established in 1967 and has done a discreet but thriving business ever since. Seating is in any of four different dining rooms, each decorated with exposed paneling and a veneer of conservative charm. Personalized culinary creations include a ragoût of seasonal mushrooms; fried goose liver with prunes; filet of beef with wine sauce; a wide variety of fish, grilled or, in some cases, flambéed; and a wide choice of desserts made with seasonal fruits imported from all over Spain.

MODERATE

Brasserie Flo. Jonqueras, 10. ☎ **93/319-31-02.** Reservations recommended. Main courses 1,800–3,600 ptas. ($14.40–$28.80); fixed-price menu 3,090 ptas. ($24.70). AE, DC, MC, V. Mon–Thurs 1–4pm and 8:30pm–midnight, Fri–Sun 1–4pm and 8:30pm–1am. Metro: Urquinaona. FRENCH/INTERNATIONAL.

Installed in a former textiles factory, this handsomely restored warehouse was opened as a restaurant in 1982 by a group of Frenchmen. It's as close as Barcelona gets to

Dining in Central Barcelona

BARCELONA

Agut d'Avignon **32**
Alt Heidelberg **13**
Beltxenea **10**
Biocenter **19**
Bodega la Plata **37**
Bodegueta **7**
Botafumeiro **3**
Brasserie Flo **14**
Burger King **15**
Ca L'Isidre **24**
Ca La María **12**
Caballito Blanco **9**
Campanas **36**
Can Culleretes **30**
Can Majó **43**
Can Pescallunes **16**
Caracoles **33**
Casa Leopoldo **23**
Chicago Pizza Pie Factory **8**
Cuineta **28**
Dama **5**
Diana **11**
Dulcinea **21**
Egipte **22**
Gambrinus **40**
Garduña **25**
Henry J. Bean's Bar & Grill **4**
Jarra **38**
Jaume de Provença **1**
Kentucky Fried Chicken **31**
Mercat de la Boquería **26**
Nou Celler **29**
Pi, Bar del **27**
Pitarra **34**
Quatre Gats **17**
Quo Vadis **20**
Ramonet (Bar Xarello) **41**
Reno **2**
Rey de la Gamba **42**
Roig Robí **6**
Siete Puertas **39**
Túnel **35**
Viena **18**

3-0320

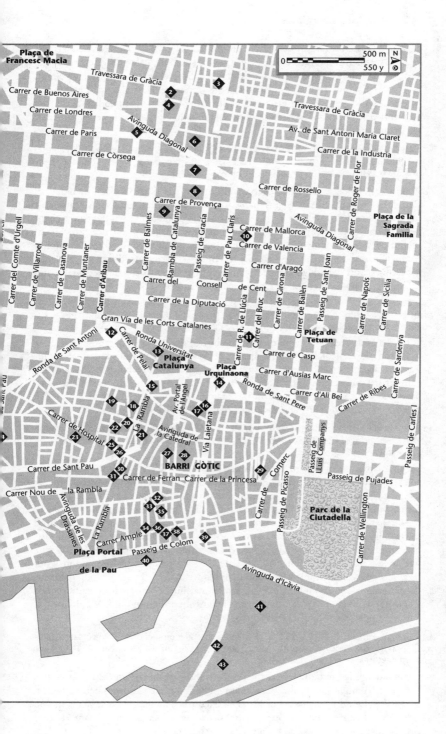

Plaça de
Francesc Macia

Travessara de Gràcia

Carrer de Buenos Aires

Carrer de Londres

Travessara de Gràcia

Carrer de Paris

Avinguda Diagonal

Av. de Sant Antoni Maria Claret

Carrer de Còrsega

Carrer de la Industria

Carrer de Rossello

Carrer de Provença

Plaça de la
Sagrada
Familia

Carrer de Balmes

Carrer de Rambla de Catalunya

Passeig de Gràcia

Carrer de Pau Claris

Carrer de Mallorca

Avinguda Diagonal

Carrer de Roger de Flor

Carrer de Valencia

Carrer del

Consell

Carrer d'Aragó

Carrer de Cent

Carrer de Girona

Carrer del Bruc

Carrer de Bailèn

Passeig de Sant Joan

Carrer de Napols

Carrer de Sicilia

Carrer de la Diputació

Gran Vía de les Corts Catalanes

Carrer de Sant Antoni

Ronda Universitat

Carrer de Pelai

Plaça
Catalunya

Carrer de R. de Llúcia

Plaça de
Tetuan

Carrer de Sardenya

Ronda de Sant Antoni

Plaça
Urquinaona

Carrer de Casp

Carrer d'Ausias Marc

Passeig de Carles I

La Rambla

Av. Portal
de l'Angel

Ronda de Sant Pere

Carrer d'Ali Bei

Carrer de Ribes

Carrer de Hospital

Via Laietana

Avinguda de
la Catedral

Passeig de
Lluis Companys

BARRI GÒTIC

Carrer de Sant Pau

Carrer de Ferran

Carrer de la Princesa

Passeig de Pujades

Carrer Nou de la Rambla

Parc de la
Ciutadella

Carrer de Wellington

Avinguda de les Drassanes

La Rambla

Carrer Ample

Carrer de Comerç

Passeig de Picasso

Plaça Portal

Passeig de Colom

de la Pau

Avinguda d'Icàvia

Plaça de
Francesc Macia

Carrer de Muntaner

Carrer d'Aribau

Carrer de Casanova

Carrer de Villarroel

Carrer del Comte d'Urgell

500 m

550 y

N

an Alsace brasserie. The art deco dining room has been compared to one on a transatlantic steamer at the turn of the century—it's spacious, palm-filled, comfortable, and air-conditioned. The food isn't overlooked either—begin with fresh foie gras. The specialty is a large plate of choucroute (sauerkraut) served with a steamed hamhock. Also good are the shrimp in garlic, salmon tartare with vodka, black rice, and stuffed sole with spinach. These dishes, each familiar fare, are nevertheless solid, satisfying, and filling.

Ⓢ **Can Culleretes.** Quintana, 5. ☎ **93/317-64-85.** Reservations recommended. Main courses 850–1,900 ptas. ($6.80–$15.20). DC, V. Tues–Sat 1:30–4pm and 9–11pm, Sun 1:30–4pm. Closed 3 weeks in July. Metro: Liceu. Bus: 14 or 59. CATALÁN.

Founded in 1786 as a *pastelería* (pastry shop) in the Barri Gòtic, this oldest of Barcelona's restaurants still retains many original architectural features. All three dining rooms are decorated in Catalán style, with tile dadoes and wrought-iron chandeliers. The well-prepared food features authentic dishes of northeastern Spain, including sole Roman style, zarzuela a la marinara (shellfish medley), canalones (cannelloni), and paella. From October to January special game dishes are available, including perdiz (partridge). Signed photographs of celebrities, flamenco artists, and bullfighters who have visited this *casa* decorate the walls.

Can Pescallunes. Carrer Magdalenas, 23. ☎ **93/318-54-83.** Reservations required for lunch. Main courses 1,800–2,300 ptas. ($14.40–$18.40). MC, V. Mon–Fri 1–3:30pm and 8:30–10:30pm. Metro: Urquinaona. FRENCH/CATALÁN.

With the look, feel, and menu of a French bistro, this 10-table restaurant is a short walk from the cathedral. In 1980 it opened its doors in this turn-of-the-century building; an elaborate street lantern marks the entrance. Richly flavorful specialties are rape (monkfish) with clams and tomatoes, a smooth vichyssoise, chateaubriand with béarnaise sauce, sole cooked in cider, steak tartare, and dessert crêpes with Cointreau. The specials change daily, and the prices remain a model of temperance.

Ⓢ **Los Caracoles.** Escudellers, 14. ☎ **93/302-31-85.** Reservations required. Main courses 1,500–3,600 ptas. ($12–$28.80). AE, DC, MC, V. Daily 1pm–midnight. Metro: Drassanes. CATALÁN/SPANISH.

Set in a labyrinth of narrow cobblestoned streets, Los Caracoles is the port's most colorful and popular restaurant—and it has been since 1835. It has won acclaim for its spit-roasted chicken and for its namesake, snails. A long, angular bar is located up front, with a two-level restaurant in back. You can watch the busy preparations in the kitchen, where dried herbs, smoked ham shanks, and garlic bouquets hang from the ceiling. In summer tables are placed outside. The excellent food features all sorts of Spanish and Catalán specialties. Everybody from Richard Nixon to John Wayne has stopped in, and Salvador Dalí was a devoted patron. Today's clientele may not be as legendary, but people keep coming in hordes to dine. Tourists often make this their number one restaurant stop in Barcelona, but it's not a tourist trap—Los Caracoles delivers the same aromatic and robust food it always did. We doubt if it has ever updated a recipe. The cookery is "the way it was."

La Cuineta. Paradis, 4. ☎ **93/315-01-11.** Reservations recommended. Main courses 2,000–3,200 ptas. ($16–$25.60); fixed-price menu 2,500 ptas. ($20). AE, DC, MC, V. Daily 1–4pm and 8pm–midnight. Metro: Jaume I. CATALÁN.

A well-established restaurant near the center of the Catalán government district, this is a culinary highlight of the Barri Gòtic. The restaurant is decorated in typical regional style and favors local cuisine. The fixed-price menu is a good value, or you can order à la carte. The most expensive appetizer is bellota (acorn-fed ham), but we suggest that you settle instead for a market-fresh Catalán dish.

Egipte. Carrer Jerusalem, 3. ☎ **93/317-74-80.** Reservations recommended. Main courses 1,200–2,400 ptas. ($9.60–$19.20); fixed-price menu 950–3,000 ptas. ($7.60–$24). AE, DC, MC, V. Mon–Sat 1–4pm and 8pm–midnight. Metro: Liceu. CATALAN/SPANISH.

A favorite among the locals, this tiny place, located right behind the central marketplace, jumps day and night. The excellent menu includes spinach vol-au-vent (traditionally served with an egg on top), *lengua de ternera* (tongue), and *berengeras* (stuffed eggplant), a chef's specialty. The local favorite is codfish in cream sauce. The ingredients are fresh and the price is right. Expect hearty market food and a total lack of pretension.

Els Quatre Gats. Montsió, 3. ☎ **93/302-41-40.** Reservations required Sat–Sun. Main courses 1,200–2,800 ptas. ($9.60–$22.40); fixed-price menu 1,800 ptas. ($14.40). AE, MC, V. Mon–Sat 1–4pm and 9pm–midnight. (Café, daily 8am–2am.) Metro: Plaça de Catalunya. CATALÁN.

A Barcelona legend since 1897, the Four Cats was the favorite of Picasso and other artists, who once hung their works on its walls. Located on a narrow cobblestone street near the cathedral, the fin-de-siècle café was the setting for poetry readings by Joán Maragall, piano concerts by Isaac Albéniz and Enric Granados, and murals by Ramón Casa. It was a base for members of the *modernismo* movement and played a major role in the intellectual and bohemian life of the city. In Catalán slang, the name of the restaurant translates as "just a few people."

Today a bar that's become a popular meeting place in the heart of the Barri Gòtic, it was long ago restored but retains its fine old look. The fixed-price meal, offered every day but Sunday, rates as one of the best bargains in town, considering the locale. The good food is prepared in an unpretentious style of Catalán cooking called *cuina de mercat* (based on whatever looked fresh at the market that day). The constantly changing menu reflects the seasons. No hot food is served on Sunday.

INEXPENSIVE

Biocenter. Pintor Fortuny, 25. ☎ **93/301-45-83.** Main courses 900–1,000 ptas. ($7.20–$8); fixed-price menu 1,075 ptas. ($8.60). No credit cards. Mon–Sat 1–5pm. (Bar, Mon–Sat 9am–11pm.) Metro: Plaça de Catalunya. VEGETARIAN.

This is the largest and best-known vegetarian restaurant in Barcelona, the creation of Catalonia-born entrepreneur Pep Cañameras, who's likely to be directing the service from his position behind the bar in front. Many clients, vegetarians or not, congregate over drinks in the front room. Some continue on for meals in one of two ground-floor dining rooms, whose walls are decorated with the paintings and artworks of the owner and his colleagues. There's a salad bar, an array of vegetarian casseroles, such soups as gazpacho and lentil, and a changing selection of seasonal vegetables. No meat and no fish of any kind are served.

⑤ Garduña. Morera, 17–19. ☎ **93/302-43-23.** Reservations recommended. Main courses 1,200–2,800 ptas. ($9.60–$22.40); fixed-price menus 975 and 1,375 ptas. ($7.80 and $11). AE, MC, V. Mon–Sat 1–4pm and 8pm–midnight, Sun 1–4pm. Metro: Liceu. CATALÁN.

This is the most famous restaurant in Barcelona's covered food market, La Boquería. Originally conceived as a hotel, it eliminated its bedrooms in the 1970s and ever since has concentrated on serving food. Battered, somewhat ramshackle, and a bit claustrophobic, it nonetheless enjoys a fashionable reputation among actors, sculptors, writers, and painters who appreciate a blue-collar atmosphere that might have been designated as bohemian in an earlier era. Because of its position near the back of the market, you'll pass endless rows of fresh produce, cheese, and meats before you reach it, a fact that adds to its allure. You can dine downstairs, near a crowded bar, or a bit more formally upstairs. The food is ultra-fresh (the chefs don't have to travel far for the ingredients) and might include "hors d'oeuvres of the sea," canalones (cannelloni) Rossini, grilled hake with herbs, rape (monkfish) marinara, paella, brochettes of veal, filet steak with green peppercorns, seafood rice, or a zarzuela (stew) of fresh fish with spices.

Ⓢ **Nou Celler.** Princesa, 16. ☎ **93/310-47-73.** Reservations required. Main courses 600–1,800 ptas. ($4.80–$14.40). MC, V. Sun–Fri 8am–midnight. Closed June 15–July 15. Metro: Jaume I. CATALÁN/SPANISH.

Near the Picasso Museum, this establishment is perfect for either a bodega-type meal or a cup of coffee. Country artifacts hang from the beamed ceiling and plaster walls. The back entrance, at Barra de Ferro, 3, is at the quieter end of the place, where dozens of original artworks are arranged into a collage. The dining room offers such "Franco era" food as fish soup, Catalán soup, zarzuela (a medley of seafood), paella, hake, and other classic dishes.

Ⓢ **Pitarra.** Avinyó, 56. ☎ **93/301-16-47.** Reservations required. Main courses 950–2,000 ptas. ($7.60–$16); fixed-price lunch 1,100 ptas. ($8.80). AE, DC, MC, V. Mon–Sat 1–4pm and 8:30–11pm. Metro: Liceu. CATALÁN.

Founded in 1890, this restaurant in the Barri Gòtic was named after the 19th-century Catalán playwright who lived and wrote his plays and poetry here in the back room. Try the grilled fish chowder or a Catalán salad, followed by grilled salmon or squid Málaga style. Valencian paella is another specialty. The cuisine doesn't even pretend to be imaginative but strictly adheres to time-tested recipes—"the type of food we ate when growing up," in the words of one diner.

SUR DIAGONAL
VERY EXPENSIVE

Beltxenea. Majorca, 275. ☎ **93/215-30-24.** Reservations recommended. Main courses 2,500–5,500 ptas. ($20–$44); *menú degustación* 6,900 ptas. ($55.20). AE, DC, MC, V. Mon–Fri 1:30–4pm and 8:30–11:30pm, Sat 8:30–11:30pm. Closed 2 weeks in Aug. Metro: Passeig de Gràcia. BASQUE.

Set in a building originally designed in the late 19th century as a *modernismo* Eixample apartment building, this restaurant celebrates the nuances and subtleties of Basque cuisine. Since the Basques are noted as the finest chefs in Spain, this is a grand cuisine indeed and is also one of the most elegantly and comfortably furnished restaurants in Barcelona. Save a visit here for that special night—it's worth the money. In a dignified dining room with parquet floors and nautical accessories, you can enjoy a cuisine that's affected by the inspiration of the chef and the availability of ingredients. Examples include hake served either fried with garlic or garnished with clams and served with fish broth. Roast lamb, grilled rabbit, and pheasant are well prepared and succulent, as are the desserts. Summer dining is possible outside in the formal garden.

✪ **Ca l'Isidre.** Les Flors, 12. ☎ **93/441-11-39.** Reservations required. Main courses 2,200–3,800 ptas. ($17.60–$30.40). AE, MC, V. Mon–Sat 1:30–4pm and 8:30–11:30pm. Closed Aug. Metro: Parallel. CATALÁN.

In spite of its seedy location (take a cab at night!), this is perhaps the most sophisticated Catalán bistro in Barcelona, drawing such patrons as King Juan Carlos and Queen Sofía. Opened in 1970, it was also visited by Julio Iglesias and the famous Catalonian band leader Xavier Cugat. Isidre Gironés, helped by his wife, Montserrat, is known for his fresh Catalán cuisine. Flowers decorate the restaurant, along with artwork, and the array of food is beautifully prepared and served. Try spider crabs and shrimp, a gourmand salad with foie gras, sweetbreads with port and flap mushrooms, or carpaccio of veal Harry's Bar style. The selection of Spanish and Catalán wines is excellent.

EXPENSIVE

✪ La Dama. Avinguda Diagonal, 423. ☎ **93/202-06-86.** Reservations required. Main courses 1,800–4,000 ptas. ($14.40–$32); fixed-price menus 4,750–7,500 ptas. ($38–$60). AE, DC, MC, V. Daily 1–4pm and 8:30–11:30pm. Metro: Provença. CATALÁN/INTERNATIONAL.

This is one of the few restaurants in Barcelona that deserves—and gets—a Michelin star. Located one floor above street level in one of the grandly iconoclastic 19th-century buildings for which Barcelona is famous, this stylish and well-managed restaurant serves a clientele of local residents and civic dignitaries with impeccable taste and confidence. You'll take an art nouveau elevator (or the sinuous stairs) up one flight to reach the dining room. The specialties might include roast filet of goat, salmon steak served with vinegar derived from cava (sparkling wine) and onions, confit of duckling, cream-of-potato soup flavored with caviar, a salad of crayfish with orange-flavored vinegar, an abundant seasonal platter of autumn mushrooms, and succulent preparations of lamb, fish, shellfish, beef, and veal. The building that contains the restaurant, designed by the *modernismo* architect Manuel Sayrach, lies 3 blocks west of the intersection of Avinguda Diagonal and Passeig de Gràcia.

✪ Jaume de Provença. Provença, 88. ☎ **93/430-00-29.** Reservations recommended. Main courses 1,950–3,000 ptas. ($15.60–$24). AE, DC, MC, V. Tues–Sat 1–4pm and 9–11:30pm, Sun 1–4pm. Closed Easter week and Aug. Metro: Estació-Sants. CATALÁN/FRENCH.

Located a few steps away from the Estació Central de Barcelona-Sants railway station at the western end of the Eixample, this is a small, cozy, and personalized restaurant with a country-rustic decor. It's the only restaurant on Avinguda Diagonal that offers food to equal that of La Dama (see below). The young-at-heart clientele is served by a polite and hardworking staff. Named after its owner/chef, Jaume Bargués, it features modern interpretations of traditional Catalán and southern French cuisine. Examples include a gratin of clams with spinach, a salad of two different species of lobster, small packets of foie gras and truffles, pig's trotters with plums and truffles, crabmeat lasagne, cod with saffron sauce, sole with mushrooms in a port-wine sauce, and a dessert specialty of orange mousse, whose presentation is an artistic statement in its own right. This establishment, incidentally, was launched during the 1940s by Jaume's forebears, who acquiesced to their talented offspring's new and successful culinary theories.

Restaurante Diana. In the Hotel Ritz, Gran Vía de les Corts Catalanes, 668. ☎ **93/318-52-00.** Reservations recommended. Main courses 2,000–3,800 ptas. ($16–$30.40); fixed-price menu 3,250 ptas. ($26) Mon–Fri, 4,450 ptas. ($35.60) Sat–Sun. AE, DC, MC, V. Daily 1:30–4pm and 8:30–11pm. Metro: Arc del Triomf. FRENCH.

At least part of the allure of dining here involves the chance to visit the most legendary hotel in Barcelona. Located on the lobby level of the Ritz, the restaurant is filled with French furnishings and accessories amid a gilt-and-blue color scheme. The polite and well-trained staff serves such dishes as seafood salad flavored with saffron; filets of sole layered with lobster; filet mignon braised in cognac, cream, and peppercorn sauce; turbot in white-wine sauce; and a wide array of delectable desserts. The cuisine is of a high international standard, although the restaurant doesn't quite reach the sublime culinary experience of La Dama or Jaume de Provença.

INEXPENSIVE

El Caballito Blanco. Majorca, 196. ☎ **93/453-10-33.** Reservations not required. Main courses 875–3,900 ptas. ($7–$31.20). AE, MC, V. Tues–Sat 1–3:45pm and 9–10:45pm, Sun 1–3:45pm. Closed Aug. Metro: Hospital Clínic. SEAFOOD/INTERNATIONAL.

This old Barcelona standby, famous for its seafood, has long been popular among locals. The fluorescent-lit dining area doesn't offer much atmosphere, but the food is good, varied, and relatively inexpensive. The "Little White Horse," in the Passeig de Gràcia area, features a huge selection, including monkfish, mussels marinara, and shrimp with garlic. If you don't want fish, try the grilled lamb cutlets. Several different pâtés and salads are offered. There's a bar to the left of the dining area.

Ca La María. Tallers, 76. ☎ **93/318-89-93.** Reservations recommended Sat–Sun. Main courses 925–1,550 ptas. ($7.40–$12.40). AE, DC, MC, V. Sun–Mon 1:30–4pm, Tues–Sat 1:30–4pm and 8:30–11pm. Metro: Plaça de la Universitat. CATALÁN.

This small blue-and-green tiled bistro (only 18 tables) is on a quiet square opposite a Byzantine-style church near Plaça de la Universitat. Look for the constantly changing daily specials. This isn't a place for haute cuisine. A bit battered in looks, the restaurant serves endearingly homelike food—providing you grew up in a family of Catalán cooks. These dishes, despite their simple origins, are often surprisingly tasty, as exemplified by the baby squid with onions and tomatoes, anglerfish with burnt garlic, and a veal sirloin cooked to taste.

NORTE DIAGONAL
VERY EXPENSIVE

✪ **Botafumeiro.** Gran de Gràcia, 81. ☎ **93/218-42-30.** Reservations recommended for dining rooms, not necessary for meals at the bar. Main courses 2,500–5,800 ptas. ($20–$46.40); fixed-price menus 8,000–9,000 ptas. ($64–$72). AE, DC, MC, V. Mon–Sat 1pm–1am, Sun 1–5pm. Metro: Enrique Cuiraga. SEAFOOD.

Although the competition is severe, this *restaurante marisquería* consistently puts Barcelona's finest seafood on the table. Much of the allure of this place comes from the attention to detail paid by the white-jacketed staff, who prepare a table setting at the establishment's bar for anyone who prefers to dine there. If you do choose to venture to the rear, you'll find a series of attractive dining rooms outfitted with light-grained panels, white napery, polished brass, potted plants, and paintings by Galician artists. These rooms are noted for the ease with which business deals seem to be arranged during the lunch hour, when international business people often make it their favorite rendezvous. The king of Spain is sometimes a patron.

Menu items include some of the most legendary seafood in Barcelona, prepared ultra-fresh in a glistening and ultramodern kitchen that's visible from parts of the dining room. The establishment prides itself on its fresh- and saltwater fish, clams, mussels, lobster, crayfish, scallops, and several varieties of crustaceans that you may never have seen before. Stored live in holding tanks or in enormous crates near the restaurant's entrance, many of the creatures are flown in every day from Galicia, home of owner Moncho Neira. In contrast to the hundred-or-so fish dishes (which might include zarzuelas, paellas, and grills), the menu lists only four or five meat dishes, including three kinds of steak, veal, and a traditional version of pork with turnips. The wine list offers a wide array of cavas from Catalonia and highly drinkable choices from Galicia.

EXPENSIVE

✪ **Neichel.** Pedralbes, 16. ☎ **93/203-84-08.** Reservations required. Main courses 2,300–3,800 ptas. ($18.40–$30.40). AE, DC, MC, V. Mon–Sat 1–4pm and 8:30–11pm. Closed Aug and all holidays. Metro: Palau Reial or María Cristina. FRENCH.

Owned and operated by Alsace-born Jean Louis Neichel, who has been called "the most brilliant ambassador French cuisine has ever had within Spain," this restaurant serves a clientele whose credentials might best be described as stratospheric. Outfitted in cool tones of gray and pastel, with its main decoration derived from a bank of windows opening onto greenery, Neichel is vastly and almost obsessively concerned with gastronomy—the savory presentation of some of the most talked-about preparations of seafood, fowl, and sweets in Spain.

Your meal might include a "mosaic" of foie gras with vegetables, a salad composed of fresh asparagus, strips of salmon marinated in sesame and served with escabeche (vinaigrette) sauce, slices of raw and smoked salmon stuffed with caviar, a prize-winning terrine of sea crab floating on a lavishly decorated bed of cold seafood sauce, escalope of turbot served with coulis (purée) of sea urchins, fricassée of Bresse chicken served with spiny lobsters, sea bass with a mousseline of truffles, Spanish milk-fed lamb served with the juice of Boletus mushrooms, a ragoût of sole containing fresh asparagus and Iranian caviar, rack of lamb gratinéed in a herb-flavored pastry crust, and an array of well-flavored game birds obtained in season from hunters throughout Catalonia and France. Both the selection of European cheeses and the changing array of freshly made desserts are nothing short of spectacular.

Reno. Tuset, 27. ☎ **93/200-91-29.** Reservations required. Main courses 1,200–3,500 ptas. ($9.60–$28). AE, DC, MC, V. Sun–Fri 1–4pm and 8:30–11:30pm. Metro: Diagonal. CATALÁN/FRENCH.

One of the finest and most enduring haute cuisine restaurants in Barcelona, Reno boasts an impeccably mannered staff (formal but not intimidating) and an under-stated modern decor accented with black leather and oversize mirrors. A discreet row of sidewalk-to-ceiling windows hung with fine-mesh lace shelters diners from the prying eyes of those on the octagonal plaza outside. Specialties, influenced by the seasons and by the traditions of France, might include partridge simmered in wine or port sauce, a platter of assorted smoked fish (each painstakingly smoked on the premises), hake with anchovy sauce, filet of sole either stuffed with foie gras and truffles or grilled with anchovy sauce, Catalán-style civet of lobster, roast duck with a sauce of honey and sherry vinegar, and an appetizing array of pastries wheeled from table to table on a trolley. Dessert might also be one of several kinds of crêpes flambéed at your table. The restaurant, incidentally, was established in 1954 by the father of the present owner.

Roig Robí. Séneca, 20. ☎ **93/218-92-22.** Reservations required. Main courses 1,950–3,250 ptas. ($15.60–$26). AE, DC, MC, V. Mon–Sat 1:30–4pm and 9–11:30pm. Metro: Diagonal. CATALÁN/FRENCH.

Excellent food from an imaginative kitchen and a warm welcome keep patrons coming back here, although we're not as excited about this restaurant as we once were. It remains, however, one of the city's most dependable choices for reliable cuisine. Begin by ordering an aperitif from the L-shaped oaken bar. Then head down a long corridor to a pair of flower-filled dining rooms. In warm weather, glass doors open onto a walled courtyard, ringed with cascades of ivy and shaded with willows and mimosa. Menu items include fresh beans with pine-nut sauce, hake al Roig Robí, codfish salad with pintos, lobster salad, ravioli stuffed with spring herbs, three different preparations of hake, chicken stuffed with foie gras, and a cockscomb salad, the latter a dish too adventuresome for many palates.

❂ Via Veneto. Granduxer, 10–12. ☎ **93/200-72-44.** Reservations required. Main courses 2,200–3,990 ptas. ($17.60–$31.90). AE, DC, MC, V. Mon–Fri 1:15–4pm and 8:45pm–midnight, Sat 8:45pm–midnight. Metro: La Bonanova. CATALÁN/INTERNATIONAL.

With a soothing and dignified decor of calming colors and baroque swirls, this restaurant is known for its solid respectability and consistently well-prepared cuisine. Set a short walk from Plaça de Francesc María, it offers such dishes as a tartare of fresh fish with caviar, roasted salt cod with potatoes, veal kidney with truffle sauce, loin of roast suckling pig with baby vegetables of the season, and filet steak served in a

👪 Family-Friendly Restaurants

Fast-Food Places   Burger King *(see p. 80)*, the Chicago Pizza Pie Factory *(see p. 80)*, and Kentucky Fried Chicken *(see p. 80)* are good bets for fast food that the kids will enjoy.

Henry J. Bean's Bar and Grill *(see p. 78)*   This place has sit-down meals that the kids will love.

Dulcinea *(see p. 82)*   This makes a great refueling stop any time of the day— guaranteed to satisfy any chocoholic.

Poble Espanyol *(see p. 90)*   A good introduction to Spanish food. All the restaurants in the "Spanish Village" serve comparable food at comparable prices— let the kids choose what to eat.

brandy, cream, and peppercorn sauce. Innovative and imaginative Catalán recipes are always being invented here. The cuisine is finely crafted based on superb local products. There's a wide array of wines to accompany any meal. Dessert might be a richly textured combination of melted chocolate, cherries, Armagnac, and vanilla ice cream.

MODERATE

Arcs de Sant Gervasi. Santaló, 103. ☎ **93/201-92-77.** Reservations recommended. Main courses 1,900–2,400 ptas. ($15.20–$19.20). AE, DC, MC, V. Tues–Sat 1–4:30pm and 9pm– midnight, Sun 1–4:30pm. Metro: Muntaner. CATALÁN.

North of the old town, Arcs de Sant Gervasi is sleekly decorated with such trappings as black lacquer chairs. A nearby gallery fills the walls with pictures that are for sale. To begin, try cream-of-crab soup or Palafrugell "black rice." For a main dish, order tender slices of veal served with wild mushrooms in a delectable cognac-flavored sauce; the kid cutlets are also juicy and superb. For dessert, try the scooped-out pineapple filled with chopped fresh fruit and crema catalana (caramel pudding).

Henry J. Bean's Bar and Grill. Carrer La Granada del Penedés, 14–16. ☎ **93/218-29-98.** Main courses 1,295–3,000 ptas. ($10.35–$24). AE, DC, MC, V. Daily 1pm–1am. Metro: Diagonal. AMERICAN.

The food is cheap, plentiful, and savory in this unassuming restaurant filled with Americana. Have a great smokehouse burger or perhaps chili con carne, stuffed mushrooms, nachos, or barbecued baby back ribs. No meal is complete without pecan or mud pie for dessert. Half-price drinks are de rigueur during happy hour, between 6 and 9pm and all night Wednesday.

MOLL DE LA FUSTA & BARCELONETA
EXPENSIVE

Can Majó. Almirante Aixada, 23. ☎ **93/221-54-55.** Reservations recommended. Main courses 1,800–3,500 ptas. ($14.40–$28); fixed-price menu 6,000 ptas. ($48). AE, DC, MC, V. Tues–Sun 1:30–4:30pm and 9–11:30pm. Metro: Barceloneta. SEAFOOD.

Located in the old fishing quarter of Barceloneta, Can Majó attracts many people from the fancier quarters who journey down here for a great seafood dinner. The Suárez-Majó family welcome you; they're still operating a business where their grandmother first opened a bar. Try a house specialty, pelada (Catalán for paella), perhaps starting with entremeses (hors d'oeuvres), from which you can select barnacles, oysters, prawns, whelks, clams, and crab—virtually whatever was caught that day. The clams with white beans are recommended. The classic all-vegetable gazpacho comes with fresh mussels and shrimp.

Ramonet (Bar Xarello). Carrer Maquinista, 17. ☎ **93/319-30-64.** Reservations recommended. Main courses 1,800–3,950 ptas. ($14.40–$31.60); fixed-price menus 4,200–5,950 ptas. ($33.60–$47.60). AE, DC, MC, V. Daily 10am–4pm and 8pm–midnight. Closed Aug 10–Sept 10. Metro: Barceloneta. SEAFOOD.

Located in a Catalán-style villa near the seaport, this rather expensive restaurant serves a large variety of fresh seafood, and has done so since 1763. The front room, with stand-up tables for seafood tapas, beer, and regional wine, is often crowded. In the two dining rooms in back, lined with wooden tables, you can choose from a wide variety of fish—shrimp, hake, and monkfish are almost always available. Other specialties include a portion of pungent anchovies, grilled mushrooms, black rice, braised artichokes, and a tortilla with spinach and beans. Mussels "from the beach" are also sold.

MODERATE

Gambrinus. Passeig del Moll de la Fusta. ☎ **93/221-96-07.** Reservations required. Main courses from 1,000 ptas. ($8). AE, DC, MC, V. Thurs–Sun 12:30–4pm and 7pm–midnight. Metro: Drassanes. SEAFOOD.

Although this restaurant is respected for the well-prepared food it serves, much of its fame derives from the enormous statue perched on its roof. Made of polychromed fiberglass by Javier Mariscal (creator of the 1992 Olympic mascot), the statue depicts a giant lobster whose waving tentacles and threatening claws attract looks of amazement from pedestrians and motorists.

Set beside the sea, in a low-slung modern building with lots of glass, the restaurant has outdoor tables on a pier, shaded with parasols. Menu items are priced from relatively inexpensive to very expensive (for example, anything made with lobster or pricey shellfish). Meals can include such dishes as fish soup, fresh oysters, fried squid, shellfish paella, and various cuts and filets of grilled fish, depending on the day's catch. Many visitors opt for a drink at the boat-shaped bar before or after their meal.

Siete Puertas (also known as 7 Portes). Passeig d'Isabel II, 14. ☎ **93/319-30-33.** Reservations required. Main courses 825–3,320 ptas. ($6.60–$26.55). AE, DC, MC, V. Daily 1pm–midnight. Metro: Barceloneta. SEAFOOD.

This is a lunchtime favorite for businesspeople (the Stock Exchange is across the way) and an evening favorite for in-the-know clients who have made it their preferred restaurant in Catalonia. It's been going since 1836. Regional dishes—the portions are enormous—include fresh herring with onions and potatoes, a different paella daily (sometimes with shellfish, for example, or with rabbit), and a wide array of fresh fish, succulent oysters, and a herb-laden stew of black beans with pork or white beans with sausage.

El Túnel. Ample, 33–35. ☎ **93/315-27-59.** Reservations recommended for lunch. Main courses 1,200–2,500 ptas. ($9.60–$20). AE, DC, MC, V. Tues–Sat 1:30–4pm and 6 to around 11:30pm, Sun 1:30–4pm. Closed Aug. Metro: San Jaume. CATALÁN.

This long-established restaurant features a delectable fish soup, cannelloni with truffles, kidney beans with shrimp, roast kid, fish stew, and filet of beef with peppers. The food is umcomplicated but delicious. The service is eager, the wine cellar extensive. El Túnel lies close to the general post office.

Fast Food & Picnic Fare

For those travelers who miss good old American food, don't fret—there are plenty of fast-food joints. It may not be as adventurous as trying authentic Spanish cuisine, but you'll definitely please the kids.

Burger King, Rambla de Canaletes, 135 (☎ **93/302-54-29;** metro: Plaça de Catalunya), is open Sunday to Friday from 10am to midnight and on Saturday from 10am to 1am. A burger, fries, and a drink costs 550 to 1,000 pesetas ($4.40 to $8).

Chicago Pizza Pie Factory, Carrer de Provença, 300 (☎ **93/215-94-15;** metro: Passeig de Gràcia), offers pizzas for 1,250 to 3,000 pesetas ($10 to $24), the latter big enough for four. It's open daily from 1pm to 1am; happy hour runs from 6 to 9pm.

Kentucky Fried Chicken, Ferran, 2 (☎ **93/412-51-54;** metro: Drassanes), is open Monday to Thursday from 11am to 11pm and Friday to Sunday from 11am to midnight. A bucket containing six pieces of chicken, enough for a meal for two, costs 1,075 ptas. ($8.60).

Viena, Rambla dels Estudis, 115 (☎ **93/317-14-92;** metro: Plaça de Catalunya), is Barcelona's most elegant fast-food place. Waiters wearing Viennese vests serve croissants with Roquefort for breakfast and, later in the day, toasted ham sandwiches, hamburgers with onions, and pasta with tomato sauce. Meals begin at 1,500 ptas. ($12). Service is Monday to Saturday from 9am to 1am and on Sunday from 2pm to midnight.

The best place in all Barcelona to buy the makings of your picnic is the **Mercat de la Boquería,** in the center of Les Rambles (metro: Liceu). This is the old marketplace of Barcelona. You'll jostle elbows with butchers and fishmongers in bloodied smocks and see salespeople selling cheeses and sausages. Much of the food is uncooked, but hundreds of items are already prepared and you can even buy a bottle of wine or mineral water.

Now for where to have your picnic. Right in the heart of Barcelona is the **Parc de la Ciutadella** (see "Parks & Gardens" in Chapter 4), in the southeast section of the district known as the Barri de la Ribera, site of the Picasso Museum. After lunch, take the kids to the park zoo and later go out on the lake in a rented rowboat.

It's more scenic to picnic in **Montjuïc,** site of several events of the 1992 Summer Olympics. After your picnic, you can enjoy the amusement park or walk through the Poble Espanyol, a re-created Spanish village.

WEST OF TIBIDABO

La Balsa. Infanta Isabel, 4. ☎ **93/211-50-48.** Reservations required. Main courses 1,500–2,600 ptas. ($12–$20.80); fixed-price menu 3,000 ptas. ($24) at lunch, 5,500–6,950 ptas. ($44–$55.60) at dinner. AE, DC, V. Mon 9–11:30pm, Tues–Sat 2–3:30pm and 9–11:30pm. Closed Easter week, reduced menu in Aug. Take a taxi to get here. INTERNATIONAL.

Poised on the uppermost level of a circular tower that was built as a water cistern, La Balsa offers a view over most of the surrounding cityscape. To reach it you must climb up to what was originally intended as the structure's rooftop. Glassed-in walls, awnings, and a verdant mass of potted plants create the decor. You're likely to be greeted by owner and founder Mercedes López before being seated. Menu items emerge from a cramped but well-organized kitchen several floors below. (The waiters here are reputedly the most athletic in Barcelona because they must run up and down the stairs carrying steaming platters.) Often booked several days in advance, the restaurant serves such dishes as a salad of broad beans (judías verdes) with strips of salmon in lemon-flavored vinaigrette, stewed veal with wild mushrooms, a salad of warm lentils with anchovies, pickled fresh salmon with chives, undercooked magret (breast) of duck served with fresh and lightly poached foie gras, and baked hake (flown in frequently from faraway Galicia) prepared in squid-ink sauce.

TASCAS

The bars listed below are known for their tapas; for further recommendations, refer to the "Barcelona After Dark" section of Chapter 4.

Alt Heidelberg. Ronda Universitat, 5. ☎ **93/318-10-32.** Tapas 250–750 ptas. ($2–$6); combination plates 1,000–1,450 ptas. ($8–$11.60). MC, V. Mon–Fri 8am–1:30am, Sat–Sun noon–2am. Metro: Plaça de la Universitat. GERMAN/TAPAS.

Since the 1930s this tasca has been an institution in Barcelona, offering German beer on tap, a good selection of German sausages, and Spanish tapas. You can also enjoy full meals here—sauerkraut garni is a specialty.

Bar del Pi. Plaça Sant Josep Oriol, 1. ☎ **93/302-21-23.** Tapas 250–550 ptas. ($2–$4.40). No credit cards. Mon–Fri 9am–11pm, Sat 9:30am–10pm, Sun 10am–10pm. Metro: Liceu. TAPAS.

One of the most famous bars in the Barri Gòtic, this establishment lies midway between two medieval squares, opening onto Església del Pi. You can sit inside at one of the cramped bentwood tables or stand at the crowded bar. In warm weather, take a table beneath the single plane tree on this landmark square. Tapas are limited; most visitors come to drink coffee, beer, or wine.

Bar Turó. Tenor Viñas, 1. ☎ **93/200-69-53.** Tapas 300–1,500 ptas. ($2.40–$12). No credit cards. Daily 9am–1am. Metro: Muntaner. TAPAS.

Set in an affluent residential neighborhood north of the old town, Bar Turó serves some of the best tapas in town. In summer you can either sit outside or retreat to the narrow confines of the inside bar. There you can select from about 20 different kinds of tapas, including Russian salad, fried squid, and Serrano ham.

Bodega la Plata. Mercè, 28. ☎ **93/315-10-09.** Tapas 180–300 ptas. ($1.45–$2.40). No credit cards. Mon–Sat 9am–11pm. Metro: Barceloneta. TAPAS.

Part of a trio of famous bodegas on this narrow medieval street, La Plata occupies a corner building whose two open sides allow richly aromatic cooking odors to permeate the neighborhood. This bodega contains a marble-topped bar and overcrowded tables. The culinary specialty is raciones (small plates) of deep-fried sardines (head and all). You can make a meal with two servings of these, coupled with the house's tomato, onion, and fresh anchovy salad.

Bodegueta. Rambla de Catalunya, 100. ☎ **93/215-48-94.** Tapas from 160 ptas. ($1.30). No credit cards. Mon–Sat 8am–2am, Sun 6:30pm–2am. Metro: Diagonal. TAPAS.

Founded in 1940, this old wine tavern specializes in Catalán sausage meats. Everything can be washed down with inexpensive Spanish wines. Beer costs 125 ptas. ($1); wine goes for 100 ptas. (80¢).

Las Campanas (Casa Marcos). Mercè, 21. ☎ **93/315-06-09.** Tapas from 250 ptas. ($2). No credit cards. Thurs–Tues noon–2am. Metro: Barceloneta. TAPAS.

No sign announces its name—from the street Las Campanas looks like a storehouse for cured hams and wine bottles. At a long and narrow stand-up bar, patrons flock here for a chorizo (spicy sausage), which is then pinioned between two pieces of bread. Sausages are usually eaten with beer or red wine. The place opened in 1952 and nothing has changed since. A tape recorder plays nostalgic favorites, everything from Edith Piaf to the Andrews Sisters.

Casa Tejada. Tenor Viñas, 3. ☎ **93/200-73-41.** Tapas 275–2,150 ptas. ($2.20–$17.20). V. Daily 9am–2am. Metro: Muntaner. TAPAS.

Covered with rough stucco and decorated with hanging hams, Casa Tejada (established in 1964) offers some of Barcelona's best tapas. Arranged behind a glass display case, they include such dishes as marinated fresh tuna, German-style potato salad, five preparations of squid (including one that's stuffed), and ham salad. For variety, quantity, and quality, this place is hard to beat. There's outdoor dining in summer.

Jamón Jamón. Mestre Nicolau, 4. ☎ **93/209-41-03.** Tapas 1,200–1,600 ptas. ($9.60–$12.80). No credit cards. Mon–Sat 9am–midnight. Metro: Muntaner. TAPAS.

Located north of Avinguda Diagonal, near Plaça de Francesc María, this establishment has a modern interior of gray granite and chrome, a deliberate contrast to the traditional pork products that are the specialty of this tasca. Entire hams from Huelva, deep in the south of Andalusia, are impaled on steel braces. The ham is laboriously carved and trimmed before you into paper-thin slices.

La Jarra. Mercè, 9. ☎ **93/315-17-59.** Tapas 200–352 ptas. ($1.60–$2.80). No credit cards. Thurs–Tues 10:30am–1am. Metro: Barceloneta. TAPAS.

La Jarra occupies a tile-covered L-shaped room that's somewhat bleak in appearance, yet residents claim that it's one of the most authentic tapas bars in the old town. You can order a ración of marinated mushrooms or well-seasoned artichokes Rioja style, but the culinary star is the ever-present haunch of jamón canario (Canary Island ham), which is carved before your eyes into lean, succulent morsels served with boiled potatoes, olive oil, and lots of salt. It resembles roast pork in flavor and appearance.

Rey de la Gamba. Joan de Borbo, 53. ☎ **93/221-75-98.** Tapas 800–1,850 ptas. ($6.40–$14.80). MC, V. Daily 10am–1am. Metro: Barceloneta. TAPAS/SHELLFISH.

The name of this place means "king of prawns," but this restaurant could also be called the House of Mussels since it sells more of that shellfish. In the old fishing village of Barceloneta, dating from the 18th century, this place packs them in, especially on weekends. A wide array of seafood is sold, along with cured ham—the combination is considered a tradition.

A SPECIAL PLACE FOR DESSERT

Dulcinea. Via Petrixol, 2. ☎ **93/302-68-24.** Cup of chocolate 325 ptas. ($2.60). No credit cards. Daily 9am–1pm and 5–9pm. Closed late July to mid-Aug. Metro: Plaça de Catalunya or Liceu. CHOCOLATE.

At this, the most famous chocolate shop in Barcelona, the specialty is melindros (sugar-topped soft-sided biscuits), which the regulars who flock here love to dunk into the very thick hot chocolate—so thick, in fact, that imbibing it feels like eating a melted chocolate bar.

Barcelona Attractions

Barcelona, long a Mediterranean center of commerce, is fast emerging as one of the focal points of European tourism, a role that reached its zenith during the 1992 Olympic Games. Spain's second-largest city is also its most cosmopolitan and avant-garde.

Because its rich history extends back for centuries, Barcelona is filled with landmark buildings and world-class museums offering many sightseeing opportunities. These include Antoni Gaudí's Sagrada Familia, the Museu Picasso, the Gothic cathedral, and Les Rambles, the famous tree-lined promenade cutting through the heart of the old quarter.

The capital of Catalonia, Barcelona sits at the northeast end of the Costa Brava, Spain's gateway to the Mediterranean. A half-hour flight east will land you on one of the Balearic Islands—Majorca, Ibiza, or Minorca. (For more information on the Balearic Islands, consult *Frommer's Spain,* 17th Edition.) You can also branch out from Barcelona to the monastery at Montserrat or the Penedés vineyards (see "Easy Excursions," later in this chapter).

To begin, however, you'll want to take in the artistic and intellectual aura of this unique seafaring city. Its residents take justifiable pride in their Catalán heritage, and they're eager to share it with you. Many of these sights can be covered on foot, and this chapter includes three walking tours.

An array of nightlife (Barcelona is a *big* bar town), shopping possibilities, and sports programs are also covered in this chapter, along with some organized tours, special events, and trips to Catalonia's wine country. It makes for some serious sightseeing; you'll need plenty of time to take it all in.

SUGGESTED ITINERARIES

If You Have 1 Day

Spend the morning following our walking tour of the Gothic Quarter (see below), taking in the highlights of this ancient district. In the afternoon visit Antoni Gaudí's unfinished cathedral, La Sagrada Familia, before returning to the heart of the city for a walk down Les Rambles. To cap your day, take the funicular to the fountains at Montjuïc or go to the top of Tibidabo for an outstanding view of Barcelona and its harbor.

Barcelona Attractions

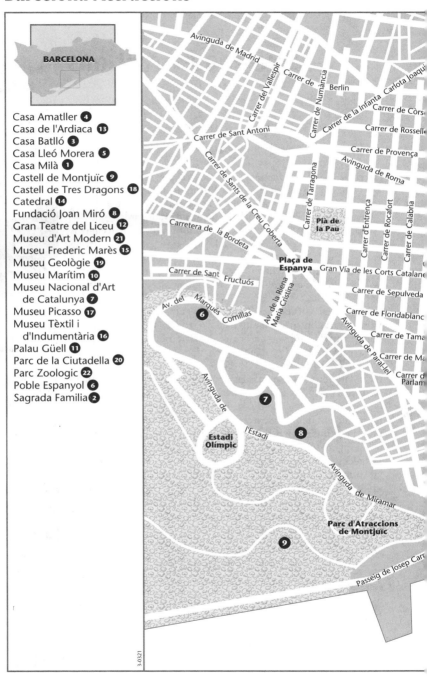

BARCELONA

Casa Amatller **4**
Casa de l'Ardiaca **13**
Casa Batlló **3**
Casa Lleó Morera **5**
Casa Milà **1**
Castell de Montjuïc **9**
Castell de Tres Dragons **18**
Catedral **14**
Fundació Joan Miró **8**
Gran Teatre del Liceu **12**
Museu d'Art Modern **21**
Museu Frederic Marès **15**
Museu Geològie **19**
Museu Marítim **10**
Museu Nacional d'Art
   de Catalunya **7**
Museu Picasso **17**
Museu Tèxtil i
   d'Indumentària **16**
Palau Güell **11**
Parc de la Ciutadella **20**
Parc Zoologic **22**
Poble Espanyol **6**
Sagrada Familia **2**

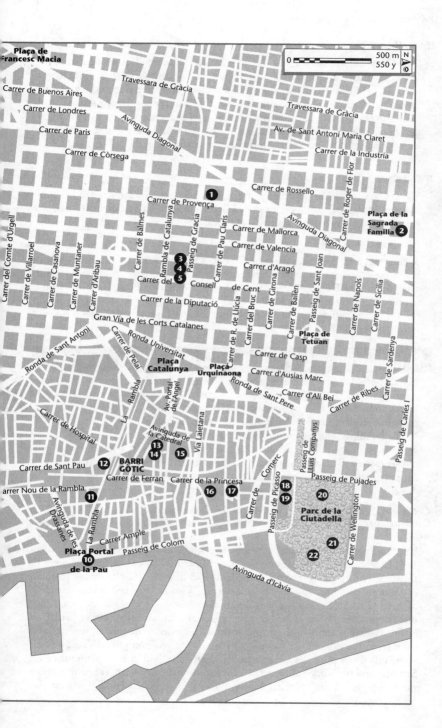

Plaça de
Francesc Macià

Carrer de Buenos Aires

Carrer de Londres

Carrer de Paris

Carrer de Còrsega

Travessara de Gràcia

Avinguda Diagonal

Travessara de Gràcia

Av. de Sant Antoni Maria Claret

Carrer de la Industria

Carrer de Rossello

Carrer de Provença

Carrer de Pau Claris

Avinguda Diagonal

Carrer de Mallorca

Plaça de la
Sagrada
Familia ❷

Carrer de Valencia

Carrer d'Aragó

de Cent

Carrer de la Diputació

Carrer de R. de Llúcia

Carrer del Bruc

Carrer de Girona

Carrer de Bailèn

Passeig de Sant Joan

Carrer de Napols

Carrer de Sicilia

Carrer de Balmes

Rambla de Catalunya

Passeig de Gracia

❸
❹
❺

Carrer del   Consell

Gran Vía de les Corts Catalanes

Ronda Universitat

Plaça de
Tetuan

Carrer de Casp

Plaça
Catalunya

Plaça
Urquinaona

Carrer d'Ausias Marc

Carrer d'Ali Bei

Carrer de Ribes

Carrer de Sardenya

Passeig de Carles I

Carrer del Comte d'Urgell

Carrer de Villarroel

Carrer de Casanova

Carrer de Muntaner

Carrer d'Aribau

Ronda de Sant Antoni

Carrer de Pelai

Ronda de Sant Pere

Carrer de Hospital

La Rambla

Av. Portal
de l'Angel

Avinguda de
la Catedral

Via Laietana

❶

❸
❹
❺

Plaça de
Francesc Macià

0   500 m
       550 y

N

BARRI
GÒTIC

❶❸
❶❹ ❶❺
❶❷

Carrer de Sant Pau

Carrer de Ferran

Carrer de la Princesa

Carrer de

Comerç

Passeig de Picasso

Passeig de
Lluis Companys

Passeig de Pujades

❶❽
❶❾

❷⓿

Parc de la
Ciutadella

Carrer de Wellington

arrer Nou de la Rambla

❶❶

❶❻ ❶❼

Avinguda de les
Drassanes

La Rambla

Carrer Ample

Plaça Portal
de la Pau

❶⓿

Passeig de Colom

Avinguda d'Icàvia

Carrer Ample

❷❶

❷❷

85

If You Have 2 Days

Spend Day 1 as described above. On Day 2, visit the Museu Picasso, housed in two Gothic mansions. Then stroll through the surrounding district, the Barri de la Ribera, which is filled with Renaissance mansions. Follow this with a ride to the top of the Columbus Monument for a panoramic view of the harborfront. Have a seafood lunch at La Barceloneta, and in the afternoon stroll up Les Rambles again. For the rest of the afternoon explore Montjuïc and visit the Museu d'Art de Catalunya. End the day with a meal at Los Caracoles, the most famous restaurant in the old city, just off Les Rambles.

If You Have 3 Days

Spend Days 1 and 2 as described above. On Day 3, make a pilgrimage to the monastery of Montserrat to see the venerated Black Virgin and a host of artistic and scenic attractions. Try to time your visit to hear the 50-member boys' choir.

If You Have 5 Days

Spend your first 3 days as described above. On Day 4, take a morning walk in *modernismo* Barcelona and have lunch on the pier. In the afternoon visit Montjuïc again to tour the Fundació Joan Miró and walk through the Poble Espanyol, a miniature village created for the 1929 World's Fair. On Day 5, take another excursion from the city, perhaps to the Penedés wine country for a sample Catalonian cava (champagne).

1 In & Around the Ciutat Vella (Old City)

The ✪ **Barri Gòtic** is the old aristocratic quarter of Barcelona, parts of which have survived from the Middle Ages. Spend at least 2 or 3 hours exploring its narrow streets and squares; start by walking up Carrer del Carme, east of Les Rambles. A nighttime stroll takes on added drama, but exercise extreme caution.

The buildings, for the most part, are austere and sober, the cathedral being the crowning achievement. Roman ruins and the vestiges of 3rd-century walls add further interest. This area is intricately detailed and filled with many attractions that are easy to miss. For a tour of the Gothic Quarter, see "Walking Tour 1," later in this chapter.

✪ **Catedral.** Plaça de la Seu. ☎ **93/315-15-54.** Cathedral, free; museum, 100 ptas. (80¢). Cathedral, daily 8am–1:30pm and 4–7:30pm; cloister museum, daily 10am–1pm. Metro: Jaume I.

Barcelona's cathedral stands as a celebrated example of Catalonian Gothic architecture. Except for the 19th-century west facade, the basilica was begun at the end of the 13th century and completed in the mid–15th century. The three naves, cleaned and illuminated, have splendid Gothic details. With its large bell towers, blending of medieval and Renaissance styles, beautiful cloister, high altar, side chapels, sculptured choir, and Gothic arches, it ranks as one of the most impressive cathedrals in Spain. Vaulted galleries in the cloister surround a garden of magnolias, medlars, and palm trees; the galleries are further enhanced by forged iron grilles. The historian Cirici called this place the loveliest oasis in Barcelona. The cloister, illuminated on Saturday and fiesta days, also contains a museum of medieval art. The most notable work displayed is the 15th-century *La Pietat* of Bartolomé Bermejo. At noon on

Sunday you can see a *sardana*, the Catalonian folk dance, performed in front of the cathedral.

Centre de Cultura Contemporania de Barcelona (Center of Contemporary Culture of Barcelona). Montalegre, 5. ☎ **93/412-07-81.** Admission 500 ptas. ($4) adults, 300 ptas. ($2.40) students and seniors 65 and over, free for children 15 and under. Tues–Sat 11am–2pm and 4–8pm, Sun 10am–3pm. Metro: Plaça de Catalunya.

Located in the Ciutat Vella, the Center of Contemporary Culture of Barcelona (or CCCB) focuses on the city itself as its subject. It explores Barcelona's culture, history, and present role as a modern European city.

Museu d'Art Comtemporani de Barcelona. Plaça dels Angels, 1. ☎ **93/412-08-10.** Admission 600 ptas. ($4.80) adults, free for children. Tues–Fri noon–8pm, Sat 10am–8pm, Sun 10am–3pm. Metro: Plaça de Catalunya.

A soaring, glistening edifice in Barcelona's shabby Raval district, the Museum of Contemporary Art is to Barcelona what the Pompidou Center is to Paris. Designed by American architect Richard Meier, the building itself is a work of art, manipulating sunlight to offer brilliant, natural interior lighting. On display in the 74,000 square feet of exhibit space is the work of such modern luminaries as Tápies, Klee, Miró, and many others. The museum has a library, bookshop, and cafeteria.

Museu d'Història de la Ciutat. Plaça del Rei. ☎ **93/315-11-11.** Admission 500 ptas. ($4). Tues–Sat 10am–2pm and 4–8pm, Sun 10am–2pm. Bus: 16, 17, 19, 22, or 45.

Connected to the Royal Palace (see below), this museum traces the history of the city from its early days as a Roman colony to its role as the city of the 1992 Summer Olympics. The museum is housed in a Catalán-Mediterranean mansion from the 1400s called the Padellás House. Many of the exhibits date from Roman days, with much else from medieval times.

Museu Frederic Marès. Plaça de Sant Iú, 5–6. ☎ **93/310-58-00.** Admission 300 ptas. ($2.40) adults, free for children 15 and under. Tues–Sat 10am–5pm, Sun 10am–2pm. Metro: Jaume I. Bus: 17, 19, or 45.

One of the biggest repositories of medieval sculpture in the region is the Frederic Marès Museum, located just behind the cathedral. It's housed in an ancient palace whose interior courtyards, chiseled stone, and soaring ceilings are impressive in their own right, an ideal setting for the hundreds of polychrome sculptures. The sculpture section dates from pre-Roman times to the 20th century. Also housed in the same building is the Museu Sentimental, a collection of everyday items that help to illustrate life in Barcelona during the past two centuries. Admission to both museums is included in the ticket price.

Palau Reial (Royal Palace). Plaça del Rei. ☎ **93/315-11-11.** Admission 500 ptas. ($4). Mon 3:30–8pm, Tues–Sat 9am–8pm, Sun 9am–1:30pm. Bus: 16, 17, 19, 22, or 45.

Former palace of the counts of Barcelona, this later became the residence of the kings of Aragón—hence, the name of its plaza (King's Square). It's believed that Columbus was received here by Isabella and Ferdinand when he returned from his first voyage to the New World. Here, some believe, the monarchs got their first look at a Native American. The Saló del Tinell, a banqueting hall with wood-paneled ceiling held up by half a dozen arches, dates from the 14th century. The hall dates from the 14th century. Rising five stories above the hall is the Torre del Rei Martí, a series of porticoed galleries.

2 Eixample

Fundació Antoni Tàpies. Aragó, 255. ☎ **93/487-03-15.** Admission 500 ptas. ($4) adults, 250 ptas. ($2) children 10–18, free for children 9 and under. Tues–Sun 11am–8pm. Metro: Passeig de Gràcia.

When it opened in 1990 this became the third museum in Barcelona devoted to the work of a single artist. In 1984 the Catalán artist Antoni Tàpies set up the foundation bearing his name, and the city of Barcelona donated an ideal site: the old Montaner i Simon publishing house near Passeig de Gràcia in the 19th-century Eixample district. One of the landmark buildings of Barcelona, the brick-and-iron structure was built between 1881 and 1884 by that exponent of Catalán art nouveau, architect Lluís Domènech i Montaner. The core of the museum is a collection of works by Tàpies (most contributed by the artist himself), covering the different stages of his career as it evolved into abstract expressionism. Here you can see the entire spectrum of mediums in which he worked: painting, assemblage, sculpture, drawing, and ceramics. His associations with Picasso and Miró are apparent. The largest of all the works by Tàpies is on top of the building itself: a gigantic sculpture made from 9,000 feet of metal wiring and tubing, entitled *Cloud and Chair.*

Museu Egipci de Barcelona. Rambla de Catalunya, 57–59. ☎ **93/488-01-88.** Admission 600 ptas. ($4.80) adults, 500 ptas. ($4) children. Mon–Sat 10am–2pm and 4–7pm. Guided tours on Sat. Closed holidays. Metro: Passeig de Gràcia.

Spain's only museum dedicated specifically to Egyptology, it contains more than 250 pieces from founder Jordi Clos's personal collection. On display are sacrophagi, jewelry, hieroglyphics, and various sculptures and artworks. Exhibits pay close attention to the everyday life of ancient Egyptians, including details regarding education, social customs, religion, and food. The museum possesses its own lab for restorations. A library with more than 3,000 works is open to the public.

✪ La Sagrada Familia. Majorca, 401. ☎ **93/455-02-47.** Church, 750 ptas. ($6), including 12-minute video on Gaudí's religious and secular works; elevator to the top (about 200 feet), 200 ptas. ($1.60). June–Aug, daily 9am–9pm; May and Sept, daily 9am–8pm; Mar–Apr and Oct, daily 9am–7pm; Nov–Feb, daily 9am–6pm. Metro: Sagrada Familia.

Gaudí's incomplete masterpiece is one of the more idiosyncratic creations of Spain— if you have time to see only one Catalán landmark, make it this one. Begun in 1882 and still incomplete at Gaudí's death in 1926, this incredible church—the Church of the Holy Family—is a bizarre wonder. The languid, amorphous structure embodies the essence of Gaudí's style, which some have described as art nouveau run rampant. Work continues on the structure, but without any sure idea of what Gaudí intended. Some say that the church will be completed by the mid–21st century.

3 In & Around the Parc de la Ciutadella

Museu d'Art Modern. Plaça d'Armes, Parc de la Ciutadella. ☎ **93/319-57-28.** Admission 300 ptas. ($2.40) adults, 200 ptas. ($1.60) students and seniors 65 and over, free for children 16 and under. Tues–Sat 10am–7pm, Sun 10am–2pm. Closed Jan 1 and Dec 25. Metro: Arc de Triomf. Bus: 14, 16, 17, 39, or 40.

This museum shares a wing of the Palau de la Ciutadella with the Catalonian parliament. Constructed in the 1700s, it was once used as an arsenal, forming part of Barcelona's defenses. It later became a royal residence before being turned into a museum early in this century. Its collection of art focuses on the early 20th century and features the work of Catalán artists, including Martí Alsina, Vayreda, Casas, Fortuny, and Rusiñol. The collection also encompasses some 19th-century

Romantic and neoclassical works, as well as *modernismo* furniture (including designs by architect Puig i Cadafalch).

✪ **Museu Picasso.** Montcada, 15–19. ☎ **93/319-63-10.** Admission 500 ptas. ($4) adults, 250 ptas. ($2) students, free for children 17 and under. Tues–Sat 10am–8pm, Sun 10am–3pm. Metro: Jaume I.

Two old palaces on a medieval street have been converted into a museum housing works by Pablo Picasso, who donated some 2,500 of his paintings, engravings, and drawings to the museum in 1970. Picasso was particularly fond of Barcelona, the city where he spent much of his formative youth. In fact, some of the paintings were done when Picasso was only 9. One portrait, dating from 1896, depicts his stern aunt, Tía Pepa. Another, completed at the turn of the century, when Picasso was 16, depicts *Science and Charity* (his father was the model for the doctor). Many of the works, especially the early paintings, show the artist's debt to van Gogh, El Greco, and Rembrandt; a famous series, *Las Meninas* (1957), is said to "impersonate" the work of Velázquez. From Picasso's blue period, the *La Vie* drawings are perhaps the most interesting. His notebooks contain many sketches of Barcelona scenes.

4 In & Around the Parc de Montjuïc

Fundació Joan Miró. Plaça de Neptú, Parc de Montjuïc. ☎ **93/329-19-08.** Admission 600 ptas. ($4.80), free for children 9 and under. June–Sept, Tues–Wed and Fri–Sat 10am–8pm, Thurs 10am–9:30pm, Sun 10:30am–2:30pm; Nov–May, Tues–Wed and Fri–Sat 11am–7pm, Thurs 11am–9:30pm, Sun 10:30am–2:30pm. Bus: 61 from Plaça d'Espanya.

Born in 1893, Joan Miró went on to become one of Spain's greatest painters, known for his whimsical abstract forms and brilliant colors. Some 10,000 works by this Catalán surrealist, including paintings, graphics, and sculptures, have been collected here. The foundation building has been greatly expanded in recent years, following the design of Catalán architect Josep Lluís Sert, a close personal friend of Miró. An exhibition in a modern wing charts (in a variety of media) Miró's complete artistic evolution from his first drawings at the age of 8 to his last works. Temporary exhibitions on contemporary art are also frequently shown.

Galería Olímpico. Passeig Olimpic, s/n, lower level. ☎ **93/426-06-60.** Admission 375 ptas. ($3). Apr–Sept, Tues–Sat 10am–2pm and 4–8pm, Sun 10am–2pm; Oct–Mar, Tues–Sat 10am–1pm and 4–6pm, Sun 10am–2pm. Metro: Espanya. Bus: 9 or 13.

An enthusiastic celebration of the 1992 Olympic Games in Barcelona, this is one of the few museums in Europe exclusively devoted to sports and sports statistics. Its exhibits include photos, costumes, and memorabilia, with heavy emphasis on the events' pageantry, the number of visitors who attended, and the fame the events brought to Barcelona. Of interest to statisticians, civic planners, and sports buffs, the gallery contains audiovisual information about the building programs that prepared the city for the onslaught of visitors. There are also conference facilities, an auditorium, video recordings of athletic events, and archives. In the cellar of the Olympic Stadium's southeastern perimeter, the museum is most easily reached by entering the stadium's southern gate (Porta Sud).

Museu Arqueològic. Passeig de Santa Madrona, 39–41, Parc de Montjuïc. ☎ **93/ 423-21-49.** Admission 200 ptas. ($1.60), free for children, free for everyone on Sun. Tues–Sat 9:30am–1:30pm and 3:30–7pm, Sun 9:30am–2pm. Metro: Espanya. Bus: 55.

Occupying the former Palace of Graphic Arts, built for the 1929 World's Fair, the Museu Arqueològic reflects the long history of this Mediterranean port city, beginning with prehistoric Iberian artifacts. The collection includes articles from the Greek, Roman (glass, ceramics, mosaics, bronzes), and Carthaginian periods. Some of the more interesting relics were excavated in the ancient Greco-Roman city of Empúries in Catalonia; other parts of the collection came from the Balearic Islands.

Museu Nacional d'Art de Catalunya. Palau Nacional, Parc de Montjuïc. ☎ **93/423-71-99.** Admission charge depends on the exhibit. Tues–Wed and Fri–Sat 10am–7pm, Thurs 10am–9pm, Sun 10am–2:30pm. Metro: Espanya.

This museum is the major depository of Catalán art, a virtual treasure trove for this important region of the world. With massive renovations recently completed, the National Art Museum of Catalonia is perhaps the most important center for Romanesque art in the world. More than 100 pieces, including sculptures, icons, and frescoes, are on display. The highlight of the museum is the collection of murals from various Romanesque churches. The frescoes and murals are displayed in apses, much as they were in the churches in which they were found. Each is placed in sequential order, providing the viewer with a tour of Romanesque art from its primitive beginnings to the more advanced, late Romanesque and early Gothic era.

Poble Espanyol. Marqués de Comillas, Parc de Montjuïc. ☎ **93/325-78-66.** Admission 950 ptas. ($7.60), free for children 6 and under; audiovisual hall, 400 ptas. ($3.20), free for children 6 and under. Mon 9am–8pm, Tues–Thurs and Sun 9am–2pm, Fri–Sat 9am–3pm. Metro: Espanya; then the free red double-decker bus.

In this re-created Spanish village, built for the 1929 World's Fair, various regional architectural styles, from the Levante to Galicia, are reproduced—in all, 115 life-size reproductions of buildings and monuments, ranging from the 10th through the 20th century. At the entranceway, for example, stands a facsimile of the gateway to the walled city of Ávila. The center of the village has an outdoor café where you can sit and have drinks. Numerous shops sell crafts and souvenir items from all the provinces, and in some of them you can see artists at work, printing fabric and blowing glass. Ever since the 1992 Olympics the village has offered 14 restaurants of varying styles, one disco, and eight musical bars. In addition, visitors can see an audiovisual presentation about Barcelona and Catalonia in general.

5 La Barceloneta / The Harbor

Monument à Colom (Columbus Monument). Portal de la Pau. ☎ **93/302-52-34.** Admission 225 ptas. ($1.80) adults, 125 ptas. ($1) children 4–12, free for children 3 and under. June–Sept 24, daily 9am–9pm; Sept 25–May, Mon–Fri 10am–1:30pm and 3:30–6:30pm, Sat–Sun and holidays 10am–6:30pm. Closed Jan 1, Jan 6, and Dec 25–26. Metro: Drassanes.

This monument to Christopher Columbus was erected on the harborfront of Barcelona on the occasion of the Universal Exhibition of 1888. It's divided into three parts, the first being a circular structure, raised by four stairways (19¹/₂ feet wide) and eight iron heraldic lions. On the plinth are eight bronze bas-reliefs depicting the principal feats of Columbus. (The originals were destroyed; the present ones are copies.) The second part is the base of the column, consisting of an eight-sided polygon, four sides of which act as buttresses; each side contains sculptures. The third part is formed by the column itself, Corinthian in style and rising 167 feet. The capital boasts representations of Europe, Asia, Africa, and America—all linked together. Finally, over a princely crown and a hemisphere recalling the newly discovered part of the globe, is a 25-foot-high bronze statue of Columbus himself by Rafael Ataché. Inside the iron column, an elevator ascends to the *mirador*. From there, a panoramic view of Barcelona and its harbor unfolds.

Museu Marítim. Avinguda de las Drassanes, s/n. ☎ **93/318-32-45.** Admission 600 ptas. ($4.80), free for children 14 and under. Tues–Sun 10am–7pm. Closed holidays. Metro: Drassanes. Bus: 14, 18, 36, 38, or 57.

Located in the former Royal Shipyards (Drassanes Reials), this 13th-century Gothic complex was used for the construction of ships for the Catalano-Aragonese rulers. The most outstanding exhibition here is a reconstruction of *La Galería Real* of Don Juan of Austria, a lavish royal galley. Another special exhibit features a map by Gabriel de Vallseca that was owned by explorer Amerigo Vespucci.

6 Outside the City Center

Museu de la Ciència (Science Museum). Teodor Roviralta, 55. ☎ **93/212-60-50.** Admission to museum and planetarium, 725 ptas. ($5.80) adults, 650 ptas. ($5.20) children 16 and under. Tues–Sun 10am–8pm. Bus: 17, 22, 58, or 73.

The Museu de la Ciència of the La Caixa Foundation is one of the most popular in Barcelona, with more than 500,000 people visiting annually. Its modern design and hands-on activities have made it the most important science museum in Spain and a major cultural attraction.

Visitors can touch, listen, watch, and participate in a variety of hands-on exhibits. From the beauty of marine life to the magic of holograms, the museum offers a world of science to discover. Watch the world turn beneath the Foucault Pendulum, ride on a human gyroscope, hear a friend whisper from 65 feet (20m) away, feel an earthquake, or use the tools of a scientist to examine intricate life forms with microscopes and video cameras.

More than 300 exhibits explore the wonders of science, from optics to space travel to the life sciences. In the Optics and Perception exhibits visitors can interact with prisms, lenses, and holograms and walk inside a kaleidoscope. In the Living Planet area baby sharks swim, a tornado swirls, and plants magically change their form when touched.

In the Mechanics exhibit, visitors can lift an 88-pound (40kg) weight with little effort. The use of lasers and musical instruments provides a fun way to learn about sound and light waves. Throughout the exhibits there are computers to help you delve deeper into various topics. Visitors can also walk inside a submarine and make weather measurements in a working weather station. For those who want to explore new worlds, there are planetarium shows where the beauty of the night sky surrounds the audience.

Monestir de Pedralbes. Baixada del Monestir, 9. ☎ **93/203-92-82.** Admission 300 ptas. ($2.40) adults, 150 ptas. ($1.20) students and seniors 65 and older, free for children 16 and under. Tues–Sun 10am–2pm. Metro: Reina Elisenda. Bus: 22, 63, 64, 75, or 114.

One of the oldest buildings in Pedralbes (the city's wealthiest residential area) is this monastery, founded in 1326 by Elisenda de Montcada, queen of Jaume II. Still a convent, the establishment is also the mausoleum of the queen, who is buried in its Gothic church. Walk through the cloisters, with nearly two dozen arches on each side, rising three stories high. A small chapel contains the chief treasure of the monastery, murals by Ferrer Bassa, who was considered the major artist of Catalonia in the 1300s.

This monastery was considered a minor attraction of Barcelona until 1993, when 72 paintings and eight sculptures from the famed Thyssen-Bornemisza collection went on permanent display here. Among the more outstanding works of art are Fra Angelico's *The Virgin of Humility* and 20 paintings from the early German Renaissance period. Italian Renaissance paintings range from the end of the 15th century to the middle of the 16th century, as exemplified by works from Dosso Dossi, Lorenzo Lotto, Tintoretto, Veronese, and Titian. The Baroque era is also represented, including such old masters as Rubens, Zurbarán, and Velázquez.

Museu de les Arts Decoratives. Palau Reial de Pedralbes, Avinguda Diagonal, 686. ☎ **93/ 280-50-24.** Admission 500 ptas. ($4) Tues and Thurs–Sun, 250 ptas. ($2) Wed, free first Sun of every month. Tues–Sun 10am–3pm. Metro: Palau Reial. Bus: 7, 63, 67, 68, or 75.

Set in a beautiful park, this palace was constructed as a municipal gift to Alfonso XIII. He didn't get to make much use of it, however, as he was forced into exile in 1931. Today it houses a collection of objets d'art, furniture, jewelry, and glassware from the 14th century to the present. More than 200 pieces, all of Spanish origin, are on display.

Torre de Collserola. Carretera de Vallvidrera, Turó de la Vilana. ☎ **93/211-79-42.** Admission 500 ptas. ($4). Wed–Sun 11am–8pm. A funicular goes to a point near the tower's parking lot; from there, free minivans make frequent runs up the mountain to the tower's base.

Some city planners considered this the most ambitious building project of the 1992 Olympics. When it was perceived that Barcelona lacked a state-of-the-art television transmitter, a team of engineers whipped up plans for a space-age needle. Completed within 24 months of its initiation, its rises 940 feet above the city's highest mountain ridge, the Collserola, beaming TV signals throughout the rest of Europe. Open now as a tourist attraction, the tower offers panoramic views over Catalonia, and an insight into some of the most bizarre engineering in town. Trussed with cables radiating outward to massive steel anchors, the tower perches delicately atop an alarmingly narrow vertical post only 14 feet wide. A high-speed elevator carries visitors from deep inside the mountain (where there's a cafeteria) to an observation platform 1,820 feet above the sea level of the (very visible) Mediterranean.

7 Parks & Gardens

Barcelona isn't just museums; much of its life takes place outside, in its unique parks and gardens, through which you'll want to stroll. The **Parc Güell** (☎ **93/ 424-38-09**) was begun by Gaudí as a real-estate venture for a friend, the wealthy, well-known Catalán industrialist Count Eusebi Güell, but it was never completed. Only two houses were constructed, but it makes for an interesting excursion nonetheless. The city took over the property in 1926 and turned it into a public park. It's open May to September, daily from 10am to 9pm; October to April, daily from 10am to 6pm. Admission is free. To reach the park, take bus no. 24, 25, 31, or 74.

One of the houses, **Casa-Museu Gaudí,** Carrer del Carmel, 28 (☎ **93/ 284-64-46**), contains models, furniture, drawings, and other memorabilia of the architect. Gaudí, however, did not design the house—Ramón Berenguer claimed that honor. Admission is 150 ptas. ($1.20). The museum can be visited Sunday to Friday from 10am to 2pm and 4 to 8pm (to 9pm April to September).

Gaudí completed several of the public areas, which today look like a surrealist Disneyland, complete with a mosaic pagoda and a lizard fountain spitting water. Originally Gaudí planned to make this a model community of 60 dwellings, somewhat like the arrangement of a Greek theater. A central grand plaza with its market below was built, as well as an undulating bench decorated with ceramic fragments. The bizarre Doric columns of the would-be market are hollow, part of Gaudí's drainage system.

Another attraction, **Tibidabo Mountain,** offers the finest panoramic view of Barcelona. A funicular takes you up 1,600 feet to the top. The ideal time to visit this summit (the culmination of the Sierra de Collcerola) north of the port is at sunset, when the city lights are on. An amusement park—with Ferris wheels swinging over Barcelona—has been opened here. (For more information on this Parc d'Atraccions, see "Especially for Kids," later in this chapter.) There's also a church, called Sacred

Heart, in this carnival-like setting, plus restaurants and mountaintop hotels. From Plaça de Catalunya, take a bus to Avinguda del Tibidabo, where you can board a special bus that will transport you to the funicular. Hop aboard to scale the mountain. The funicular runs daily from 7:15am to 9:45pm and costs 400 ptas. ($3.20) each way.

Located in the south of the city, the mountain park of **Montjuïc** (Montjuch in Spanish) has splashing fountains, gardens, outdoor restaurants, and museums, making for quite an outing. The re-created Spanish village, the Poble Espanyol, and the Joan Miró Foundation are also in the park. There are many walks and vantage points for viewing the Barcelona skyline.

The park was the site of several events during the 1992 Summer Olympics. An illuminated fountain display, the Fuentes Luminosas, at Plaça de la Font Magica, near Plaça d'Espanya, is on view from 8 to 11pm every Saturday and Sunday from October to May, and from 9pm to midnight on Thursday, Saturday, and Sunday from June to September. See the individual attractions in the park for their various hours of opening. To reach the top, take bus no. 61 from Plaça d'Espanya or the Montjuïc funicular.

The **Parc de la Ciutadella,** Avenida Wellington, s/n (☎ **93/221-25-06**), gets its name, Park of the Citadel, because it's the site of a former fortress that defended the city. After Philip V won the War of the Spanish Succession (Barcelona was on the losing side), he got his revenge. He ordered that the "traitorous" residential suburb be leveled. In its place rose a citadel. In the mid–19th century it, too, was leveled, though some of the architectural evidence of that past remains in a governor's palace and an arsenal. Today most of the park is filled with lakes, gardens, and promenades, but it includes a zoo (see "Especially for Kids," below) and the Museu d'Art Modern (see "In & Around the Parc de la Ciutadella," earlier in this chapter). Gaudí is said to have contributed to the monumental "great fountain" in the park when he was a student. The park is open, without charge, daily from 8am to 9pm. To reach the park, take the metro to Ciutadella.

The **Parc de Joan Miró,** lying near Plaça de Espanya, is dedicated to one of the most famous artists of Catalonia, Joan Miró. It occupies an entire city block. One of the parks added in the 1990s and one of Barcelona's most popular, it's often called Parc de l'Escorxador (slaughterhouse), a reference to what the park used to be. Its main features are an esplanade and a pond from which a sculpture by Miró, *Woman and Bird,* rises up. Palm, pine, and eucalyptus trees, as well as playgrounds and pergolas, complete the picture. To reach the park, take the metro to Espanya. It's open throughout the day.

8 Especially for Kids

The Cataláns have a great affection for children, and although many of the attractions of Barcelona are for adults only, there is an array of amusements designed for the young or the young at heart.

Children from 3 to 7 have their own special place at the **Museu de la Ciència,** Teodor Roviralta, 55 (☎ **93/212-60-50**). Clik del Nens is a playground of science. Children walk on a giant piano, make bubbles, lift a hippopotamus, or enter an air tunnel. They observe, experiment, and examine nature in an environment created just for them. Special 1-hour guided sessions are given daily. (For further details, see "Outside the City Center," earlier in this chapter.)

The **Poble Espanyol,** Marqués de Comillas, Parc de Montjuïc (☎ **93/ 325-78-66**), is described in "In & Around the Parc de Montjuïc," earlier in this chapter. Kids compare a visit here to a Spanish version of Disneyland. Frequent fiestas enliven the place, and it's fun for everybody, young and old.

Parc Zoologic. Parc de la Ciutadella. ☎ **93/221-25-06.** Admission 1,000 ptas. ($8), free for children 2 and under. Summer, daily 9:30am–7:30pm; off-season, daily 10am–5pm. Metro: Ciutadella.

Modern, with barless enclosures, this ranks as Spain's top zoo. One of the most unusual attractions is the famous albino gorilla, Snowflake (Copito de Nieve), the only one of its kind in captivity in the world. The main entrances to the Ciutadella Park are via Passeig de Pujades and Passeig de Picasso.

Parc d'Atraccions (Montjuïc). Parc de Montjuïc. ☎ **93/441-70-24.** Admission 600 ptas. ($4.80); ticket for all rides, 1,800 ptas. ($14.40). Oct–Mar, Sat–Sun 11:30am–8pm; Apr–May, Sat–Sun 11am–9pm; June–Aug, Tues–Fri 5–10pm, Sat 6pm–1am, Sun noon–11pm; Sept, days and hours vary. Metro: Paral-lel; then take the funicular.

This place becomes a festival in summer, with open-air concerts and more than three dozen rides for the kids. Everything is set against a wide view of Barcelona and its harbor. Children love the nightly illuminated fountain displays and the music.

Parc d'Atraccions (Tibidabo). Plaça Tibidabo, 3–4, Cumbre del Tibidabo. ☎ **93/211-79-42.** Free admission; ticket for all rides, 1,800 ptas. ($14.40) adults, 300 ptas. ($2.40) seniors 65 and over, free for children 4 and under. May to mid-June, Wed–Sun noon–8pm; mid-June to Sept, Tues–Sun noon–8pm; off-season, Sat–Sun and holidays 11am–8pm. Take the Ferrocarrils de la Generalitat railway line to Avinguda Tibidabo to Tramvía Blau; then take the funicular.

On top of Tibidabo, this park combines tradition with modernity—rides from the beginning of the century complete with 1990s novelties. In summer the place takes on a carnival-like atmosphere.

9 For the Architecture Enthusiast

The **Casa Milà,** Passeig de Gràcia, 92 (☎ **93/484-59-80;** metro: Diagonal), commonly called La Pedrera, is the most famous apartment-house complex in Spain. Antoni Gaudí's imagination went wild when planning its construction; he even included vegetable and fruit shapes in his sculptural designs. Controversial and much criticized upon its completion, today it stands as a classic example of *modernismo* architecture. The entire building was restored in 1996. The ironwork around the balconies forms an intricate maze, and the main gate has windowpanes shaped like turtle shells. The rooftop is filled with phantasmagorical chimneys known in Spanish as *espantabrujas* (witch-scarers). Tours of the famous rooftops are available Tuesday to Saturday at 10am, 11am, noon, and 1pm, but they have to be arranged in advance by calling the number above. Tours are free, but a tip is expected. From the rooftop you'll also have a view of Gaudí's unfinished church, La Sagrada Familia.

Casa Lleó Morera, Passeig de Gràcia, 35 (no phone; metro: Passeig de Gràcia), lying between Carrer del Consell de Cent and Carrer d' Aragó, is one of the most famous buildings of the *modernismo* movement. It's one of the trio of structures called the Mançana de la Discòrdia (Block of Discord), an allusion to the mythical judgment of Paris. Three of the most famous *modernismo* architects of Barcelona, including Gaudí, competed with their various works along this block. In florid *modernismo* design, the Casa Lleó, designed by Domènech i Montaner in 1905, was considered extremely revolutionary in its day. Perhaps that assessment still stands. Today the building is private; no visits to the interior are possible.

Constructed in a cubical design, with a Dutch gable, the **Casa Amatller,** Passeig de Gràcia, 41 (☎ **93/216-01-75;** metro: Passeig de Gràcia), was created by Puig i

Cadafalch in 1900. It stands in sharp contrast to its neighbor, the Gaudí-designed Casa Batlló. The architecture of the Casa Amatller, actually imposed on an older structure, is a vision of ceramic, wrought iron, and sculptures. Admission to the Gothic-style interior is free. It's open Monday to Friday from 9am to 2pm.

Next door to the Casa Amatller, the **Casa Batlló,** Passeig de Gràcia, 43 (☎ 93/ 216-01-12; metro: Passeig de Gràcia), was designed by Gaudí in 1905. Using "sensuous" curves in iron and stone, the architect gave the facade a lavish baroque exuberance. The balconies have been compared to "sculpted waves." The upper part of the facade evokes animal forms, and delicate tiles spread across the design—a poly-chromatic exterior extraordinaire. The downstairs building is the headquarters of an insurance company. Although visitors are not always welcome, many tourists walk inside for a view of Gaudí's interior, which is basically as he designed it. Since this *is* a place of business, be discreet.

The **Casa de la Ciutat/Ayuntamiento,** Plaça de Sant Jaume (☎ 93/402-73-62; metro: Jaume I), originally constructed at the end of the 14th century, is considered one of the best examples of Gothic civil architecture in the Catalán-Mediterranean style. Across this landmark square from the Palau de la Generalitat, it has been end-lessly renovated and changed since its original construction. Behind a neoclassical facade, the building has a splendid courtyard and staircase. Its major architectural highlights are the 15th-century Salón de Ciento (Room of the 100 Jurors) and the Salón de las Cronicas (Room of the Chronicles), the latter decorated with black marble. The Salón de Ciento, in particular, represents a medley of styles. You can enter the building on Saturday and Sunday from 10am to 2pm or by special arrange-ment; it's closed from mid-December to mid-January.

WALKING TOUR 1
Gothic Quarter

Start: Plaça Nova.
Finish: Plaça de la Seu.
Time: 3 hours.
Best Times: Any sunny day.
Worst Times: Rush hours (Mon–Sat 7–9am and 5–7pm), because of traffic.

Begin at:

1. Plaça Nova, set in the shadow of the cathedral. This is the largest open-air space in the Gothic Quarter and the usual site of the Barcelona flea market. Opening onto this square is the Portal del Bisbe, a gate flanked by two round towers that have survived from the ancient Roman wall that once stood here. From Plaça Nova, climb the incline of the narrow asphalt-covered street (Carrer del Bisbe) lying between these massive walls. On your right, notice the depth of the foun-dation, which indicates how much the city has risen since the wall was constructed.

At the approach of the first street, Carrer de Santa Llúcia, turn left, noticing the elegant simplicity of the corner building with its Romanesque facade, the:

2. Capilla de Santa Llúcia (☎ 93/315-15-54), open daily from 9am to 1:15pm and 4 to 6:45pm. Its solidly graceful portal and barrel-vaulted interior were completed in 1268. Continue down Carrer de Santa Llúcia a few paces, noticing the:

3. Casa de l'Ardiaca (Archdeacon's House), constructed in the 15th century as a residence for Archdeacon Despla. The Gothic building has sculptural reliefs with Renaissance motifs. In its cloisterlike courtyard are a fountain and a palm tree. Notice the mail slot, where five swallows and a turtle carved into stone await the arrival of important messages. Since 1919 this building has been home to the Museu d'Història de la Ciutat (Municipal Institute of the History of the City).

As you exit the Archdeacon's House, continue in the same direction several steps until you reach:

4. **Plaça de la Seu,** the square in front of the main entrance to the Catedral de Barcelona (see "In & Around the Ciutat Vella," earlier in this chapter). Here you can stand and admire the facade of Mediterranean Gothic architecture. On each side of Plaça de la Seu you can see the remains of Roman walls.

After touring the cathedral, exit from the door you entered and turn right onto Carrer dels Comtes, admiring the gargoyles along the way. After about 100 paces, you'll approach the:

5. **Museu Frederic Marès** on Plaça de Sant Iú. On the lower floors are Punic and Roman artifacts, but most of the museum is devoted to the works of this Catalán sculptor. Exit through the same door you entered and continue your promenade in the same direction. You'll pass the portal of the cathedral's side, where the heads of two rather abstract angels flank the throne of a seated female saint. A few paces farther, notice the stone facade of the:

6. **Arxiu de la Carona d'Aragó,** the archives building of the crown of Aragón. Formerly called the Palacio del Lugarteniente (Deputy's Palace), this Gothic building was the work of Antonio Carbonell. On some maps it also appears as the Palacio de los Virreyes (Palace of the Viceroys). The palace contains medieval and royal documents. Enter its courtyard, admiring the century-old grapevines. Then climb the 11 monumental steps to your left, facing a modern bronze sculpture by a Catalán artist. It represents, with a rather abstract dateline and map, the political history and imperial highlights of Catalonia.

As you exit from the courtyard, you'll find yourself back on Carrer dels Comtes. Continue in the same direction, turning left at the intersection of Baixada de Santa Clara. This street, in one short block, will bring you to one of the most famous squares of the Gothic Quarter:

7. **Plaça del Rei.** The Great Royal Palace, an enlarged building of what was originally the residence of the counts of Barcelona, stands at the bottom of this square. Here at the King's Square you can visit both the Palau Reial and the Museu d'Història de la Ciutat (see "In & Around the Ciutat Vella," earlier in this chapter). On the right side of the square stands the Palatine Chapel of Santa Agata, a 14th-century Gothic temple that's part of the Palau Reial. In this chapel is preserved the altarpiece of the lord high constable, a 15th-century work by Jaume Huguet.

Retrace your steps up Baixada de Santa Clara, crossing Carrer dels Comtes, and continue straight to Carrer de la Pietat, which will skirt the semicircular, massively buttressed rear of the cathedral. With the cathedral's buttresses to your right, pass the 14th-century:

8. **Casa del Canonge (House of the Canon),** opening onto Carrer Arzobispo Irurita. This building was erected in the Gothic style and restored in 1929; escutcheons from the 15th and 16th centuries remain. Notice the heraldic symbols of medieval Barcelona on the building's stone plaques—twin towers supported by winged goats with lion's feet. On the same facade, also notice the depiction of twin angels. Today the building is used as a women's training school, the Escola Professional per a la Doña.

Continue walking along Carrer de la Pietat, which makes a sudden sharp left. Notice the carved *Pietà* above the Gothic portal leading into the rear of the

Walking Tour— Gothic Quarter

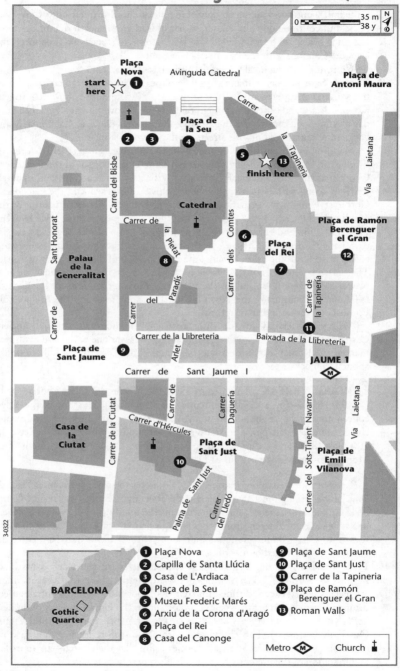

0   35 m
38 y

N

Plaça Nova ①
start here ☆

Avinguda Catedral

Plaça de Antoni Maura

Carrer de la Tapineria

Plaça de la Seu

② ③ ④

⑤ ☆ ⑬
finish here

Carrer del Bisbe

Sant Honorat

Catedral

Carrer de la Pietat

Palau de la Generalitat

⑧

Paradis

Carrer del

Carrer dels Comtes

⑥

Plaça del Rei
⑦

Plaça de Ramón Berenguer el Gran
⑫

Carrer de la Tapineria

⑪

Via Laietana

Carrer de

Plaça de Sant Jaume
⑨

Carrer de la Llibreteria

Arlet

Baixada de la Llibreteria

JAUME 1 Ⓜ

Carrer de Sant Jaume I

Casa de la Ciutat

Carrer de la Ciutat

Carrer de

Carrer d'Hércules

Carrer Dagueria

Plaça de Sant Just
⑩

Palma de Sant Just

Carrer del Lledó

Carrer del Sots-Tinent Navarro

Plaça de Emili Vilanova

Via Laietana

3-0322

BARCELONA

Gothic Quarter

① Plaça Nova
② Capilla de Santa Llúcia
③ Casa de L'Ardiaca
④ Plaça de la Seu
⑤ Museu Frederic Marés
⑥ Arxiu de la Corona d'Aragó
⑦ Plaça del Rei
⑧ Casa del Canonge

⑨ Plaça de Sant Jaume
⑩ Plaça de Sant Just
⑪ Carrer de la Tapineria
⑫ Plaça de Ramón Berenguer el Gran
⑬ Roman Walls

Metro Ⓜ   Church ✝

cathedral. Continue walking straight. One block later, turn left onto Carrer del Bisbe and continue downhill. Your path will lead you beneath one of the most charming bridges in Spain. Carved into lacy patterns of stonework, it connects the Casa del Canonge with the Palau de la Generalitat.

Continue walking until Carrer del Bisbe opens into:

9. Plaça de Sant Jaume, in many ways the political heart of Catalán culture. Across this square, constructed at what was once a major junction for two Roman streets, race politicians and bureaucrats intent on Catalonian government affairs. On Sunday evenings you can witness the sardana, the national dance of Catalonia. Many bars and restaurants sit on side streets leading from this square.

Standing in the square, with your back to the street you just left (Carrer del Bisbe), you'll see, immediately on your right, the Doric portico of the Palau de la Generalitat, the parliament of Catalonia. With its large courtyard and open-air stairway, along with twin arched galleries, this exquisite work in the Catalonian Gothic style began construction in the era of Jaume I. A special feature of the building is the Chapel of St. George, built in flamboyant Gothic style between 1432 and 1435 and enlarged in 1620 with the addition of vaulting and a cupola with hanging capitals. The back of the building encloses an orangery courtyard begun in 1532. In the Salón Dorado, the Proclamation of the Republic was signed. The palace bell tower houses a carillon on which both old and popular music is played each day at noon. Across the square are the Ionic columns of the Casa de la Ciutat/Ayuntamiento, the Town Hall of Barcelona (see "For the Architecture Enthusiast," earlier in this chapter).

With your back to Carrer del Bisbe, turn left onto the narrow and very ancient Carrer de la Llibreteria. Two thousand years ago this was one of the two roads that marked the Roman center of town. Walk uphill on Carrer de la Llibreteria for about 1¹/₂ blocks.

☕ **TAKE A BREAK**   Founded in 1909, the **Mesón del Café,** Llibreteria, 16 (☎ **93/315-07-54**), specializes in coffee and cappuccino. It's one of the oldest coffeehouses in the neighborhood, sometimes crowding 50 people into its tiny precincts. Some regulars perch on stools at the bar and order breakfast. Coffee costs 100 ptas. (80¢) and a cappuccino goes for 235 ptas. ($1.90). The café is open Monday to Saturday from 7am to 11pm.

Retrace your steps along Carrer de la Llibreteria and once again enter Plaça de Sant Jaume. Facing the Town Hall, take the street that parallels its left side, Carrer de la Ciutat. Note the elegant stonework on the building's side, which is carved in a style radically different from the building's neoclassical facade. At the first left, turn onto Carrer d'Hercules, and walk along it for 1 block until you enter the quiet, somewhat faded beauty of:

10. Plaça de Sant Just, dominated by the entrance to the Església dels Sants Just i Pastor (☎ 93/301-73-33). Visiting hours are erratic; you'll find that its doors are usually closed except during Sunday mass. Above the entrance portal, an enthroned Virgin is flanked by a pair of protective angels. The Latin inscription hails her as VIRGO NIGRA ET PULCHRA, NOSTRA PATRONA PIA (Black and Beautiful Virgin, Our Holy Patroness). This church dates from the 14th century, although work continued into the 16th. Some authorities claim that the church—in an earlier manifestation of the present structure—is the oldest in Barcelona.

Opposite the facade of the church, at Plaça de Sant Just, 4, is an aristocratic town house covered with faded but still elegant frescoes of angels cavorting among garlands, an example of the artistry, taste, and wealth of a bygone era. With your back to the Black Virgin, turn right onto the narrow cobblestone street, Carrer del Lledo, which begins at the far end of the square. One short block later, turn left onto Baixada de Cassador. As you descend the steep slope of this narrow street, notice the blue-and-white covering of the House of the Blue Tiles at the bottom of the hill.

Turn left onto Carrer del Sots Tinent Navarro. The massive gray-stone wall rising on your left is the base of an ancient Roman fort. Note the red bricks of a 13th-century palace on top of the Roman wall. The solitary Corinthian column rising from the base is another reminder of Barcelona's Roman past.

Continue on to Plaça d'Emili Vilanova. Near the top of the Roman wall, note the pair of delicate columns of a Gothic window. Continue another block to the cross street, Carrer Jaume I. Cross it and approach Plaça de l'Angel. Continue walking to:

11. **Carrer de la Tapineria.** For centuries, Catalonia has been the center of Spain's footwear industry. In medieval times this was the street of the shoemakers. In fact, the industry is so entrenched that there's even a museum devoted to antique footwear, the Museu del Calcat Antic, Plaça Sant Felip Neri, 5 (☎ 93/301-45-33), open Monday to Saturday from 11am to 2pm and 4 to 7pm and on Sunday from 11am to 2pm.

In 1 short block Carrer de la Tapineria leads to:

12. **Plaça de Ramón Berenguer el Gran.** An equestrian statue dedicated to this hero (1096–1131) is ringed with the gravel of a semicircular park, whose backdrop is formed by the walls of the ancient Roman fort and, nearby, a Gothic tower.

Traverse the park, crossing in front of the equestrian statue, until you once again reach the edge of the Roman wall as you head toward the park's distant end. There Carrer de la Tapineria will lead you on a path paralleling the ancient:

13. **Roman Walls,** one of Barcelona's most important treasures from its past. The walls, known as Las Murallas in Spanish, were constructed between A.D. 270 and 310. The walls followed a rectangular course, and were built so that their fortified sections would face the sea. By the 11th and 12th centuries Barcelona had long outgrown their confines. Jaume I ordered the opening of the Roman walls, and the burgeoning growth that ensued virtually destroyed them, except for the foundations you see today.

Continue your promenade, but turn left at the narrow Baixada de la Canonja. A short walk down this cobblestoned alleyway will return you to Plaça de la Seu, not far from where you began this tour.

WALKING TOUR 2
Barcelona Harborfront

Start: Plaça Portal de la Pau.
Finish: Parc de la Ciutadella.
Time: 2 hours.
Best Times: Any sunny day.
Worst Times: Rush hours (Mon–Sat 7–9am and 5–7pm), because of traffic.

This tour begins near the harborfront at the end of Les Rambles in the shadow of the Columbus Monument at:

1. **Plaça Portal de la Pau.** Here at the base of the Columbus Monument, look at the quartet of nymphs seeming to offer laurel garlands to whomever approaches.

If you haven't already done so, you may want to take the elevator to the top for a bird's-eye view of the harborfront you're about to traverse.

Afterward, head east along:

2. **Passeig de Colom,** which, at this point, is raised on stilts high above a yacht basin. The waterside promenade adjacent to the yacht basin, far below you on your right, is called:

3. **Passeig del Moll de la Fusta,** originally the timber wharf. It stands as an excellent symbol of the recovery of Barcelona's formerly seedy waterfront. Several bars and restaurants enliven this balcony over the Mediterranean, from which one can descend via bridges to the level of a pedestrian wharf, where palm trees arise from the cobbled pavement.

Continue along Passeig de Colom until you reach the slightly faded but very grand:

4. **Plaça del Duc de Mendinaceli,** on the inland (left) side of the boulevard. When traffic permits, cross Passeig de Colom, perhaps resting a moment on one of the park benches in the square, whose focal point is a column ringed with mermen (half fish, half men). Continue walking east, passing pigeons, children, and grandparents sunning themselves.

You can now begin a brisk 7-block stroll eastward along the left (inland) side of Passeig de Colom. After about $2^1/_2$ blocks, glance to your right at an enormous sculpture of a lobster waving a claw from atop the low-slung modern restaurant called Gambrinus. The lobster, crafted from fiberglass by a local sculptor, has become one of Barcelona's conversation pieces.

You'll eventually reach a monumental square called:

5. **Plaça d'Antoni López,** whose northern end is dominated by Barcelona's main post office (Correos y Telegrafos). Cross Carrer de la Fustería, heading toward the front side of the post office, then pass in front of the building, traversing the busy Vía Laietana, which borders the post office's eastern edge.

Continue to walk straight ahead, always east. The quiet street you'll enter is Carrer del Consolat del Mar, more interesting than the broader Passeig d'Isabel II, which runs parallel and a short distance to the right. Walk east along Carrer del Consolat del Mar. The neoclassical doorway on your right marks the entrance to:

6. **La Lonja,** the stock exchange of Barcelona. It has a central courtyard with allegorical statues. The stock exchange dates from the 14th century. Once it was a fine arts school attended by Picasso and Miró.

Half a block later Carrer del Consolat del Mar opens onto:

7. **Plaça de Palau,** a gracefully proportioned square reminiscent of another era's political and cultural glory. Midway down the length of this square, head north (left) on Carrer de l'Espasería, at the end of which you'll come upon:

8. **Santa María del Mar,** in Plaça de Santa María, a Catalonian Gothic church with a soaring interior dating from the 14th century. After your visit, turn left as you exit, then left again, so that your footsteps along Carrer de Santa María flank the southern exterior of the church.

After half a block Carrer de Santa María opens onto one of the most bizarre monuments in Barcelona:

9. **Carrer del Fossar de los Moreres.** Occupying most of a medieval square, the plaza incorporates a sprawling and steeply inclined red-brick pavement, fronted by a low wall of reddish porphyry, inscribed with a memorial to Catalonian martyrs who died in an uprising against Castilian Spain in 1714. As you enter the square, note on your left a narrow street.

Walking Tour—Barcelona Harborfront

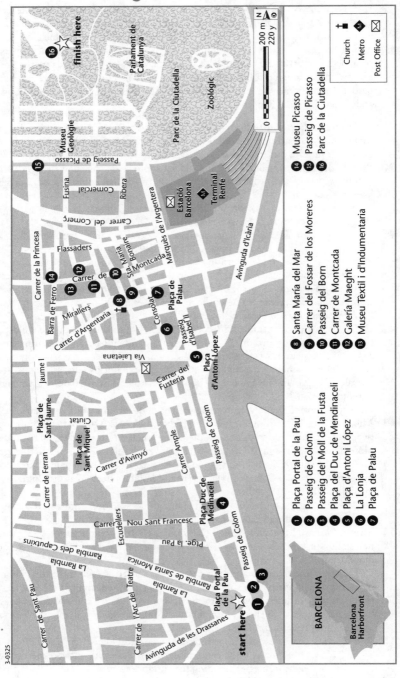

start here

finish here

1. Plaça Portal de la Pau
2. Passeig de Colom
3. Passeig del Moll de la Fusta
4. Plaça del Duc de Mendinaceli
5. Plaça d'Antoni López
6. La Lonja
7. Plaça de Palau
8. Santa María del Mar
9. Carrer del Fossar de los Moreres
10. Passeig del Born
11. Carrer de Montcada
12. Galería Maeght
13. Museu Tèxtil i d'Indumentaria
14. Museu Picasso
15. Passeig de Picasso
16. Parc de la Ciutadella

Church | Metro | Post Office

BARCELONA

Barcelona Harborfront

3-0325

☕ **TAKE A BREAK**   The **Pâtissería Güell La Mallorquina,** Plaça de Les Olles, 7 (☎ **93/319-39-83**), was established in 1878 in a 16th-century building on this narrow street. Sample the llunes, half-moon–shaped pastries filled with almonds and sprinkled with powdered sugar. Or take out an order of coques, sprinkled with sugar and topped with pine nuts. All pastries are made on the premises, and the dough is rolled out on marble tables. You can stop in here and buy pastries Monday and Wednesday to Saturday from 8am to 2pm and 5 to 8:30pm and on Sunday from 8am to 3pm.

Return to the square of the martyrs and continue walking along Carrer de Santa María until you reach the rear of the Church of Santa María del Mar, where you'll notice the massive buttresses. You've arrived at:

10. Passeig del Born, one of the colorful old squares of Barcelona and the residence of some appealing and nostalgic bars. But this square doesn't come alive until much later at night.

Turn left after 1 very short block onto Placeta de Montcada, which narrows after about 30 paces and changes its name to:

11. Carrer de Montcada, which represents the aristocratic heart of Barcelona during the height of its prestige and power. Notice the semifortified palace at no. 20, which served during the 18th century as the Barcelona residence of the Catalonian ambassador from Great Britain. Also note the nine gargoyles adding visual interest to the fourth and uppermost floor of the palace, whose forbidding exterior seems even more severe because of the narrow street it sits on.

A few steps later, on your right, is the:

12. Galería Maeght, Montcada, 25 (☎ 93/310-42-45), established by the children of the couple who created one of the most famous museums of modern art in Europe, the Foundation Maeght in St-Paul-de-Vence in France. Many well-known and unknown painters are exhibited under the gallery's brick vaults, and works are for sale. The showrooms are open Tuesday to Saturday from 10am to 2pm and 4 to 8pm.

As you leave the gallery, turn right and continue walking until you reach the:

13. Museu Tèxtil i d'Indumentaria, Montcada, 12 (☎ 93/310-45-16), occupying two 13th-century Gothic palaces. Many of the articles in this textile and costume museum are Egyptian and Hispano-Muslim. Textiles range from the Gothic era to the 20th century; many of the garments are liturgical. It's open Tuesday to Saturday from 10am to 5pm and on Sunday and holidays from 10am to 2pm. Admission is 300 ptas. ($2.40).

After exiting the museum, turn left and continue walking until you reach the most visited museum in Barcelona, the:

14. Museu Picasso, Montcada, 15–19 (☎ 93/319-63-10), ensconced in two Gothic mansions (see "In & Around the Parc de la Ciutadella," earlier in this chapter, for more details).

Exit from the museum and turn right along Carrer de Montcada. In 1 short block, turn right again onto Carrer de la Princesa and walk straight for 4 blocks, traversing a confusing five-way intersection. You'll soon arrive at the wide and busy Carrer del Comerç, which you should cross. Continue walking along Carrer de la Princesa until it dead-ends at:

15. Passeig de Picasso, designed by architects Amadó and Domènech. A sculpture by Tàpies, *Homage to Picasso,* is the centerpiece. Cross Passeig de Picasso and notice the ornate wrought-iron gates guarding the entrance to the:

16. Parc de la Ciutadella, which was the site of the 1888 Universal Exposition (see "Parks & Gardens," earlier in this chapter, for more details). If you enter the park through its main entrance on Passeig Lluís Companys, you can still see some of the relics from that great fair. The park is filled with museums, a zoo, and many attractions. Since it covers a large area, these attractions are signposted, and you can follow the directions and take in whatever interests you—or whatever you have time to explore.

WALKING TOUR 3
Les Rambles

Start: Plaça Portal de la Pau.
Finish: Plaça de Catalunya.
Time: 1¹/₂ hours.
Best Times: Any time during daylight.
Worst Times: Midnight to dawn, which might be unsafe.

This most famous promenade in Spain was laid out in the 18th century. Begin at:

1. Plaça Portal de la Pau, with its Columbus Monument, which you can scale for a view of the harbor (see "La Barceloneta / The Harbor," earlier in this chapter). You can also book a harbor cruise of the port here or even take a horse-and-carriage ride.

With your back to the monument to Columbus, head up Les Rambles, the first of which is the:

2. Rambla de Santa Mònica, where it's recommended that you walk with care late at night; this Rambla borders the Barri Xinès, long known as a center of drugs, prostitution, and criminal activity. Hookers, pimps, beggars, transvestites, and various immigrants live in this quarter, along with some hardworking and respectable poor people. If you have children with you (or even if you don't), you may want to turn right at Passatge de la Banca and visit the:

3. Museu de Cera (☎ 93/317-26-49), a wax museum with some 300 figures—past and present—from Barcelona's history. Admission is 750 ptas. ($6) for adults, 450 ptas. ($3.60) for children 5 to 11; it's open Monday to Friday from 10am to 1:30pm and 4 to 7pm and on Saturday, Sunday, and holidays from 10am to 1:20pm and 4:30 to 8pm.

☕ **TAKE A BREAK** In warm weather, the tables of the **Café Opera,** Les Rambles, 74 (☎ **93/317-75-85**), spill out onto the Rambles, but for most of the year clients pack into a narrow stand-up area beside a marble-topped bar or head to the tables in back. Everywhere, reminders of the café's belle époque past sheath the slightly seedy room with its tarnished crystal chandeliers and turn-of-the-century frescoes. International gays mingle with unionists, trade leaders, anarchists, vacationing American students, and French schoolteachers. It's the most famous café along Les Rambles. Waiters in black vests bring beer or other drinks to the tables either inside or outside. The café is open daily from 8am to 3am.

The next Rambla is the:

4. Rambla dels Caputxins, which begins at Plaça del Teatre. This was once the heart of the old theater district, but only the rather bleak Teatro Principal survives. Philip II launched this area on its theatrical career when he granted permission for the construction of a playhouse here to raise money for the city. In Plaça del Teatre you can see a monument to Serafi Pitarra, "the father" of contemporary theater in Catalonia.

Turn left here to reach the:

5. Güell Palace, Nou de La Rambla, 3 (☎ 93/317-39-74). Constructed for Gaudí's patron Eusebi Güell in the 1880s, this is one of the masterpieces of Antoni Gaudí. His tastes, although essentially Gothic, show even Moorish influences in this strange building. The main hall is usually open to the public, who can wander in and look about—and up. Its perforated cupola is adorned with broken fragments of ceramic tiles and crowned with a curious melange of balustrades, multiform chimneys, and crenels. The building houses theatrical archives containing such items as the memoirs of Catalán literary figures, props left over from long-forgotten hits of yesteryear, and antique theater posters. The archives are open Monday to Saturday from 10am to 1:30pm and 4 to 7:30pm, charging 300 ptas. ($2.40) for admission.

Walking back to Les Rambles, continue up the promenade but veer right onto Carrer de Colom on the other side of the esplanade, entering the landmark:

6. Plaça Reial (Royal Square). At first you'll think you've been transported to Andalusia. Constructed in a neoclassical style during the 19th century, this plaza has palms and elaborate facades, even ocher-painted arcades, and in the center is a fountain dedicated to the Three Graces. The lampposts are attributed to the young Gaudí. You'll see old men sunning themselves on the benches in this square, which was built on the site of a former Capuchin monastery, one of many religious edifices that lined the Rambles until they were suppressed in 1835. Sunday morning brings out a coin and stamp market.

Returning to Les Rambles, continue north from the harbor until you reach, on the left side, the:

7. Gran Teatre del Liceu, Rambla dels Caputxins, which, although destroyed by fire in January 1994, nevertheless remains one of the sightseeing targets of Barcelona, mainly because of rubber-neckers wanting to see the destruction. A workman's blowtorch ignited a curtain and the rest is theatrical history. Saved from the flames were some 85 valuable paintings and at least three dozen art objects that will be used to decorate the new opera house when it's rebuilt. Projected date? 2001. Before the fire this 1847 theater with 2,700 seats was Europe's largest opera house.

After viewing the site (perhaps a construction site at the time of your visit), continue north along Les Rambles to the:

8. Rambla de Sant Josep, also known as the Rambla de les Flors. Flower stands line this part of Les Rambles. This Rambla begins at Plaça de la Boquería, where you can visit the centuries-old market that bears the same name as the square.

At Rambla de Sant Josep, 99, stands the neoclassical Palau de la Virreina dating from 1778, named after a vicereine of Peru. Frequent contemporary exhibitions are staged here.

Next comes the:

9. Rambla dels Estudis, beginning at Carrer del Carme. The esplanade of the students takes its name from a university that once stood there until Philip V converted it into army barracks. Because so many birds are sold here, some people call this (in Spanish) the Rambla de los Pajaros (Boulevard of the Birds).

The final Rambla is the:

10. Rambla de Canaletes, which begins at Carrer del Santa Anna. This Rambla takes its name from a famous fountain. If you take a drink from it, it's said that you will never leave Barcelona. The fountain stands near the intersection of the Rambla and Carrer del Pelai.

At the end of this promenade you'll have arrived at:

Walking Tour—Les Rambles

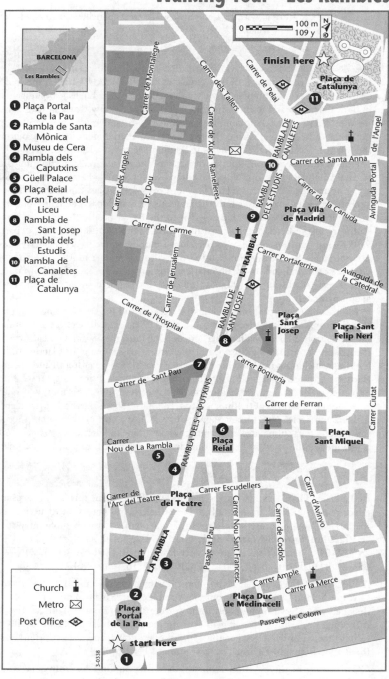

BARCELONA
Les Rambles

1 Plaça Portal de la Pau
2 Rambla de Santa Mònica
3 Museu de Cera
4 Rambla dels Caputxins
5 Güell Palace
6 Plaça Reial
7 Gran Teatre del Liceu
8 Rambla de Sant Josep
9 Rambla dels Estudis
10 Rambla de Canaletes
11 Plaça de Catalunya

0   100 m
    109 y

finish here

Plaça de Catalunya

Carrer de Montalegre

Carrer dels Tallers

Carrer de Pelai

Carrer dels Angels

Dr. Dou

Carrer de Xuclà Ramelleres

RAMBLA DE CANALETES

Carrer del Santa Anna

Avinguda Portal de l'Angel

RAMBLA DELS ESTUDIS

Carrer de la Canuda

Plaça Vila de Madrid

Carrer del Carme

LA RAMBLA

Carrer Portaferrisa

Avinguda de la Catedral

Carrer de Jerusalem

Carrer de l'Hospital

RAMBLA DE SANT JOSEP

Plaça Sant Josep

Plaça Sant Felip Neri

Carrer Boqueria

Carrer de Sant Pau

Carrer de Ferran

Carrer Ciutat

Carrer Nou de La Rambla

RAMBLA DELS CAPUTXINS

Plaça Reial

Plaça Sant Miquel

Carrer Escudellers

Carrer d'Avinyo

Carrer de Codols

Carrer de l'Arc del Teatre

Plaça del Teatre

Carrer Nou Sant Francesc

Pasaje la Pau

LA RAMBLA

Carrer Ample

Carrer la Merce

Plaça Duc de Medinaceli

Passeig de Colom

Church †
Metro ⊠
Post Office ◈

start here

Plaça Portal de la Pau

3-0338

105

11. Plaça de Catalunya, with its fountains, shade trees, benches, chairs, and—most important—public toilets.

10 Organized Tours

Pullmantur, Gran Vía de les Corts Catalanes, 635 (☎ **93/317-12-97;** metro: Plaça de Catalunya), offers a number of tours and excursions (with English-speaking guides) in both Barcelona and its environs. For a preview of the city, you can take a morning tour departing from the company's terminal at the above address at 9:30am, taking in the cathedral, the Gothic Quarter, Les Rambles, the monument to Columbus, the Spanish Village, and the Olympic Stadium. It costs 4,180 ptas. ($33.45). An afternoon tour leaves at 3:30pm, with visits to some of the most outstanding architectural examples in the Eixample, including Gaudí's Sagrada Familia, the Parc Güell, and a stop at the Picasso Museum. This tour costs 4,190 ptas. ($33.50). Pullmantur also offers several excursions into the environs of Barcelona. The daily tour of the monastery of Montserrat includes a visit to the Royal Basilica to view the famous sculpture of the Black Virgin. This tour, costing 5,300 ptas. ($42.40), departs at 9:30am and returns at 2:30pm to Barcelona's harbor, where passengers have the option to remain for the afternoon. A full-day Girona-Figueres tour includes a visit to Girona's cathedral and its Jewish quarter, plus a trip to the Salvador Dalí museum. This excursion, costing 10,700 ptas. ($85.60), leaves Barcelona at 9am and returns at approximately 6pm.

Another company that offers tours of Barcelona and the surrounding countryside is **Juliatours,** Ronda Universitat, 5 (☎ **93/317-64-54**). Itineraries are similar to those mentioned above, with similar prices. One tour, the "Visita Ciudad Artistica," focuses on the artistic significance of the city. It passes many of Gaudí's brilliant buildings, including the Casa Lleó Morera, Casa Milá (La Perdrera), and his unfinished masterpiece, La Sagrada Familia. Also included is a visit to the Museu Picasso or Museu d'Art Modern, depending on the day of your tour. This tour, which leaves at 3:30pm and returns at 6:30pm, costs 4,180 ptas. ($33.45). Another popular tour is the "Panorámica Nocturna y Show Flamenco." At a cost of 7,950 ptas. ($63.60), this evening tour culminates in a flamenco show at one of Barcelona's *tablaos*. A drink is included in the price of the tour, and dinner is available for an additional charge.

11 Outdoor Activities

BULLFIGHTING The Cataláns of Barcelona don't pursue this "art" with as much fervor as do the Castilians of Madrid. Nevertheless, you may want to attend one of the *corridas*. Bullfights are held from April to September, usually on Sunday at 6pm at **Plaça de Toros Monumental,** Gran Vía de les Corts Catalanes (☎ **93/245-58-04**). Purchase tickets in advance from the office at Muntaner, 24 (☎ **93/453-38-21**). Tickets cost 2,100 to 12,000 ptas. ($16.80 to $96).

A FITNESS CENTER The city's most obvious fitness center lies adjacent to the Olympic Stadium, in an indoor-outdoor complex whose main allure is its beautifully designed pair of swimming pools. Built for the 1992 Summer Olympics, the facility contains a health club and gym open to members of the public for 1,100 ptas. ($8.80) for a full-day pass. For the address, open hours, and a description, refer to the Piscina Bernardo Picornell in "Swimming," below.

GOLF One of the city's best courses, the **Club de Golf Vallromanas,** Afueras, s/n, Vallromanas (Barcelona) (☎ **93/572-90-64**), is about a 20-minute drive north of the town center. Nonmembers who reserve tee-off times in advance are welcome to play for a greens fee of 6,000 ptas. ($48) on weekdays and 12,000 ptas. ($96) on weekends. The club is open Wednesday to Monday from 9am to 8:30pm.

JOGGING   In the heart of Barcelona, the **Parc de la Ciutadella** (see "Parks & Gardens," earlier in this chapter) is the jogger's favorite. You can also use the paths surrounding Montjuïc.

SQUASH   Your best bet is the **Squash Club Barcelona,** Doctor Gregoria Maranon, 17 (☎ **93/334-02-58;** metro: Plaça de la Universitat), which accepts non-members and is open Monday to Friday from 9am to midnight, on Saturday from 10am to 10pm, and on Sunday from 10am to 8pm. Squash courts can be rented by anyone for 1,330 ptas. ($10.65) per half hour of play time. There are 15 courts in all. The swimming pool and gym, however, are reserved for members.

SWIMMING   Most city residents head out to the beaches of Sitges when they feel like swimming, but if you're looking for a not-very-crowded pool, you'll find one at the **Esportiu Piscina DeStampa,** Calle Rosich, s/n, in the Hospitalete district (☎ **93/334-56-00**). It's open Monday to Friday from 1 to 3pm and 7 to 9pm, on Saturday from 10am to 2pm and 4 to 8pm, and on Sunday from 10am to 2pm. Monday to Friday admission is 315 ptas. ($2.50); on Saturday and Sunday, 365 ptas. ($2.90).

A much better choice, however, allows you to swim where some of the events of the 1992 Summer Olympics took place, at **Piscina Bernardo Picornell,** Avinguda de Estadi, 30–40, on Montjuïc (☎ **93/423-40-41**). Set adjacent to the Olympic Stadium, it incorporates two of the best and most state-of-the-art swimming pools in Spain, each custom-built for the 1992 Olympics, and now open to the public Monday to Friday from 7am to midnight, on Saturday from 7am to 9pm, and on Sunday from 7:30am to 2:30pm. (One pool is outdoors; the other is indoors.) Entrance costs 600 ptas. ($4.80) and allows full use throughout the day of whichever pool is open, plus the gymnasium, the sauna, and the Jacuzzis. Bus no. 61 makes frequent runs from Plaça d'Espanya.

TENNIS   The neighborhoods of Barcelona don't contain as many tennis courts as you might have expected from a city of its size. Those that do exist are organized in often unexpected places, usually in a cluster of two or three courts. Many of them are private; others are associated with hotels or some of the city's schools and universities. One of the city's largest clubs is technically private, but sometimes allows qualified players to use its facilities for an hour if the courts aren't busy. The **Open Tennis Club** (also known as Club Open) (☎ **93/379-42-46**) is in the village of Castel de Fels, 3$^{1}/_{2}$ miles (5.5km) beyond the airport, beside the road leading to Sitges (signs will guide you from the highway). If space is not available at the time of your call, your hotel concierge, the Barcelona tourist office, or the operators at phone line "010" might be able to tell you of other courts allowing short-term access to nonmembers.

12 Shopping

Barcelonans look more to Paris than to Madrid for their fashions and style and, of course, create much of their style themselves. *Moda joven* (young fashion) is all the rage in Barcelona.

If your time and budget are limited, you may want to patronize Barcelona's major department store, El Corte Inglés, for an overview of Catalán merchandise at reasonable prices. Barcelona is filled with boutiques, but clothing is an expensive item here, even though the city has been a textile center for centuries.

Markets (see below) are very popular in Barcelona and are suitable places to search for good buys.

THE SHOPPING SCENE   If you're a window shopper, stroll along **Passeig de Gràcia** from Avinguda Diagonal to Plaça de Catalunya. Along the way you'll see some of the most elegant and expensive shops in Barcelona, plus an assortment of splendid turn-of-the-century buildings and cafés, many with outdoor tables.

Another shopping expedition is to the **Mercat de la Boquería,** Rambla, 101 (☎ 93/318-25-84), near Carrer del Carme. Here you'll see a wide array of straw bags and regional products, along with a handsome display of the food that you're likely to be eating later in a local restaurant: fruits, vegetables (artfully displayed), breads, cheeses, meats, and fish. Venders sell their wares Monday to Saturday from 7am to 8pm.

In the **old quarter** the principal shopping streets are all five Rambles, plus Carrer del Pi, Carrer de la Palla, and Avinguda Portal de l'Angel, to cite only some of the major ones. Moving north in the Eixample are Passeig de Catalunya, Passeig de Gràcia, and Rambla de Catalunya. Going even farther north, Avinguda Diagonal is a major shopping boulevard. Other prominent shopping streets include Bori i Fontesta, Vía Augusta, Carrer Muntaner, Travessera de Gràcia, and Carrer de Balmes.

In general, shops are open Monday to Saturday from 9am to 8pm. Some smaller shops close from 1:30 to 4pm.

The **American Visitors Bureau,** Gran Vía de les Corts Catalanes, 591 (☎ 93/301-01-50), between Rambla de Catalunya and Calle de Balmes, will pack and ship your purchases and gifts and even handle excess luggage and personal effects. The company also operates a travel agency here, booking flights and hotel accommodations for those needing it. It's open Monday to Friday from 9am to 1pm and 4 to 7pm and on Saturday from 9am to 1pm.

Watch for summer **sales** (*rebajas*) in late July and August. Merchandise is often heavily discounted by stores getting rid of their summer stock before fall.

SHOPPING A TO Z

Barcelona, a city of design and fashion, offers a wealth of shopping opportunities. In general, prices tend to be slightly lower than those in London, Paris, and Rome.

In addition to modern, attractively designed, and stylish clothing, shoes and decorative objects are often good buys. In the city of Miró, Tàpies, and Picasso, art is a major business, and the reason so many gallery owners from around the world come to visit. You'll find dozens of galleries, especially in the Barri Gòtic and around the Picasso Museum. Barcelona is also noted for its flea markets, where good purchases are always available if you search hard enough.

Antiques abound here, but rising prices have put them beyond the means of the average shopper. However, the list below includes some shops where you can look, if nothing else. Most shoppers from abroad settle happily for handcrafts, and the city is rich in offerings, ranging from simple pottery to handmade furniture. Barcelona has been in the business of creating and designing jewelry since the 17th century, and its offerings in this field are of the widest possible range—as are the prices.

What follows is only a limited selection of some of the hundreds of shops in Barcelona.

ANTIQUES

Artur Ramón Anticuario. Carrer de la Palla, 25. ☎ **93/302-59-70.** Metro: Jaume I.

One of the finest antiques stores in Barcelona is this three-level emporium with high ceilings and a medieval kind of grace. Set on a narrow flagstone-covered street near

Plaça del Pi (the center of the antiques district), it stands opposite a tiny square, Placeta al Carrer de la Palla, whose foundations were laid by the Romans. The store, which has been operated by four generations of men named Artur Ramón, contains everything from Romanesque works to Picasso pieces. The prices are high, as you'd expect, for items of quality and lasting value. Open Monday to Saturday from 10am to 1:30pm and 5 to 8pm.

El Bulevard des Antiquaris. Passeig de Gràcia, 55. No central phone. Metro: Passeig de Gràcia.

This 70-unit shopping complex, just off one of the town's most aristocratic avenues, has a huge collection of art and antiques assembled in a series of boutiques. There's a café/bar on the upper level. In summer it's open Monday to Friday from 9:30am to 8:30pm; in winter, on Monday from 4:30 to 8:30pm and Tuesday to Saturday from 10:30am to 8:30pm. Some boutiques, however, keep "short" hours.

Urbana. Còrsega, 258. ☎ **93/218-70-36.** Metro: Hospital Sant Pau.

Urbana sells an array of architectural remnants (usually from torn-down mansions), antique furniture, and reproductions of brass hardware. There are antique and reproduction marble mantelpieces, wrought-iron gates and garden seats, even carved-wood fireplaces with the *modernismo* look. It's an impressive, albeit costly, array of merchandise rescued from the architectural glory of yesteryear. Open Monday to Friday from 10am to 2pm and 4:30 to 8pm.

CAMERAS

Casa Arpi. Rambla dels Caputxins, 38. ☎ **93/301-74-04.** Metro: Liceu.

This is one of the most famous camera shops in Spain. A multilingual staff will guide you to the best buys in new and used cameras, including familiar brand-name products. The firm also does quality processing, ready within 24 to 48 hours. Open Monday to Saturday from 9:30am to 1:30pm and 4:30 to 8pm.

DEPARTMENT STORES

El Corte Inglés. Plaça de Catalunya, 14. ☎ **93/302-12-12.** Metro: Plaça de Catalunya.

Part of the largest and most glamorous department store chain in Spain, this store sells a wide variety of merchandise, ranging from Spanish handcrafts to high-fashion items, from Spanish or Catalán records to food. The store also has restaurants and cafés and offers a number of consumer-related services, such as a travel agent. It has a department that will arrange the mailing of your purchases back home. Open Monday to Friday from 10am to 9:30pm.

DESIGNER HOUSEWARES

Vincón. Passeig de Gràcia, 96. ☎ **93/215-60-50.** Metro: Passeig de Gràcia.

Fernando Amat's Vincón is the best in the city, with 10,000 products—everything from household items to the best in Spanish contemporary furnishings. Housed in the former home of artist Ramón Casas, with gilded columns and mosaic-inlaid floors, the showroom is filled with the best Spain has, each item personally selected because of its quality and craft. The window display alone is worth the trek there: Expect *anything*. Open Monday to Saturday from 10am to 1:30pm and 5 to 8pm.

FABRICS & WEAVINGS

Coses de Casa. Plaça de Sant Josep Oriol, 5. ☎ **93/302-73-28.** Metro: Jaume I.

Appealing fabrics and weavings are displayed in this 19th-century store. Many are hand-woven in Majorca, their boldly geometric patterns inspired by Arab motifs of centuries ago. The fabric, for the most part, is 50% cotton, 50% linen; much of it would make excellent upholstery material. Open Monday to Friday from 9:45am to 1:30pm and 4:30 to 8pm and on Saturday from 10am to 2pm and 5 to 8pm.

FASHION

Groc. Ramble de Catalunya, 100. ☎ **93/215-74-74.** Metro: Plaça de Catalunya.

Designs for both women and men are sold here. One of the most stylish shops in Barcelona, it's expensive but filled with high-quality apparel made from the finest of natural fibers. The men's store is downstairs, the women's store one flight up. Open Monday to Saturday from 10am to 2pm and 4:30 to 8pm. The men's department is closed Monday from 10am to 2pm; the women's department is closed Saturday from 4:30 to 8pm. The entire store is closed in August.

Roser-Francesc. Roger de Llúria, 87. ☎ **93/215-78-67.** Metro: Urquinaona.

With an inventory scattered over two floors of a narrow storefront in the Eixample district, this establishment is the quintessential boutique. It stocks only a limited selection of casually elegant clothes for both men and women, each chosen carefully with an alert consciousness of what's currently fashionable in Rome, Paris, Düsseldorf, and Los Angeles. Most of the garments are crafted from cotton, and are ideal for such warm-weather resorts as Sitges, a short car ride to the south of Barcelona. Open Monday to Saturday from 10am to 2:30pm and 4:30 to 8:30pm.

GALLERIES

Art Picasso. Tapineria, 10. ☎ **93/310-49-57.** Metro: Jaume I.

Here you can get good lithographic reproductions of works by Picasso, Miró, and Dalí, as well as T-shirts emblazoned with the designs of these masters. Tiles sold here often carry their provocatively painted scenes. Open Monday to Saturday from 9:30am to 8pm and on Sunday from 9:30am to 3pm.

Sala Parés. Petritxol, 5. ☎ **93/318-70-20.** Metro: Plaça de Catalunya.

Established in 1840, this is the finest art gallery in the city, recognizing and promoting the work of many Spanish and Catalán painters and sculptors who have gone on to acclaim. The Maragall family has been the "talent" recognizing all this budding genius. Paintings are displayed in a two-story amphitheater, whose high-tech steel balconies are supported by a quartet of steel columns evocative of Gaudí. Exhibitions of the most avant-garde art in Barcelona change about every 3 weeks. Open Monday to Saturday from 10:30am to 2pm and 4:30 to 8:30pm and on Sunday from 11am to 2pm.

GIFTS

Beardsley. Petritxol, 12. ☎ **93/301-05-76.** Metro: Plaça de Catalunya.

Named after the Victorian English illustrator, this store is on the same street where the works of Picasso and Dalí were exhibited before they became world famous. The wide array of gifts, perhaps the finest selection in Barcelona, includes a little bit of everything—dried flowers, writing supplies, silver dishes, unusual bags and purchases, and lots more. Open Monday to Friday from 9:30am to 1:30pm and 4:30 to 8pm and on Saturday from 10am to 2pm and 5 to 8pm.

LEATHER

Loewe. Passeig de Gràcia, 35. ☎ **93/216-04-00.** Metro: Passeig de Gràcia.

The biggest branch in Barcelona of this prestigious nationwide leather-goods chain is in one of the best-known *modernismo* buildings in the city. Everything is top-notch, from the elegantly spacious showroom to the expensive merchandise to the helpful salespeople. The company exports its goods to branches throughout Asia, Europe, and North America. Open Monday to Saturday from 9:30am to 2pm and 4:30 to 8pm.

MARKETS

El Encants antiques market is held every Monday, Wednesday, Friday, and Saturday in Plaça de les Glóries Catalanes (metro: Glóries). There are no specific times—go any time during the day to survey the selection.

Coins and postage stamps are traded and sold in **Plaça Reial** on Sunday from 10am to 2pm. The location is off the southern flank of Les Rambles (metro: Drassanes).

A book-and-coin market is held at the **Ronda Sant Antoni** every Sunday from 10am to 2pm (metro: Plaça de la Universitat).

MUSIC

Casa Beethoven. Rambles, 97. ☎ **93/301-48-26.** Metro: Liceu.

Probably the most complete collection of sheet music in town can be found here. In a narrow store established in 1920, the collection naturally focuses on the works of Spanish and Catalán composers. Music lovers might make some rare discoveries here. Open Monday to Friday from 9am to 1:30pm and 4 to 8pm and on Saturday from 9am to 1:30pm and 5 to 8pm.

PORCELAIN

Kastoria 2. Avinguda Catedra, 6–8. ☎ **93/310-04-11.** Metro: Plaça de Catalunya.

This large store near the cathedral carries many kinds of leather goods, including purses, suitcases, coats, and jackets. But most people come here to look at its famous Lladró porcelain—they're authorized dealers and have a big selection. Open Monday to Saturday from 10am to 2pm and 3 to 8pm and on Sunday from 10am to 2pm.

POTTERY

Artesana I Coses. Placeta de Montcada, 2. ☎ **93/319-54-13.** Metro: Jaume I.

Here you'll find pottery and porcelain from every major region of Spain. Most of the pieces are heavy and thick-sided—designs in use in the country for centuries. Open Monday to Saturday from 10:30am to 2pm and 4:30 to 8pm.

Itaca. Carrer Ferran, 26. ☎ **93/301-30-44.** Metro: Liceu.

Here you'll find a wide array of handmade pottery, not only from Catalonia and other parts of Spain, but also from Portugal, Mexico, and Morocco. The merchandise has been selected for its basic purity, integrity, and simplicity. Open Monday to Friday from 10am to 2pm and 4:30 to 8pm and on Saturday from 10am to 2pm and 5 to 8:30pm.

SHOPPING CENTERS/MALLS

The landscape of Barcelona has exploded since the mid-1980s with the construction of several American-style shopping malls, some of which are too far from the city's historic core to be convenient to most foreign visitors. Here's a description, however, of some of the city's best:

Centre Comercial Barcelona Glories. Avinguda Diagonal, 208. ☎ **93/486-06-39.** Metro: Glories.

Built in 1995, this is the largest shopping center in downtown Barcelona, a three-story emporium of the good life as based on California models, but crammed into a distinctly urban neighborhood. More than 100 shops are contained inside: some posh, others much less so. Although there's a typical shopping-mall anonymity to some aspects of this place, you'll still be able to find virtually anything you might have forgotten while packing for your trip. It's open Monday to Saturday from 10am to 10pm.

Diagonal Center (Illa). Avinguda Diagonal, 557. ☎ **93/444-00-00.** Metro: María Cristina.

Smaller than the above-mentioned Centre Comercial Barcelona Glories, with about half the number of shops, this two-story mall contains stores devoted to luxury products, as well as a scattering of bars, cafés, and simple but cheerful restaurants favored by office workers and shoppers. Built in the early 1990s, it even has an area devoted to video games, where teenagers can make as much electronic noise as they want while their guardians go shopping. It's open Monday to Saturday from 10am to 9pm.

Maremagnum. Moll d'Espanya, s/n. ☎ **93/225-81-00.** Metro: Drassanes.

The best thing about this place is its position adjacent to the waterfront of Barcelona's historic seacoast, plus the fact that it's well suited to outdoor promenades. Built in the early 1990s near the Columbus Monument, it contains a handful of shops selling touristy items and lots of cafés, bars, and places to sit. You might get the idea that only a few of the people who come here are really interested in shopping, despite the fact that the place defines itself as a shopping mall.

Poble Espanyol. Marqués de Comilias, Parc de Montjuïc. ☎ **93/325-78-66.** Metro: Espanya; then take the free red double-decker bus to Montjuïc.

This is not technically a shopping mall but a "village" (see "In & Around the Parc de Montjuïc," earlier in this chapter) with about 35 stores selling typical folk crafts from every part of Spain: glassware, leather goods, pottery, paintings, and carvings—you name it. Stores keep various hours, but you can visit any time during the day.

STRAW PRODUCTS
La Manual Alpargatera. Aviño, 7. ☎ **93/301-01-72.** Metro: Jaume I or Liceu.

In addition to its large inventory of straw products, such as hats and bags, this shop is known mainly for its footwear, called *espadrilles* (*alpargatas* in Spanish). This basic rope-soled shoe (said to go back 1,000 years) is made on the premises. Some Cataláns wear only espadrilles when performing the sardana, their national dance. To find La Manual Alpargatera, turn off Les Rambles at Carrer Ferran, walk two blocks, and make a right. Open Monday to Saturday from 9:30am to 1:30pm and 4:30 to 8pm.

UMBRELLAS
Julio Gomez. Rambla de Sant Josep (also called Rambla de las Flors), 104. ☎ **93/301-33-26.** Metro: Liceu.

For more than a century Julio Gomez has rung up umbrella sales here. In a workshop out back, women labor over these unique umbrellas or lace-trimmed silk or cotton parasols. There are also Spanish fans, walking sticks capped with silver, and other memorabilia—all adding up to an evocative piece of shopping nostalgia. Open Monday to Saturday from 9:30am to 1:30pm and 4 to 8pm.

13 Barcelona After Dark

Barcelona comes alive at night—the funicular ride to Tibidabo or the illuminated fountains of Montjuïc are especially popular. During the Franco era the center of club life was the cabaret-packed district near the south of Les Rambles, an area, incidentally, known for nighttime muggings—so use caution if you go there. But the most fashionable clubs long ago deserted this seedy area and have opened in nearly every major district of the city.

Your best source of local information is a little magazine called *Guía del Ocio,* which previews "La Semana de Barcelona" (This Week in Barcelona). It's in Spanish, but most of its listings will probably be comprehensible. The magazine is sold at virtually every news kiosk along Les Rambles.

Nightlife begins for Barcelonans with a promenade (*paseo*) along Les Rambles in the early evening, usually from 5 to 7pm. Then things quiet down a bit, until a second surge of energy brings out Les Rambles crowds again, from 9 to 11pm. After that the esplanade clears out quite a bit.

If you've been scared off by press reports of Les Rambles between Plaça de Catalunya and the Columbus Monument, you'll feel safer along the Rambla de Catalunya, in the Eixample, north of Plaça de Catalunya. This street and its offshoots are lively at night, with many cafés and bars.

The array of nighttime diversions in Barcelona is staggering. There's something to interest almost everyone and to fit most pocketbooks. For families, the amusement parks are the most frequented venues. Sometimes locals opt for an evening in the *tascas* (taverns) or pubs, perhaps settling for a bottle of wine at a café, an easy and inexpensive way to spend an evening of people watching. Serious drinking in pubs and cafés begins by 10 or 11pm. But for the most fashionable bars and discos, Barcelonans delay their entrances until at least 1am.

Cultural events are big in the Catalonian repertoire, and the old-fashioned dance halls, too, still survive in some places. Although disco has waned in some parts of the world, it's still going strong in Barcelona. Decaying movie houses, abandoned garages, and long-closed vaudeville theaters have been taken over and restored to become nightlife venues for *la movida,* that after-dark movement that sweeps across the city until dawn.

Flamenco isn't the rage here that it is in Seville and Madrid, but it still has its devotees. The city is also filled with jazz aficionados. Best of all, the old tradition of the music hall with vaudeville lives on in Barcelona.

SPECIAL EVENTS & DISCOUNTS In the summer you'll see plenty of free entertainment just by walking the streets—everything from opera to monkey acts. Les Rambles are a particularly good place to watch.

There's almost always a **festival** happening in the city, and many of the events can be enjoyed for free. The tourist office can give you details of when and where.

Some **theaters** advertise discount or half-price nights. Check in the weekly *Guía del Ocio.*

THE PERFORMING ARTS

Culture is deeply ingrained in the Catalán soul. The performing arts are strong here—some, in fact, taking place on the street, especially along Les Rambles. Crowds will often gather around a singer or mime. A city square will suddenly come alive on Saturday night with a spontaneous festival—"tempestuous, surging, irrepressible life and brio" is how the writer Rose MacCauley described it.

Long a city of the arts, Barcelona experienced a cultural decline during the Franco years, but now it's filled once again with the best opera, symphonic, and choral music.

The **Gran Teatre del Liceu,** Rambla dels Caputxins (metro: Liceu), was a monument to belle époque extravagance, a 2,700-seat century opera house and one of the grandest theaters in the world. It was designed by Catalán architect Josep Oriol Mestves. In January 1994 the opera house was gutted by fire, which shocked

Catalonia, many of whose citizens regarded this place as the citadel of their culture. To borrow from Shakespeare, the old Liceu now belongs to the "Bare ruin'd choirs, where late the sweet birds sang." The government of Catalonia has vowed that "the Liceu will be rebuilt—right here, in the same place, and just as it was." Even as Barcelona debates the future of this world-famous opera house, visitors to the city view its ruins as a sightseeing oddity. Stay tuned for future developments.

CLASSICAL MUSIC

Palau de la Música Catalán. Sant Francest de Paula, 2. ☎ **93/268-10-00.** Ticket prices depend on event.

In a city chock-full of architectural highlights, this one stands out. In 1908 Lluís Domènech i Montaner, a Catalán architect, designed this structure, including stained glass, ceramics, statuary, and ornate lamps, among other elements. It stands today, restored, as a classic example of *modernismo*. Concerts and leading recitals are presented here. The box office is open Monday to Friday from 10am to 9pm and on Saturday from 3 to 9pm.

THEATER

Theater is presented in the Catalán language and therefore will not be of interest to most visitors. However, for those who speak the language, or perhaps who are fluent in Spanish, here are some recommendations:

Companyia Flotats. Teatre Poliorama, Rambla dels Estudis, 115. ☎ **93/317-75-99.** Tickets 1,500–2,500 ptas. ($12–$20). Closed Aug. Metro: Liceu.

This leading company is directed by Josep María Flotats, an actor-director who was trained in the tradition of theater repertory, working in such theaters in Paris as the Théâtre de la Villa and the Comédie-Française. He founded his own company in Barcelona, where he presents both classic and contemporary plays.

Mercat de Los Flors. Lleida, 59. ☎ **93/426-18-75.** Tickets 1,100–2,500 ptas. ($8.80–$20). Metro: Espanya.

Housed in a building constructed for the 1929 International Exhibition at Montjuïc is this other major Catalán theater. Peter Brook first used it as a theater for a 1983 presentation of *Carmen.* Innovators in drama, dance, and music are showcased here, as are modern dance companies from Europe, including troupes from Italy and France. The 999-seat house also has a restaurant overlooking the rooftops of the city.

Teatre Lliure. Montseny, 47. ☎ **93/218-92-51.** Tickets 1,600 ptas. ($12.80) Tues–Thurs, 2,000 ptas. ($16) Fri–Sun. Metro: Passeig de Gràcia.

This self-styled free theater is the leading Catalán-language theater in Barcelona. Once a workers' union, since 1976 the building has been the headquarters of a theater cooperative. Its directors are famous in Barcelona for their bold presentations here, including works by Bertolt Brecht, Luigi Pirandello, Jean Genet (who wrote about Barcelona), and even Molière and Shakespeare. New dramas by Catalán playwrights are also presented. The house seats 200 to 350.

FLAMENCO

El Tablao de Carmen. Poble Espanyol de Montjuïc. ☎ **93/325-68-95.** Dinner and show, 7,500 ptas. ($60); drink and show, 4,000 ptas. ($32).

This club provides a highly rated flamenco cabaret in the re-created village. You can go early and explore the village if you wish, and even have dinner here. This place has long been a tourist favorite. The club is open Tuesday to Sunday from 8pm to past midnight. During the week it sometimes closes around 1am, but often stays open until 2 or 3am on weekends, depending on business. The first show is always at 9:30pm; the second show Tuesday to Thursday and Sunday is at 11:30pm, on Friday and Saturday at midnight. Reservations are encouraged.

Tablao Flamenco Cordobés. Les Rambles, 35. ☎ **93/317-66-53.** Dinner and show, 7,500 ptas. ($60); one drink and show, 4,000 ptas. ($32). Metro: Drassanes.

At the southern end of Les Rambles, a short walk from the harborfront, you'll hear the strum of the guitar, the sound of hands clapping rhythmically, and the haunting sound of the flamenco, a tradition here since 1968. Head upstairs to an Andalusian-style room where performances take place with the traditional *cuadro flamenco*—singers, dancers, and guitarist. Cordobés is said to be the best showcase for flamenco in Barcelona. November to March (except for 1 week in December), the show with dinner begins at 8:30pm and the show without dinner at 10pm. April to October and December 25–31, four shows are offered nightly: with dinner at 8 and 9:45pm; without dinner at 9:30 and 11:15pm. Reservations are required. It's closed in January.

THE CLUB & MUSIC SCENE
CABARET
Arnau. Avinguda del Paral-lel, 60. ☎ **93/442-28-04.** Cover (including the first drink) 2,500 ptas. ($20). Metro: Paral-lel.

A veteran at surviving the many changes that have affected the worlds of cabaret and entertainment since its heyday in the 1970s, this place has managed to keep up with the times and the demands of the marketplace. Shows mingle touches of Catalán folklore with glitz and glitter, hints of family nostalgia, and doses of melodrama. Two shows are presented every night, at 9pm and midnight.

Bodega Bohemia. Lancaster, 2. ☎ **93/302-50-61.** Metro: Liceu.

This cabaret extraordinaire, off Les Rambles, is a Barcelona institution, and everybody who is anybody has been here. The Bodega Bohemia rates as high camp—a talent showcase for theatrical personalities whose joints aren't so flexible but who perform with bracing dignity. Curiously, most audiences fill up with young people, who cheer, boo, catcall, and scream with laughter—and the old-timers on stage love it. The show stretches on forever. In all, it's an incredible entertainment bargain if your tastes lean slightly to the bizarre. The street outside is none too safe; take a taxi right to the door. Open daily from 11pm to 4am.

DANCE CLUBS & DISCOS
Estudio 54. Avinguda del Paral-lel, 64. ☎ **93/329-54-54.** Cover 1,200 ptas. ($9.60). Metro: Paral-lel.

Barcelona's version of New York's ill-fated and long-defunct Studio 54 continues to jump with a slightly faded version of the same energy as its namesake. It lies on the opposite side of the Barri Xinés from Les Rambles. Inside, you'll find a creative array of lighting effects and an energetic dance floor that thrives on eccentric styles of personal expression. The place is at its most appealing Thursday to Saturday from 11:30pm to 5am.

Up and Down. Numancia Diagonal, 179. ☎ **93/280-29-22.** Cover (including the first drink) 2,000 ptas. ($16). Metro: Sants Estació.

The chic atmosphere of this disco attracts the elite of Barcelona, spanning a generation gap. The more mature patrons, specifically the black-tie, post-opera crowd, head for the upstairs section, leaving the downstairs to the loud music and "flaming youth."

Up and Down is the most cosmopolitan disco in Barcelona, with a carefully planned ambience, impeccable service, and a welcoming atmosphere. Every critic who comes here comments on the piquant, sassy antics of the waiters, whose theatricality is part of the carnival-like atmosphere pervading this place. The disco is enhanced by audiovisual techniques; the decor is black and white. Dress can be your own selection, but men must always—regardless of their outfit—wear a tie.

Technically, this is a private club and you can be turned away at the door. The restaurant is open Monday to Saturday from 10pm to 2am, serving meals costing 4,500 ptas. ($36) and up. The disco is open Tuesday to Saturday from 12:30am to anytime between 5 and 6:30am, depending on business. Drinks in the disco cost 1,400 ptas. ($11.20) for a beer; 1,900 ptas. ($15.20) and up for a hard drink.

A DANCE HALL

La Paloma. Tigre, 27. ☎ **93/301-68-97.** Cover 400–800 ptas. ($3.20–$6.40). Metro: Plaça de la Universitat.

Those feeling nostalgic may want to drop in on the most famous dance hall of Barcelona. It was young in 1903. The iron for the famed Barcelona statue of Columbus was smelted in La Paloma before it became the dance hall it is today. Remember the fox trot? The mambo? If not, learn about them at La Paloma, where they're still danced, along with the tango, the cha-cha, and the bolero. Tuesday is boxing night: A boxing match actually takes place in a ringed-off area of the dance floor. Live orchestras provide the music for this old hall with its faded but flamboyant trappings, including gilded plaster angels, crystal chandeliers, and opera-red draperies. "Matinees" are from 6 to 9:30pm; night dances are from 11:30pm to 5am.

THE BAR SCENE
PUBS & BARS

In addition to the bars listed below, several Barcelona tapas bars are recommended in the "Dining" section of Chapter 3.

El Born. Passeig del Born, 26. ☎ **93/319-53-33.** Metro: Jaume I.

Facing a rural-looking square, this place, once a fish store, has been cleverly converted. There are a few tables near the front, but our preferred spot is the inner room, decorated with rattan furniture, ceramic jugs, books, and modern paintings. The music here could be anything from Louis Armstrong to classic rock-and-roll. Dinner can also be had at the upstairs buffet. The room is somewhat cramped, but there you'll find a simple but tasty collection of fish, meat, and vegetable dishes, all carefully laid out; a full dinner without wine costs around 3,000 ptas. ($24). Open Monday to Saturday from 7:30am to 2:30am.

Café Bar Padam. Rauric, 9. ☎ **93/302-50-62.** Metro: Liceu.

The tapas served here are derived from time-honored Catalán culinary traditions, but the clientele and decor are modern, hip, and often gay. The bar is on a narrow street in the Ciutat Vella, about 3 blocks east of the Rambla dels Caputxins. The only color in the black-and-white rooms comes from fresh flowers and modern paintings. Tapas include fresh anchovies and tuna, plus cheese platters. Jazz is sometimes featured. Open Monday to Saturday from 7pm to 2am.

Cocktail Bar Boadas. Tallers, 1. ☎ **93/318-95-92.** Metro: Plaça de Catalunya.

This intimate and conservative bar is usually filled with regulars. Established in 1933, it lies near the top of Les Rambles. Many visitors stop here for a before-dinner drink and snack prior to wandering to one of the district's many restaurants. You can choose among a wide array of Caribbean rums, Russian vodkas, and English gins—the skilled bartenders know how to mix them all. The place is especially well known for its daiquiris. Open daily from noon to 2am.

Dirty Dick's, Taberna Inglesa. Carrer Marc Aureli, 2. ☎ **93/200-89-52.** Metro: Muntaner.

An English-style pub behind an inwardly curving bay window in a residential part of town, Dirty Dick's has an interior of dark paneling and exposed brick, with banquettes for quiet conversation. If you sit at the bar you'll be faced with a tempting array of tiny sandwiches that taste as good as they look. The pub is set at the corner of Vía Augusta, a main thoroughfare leading through the district. Open daily from 6pm to 2:30am.

Pub 240. Aribau, 240. ☎ **93/209-09-67.** Cover 2,500 ptas. ($20).

This elegant bar, which bears absolutely no resemblance to an English pub, is arranged in three sections: a bar, a small amphitheater, and a lounge for talking and listening to music. Rock and South American folk music are played here, and the place is jammed almost every night. Open daily from 7pm to 5am.

Zig-Zag Bar. Platón, 13. ☎ **93/201-62-07.** Metro: Muntaner.

Favored by actors, models, cinematographers, and photographers, this bar claims to have inaugurated Barcelona's trend toward high-tech minimalism in its watering holes. Owned by the same entrepreneurs who developed the state-of-the-art nightclub Otto Zutz, it offers an unusual chance to see Spain's *movida* in action. Open Monday to Thursday from 7:30pm to 2:30am and on Friday and Saturday from 7:30pm to 3am.

SPECIALTY BARS
Champagne Bars

The growing popularity of champagne bars during the 1980s was an indication of Spain's increasing cosmopolitanism. The Cataláns call their own version of champagne *cava.* In Spanish, champagne bars are called *champanerías,* and in Catalán the name is *xampanyerías.* These Spanish wines are often excellent, said by some to be better than their French counterparts. With more than 50 companies producing cava in Spain and with each bottling up to a dozen different grades of wine, the best way to learn about Spanish champagne is either to visit the vineyard or to sample the products at a xampanyería.

Champagne bars usually open at 7pm and stay open into the wee hours of the morning. Tapas are served, ranging from caviar to smoked fish to frozen chocolate truffles. Most establishments sell only a limited array of house cavas by the glass—you'll be offered a choice of *brut* or *brut nature* (*brut* is slightly sweeter). More esoteric cavas must be purchased by the bottle. The most acclaimed brands include Mont-Marçal, Gramona, Mestres, Parxet, Torello, and Recaredo.

La Cava del Palau. Verdaguer I Callis, 10. ☎ **93/310-09-38.** Metro: Urquinaona.

Located in an old part of Barcelona, this large champagne bar is a favorite of the after-concert crowd (the Palace of Music is just around the corner). Live music is sometimes presented, accompanied by a wide assortment of cheeses, cold cuts, pâtés, and fresh anchovies. Open Monday to Friday from 1:30 to 4pm and 8pm to 2am and on Saturday from 8pm to 2am.

Xampanyería Casablanca. Bonavista, 6. ☎ **93/237-63-99.** Metro: Passeig de Gràcia.

Someone had to fashion a champagne bar after the Bogart-Bergman film, and this is it. Four kinds of house cava are served by the glass. The staff also serves a good selection of tapas, especially pâtés. The Casablanca is close to Passeig de Gràcia. Open Sunday to Thursday from 6:45pm to 2:30am and on Friday and Saturday from 6:45pm to 3am.

Xampú Xampany. Gran Vía de les Corts Catalanes, 702. ☎ **93/265-04-83.** Metro: Girona.

At the corner of Plaça de Tetuan, this xampanyería offers a variety of hors d'oeuvres in addition to the wine. Abstract paintings, touches of high tech, bouquets of flowers, and a pastel color scheme create the decor. Open daily from 6:30pm to 3:30am.

Grand Chic Bars

In Barcelona they speak of a "bar boom"—the weekly entertainment guide, *Guía del Ocio,* has estimated that 500 new bars opened before the 1992 Olympics. A staff writer said, "The city has put her ambition and energy into designing bars and hopping from bar to bar. The inauguration of a new watering hole interests people more than any other social, cultural, or artistic event." The bars are stylish and often avantgarde in design. We'll sample only a few of the better ones, but know that there are literally hundreds more.

Nick Havanna. Roselló, 208. ☎ **93/237-54-05.** No cover: Sun–Thurs; 900 ptas. ($7.20) Fri–Sat, including the first drink. Metro: Diagonal.

Like a high-tech cathedral, it has a soaring ceiling supported by vaguely ecclesiastical concrete columns off which radiate four arms. There's a serpentine-shaped curve of two different bars upholstered in black-and-white cowhide, plus a bank of at least 30 different video scenes. To keep patrons in touch with world events between drinks, a Spanish-language teletype machine chatters out news events. Some women have admitted to detouring to the men's room for a view of the famous mirrored waterfall cascading into the urinal. This has become one of Barcelona's most talked-about and most frequented watering holes. It's hip and happening—so dress accordingly, and go late or you'll have the place to yourself. Open daily from 11pm to 5:30am.

Otto Zutz Club. Carrer Lincoln, 15. ☎ **93/238-07-22.** Cover 2,000 ptas. ($16). Metro: Passeig de Gràcia or Fontana.

Sheathed in one of the most carefully planned neoindustrial decors in Spain, this nightspot is the last word in hip and a magnet for the city's artists and night people. Facetiously named after a German optician and the recipient of millions of pesetas' worth of interior drama, it sits behind an angular facade that reminds some visitors of a monument to some mid–20th-century megalomaniac. Originally built to house a textile factory, the building contains a labyrinth of metal staircases decorated in shades of blue, highlighted with endless spotlights and warmed with lots of exposed wood. On the uppermost floor a high-tech restaurant serves supper-club food (brochettes, light pastas, and platters of smoked fish) for around 3,000 ptas. ($24) for a full meal. Open Tuesday to Saturday from 11pm to 6am—but don't even think of showing up before midnight.

Ticktacktoe. Roger de Llúria, 40. ☎ **93/318-99-47.** Metro: Passeig de Gràcia.

In the Eixample district, this bar/restaurant is one of the most talked-about rendezvous spots in the city. The decor is definitely tongue-in-cheek—everything from a marble whale to a bar in the form of a female breast. Frequented by TV personalities, Ticktacktoe draws a fashionable crowd, most of whom are under 35. Regular competitions are held at the snooker and the billiards tables. The bar is open Monday to Thursday from 8pm to midnight and on Friday and Saturday from 8pm to 1am; the restaurant, from 1 to 4pm and 8:30pm to midnight. Closed from August 15 to 30.

In case you want to see the world.

At American Express, we're here to make your journey a smooth one. So we have over 1,700 travel service locations in over 120 countries ready to help. What else would you expect from the world's largest travel agency?

do more

http://www.americanexpress.com/travel

In case you want to be welcomed there.

We're here to see that you're always welcomed at establishments everywhere. That's why millions of people carry the American Express® Card – for peace of mind, confidence, and security, around the world or just around the corner.

do more®

Cards

In case you're running low.

We're here to help with more than 118,000 Express Cash

locations around the world. In order to enroll, just call

American Express before you start your vacation.

do more

Express Cash

And just in case.

We're here with American Express® Travelers Cheques and Cheques *for Two*.® They're the safest way to carry money on your vacation and the surest way to get a refund, practically anywhere, anytime.

Another way we help you...

do more

Travelers Cheques

Zsa Zsa. Roselló, 156. ☎ **93/453-85-66.** Metro: Provença.

This is a favorite bar with journalists, writers, and advertising executives, who mingle, drink, converse, and make or break deals. A light system creates endlessly different patterns that seem to change with the mood of the crowd. Chrome columns capped with stereo speakers dot the room like a high-tech forest. Open daily from 7pm to 3am.

Nostalgia Bars

Bar Pastis. Calle Santa Mònica, 4. ☎ **93/318-79-80.** Metro: Drassanes.

Just off the southern end of Les Rambles, this tiny bar was opened in 1947 by Carme Pericás and Quime Ballester, two Valencianos. They made it a shrine to Edith Piaf, and her songs are still played on an old phonograph in back of the bar. If you look at the dusty art in this dimly lit place, you'll see some of Piaf. But mainly the decor consists of paintings by Quime Ballester, who had a dark, rather morbid vision of the world. You can order four different kinds of pastis in this "corner of Montmartre." Outside the window, check out the view, usually a parade of transvestite hookers. The crowd is likely to include almost anyone, especially people who used to be called "bohemians"; they live on in this bar of yesterday. Live music is performed Sunday to Thursday—go after 11:30pm. Open Monday, Wednesday, and Thursday from 7:30pm to 2:30am, on Friday and Saturday from 7:30pm to 3am, and on Sunday from 6:30pm to 1:30am.

Els Quatre Gats. Montsió, 3. ☎ **93/302-41-40.** Metro: Urquinaona.

The Four Cats has been called "the best bar in Barcelona" (see also the restaurant listing under "Dining" in Chapter 3). In 1897 Pere Romeu and three of his friends—painters Ramón Casas, Santiago Rusiñol, and Miguel Utrillo—opened a café for artists and writers at the edge of the Barri Gòtic. Early in the history of the café they staged a one-man show for a young artist, Pablo Picasso, but he didn't sell a single painting. However, Picasso stayed around to design the art nouveau cover of the menu. The café folded in 1903, becoming a private club and art school and attracting Joan Miró.

In 1978 two Cataláns reopened the café in the Casa Martí, a building designed by Josep Puig i Cadafalch, one of the leading architects of *modernismo*. The café displays works by major modern Catalán painters, including Tàpies. You can come in to drink coffee at the café, taste some wine, eat a full meal—and even try, if you dare, a potent Marc de Champagne, an eau-de-vie distilled from the local cava. The café is open daily from 8am to 2am.

Gay & Lesbian Bars

Chaps. Avinguda Diagonal, 365. ☎ **93/215-53-65.** Metro: Diagonal.

Gay residents of Barcelona refer to this saloon-style watering hole as the premier leather bar of Catalonia. But in fact the dress code usually steers more toward boots and jeans than leather and chains. Set behind a pair of swinging doors evocative of the old American West, Chaps contains two different bar areas. Open daily from 7pm to 3am.

El Convento. Carrer Bruniquer, 59 (Plaça Joanic). No phone. Cover (including the first drink) 1,100 ptas. ($8.80). Metro: Joanic.

This may be like no disco you've ever seen. The decoration is like a church, with depictions of the Virgin Mary and even candles adding to the ecclesiastical atmosphere. But the clientele consists mainly of young gay males in a party mood. Often shows and organized parties are presented here. A novelty, to say the least. Open daily from midnight to 6am.

Martin's Disco. Passeig de Gràcia, 130. ☎ **93/218-71-67.** Cover (including the first drink) 1,000 ptas. ($8). Metro: Passeig de Gràcia.

Behind a pair of unmarked doors, in a neighborhood of art nouveau buildings, this is one of the more popular gay discos in Barcelona. In a series of all-black rooms, you'll wander through a landscape of men's erotic art, upended oil drums (used as cocktail tables), and the disembodied front-end chassis of yellow cars set amid the angular surfaces of the drinking and dancing areas. Another bar supplies drinks to a large room where films are shown. Open daily from midnight to 6am.

Santanassa. Carrer Aribau, 27. ☎ **93/451-00-52.** No Cover: Sun–Thurs; 1,000 ptas. ($8) Fri–Sat, including the first drink. Metro: Plaça de la Universitat.

This is a regular staple on Barcelona's gay circuit, with at least one bar, a dance floor, provocative art, and a clientele whose percentage of gay women has greatly increased in the past several years. Open nightly from 11pm to 3am.

MORE ENTERTAINMENT

MOVIES   Recent cinematic releases from Paris, New York, Rome, Hollywood, and even Madrid come quickly to Barcelona, where an avid audience often waits in long lines for tickets. Most foreign films are dubbed into Catalán, unless they're indicated as *VO* (original version). Movie listings are published in the *Guía de Ocio,* available at any newsstand along Les Rambles.

If you're a movie buff, the best time to be in Barcelona is June and early July for the annual film festival.

A CASINO   Midway between the coastal resorts of Sitges and Villanueva, about 25 miles (40km) southwest of Barcelona and about 2 miles (3km) north of Sitges, stands the **Gran Casino de Barcelona,** Sant Pere (San Pedro) de Ribes (☎ **93/893-36-66**). The major casino in all of Catalonia, it's housed in a villa originally built during the 1800s. Elegant, with gardens, it attracts restaurant clients as well as gamblers. A set menu in the restaurant (reservations recommended) costs 5,000 ptas. ($40). For admission to the casino, you'll pay 550 ptas. ($4.40) and must show your passport. The casino is open year-round, Sunday to Thursday from 5pm to 4am and on Friday and Saturday from 5pm to 5am.

14 Easy Excursions

Major 1-day excursions include the monastery of Montserrat, the Penedés vineyards, and the canonical church in Cardona. Among other popular stopovers are the resorts north of Barcelona along the Costa Brava, which are covered extensively in *Frommer's Spain,* 17th Edition.

MONTSERRAT

35 miles (56km) NW of Barcelona, 368 miles (592km) E of Madrid

Montserrat, sitting atop an impressive 4,000-foot mountain 7 miles (11km) long and $3^1/2$ miles (5.5km) wide, is one of the most important pilgrimage spots in Spain, ranking with Zaragoza and Santiago de Compostela. Thousands travel here every year to see and touch the 12th-century statue of La Moreneta (The Black Virgin), the patron saint of Catalonia. So many newly married couples flock here for her blessings that Montserrat has become Spain's Niagara Falls.

ESSENTIALS

GETTING THERE   **By Train**   The best and most exciting way to go is via the Catalán railway—**Ferrocarrils de la Generalitat de Catalunya** (Manresa line), with

five trains a day leaving from Plaça d'Espanya in Barcelona. The central office is at Plaça de Catalunya, 1 (☎ **93/205-15-15**). The train connects with an aerial cableway (Aeri de Montserrat), included in the rail passage. Expect to spend 1,635 ptas. ($13.10), including the funicular.

By Bus   The train with its funicular tie-in has taken over as the preferred means of transport. However, at certain times long-distance bus service is provided by **Autocars Julià,** on Carrer Viriato (☎ **93/490-40-00**), in Barcelona. Daily service from Barcelona to Montserrat is generally operated, with departures near Estacio Central de Barcelona-Sants, at Plaça de Països Catalanes. The bus departs at 9am and returns to Barcelona at 5pm.

By Car   Take A-2 southwest of Barcelona toward Tarragona, turning west at the junction with N-II. The signs and exit to Montserrat will be on your right. From the main road, it's 9 miles (14.5km) up to the monastery through dramatic, eerie rock formations.

VISITOR INFORMATION   The **tourist information office** is at Plaça de la Creu (☎ **93/835-02-51**). It's open from 10am to 1:45pm and 3 to 5:30pm.

WHEN TO GO   Avoid visiting Montserrat on Sunday, if possible. Thousands of locals pour in then, especially if the weather is nice. Remember that the winds blow cold at Montserrat. Even in summer, visitors should take along warm sweaters, jackets, or coats. In winter, thermal underwear might not be a bad idea.

WHAT TO SEE & DO

The 50-member ✪ *Escolanía* (boys' choir) is one of the oldest and most renowned in Europe, dating from the 13th century. At 1pm daily you can hear them singing *Salve Regina* and the *Virolai* (hymn of Montserrat) in the **Basilica Santuari de Nostra Senyora de Montserrat.** The basilica is open daily from 8 to 10:30am and noon to 6:30pm and admission is free. To view the 12th- or 13th-century Black Virgin statue, enter the church through a side door to the right. At Plaça de Santa María you can also visit the **Museu de Montserrat,** known for its collection of ecclesiastical paintings, including works by Caravaggio and El Greco. Modern Spanish and Catalán artists are also represented (see Picasso's early *El Viejo Pescador,* dating from 1895). Works by Dalí and such French impressionists as Monet, Sisley, and Degas are also shown. The collection of biblical artifacts is also interesting; look for the crocodile mummy, at least 2,000 years old. Charging 400 ptas. ($3.20) admission, the museum is open daily from 10:30am to 2pm and 3 to 6pm.

The 9-minute funicular ride to the 4,119-foot-high peak, **Sant Jeroni,** makes for an exciting trip. The funicular operates April to October, daily about every 20 minutes from 10am to 6:40pm. The cost is 700 ptas. ($5.60) round-trip. From the top you'll see not only the whole of Catalonia but also the Pyrenees and the islands of Majorca and Ibiza.

You can also make an excursion to the **Santa Cova (Holy Grotto),** the alleged site of the discovery of the Black Virgin. The grotto dates from the 17th century and was built in the shape of a cross. Many famous Catalán artists, such as Puig i Cadafalch and Gaudí, exhibited religious works on the road to the shrine. You go halfway by funicular but must complete the trip on foot.

The chapel is open April to October, daily from 9am to 6:30pm; off-season, daily from 10am to 5:30pm. The funicular operates April to October only, daily every 15 minutes from 10am to 7pm, charging 300 ptas. ($2.40) round-trip.

WHERE TO STAY & DINE

Few people spend the night here, but most visitors will want at least one meal. If you don't want to spend a lot, purchase a picnic lunch in Barcelona or ask your hotel to pack a meal.

Abat Cisneros. Plaça de Monestir, 08691 Montserrat. ☎ **93/835-02-01.** Fax 93/828-40-06. 41 rms. TV TEL. 7,700 ptas. ($61.60) double. AE, DC, MC, V. Parking 300 ptas. ($2.40).

Set on the main square of Montserrat, this is a well-maintained, modern hotel with few pretensions and a history of family management dating back to 1958. The bedrooms are simple, clean, and well maintained. The in-house restaurant serves fixed-price meals for around 2,675 ptas. ($21.40) per person. The hotel's name is derived from a title given to the head of any Benedictine monastery during the Middle Ages.

PENEDÉS WINERIES

From the Penedés wineries comes the famous cava (Catalán champagne), which can be sampled in the champagne bars of Barcelona. You can see where this wine originates by journeying 25 miles (40km) from Barcelona via highway A-2, Exit 27. There are also daily trains to Sant Sadurní d'Anoia, home to 66 cava firms. Trains depart from Barcelona Sants.

The firm best equipped to receive visitors is **Codorníu** (☎ **93/818-32-32**), the largest producer of cava (some 40 million bottles a year). Codorníu is ideally visited by car because of unreliable public transportation. However, it's sometimes possible to get a taxi from the station at Sant Sadurní d'Anoia.

Groups are welcomed at Codorníu (but there must be at least four people present before a tour is conducted). It's not necessary to make an appointment before showing up. Tours are presented in English, among other languages, and take 1 $^1/_2$ hours; they visit some of the 10 miles (16km) of underground cellars by electric cart (take a sweater, even on a hot day). A former pressing section has been turned into a museum, exhibiting wine-making instruments through the ages. The museum is housed in a building designed by the great *modernismo* architect Puig i Cadafalch.

King Juan Carlos has declared the plant a national historic and artistic monument. The tour ends with a cava tasting. Tours are conducted Monday to Friday at 8am, 12:30pm, and 3:45pm. Call the number above for more information. The ideal time for a visit is for the autumn grape harvest. Codorníu is closed in August.

CARDONA

60 miles (97km) NW of Barcelona

Another popular excursion from Barcelona is to Cardona, 60 miles away. Take N-II west, then head north on C-1411 to Manresa. Cardona, reached along C-1410, lies 20 miles (32km) northwest of Manresa.

The home of the dukes of Cardona, the town is known for its canonical church, **Sant Vicenç de Cardona,** placed inside the walls of the castle. The church was consecrated in 1040. The great Catalán architect Josep Puig i Cadafalch wrote, "There are few elements in Catalán architecture of the 12th century that cannot be found in Cardona, and nowhere better harmonized." The church reflects the Lombard style of architecture. The castle (now the parador—see below) was the most important fortress in Catalonia.

WHERE TO STAY & DINE

Parador Nacional Duques de Cardona. Castillo de Carona, s/n, 08261 Cardona. ☎ **93/869-12-75.** Fax 93/869-16-36. 56 rms, 2 suites. A/C TV TEL. 9,000–12,000 ptas. ($72–$96) double; 13,765–17,600 ptas. ($110.10–$140.80) suite. AE, DC, MC, V. Free parking.

Sitting atop a cone-shaped mountain that towers 330 feet above Cardona, this restored castle opened as a four-star parador in 1976. Once the seat of Ludovici Pio (Louis the Pious) and a stronghold against the Moors, it was later expanded and strengthened by Guifré el Pilós (Wilfred the Hairy). In the 9th century the palace went to Don Ramón Folch, nephew of Charlemagne. The massive fortress castle proved impregnable to all but the inroads of time, and several ancient buildings in this hilltop complex have been restored and made part of the parador.

The spacious accommodations, some with minibars, are furnished with hand-carved wooden canopied beds and woven bedspreads and curtains. The bedrooms command panoramic views. The public rooms are decorated with antique furniture, tapestries, and paintings from various periods. The bar is in a former castle dungeon, with meals served in the lone stone-arched medieval dining room where the counts once took their repasts. Offered on the menu are regional dishes costing 3,200 ptas. ($25.60) for a complete meal. Try the Catalán bouillabaisse, accompanied by wines whose taste would be familiar to the Romans. Service is daily from 1 to 4pm and 8 to 10:30pm.

5 Settling into Madrid

Madrid was conceived, planned, and built when Spain was at the peak of its confidence and power, the solid and severely dignified seat of a great empire that stretched around the world. It's a monumental city that glitters almost as much as Paris, Rome, or London. Although the city lacks the spectacular Romanesque or Gothic monuments that pepper the landscape of older Spanish cities, it never fails to convey a sense of raw and rarely subtle power.

Madrid has the highest altitude of any European capital, with a climate that's blisteringly hot in summer but often quite cold in winter. Traffic roars down wide, exhaust-polluted boulevards that stretch for miles—from the narrow streets of the city's historic 17th-century core to the ugly concrete suburbs that have mushroomed in recent years.

Most striking is how the city has blossomed since Franco's demise. Madrid was at the forefront of *la movida* (the movement), Spain's drive to resuscitate its artistic tradition after years of creative repression. More world-class art is concentrated in the neighborhood around the stellar Prado than in virtually any equivalent area in the world: the Caravaggios and Rembrandts at the Thyssen-Bornemisza; the El Grecos and Velázquezes at the Prado itself; and the Dalís and Mirós—not to mention Picasso's wrenching *Guernica*—at the Reina Sofia. Ironically, much of the city's art was collected by 18th-century Spanish monarchs whose artistic sense was frequently more astute than their political savvy.

Regrettably, within the city limits you'll also find sprawling expanses of concrete towers, sometimes paralyzing traffic, a growing incidence of street crime, and entire districts that, as in every other metropolis, bear virtually no historic or cultural interest for a temporary visitor. So, seek out the city's gems: the opulent grandeur of the Palacio Real, the uncontained bustle of El Rastro's flea market, the sultry fever of late-night flamenco. And when urban bustle starts to overwhelm, seek respite in the Parque del Retiro, a vast, verdant oasis in the heart of the city.

If your time in Spain is limited, a stopover in Madrid—coupled with day trips to its environs—can provide a primer in virtually every major period and school of Spanish art and architecture dating back to the Roman occupation. At least nine world-class destinations are less than 100 miles away; for more information on these day trips, see Chapter 7, "Easy Excursions from Madrid."

1 Orientation

ARRIVING

BY PLANE Lying 9 miles east of the center, **Barajas** (☎ **91/305-83-43** for airport information), Madrid's international airport, has two terminals—one international, the other domestic. A conveyor belt connects the two.

Air-conditioned yellow airport buses take you from the arrival terminal to the bus depot under Plaza de Colón. You can also get off at stops along the way, provided that your baggage isn't stored in the hold. The buses leave every 15 minutes, either to or from the airport.

If you go into town by taxi, expect to pay 2,500 ptas. ($20) and up, plus surcharges (in either direction), for the trip and for baggage handling. If you take an unmetered limousine, negotiate the price in advance.

BY TRAIN Madrid has three major railway stations: **Atocha,** at Avenida Ciudad de Barcelona (metro: Atocha RENFE), for trains to Lisbon, Toledo, Andalusia, and Extremadura; **Chamartín,** in the northern suburbs at Augustín de Foxá (metro: Chamartín), for trains to and from Barcelona, Asturias, Cantabria, Castille-León, the Basque country, Aragón, Catalonia, Levante (Valencia), Murcia, and the French frontier; and **Estación Príncipe Pío** or Norte, at Paseo del Rey, 30 (metro: Príncipe Pío), for trains to and from northwest Spain (Salamanca and Galicia).

For information about connections from any of these stations, or for rail tickets, contact the principal office of **RENFE** (Spanish Railways), Alcalá, 44 (☎ **91/328-90-20;** metro: Banco de España). The office is open Monday to Friday from 9am to 8pm, but the information phone is manned daily from 7am to 11pm.

BY BUS Madrid has at least eight major bus terminals, including the large **Estación Sur de Autobuses,** Calle Canarias, 17 (☎ **91/468-45-11;** metro: Palos de la Frontera). Most buses pass through this station.

BY CAR All highways in Spain radiate outward from Madrid. The accompanying table shows the major highways into Madrid, with information on driving distances to the city:

Highways to Madrid

Route	From	Distance to Madrid
N-I	Irún	315 miles (505km)
N-II	Barcelona	389 miles (622km)
N-III	Valencia	217 miles (347km)
N-IV	Cádiz	388 miles (621km)
N-V	Badajoz	254 miles (406km)
N-VI	Galicia	374 miles (598km)

VISITOR INFORMATION

The most convenient tourist office is on the ground floor of the 40-story **Torre de Madrid,** Plaza de España (☎ **91/541-23-25;** metro: Plaza de España), open Monday to Friday from 9am to 7pm and on Saturday from 9:30am to 1:30pm. Ask for a street map of the next town on your itinerary, especially if you're driving. The staff here can give you a list of hotels and hostals but cannot recommend any particular establishment.

CITY LAYOUT

In modern Spain all roads, rails, and telephone lines lead to Madrid. The capital has outgrown all previous boundaries and is branching out in all directions.

MAIN ARTERIES & SQUARES Every new arrival must find the **Gran Vía,** which cuts a winding pathway across the city beginning at **Plaza de España,** where you'll find one of Europe's tallest skyscrapers, the Edificio España. On this principal avenue is the largest concentration of shops, hotels, restaurants, and movie houses in the city. **Calle de Serrano** is a runner-up.

South of the avenue lies the **Puerta del Sol.** All road distances within Spain are measured from this square. However, its significance has declined, and today it's a prime hunting ground for pickpockets and purse snatchers. Here **Calle de Alcalá** begins and runs for $2^{1}/_{2}$ miles.

Plaza Mayor is the heart of Old Madrid, an attraction in itself with its mix of French and Georgian architecture. (Again, be wary, especially late at night.) Pedestrians pass under the arches of the huge square onto the narrow streets of the old town, where you can find some of the capital's most intriguing restaurants and tascas, serving tasty tapas with drinks. On the colonnaded ground level of the plaza are shops, many selling souvenir hats of turn-of-the-century Spanish sailors or army officers.

The area south of Plaza Mayor—known as *barrios bajos*—merits exploration. The narrow cobblestone streets are lined with 16th- and 17th-century architecture. Directly south of the plaza is **Arco de Cuchilleros,** a street packed with markets, restaurants, flamenco clubs, and taverns.

The Gran Vía ends at Calle de Alcalá, and at this juncture lies **Plaza de la Cibeles,** with its fountain to Cybele, "the mother of the gods," and what has become known as "the cathedral of post offices." From Cibeles, the wide **Paseo de Recoletos** begins a short run to **Plaza de Colón.** From this latter square rolls the serpentine **Paseo de la Castellana,** flanked by expensive shops, apartment buildings, luxury hotels, and foreign embassies.

Back at Cibeles again: Heading south is **Paseo del Prado,** where you'll find Spain's major attraction, the Museo del Prado, as well as the Jardín Botánica (Botanical Garden). The *paseo* also leads to the Atocha Railway Station. To the west of the garden lies the **Parque del Retiro,** once reserved for royalty, with restaurants, nightclubs, a rose garden, and two lakes.

FINDING AN ADDRESS Madrid is a city of grand boulevards that extend for long distances and cramped meandering streets that seem to follow no plan. Finding an address can sometimes be a problem, primarily because of the way buildings are numbered.

On most streets the numbering begins on one side and runs consecutively until the end, then it resumes on the other side, going in the opposite direction, rather as a farmer plows a field—up one side, down the other. Thus, no. 50 could be opposite no. 250. But there are many exceptions to this system of numbering. That's why it's important that you know the cross street as well as the number of the address you're looking for. To complicate matters, some addresses don't have a number at all. What they have instead is the designation *s/n,* meaning *sin número* (without number). For example, the address of the Panteón de Goya (Goya's Tomb) is Glorieta de San Antonio de la Florida, s/n (see Chapter 6, "Madrid Attractions"). Note also that in Spain, as in many other European countries, the building number comes after the street name.

STREET MAPS Arm yourself with a good map before setting out. The best is published by **Falk,** and it's available at most newsstands and kiosks in Madrid. Those given away free by tourist offices and hotels aren't adequate, as they don't list the maze of little streets.

Neighborhoods In Brief

Madrid can be divided into three principal districts: Old Madrid, which holds the most tourist interest; Ensanche, the new district, often with the best shops and hotels; and the periphery, which is of little interest to visitors.

Plaza Mayor / Puerta del Sol This is the heart of Old Madrid, often called "the tourist zone." Filled with taverns and bars, it's bounded by Carrera de San Jerónimo, Calle Mayor, Cava de San Miguel, Cava Baja, and Calle de la Cruz. From Plaza Mayor, Arco de Cuchilleros is filled with Castilian restaurants and taverns; more *cuevas* lie along Cava de San Miguel, Cava Alta, and Cava Baja. To the west of this old district is the Manzanares River. Muslim Madrid centers on the present-day Palacio de Oriente and Las Vistillas. What is now Plaza de la Paja was the heart of the city and its main marketplace during the medieval and Christian period. In 1617 Plaza Mayor became the hub of Madrid, and it remains the nighttime center of tourist activity, more so than the Puerta del Sol.

The Salamanca Quarter Ever since Madrid's city walls came tumbling down in the 1860s, the district of Salamanca to the north has been a fashionable address. Cutting through it is Calle de Serrano, a street lined with stores and boutiques. The U.S. Embassy is also here.

Gran Vía / Plaza de España The Gran Vía is the city's main street, lined with cinemas, department stores, and the headquarters of banks and corporations. It begins at Plaza de España, with its bronze figures of Don Quixote and his faithful squire, Sancho Panza.

Argüelles/Moncloa The university area is bounded by Pintor Rosales, Cea Bermúdez, Bravo Murillo, San Bernardo, and Conde Duque. Students haunt its famous ale houses.

Chueca This is an old and decaying area north of the Gran Vía. Its main streets are Hortaleza, Infantas, Barquillo, and San Lucas. It's the center of gay nightlife, with many clubs and cheap restaurants. It can be dangerous at night, however, although the police presence has increased.

Castellana / Recoletos / Paseo del Prado Not a real city district, this is Madrid's north-south axis, its name changing along the way. The Museo del Prado and some of the city's more expensive hotels are found here. Many restaurants and other hotels are located along its side streets. In summer the several open-air terraces are filled with animated crowds. The most famous café is the Gran Café Gijón (see "Dining," later in this chapter).

2 Getting Around

Getting around Madrid isn't easy, because everything is spread out. Even many Madrileño taxi drivers, often new arrivals from a foreign country, are unfamiliar with their own city once they're off the main boulevards.

BY SUBWAY The metro system is easy to learn. The central converging point is the Puerta del Sol. The metro operates from 6am to 1:30am. Avoid rush hours. For

Madrid Metro

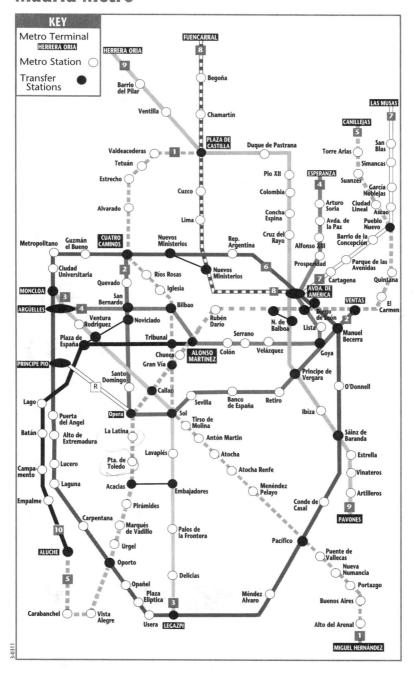

information, call **91/552-49-00.** You can save money on public transportation by purchasing a 10-trip ticket known as a *bonos*.

BY BUS   A bus network also services the city and suburbs, with routes clearly shown at each stop on a schematic diagram. Both red and yellow buses are fast and efficient because they travel along special lanes.

You can also purchase a 10-trip ticket (but without transfers) for Madrid's bus system. It's sold at **Empresa Municipal de Transportes,** Plaza de la Cibeles (☎ **91/ 401-99-00**), where you can also purchase a guide to the bus routes. The office is open daily from 8am to 8:30pm.

BY TAXI   Even though cab fares have risen recently, they're still reasonable. When you flag down a taxi, the meter should register the basic charge, and the meter increases for every kilometer thereafter. Supplements are charged for trips to the airport, the railway station, and the bullring, as well as for trips at night and on Sunday and holidays. It's customary to tip at least 10% of the fare.

Warning: Make sure that the meter is turned on when you get into a taxi. Otherwise, some drivers will "assess" the cost of the ride, and their assessment, you can be sure, will involve higher mathematics.

Also, there are unmetered taxis that hire out for the day or the afternoon. These are legitimate, but some drivers will operate as gypsy cabs. Since they're unmetered, they can charge high rates. They're easy to avoid, though—take either a black taxi with horizontal red bands or a white one with diagonal red bands instead.

If you take a taxi outside the city limits, the driver is entitled to charge you twice the rate shown on the meter.

To call a taxi, dial **91/445-90-08** or **91/447-51-80.**

BY CAR   Driving is a nightmare and potentially dangerous in congested Madrid. It always feels like rush hour in Madrid (theoretically, rush hours are 8 to 10am, 1 to 2pm, and 4 to 6pm Monday to Saturday). Parking is next to impossible, except in expensive garages. About the only time you can drive around Madrid with a minimum of hassle is in hot August, when thousands of Madrileños have taken their automobiles and headed for Spain's vacation oases. Save your car rentals (see "Fast Facts: Madrid," below) for 1-day excursions from the capital. If you drive into Madrid from another city, ask at your hotel for the nearest garage or parking facility and park your vehicle there until you're ready to leave.

BY BICYCLE   Ever wonder why you see so few people riding bicycles in Madrid? Those who tried were overcome by the traffic pollution. It's better to walk.

ON FOOT   This is the perfect way to see Madrid, especially the ancient narrow streets of the old town. If you're going to another district—and chances are that your hotel will be outside the old town—you can take the bus or metro. For such a large city, Madrid can be covered amazingly well on foot, because so much of what will interest a visitor lies in various clusters.

FAST FACTS: Madrid

American Express   For your mail or banking needs, you can go to the American Express office at Plaza de las Cortes, 2, at the corner of Marqués de Cubas and across the street from the Palace Hotel (☎ 91/322-55-00; metro: Gran Vía). It's open Monday to Friday from 9am to 5:30pm and on Saturday from 9am to noon.

Area Code   For phone calls within Spain, Madrid's area code is **91.** If you're calling from the United States, dial 011, the country code (34), Madrid's city code (1), and then the local number.

Bookstores   Turner's, at Genova, 3 and 5 (☎ 91/319-28-67; metro: Alonso Martinez), has one of the largest collections of English-language books in the city, as well as a good selection of Spanish CDs. Open Monday to Friday from 10am to 8pm and on Saturday from 10am to 2pm.

Car Rentals   Should you want to rent a car while in Madrid, you'll have several choices. In addition to the Avis office at Barajas Airport (☎ 91/305-42-73), the main office downtown is at Gran Vía, 60 (☎ 91/348-03-48). Hertz, too, has an office at Barajas Airport (☎ 91/305-84-52) and another in the heart of Madrid in the Edificio España, Gran Vía, 88 (☎ 91/542-58-05). Budget Rent-a-Car maintains its headquarters at Gran Vía, 49 (☎ 91/401-12-54).

Crime   See "Safety," below.

Currency Exchange   The currency exchange at Chamartín railway station (metro: Chamartín) is open 24 hours and gives the best rates in the capital. If you exchange money at a bank, ask about the minimum commission charged.

Dentist   For an English-speaking dentist, contact the U.S. Embassy, Serrano, 75 (☎ 91/587-22-00); it maintains a list of dentists who have offered their services to Americans abroad. For dental services, you can also consult Unidad Médica Anglo-Americana, Conde de Arandá, 1 (☎ 91/435-18-23), in back of Plaza de Colón. Office hours are Monday to Friday from 9am to 8pm and on Saturday from 10am to 1pm, and there's a 24-hour daily answering service.

Doctor   For an English-speaking doctor, contact the U.S. Embassy, Serrano, 75 (☎ 91/587-22-00).

Drugstores   For a late-night pharmacy, dial 098 or look in the daily newspaper under "Farmacias de Guardia" to learn what drugstores are open after 8pm. Another way to find out is go to any pharmacy, even if it's closed—it will always post a list of nearby pharmacies that are open late that day. Madrid contains hundreds of pharmacies, but one of the most central is the Farmacia Gayoso, Arenal, 2 (☎ 91/521-28-60; metro: Puerta del Sol), open Monday to Saturday, 24 hours a day.

Embassies/Consulates   If you lose your passport, fall seriously ill, get into legal trouble, or have some other serious problem, your embassy or consulate will probably have the means to provide assistance. These are the Madrid addresses and hours: The Embassy of the **United States,** at Calle Serrano, 75 (☎ 91/577-40-00; metro: Núñez de Balboa), is open Monday to Friday from 9:30am to 1pm and 2:30 to 5pm. The Embassy of **Canada,** Núñez de Balboa, 35 (☎ 91/431-43-00; metro: Velázquez), is open Monday to Friday from 8:30am to 5pm. The Embassy of the **United Kingdom,** Fernando el Santo, 16 (☎ 91/319-02-00; metro: Colón), is open Monday to Friday from 9am to 2pm and 3:30 to 6pm. The **Republic of Ireland** has its embassy at Claudio Coello, 73 (☎ 91/576-35-00; metro: Serrano); it's open Monday to Friday from 10am to 2pm. The Embassy of **Australia,** Paseo de la Castellana, 143 (☎ 91/579-04-28; metro: Cuzco), is open Monday to Thursday from 8:30am to 1:30pm and 2:30 to 5pm and on Friday from 8:30am to 2pm. Citizens of **New Zealand** can go to their embassy at Plaza de la Lealtad, 2 (☎ 91/523-02-26; metro: Banco de España); it's open Monday to Friday from 9am to 1:30pm and 2:30 to 5:30pm.

Emergencies   In an emergency, to report a **fire** call 080; to reach the **police,** 091; and to call for an **ambulance,** 91/734-25-54.

Hospitals/Clinics   Unidad Médica Anglo-Americana, Conde de Arandá, 1 (☎ 91/435-18-23; metro: Usera), is not a hospital but a private outpatient clinic, offering the services of various specialists. This is not an emergency clinic, although someone on the staff is always available. The daily hours are 9am to 8pm. For a real medical emergency, call 91/734-25-54 for an ambulance.

Information   See "Visitor Information" in "Orientation," earlier in this chapter.

Laundry/Dry Cleaning   Try a self-service facility, Lavandería Donoso Cortes, Donoso Cortes, 17 (☎ 91/446-96-90; metro: Quevedo), open Monday to Friday from 9am to 7pm and on Saturday from 9am to 1pm. A good dry-cleaning service is provided by El Corte Inglés department store at Calle Preciados, 3 (☎ 91/532-18-00; metro: Callos), where the staff speaks English.

Libraries   The British Cultural Center, Almagro, 5 (☎ 91/337-35-00; metro: Alonso Martínez), has a large selection of English-language reading material. It's open Monday to Friday from 9am to 1pm and 3 to 6pm (in winter, Monday to Thursday from 9am to 7pm and on Friday from 9am to 3pm).

Luggage Storage/Lockers   These can be found at both the Atocha and Chamartín railway terminals, as well as the major bus station, the Estación Sur de Autobuses, Calle Canarias, 17 (☎ 91/468-45-11; metro: Palos de la Frontera). Storage is also provided at the air terminal underneath Plaza de Colón.

Police   In an emergency, dial **091.**

Post Office   If you don't want to receive your mail at your hotel or the American Express office, have it marked LISTA DE CORREOS and sent to the central post office in Madrid. To pick up mail, go to the window marked LISTA, where you'll be asked to show your passport. Madrid's central office is in "the cathedral of the post offices" at Plaza de la Cibeles (☎ 91/536-01-11).

Rest Rooms   Some public rest rooms are available, including those in the Parque del Retiro and on Plaza de Oriente across from the Palacio Real. Otherwise, you can always go into a bar or tasca, but you should order something. The major department stores, such as Galerías Preciados and El Corte Inglés, have good, clean rest rooms.

Safety   Because of an increasing crime rate in Madrid, the U.S. Embassy has warned visitors to leave valuables in a hotel safe or other secure place when going out. Your passport may be needed, however, as the police often stop foreigners for identification checks. The embassy advises against carrying purses and suggests that you keep valuables in front pockets and carry only enough cash for the day's needs. Be aware of those around you and keep a separate record of your passport number, traveler's check numbers, and credit/charge-card numbers.

Purse snatching is common, and the criminals often work in pairs, grabbing purses from pedestrians, from cyclists, and even from cars. A popular scam involves one miscreant's smearing the back of the victim's clothing, perhaps with mustard, ice cream, or something worse. An accomplice pretends to help clean up the mess while picking all the victim's pockets.

Every car can be a target, whether parked or just stopped at a light, so don't leave anything in sight in your car. If your vehicle is standing still, a thief may open the door or break a window in order to snatch a purse or package, even from under the seat. Place all your valuables in the trunk when you park and always assume that someone is watching you to see whether you're putting something away for safe-keeping. Keep the car locked while you're driving.

Taxes   There are no special city taxes for tourists, except for the VAT (central government tax; known as IVA in Spain) levied nationwide on all goods and services, ranging from 7% to 33%. For information on how to recover VAT, see "Shopping" in Chapter 6.

Taxis   See "Getting Around," earlier in this chapter.

Telephone   If you don't speak Spanish, you'll find it easier to telephone from your hotel, but remember that this is often very expensive because hotels impose a surcharge on every operator-assisted call. In some cases this can be as high as 40% or more. On the street, phone booths (known as *cabinas*), have dialing instructions in English; you can make locals calls by inserting a 25-pta. coin (20¢) for 3 minutes. In Spain many smaller establishments, especially bars, discos, and a few low-cost restaurants, don't have phones. For long-distance calls, especially transatlantic ones, it may be best to go to the main telephone exchange, Locutorio Gran Vía, Gran Vía, 30; or Locutorio Recoletos, Paseo de Recoletos, 37–41. You may not be lucky enough to find an English-speaking operator, but you can fill out a simple form that will facilitate the placement of your call.

Transit Information   For metro information, call 91/552-49-00.

3 Best Hotel Bets

- **Best Historic Hotel:** Inaugurated by Alfonso XIII in 1910, the **Ritz** (☎ **800/ 225-5843** in the U.S. and Canada, or 91/521-28-57), this gathering place of Madrid society, is still the capital's leading luxury hotel. This Edwardian grandee is mellower than ever before, the old haughtiness of former managements gone with the wind—it long ago rescinded its policy of not allowing movie stars as guests. The rich and famous continue to parade through its portals; today in the lobby you're likely to encounter virtually anyone, from the secretary-general of NATO to Paloma Picasso.

- **Best Hotel for Business Travelers:** The concierge at the **Park Hyatt Villa Magna** (☎ **800/223-1234** in North America, or 91/587-12-34) is one of the most skillful in Madrid, well versed in procuring virtually anything a traveler could conceivably need during a trip to the Spanish capital. One floor below lobby level, this five-star hotel's business center is well stocked with access to translators, word processors, fax machines, and photocopiers. There's a branch of Hertz car rental on the premises, and enough stylish conference rooms (staffed with butlers and stocked with caviar if the nature of your business meeting calls for it) to provide a venue for virtually any sales or executive meeting; limousines with drivers are available.

- **Best for a Romantic Getaway:** The **Santo Mauro Hotel** (☎ **91/319-69-00**) opened in 1991 in a villa built in 1894 for the duke of Santo Mauro. The lavish property has an ageless grace, although it's been brought up to a state-of-the-art condition. In good weather guests retreat to a beautiful garden pavilion and enjoy many facilities such as a gym and indoor pool. It's resortlike in nature, although situated in Madrid. If you can afford it, go for one of the suites with a fireplace.

- **Best Trendy Hotel:** A former rundown apartment house, the **Hotel Destiny Villa Real** (☎ **91/420-37-67**) has blossomed into a fashionable address, opposite the Cortes and next to the Palace Hotel. This is a 19th-century building of classic French architecture. Some of the town's most important movers and shakers can be found in the cocktail bar. A chic rendezvous patronized by the cognoscenti of Spain, it's where you'd invite the duchess of Alba for tea.

- **Best Lobby for Pretending You're Rich:** The **Palace Hotel** (☎ **800/325-3535** in the U.S., 800/325-3589 in Canada, or 91/429-75-51), between the Prado and the Cortes, is a Victorian wedding cake of a place. To sit and people-watch in this lobby—the grandest belle époque lobby in Madrid—is to be at the epicenter of Spanish political life. Head for the dazzling stained-glass cupola of the main rotunda lounge, and take in the fanciful ceiling frescoes and the custom-made carpets along the way.

- **Best for Families:** Family friendly, the chain-run **Novotel** (☎ **800/221-4542** in the U.S. and Canada, or 91/405-46-00) on the outskirts of town is a good place for the whole family. Rates are reasonable, and the bedrooms can easily be arranged to sleep children. There's also a pool, and the breakfast buffet is one of the most generous in Madrid. Children 15 and under stay free in their parents' room.

- **Best Moderately Priced Hotel:** Built in 1966 and still going strong, the reasonably priced **Gran Hotel Colón** (☎ **91/573-59-00**) lies west of Retiro Park in a relatively safe area of Madrid that's easily connected to the center by subway. It's well maintained and kept up-to-date, offering some well-designed bedrooms with comfortably traditional furnishings.

- **Best Budget Hotel:** The **Hostal Cervantes** (☎ **91/429-27-45**) is a family-run hotel that has long been a favorite with Frommer readers. Reached by a tiny birdcage-style elevator, the hostal is conveniently located near such fabled and pricey citadels as the Palace Hotel. But here rates are amazingly reasonable. True, it's a bit spartan and no breakfast is served, but for the location and the price it's virtually unbeatable.

- **Best B&B:** Of the numerous budget accommodations housed in a single 19th-century building on the Gran Vía (the main street of Madrid), the **Hostal-Residencia Continental** (☎ **91/521-46-40**) is the best. Located on the building's third and fourth floors, this long-established B&B has comfortable, tidy, and recently renovated rooms.

- **Best Service:** There are grander hotels in Madrid, but it's hard to find a staff as highly motivated, professional, and efficient as the one at the **Castellana Inter-Continental Hotel** (☎ **800/327-0200** in the U.S., or 91/310-02-00). Room service is offered around the clock, and the staff seems adept at solving your Madrid-related problems. Nothing seems to make them lose their cool, even when there's a line at the desk.

- **Best Location:** The **Gran Hotel Reina Victoria** (☎ **91/531-45-00**) is for those who want to be in the heartbeat of Old Madrid, within easy walking distance of all those midtown Hemingway haunts. Dozens of the finest tapas bars are virtually at your doorstep, and you can walk among the flower vendors, cigarette peddlers, and lottery ticket hawkers, enjoying an atmosphere that's missing from the newer and more modern section of Madrid.

- **Best Health Club:** The **Hotel Ritz** (☎ **800/225-5843** in the U.S. and Canada, or 91/521-28-57) is not only the most historic hotel in Madrid, but it's got a state-of-the-art fitness center on its top floor. The 1,727-square-foot gym overlooks the Prado Museum, Los Jerónimos Church, and the tree-lined Paseo del Prado. All Ritz guests have complimentary use of most of the center's services and facilities, which include English-speaking professional trainers, the latest exercise equipment, hot saunas, UVA rays, dressing rooms, showers, lockers, and an outside jogging trail that's open March to October.

- **Best Hotel Pool:** The swimming pool at the **Meliá Castilla** (☎ **800/336-3542** in the U.S., or 91/567-50-00) isn't the largest in Madrid, but because of the hotel's location (in the heart of the city's business district), and because it's an oasis of good service and greenery in an otherwise congested neighborhood, it's a favorite. Set in the center of the hotel's courtyard, with 15 carefully manicured stories that rise around it, it offers cool refreshments from the nearby bar, snacks and platters from the nearby restaurant, and a welcome calm and quiet after a day navigating through the crowds of central Madrid. It's open only to residents of the hotel from April to October.
- **Best Views:** Often called the Waldorf-Astoria of Spain, the 26-story **Hotel Plaza** (☎ **91/547-12-00**) has been one of Madrid's massive landmarks since 1953. From its bedroom windows you'll have views of the city skyline. Try for one of the units on the eighth floor with a balcony.

4 Accommodations

Madrid's hotels, though expensive, are among the finest in the world. The city's much-maligned reputation, earned in the days of Franco, is but a distant, unpleasant memory: no more rooms last renovated in 1870 or food that tastes of acidic olive oil left over from the Spanish-American War.

More than 50,000 hotel rooms blanket the city—from *grand luxe* bedchambers fit for a prince to bunker-style beds in the hundreds of neighborhood *hostales* and *pensiones* (low-cost boardinghouses). Three-quarters of our recommendations are modern, yet many guests prefer the landmarks of yesteryear, including those grand old establishments, the Ritz and the Palace (ca. 1910–12). But beware: Many older hostelries in Madrid haven't kept abreast of the times; a handful haven't added improvements or overhauled bedrooms substantially since the 1960s.

Traditionally, hotels are clustered around the Atocha Railway Station and the Gran Vía. In our search for the most outstanding hotels, we've almost ignored these two popular, but noisy, districts. The newer hotels have been built away from the center, especially on residential streets jutting off from Paseo de la Castellana. Bargain seekers, however, will still find great pickings in the Atocha district and along the Gran Vía.

RESERVATIONS   Most hotels require at least a day's deposit before they will reserve a room for you. Preferably, this can be accomplished with an international money order or, if agreed to in advance, with a personal check or credit/charge-card number. You can usually cancel a room reservation 1 week ahead of time and get a full refund. A few hotelkeepers will return your money 3 days before the reservation date, but some will take your deposit and never return it, even if you cancel far in advance. Many budget hotel owners operate on such a narrow margin of profit that they find just buying stamps for airmail replies too expensive by their standards. Therefore it's most important that you enclose a prepaid International Reply Coupon with your payment, especially if you're writing to a budget hotel. Better yet, call and speak to the hotel of your choice or send a fax.

If you're booking into a chain hotel, such as a Hyatt or a Forte, you can call toll free in North America and easily make reservations over the phone. Whenever such a service is available, toll-free numbers are indicated in the individual hotel descriptions.

If you arrive without a reservation, begin your search for a room as early in the day as possible. If you arrive late at night, you have to take what you can get, often for a much higher price than you'd like to pay.

A Note on Making Hotel Reservations: The telephone area code for Madrid is 91 if you're calling from within Spain. If you're calling from the United States, dial 011, the country code (34), Madrid's city code (1), and then the local number.

PRICE CLASSIFICATIONS   The following prices are for double rooms with private bath. Hotels rated **Very Expensive** charge 30,000 ptas. ($240) and up for a double, although some establishments in this bracket, including the Villa Magna, the Santo Mauro, and the Ritz, can ask twice that price. Hotels judged **Expensive** charge 17,000 to 30,000 ptas. ($136 to $240) for a double, and **Moderate** hotels—at least moderate in the sense of Madrid's hotel price scale—charge from a low of 10,000 ptas. ($80) to a high of 17,300 ptas. ($138.40) for a double. Hotels considered **Inexpensive**—again, by Madrid's pricing standards—ask 10,000 ptas. ($80) or less for a double.

Note: All hotels in the "Very Expensive" and "Expensive" categories include private bath with their guest rooms unless otherwise specified. Hotels in the other categories may or may not include bath, and that information is supplied for each entry. Also, breakfast is not included in the quoted rates unless otherwise specified. A 7% government room tax is added to all rates.

RATINGS   Spain officially rates its hotels by star designation, from one to five stars. Five stars is the highest rating in Spain, signaling a deluxe establishment complete with all the amenities and the high tariffs associated with such accommodations.

Most of the establishments recommended in this guide are three- and four-star hotels falling into that vague "middle-bracket" category. Hotels granted one and two stars, as well as pensions (guesthouses), are far less comfortable, with limited plumbing and other physical facilities, although they may be perfectly clean and decent places. The latter category is strictly for dedicated budgeters.

PARKING   As mentioned, this is a serious problem, as so few hotels have garages; many buildings turned into hotels were constructed before the invention of the automobile. Street parking is rarely available, and even if it is, you run the risk of having your car broken into. If you're driving into Madrid, most hotels (or most police) will allow you to park in front of the hotel long enough to unload your luggage. Someone on the staff will pinpoint the location of the nearest garage in the neighborhood, often giving you a map showing the way. In instances where a hotel has its own parking, charges are given.

NEAR PLAZA DE LAS CORTÉS
VERY EXPENSIVE

✪ **Hotel Villa Real.** Plaza de las Cortes, 10, 28014 Madrid. ☎ **91/420-37-67.** Fax 91/420-25-47. 115 rms, 19 suites. A/C MINIBAR TV TEL. 34,400 ptas. ($275.20) double; 65,000 ptas. ($520) suite. Rates include breakfast. AE, DC, MC, V. Parking 1,600 ptas. ($12.80). Metro: Plaza de la Cibeles.

Until 1989 the Villa Real was little more than a rundown 19th-century apartment house auspiciously located across a three-sided park from the Spanish parliament (Congreso de los Diputados) between Puerta del Sol and Paseo del Prado. Its developers poured billions of pesetas into renovations to produce a stylish hotel today patronized by the cognoscenti of Spain. The eclectic facade combines an odd mixture of neoclassical and Aztec motifs; footmen and doormen dressed in uniforms of buff and forest green are stationed out front. The Villa Real's rooms are more consistent in quality than those offered by its neighbor, the Palace (see below), which can have very good or very bad rooms. But the Villa Real lacks the mellow charm and patina of the Palace. The interior contains a scattering of modern paintings amid neoclassical moldings and details.

Accommodations in Central Madrid

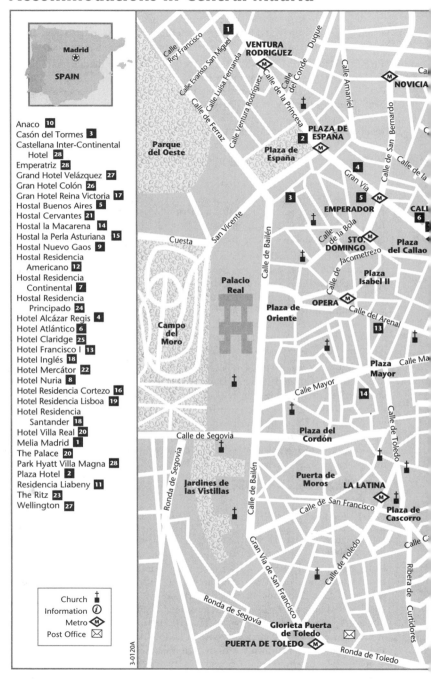

Anaco **10**
Casón del Tormes **3**
Castellana Inter-Continental
    Hotel **28**
Emperatriz **28**
Grand Hotel Velázquez **27**
Gran Hotel Colón **26**
Gran Hotel Reina Victoria **17**
Hostal Buenos Aires **5**
Hostal Cervantes **21**
Hostal la Macarena **14**
Hostal la Perla Asturiana **15**
Hostal Nuevo Gaos **9**
Hostal Residencia
    Americano **12**
Hostal Residencia
    Continental **7**
Hostal Residencia
    Principado **24**
Hotel Alcázar Regis **4**
Hotel Atlántico **6**
Hotel Claridge **25**
Hotel Francisco I **13**
Hotel Inglés **18**
Hotel Mercátor **22**
Hotel Nuria **8**
Hotel Residencia Cortezo **16**
Hotel Residencia Lisboa **19**
Hotel Residencia
    Santander **18**
Hotel Villa Real **20**
Melia Madrid **1**
The Palace **20**
Park Hyatt Villa Magna **28**
Plaza Hotel **2**
Residencia Liabeny **11**
The Ritz **23**
Wellington **27**

Church ✝
Information ⓘ
Metro Ⓜ
Post Office ✉

3-0120A

136

Each of the accommodations offers a TV with video movies and satellite reception, a safe for valuables, soundproofing, a sunken salon filled with leather-upholstered furniture, and built-in furniture accented with burlwood inlays.

Dining/Entertainment: The social center is the high-ceilinged formal bar. The hotel's formal restaurant, Europa, serves both lunch and dinner, with meals consisting of a Spanish and international cuisine.

Services: Room service (24 hours), laundry/valet, baby-sitting, express checkout.

Facilities: Sauna, foreign currency exchange, business center.

Palace. Plaza de las Cortes, 7, 28014 Madrid. ☎ **800/325-3535** in the U.S., 800/325-3589 in Canada, or 91/429-75-51. Fax 91/429-86-55. 424 rms, 31 suites. A/C MINIBAR TV TEL. 40,000–46,000 ptas. ($320–$368) double; 75,000–175,000 ptas. ($600–$1,400) suite. AE, DC, MC, V. Parking 2,300 ptas. ($18.40). Metro: Banco de España.

The Palace, an ornate Victorian wedding cake, is known as the "grand *dueña*" of Spanish hotels. The establishment had an auspicious beginning, inaugurated by Alfonso XIII in 1912. Covering an entire city block, it faces the Prado and Neptune Fountain, in the historic and artistic area, within walking distance of the main shopping center and the best antiques shops. Some of the city's most intriguing tascas and restaurants are only a short stroll away.

Architecturally, the Palace captures the grand pre–World War I hotel style, with an emphasis on space and comfort. But it doesn't achieve the snobby appeal and chic of its nearby sibling, the Ritz (under the same management), or even of the Villa Real. Even though it's one of the largest hotels in Madrid, it retains first-class service. The hotel is air-conditioned with a formal, traditional lobby. The rooms are also conservative and traditional, boasting plenty of space and large bathrooms with lots of amenities. As was the style when the hotel was built, the accommodations vary widely, with the best rooms on the fourth, fifth, and sixth floors. The noisy rooms are on the side; they also lack views. Many rooms appear not to have been renovated for two decades or so.

Dining/Entertainment: The elegant dining choice is La Cupola, serving Italian specialties along with some of the more famous dishes of the Spanish cuisine. Piano music and other entertainment are featured.

Services: Room service (24 hours), laundry/valet, baby-sitting, express checkout.

Facilities: Foreign currency exchange, business center.

INEXPENSIVE

Ⓢ **Hostal Cervantes.** Cervantes, 34, 28014 Madrid. ☎ **91/429-27-45.** 12 rms. 6,000 ptas. ($48) double. No credit cards. Metro: Banco de España.

One of Madrid's most pleasant family-run hotels, the Cervantes has been widely appreciated by our readers for years. You'll take a tiny birdcage-style elevator to the immaculately maintained second floor of this stone-and-brick building. Each accommodation contains a bed and spartan furniture. No breakfast is served, but the owners, the Alfonsos, will direct you to a nearby café. The establishment is convenient to the Prado, Retiro Park, and the older sections of Madrid.

NEAR PLAZA DE ESPAÑA
EXPENSIVE

Plaza Hotel. Plaza de España, 8, 28013 Madrid. ☎ **91/547-12-00.** Fax 91/548-23-89. 231 rms, 75 suites. A/C MINIBAR TV TEL. 21,200 ptas. ($169.60) double; from 25,600 ptas. ($204.80) suite. AE, DC, MC, V. Parking 2,500 ptas. ($20). Metro: Plaza de España.

Atop a city garage, the Plaza Hotel, built in 1953, could be called the Waldorf-Astoria of Spain. A massive rose-and-white structure, it soars upward to a central tower that's

26 stories tall. It's a landmark visible for miles around and one of the tallest sky-scrapers in Europe. Once one of the best hotels in Spain, the Plaza has declined in recent years in spite of a 1992 renovation. It's aging and a bit dreary, and not at all in the same class as the hotels previously recommended. The hotel's accommodations include conventional doubles as well as luxurious suites, each of which contains a sitting room and abundant amenities. Each accommodation, regardless of its size, has a marble bathroom. The furniture is usually of a standardized modern style, in harmonized colors. The quieter rooms are on the upper floors.

Dining/Entertainment: The Azalea Restaurant offers either buffet or à la carte dining, and the Express Bar provides a complete buffet breakfast—even a "diet corner." There's also a piano bar.

Service: Room service, laundry, money exchange, medical service, hairdresser.

Facilities: Shopping arcade.

MODERATE

Casón del Tormes. Calle del Río, 7, 28013 Madrid. ☎ **91/541-97-46.** Fax 91/541-18-52. 63 rms. A/C TV TEL. 12,000 ptas. ($96) double; 15,300 ptas. ($122.40) triple. MC, V. Parking 1,200 ptas. ($9.60). Metro: Plaza de España.

The attractive three-star Casón del Tormes is around the corner from the Royal Palace and Plaza de España. Set behind a four-story red-brick facade with stone-trimmed windows, it overlooks a quiet one-way street. The long, narrow lobby contains vertical wooden paneling, a marble floor, and a bar opening into a separate room. The bedrooms are not spectacular, but generally roomy and comfortable. Motorists appreciate the public parking lot near the hotel. Laundry service is provided.

ON OR NEAR THE GRAN VÍA
MODERATE

Hotel Atlántico. Gran Vía, 38, 28013 Madrid. ☎ **800/528-1234** in the U.S. and Canada, or 91/522-64-80. Fax 91/531-02-10. 80 rms. A/C MINIBAR TV TEL. 13,305 ptas. ($106.45) double. Rates include breakfast. AE, DC, MC, V. Metro: Gran Vía.

Refurbished in stages between the late 1980s and 1994, this hotel occupies five floors of a grand turn-of-the-century building on one of Madrid's most impressive avenues. Established in 1989 as a Best Western affiliate, it offers security boxes in relatively unadorned but well-maintained bedrooms, which have been insulated against noise. The rooms are rather small. The hotel contains an English-inspired bar serving drinks and snacks that's open 24 hours a day. Don't judge the hotel by its rather bleak check-in area or the rather shabby third-floor lounge.

Residencia Liabeny. Salud, 3, 28013 Madrid. ☎ **91/531-90-00.** Fax 91/532-74-21. 224 rms. A/C MINIBAR TV TEL. 9,600–14,000 ptas. ($76.80–$112) double; 16,000–21,000 ptas. ($128–$168) triple. AE, MC, V. Parking 1,400 ptas. ($11.20). Metro: Puerta del Sol, Callao, or Gran Vía.

This hotel, behind a stone-sheathed, austere rectangular facade, is in a prime location midway between the tourist highlights of the Gran Vía and the Puerta del Sol. Named after the original owner of the hotel, it contains seven floors of comfortable, contemporary bedrooms, which even though newly redecorated are a bit too pristine for our taste. The cocktail bar is more warming, although in a rather macho style, and the dining room is strictly for convenience. A coffee shop is also on the premises, and good laundry service and rather personalized attention from the staff add to the allure of the place.

INEXPENSIVE

Anaco. Tres Cruces, 3, 28013 Madrid. ☎ **91/522-46-04.** Fax 91/531-64-84. 39 rms. A/C TV TEL. 9,000–9,500 ptas. ($72–$76) double; 10,500–12,000 ptas. ($84–$96) triple. AE, DC, MC, V. Metro: Gran Vía, Callao, or Puerta del Sol.

A modest yet modern hotel, the Anaco is just off the main shopping thoroughfare, the Gran Vía. Opening onto a tree-shaded plaza, it attracts those seeking a clean resting place. The bedrooms are compact and contemporary, with built-in headboards, reading lamps, and lounge chairs. A useful tip: Ask for one of the five terraced rooms on the top floor, which rent at no extra charge. The hotel has a bar/cafeteria/restaurant open daily. English is spoken here. Nearby is a municipally operated garage.

Hostal Buenos Aires. Gran Vía, 61, 28013 Madrid. ☎ **91/542-01-02.** Fax 91/542-28-69. 25 rms. A/C TV TEL. 7,000 ptas. ($56) double. AE, DC, MC, V. Metro: Plaza de España. Bus: 1, 2, or 44.

To reach this place, you pass through a marble-covered street-floor lobby in a 1955 building, then take the elevator to the second floor. The hostal occupies two floors. One of its best features is a wood-sheathed café/bar that's open 24 hours a day. The bedrooms are comfortable, modern, and clean, although a bit small, with safety deposit boxes, balconies, and hair dryers.

Hostal Nuevo Gaos. Calle Mesonero Romanos, 14, 28013 Madrid. ☎ **91/532-71-07.** Fax 91/522-70-98. 23 rms. A/C MINIBAR TV TEL. 6,200–7,500 ptas. ($49.60–$60) double. AE, DC, MC, V. Metro: Callao. Bus: 1, 2, or 44.

On the second, third, and fourth floors of a 1930s building just off the Gran Vía, this residencia offers guests the chance to enjoy a comfortable standard of living at moderate rates. The place lies directly north of the Puerta del Sol, across the street from the popular flamenco club Torre Bermejas. Breakfast can be taken at a nearby café.

⑤ Hostal Residencia Continental. Gran Vía, 44, 28013 Madrid. ☎ **91/521-46-40.** Fax 91/521-46-49. 29 rms. TV TEL. 5,000 ptas. ($40) double. AE, DC, MC, V. Metro: Callao. Bus: 1, 2, 36, or 46.

Sprawling over the third and fourth floors of Gran Vía, 44, this hostal is a bit more expensive than the other accommodations in the building, but the rooms are comfortable, tidy, and renovated. The desk clerk speaks English. The Continental is in a virtual "casa of budget hotels," a 19th-century building filled exclusively with small hotels and pensions. If no room is available at the Continental, you can ring the doorbells of the other establishments because this "house of hotels" is a good bet for the budget tourist. No breakfast is served.

Hotel Alcázar Regis. Gran Vía, 61, 28013 Madrid. ☎ **91/547-93-17.** 25 rms, none with bath. 5,500 ptas. ($44) double; 7,000 ptas. ($56) triple. AE. Metro: Plaza de España or Santo Domingo.

Conveniently located in the midst of Madrid's best shops is this post–World War II building, complete with a circular Greek-style temple as its crown. On the building's fifth floor you'll find long and pleasant public rooms, wood paneling, leaded-glass windows, parquet floors, crystal chandeliers, and high-ceilinged guest rooms, each with hot and cold running water.

Hotel Nuria. Fuencarral, 52, 28004 Madrid. ☎ **91/531-92-08.** Fax 91/532-90-05. 80 rms. TV TEL. 6,200–6,350 ptas. ($49.60–$50.80) double. Rates include breakfast. AE, DC, MC, V. Metro: Gran Vía or Tribunal. Bus: 3, 7, or 40.

The Hotel Nuria, just 3 blocks from the Gran Vía, has some bedrooms with especially interesting views of the capital. Furnishings are simple and functional. A bar, restaurant, and TV lounge are available to guests. The hotel was last renovated in 1986.

NEAR THE PUERTA DEL SOL
EXPENSIVE

Gran Hotel Reina Victoria. Plaza Santa Ana, 14, 28012 Madrid. ☎ **91/531-45-00.** Fax 91/522-03-07. 197 rms, 4 suites. A/C MINIBAR TV TEL. From 21,900 ptas. ($175.20) double; from 55,100 ptas. ($440.80) suite. Rates include breakfast. AE, DC, MC, V. Parking 1,700 ptas. ($13.60). Metro: Tirso de Molina or Puerta del Sol.

This establishment is about as important to the legends of Madrid as the famous bullfighter Manolete himself. He used to stay here, giving lavish parties in one of the reception rooms and attracting mobs in the square below when he went out on his balcony for morning coffee. Since the recent renovation and upgrading of this property by Spain's Tryp Hotel Group, it's less staid and more impressive than ever.

Originally built in 1923 and named after the grandmother of the present king of Spain, Juan Carlos, the hotel sits behind an ornate and eclectic stone facade, which the Spanish government protects as a historic monument. Although it's located in a congested and noisy neighborhood in the center of town, the Reina Victoria opens onto its own sloping plaza, once a meeting place for 17th-century intellectuals. Today the area is usually filled with flower vendors, seniors reclining in the mid-afternoon sun, and young people resting between bouts at the dozens of neighborhood tapas bars.

Each of the hotel's bedrooms contains sound-resistant insulation, a safe for valuables, and a private bathroom with many amenities.

Dining/Entertainment: Guests enjoy the hotel's stylish and popular lobby bar, the Manuel Gonzalez Manolete; the lavishly displayed bullfighting memorabilia and potent drinks add another attraction to an already memorable hotel. The in-house restaurant is El Ruedo.

Services: Concierge, room service (24 hours), baby-sitting.

Facilities: Because of the hotel's position in one of Madrid's most interesting neighborhoods, almost anything is available within a few minutes' walk.

INEXPENSIVE

Ⓢ Hostal la Macarena. Cava de San Miguel, 8, 28005 Madrid. ☎ **91/365-92-21.** Fax 91/364-27-57. 18 rms. TEL. 6,000 ptas. ($48) double; 7,500 ptas. ($60) triple; 8,000 ptas. ($64) quad. MC, V. Metro: Puerta del Sol, Opera, or La Latina.

Known for its reasonable prices and praised by readers for the warmth of its reception, this unpretentious, clean hostal is run by the Ricardo González family. Its 19th-century facade, accented with belle époque patterns, stands in ornate contrast to the chiseled simplicity of the ancient buildings facing it. The location is one of the hostal's assets: It's on a street (admittedly, a noisy one) immediately behind Plaza Mayor, near one of the best clusters of tascas in Madrid. Windows facing the street have double panes.

Hostal la Perla Asturiana. Plaza de Santa Cruz, 3, 28012 Madrid. ☎ **91/366-46-00.** Fax 91/366-46-08. 33 rms. TV TEL. 4,900 ptas. ($39.20) double; 7,000 ptas. ($56) triple. AE, DC, MC, V. Metro: Puerta del Sol.

Ideal for those who want to stay in the heart of Old Madrid (1 block off Plaza Mayor and 2 blocks from the Puerta del Sol), this small family-run establishment has a courteous staff member at the desk 24 hours a day for security and convenience. You can socialize in the small, comfortable lobby that's adjacent to the reception desk. The bedrooms are clean and simple, but often cramped, with fresh towels supplied daily. Many inexpensive restaurants and tapas bars are nearby. No breakfast is served.

Hostal Residencia Americano. Puerta del Sol, 11, 28013 Madrid. ☎ **91/522-28-22.** 43 rms. TV TEL. 4,700 ptas. ($37.60) double; 7,000 ptas. ($56) triple; 8,000 ptas. ($64) quad. No credit cards. Metro: Puerta del Sol.

The Hostal Residencia Americano, on the third floor of a five-story building, is suitable for those who want to be in the Puerta del Sol. Owner/manager A. V. Franceschi has refurbished all the guest rooms, most of them outside chambers with balconies facing the street. Mr. Franceschi promises hot and cold running water 24 hours a day. No breakfast is served.

Ⓢ **Hostal Residencia Principado.** Zorrilla, 7, 28014 Madrid. ☎ **91/429-81-87.** 15 rms. TV. 5,800 ptas. ($46.40) double. AE, MC, V. Metro: Sevilla or Banco de España. Bus: 5, 9, or 53.

The two-star Hostal-Residencia Principado is a real find. Located in a well-kept town house, it's run by a gracious owner, who keeps everything clean and inviting. New tiles, attractive bedspreads, and curtains give the guest rooms a fresh look. Safety deposit boxes are provided. For breakfast you can go to a nearby café. English is spoken.

Hotel Francisco I. Arenal, 15, 28013 Madrid. ☎ **91/548-43-14.** Fax 91/542-28-99. 58 rms. TV TEL. 9,700 ptas. ($77.60) double. Rates include breakfast. MC, V. Metro: Puerta del Sol or Ópera.

Here you can rent modern, clean rooms. There's a pleasant lounge and a bar, and on the sixth floor you'll find a comfortable, rustically decorated restaurant. The hotel was considerably modernized in 1993, with the addition of new bathrooms as well as air conditioning in most of the bedrooms. The hotel provides 24-hour room service and laundry and valet service.

Ⓢ **Hotel Inglés.** Calle Echegaray, 8, 28014 Madrid. ☎ **91/429-65-51.** Fax 91/420-24-23. 50 rms, 8 suites. TV TEL. 10,000 ptas. ($80) double; 13,600 ptas. ($108.80) suite. AE, DC, MC, V. Parking 1,200 ptas. ($9.60). Metro: Puerta del Sol or Sevilla.

You'll find the Hotel Inglés on a central street lined with tascas, although the hotel operates its own 24-hour cafeteria. It's more modern and impersonal than it was when Virginia Woolf made it her address in Madrid. Behind its red-brick facade you'll find unpretentious and contemporary bedrooms, all well maintained. The comfortable armchairs in the TV lounge are likely to be filled with avid soccer fans. The lobby is air-conditioned, although the guest rooms are not. Guests who open their windows at night are likely to hear noise from the enclosed courtyard, so light sleepers beware.

Hotel Residencia Lisboa. Ventura de la Vega, 17, 28014 Madrid. ☎ **91/429-98-94.** Fax 91/369-41-96. 27 rms. 6,000 ptas. ($48) double. AE, DC, MC, V. Metro: Puerta del Sol.

The Lisboa, on Madrid's most famous restaurant street, can be a bit noisy, but that's our only complaint. The hotel is a neat, modernized town house with compact rooms and central heating in the cooler months. The staff members speak five languages. The Lisboa does not serve breakfast, but it's surrounded by budget dining rooms, cafés, and tascas.

Hotel Residencia Santander. Calle Echegaray, 1, 28014 Madrid. ☎ **91/429-95-51.** 38 rms. TEL. 7,000 ptas. ($56) double. MC, V. Metro: Puerta del Sol.

A snug little hotel just off the Puerta del Sol, the Santander is a refurbished 1930 house with adequate rooms, some of which contain TVs. Although it's on a teeming street, you might appreciate the nonstop local atmosphere. Restaurants and bars in the area are active day and night. No breakfast is served.

NEAR ATOCHA STATION
MODERATE

Hotel Mercátor. Calle Atocha, 123, 28012 Madrid. ☎ **91/429-05-00.** Fax 91/369-12-52. 89 rms, 3 suites. MINIBAR TV TEL. 11,350 ptas. ($90.80) double; 12,750 ptas. ($102) suite. AE, DC, MC, V. Parking 1,320 ptas. ($10.55). Metro: Atocha or Antón Martín.

Only a 3-minute walk from the Prado, Centro de Arte Reina Sofía, and the Thyssen-Bornemisza Museum, the Mercátor draws a clientele seeking a good hotel—orderly, well run, and clean, with enough comforts and conveniences to please the weary traveler. The public rooms are simple, outfitted in a vaguely modern type of minimalism. Some of the guest rooms are more inviting than others, especially those with desks and armchairs. And 21 rooms are air-conditioned. The Mercátor is a *residencia*—that is, it offers breakfast only and does not have a formal restaurant for lunch and dinner; however, it has a bar and cafeteria serving light meals, such as *platos combinados* (combination plates). The hotel has a garage and is within walking distance of American Express. Laundry service is provided, plus room service from 7am to 10pm.

INEXPENSIVE

Hotel Residencia Cortezo. Doctor Cortezo, 3, 28012 Madrid. ☎ **91/369-01-01.** Fax 91/369-37-74. 86 rms, 4 suites. A/C MINIBAR TV TEL. 10,000 ptas. ($80) double; 14,750 ptas. ($118) suite. AE, MC, V. Parking 1,000 ptas. ($8). Metro: Tirso de Molina.

Just off Calle de Atocha, which leads to the railroad station of the same name, the Cortezo is a short walk from Plaza Mayor and the Puerta del Sol. The accommodations are comfortable but very simply furnished, with contemporary baths. The beds are springy, the colors are well chosen, and the furniture is pleasantly modern; often there's a sitting area with a desk and armchair. The public rooms match the guest rooms in freshness. The hotel was built in 1959 and last renovated in 1989.

NEAR RETIRO/SALAMANCA
VERY EXPENSIVE

✪ **Park Hyatt Villa Magna.** Paseo de la Castellana, 22, 28046 Madrid. ☎ **800/223-1234** in the U.S. and Canada, or 91/587-12-34. Fax 91/431-22-86. 164 rms, 18 suites. A/C MINIBAR TV TEL. 42,000 ptas. ($336) double; from 78,000 ptas. ($624) suite. AE, DC, MC, V. 2-night weekend package available for 40,000 ptas. ($320) double. Parking 2,000 ptas. ($16). Metro: Rubén Darío.

One of the finest hotels in Europe, the nine-story Park Hyatt is faced with slabs of rose-colored granite and set behind a bank of pines and laurels on the city's most fashionable boulevard. It was already a supremely comfortable and elegant modern hotel when Hyatt International took over its management in 1990. Today it's an even finer choice than the Palace or the Villa Real and is matched in luxury, ambience, and tranquillity only by the Ritz (see below), which has a greater patina because it's much older.

It was originally conceived when a handful of Spain's elite teamed up to create a setting in which their special friends, along with an array of discriminating international visitors, would be pleased to live and dine. They hired an architect, imported a French decorator (whose style is a contemporary version of neoclassicism), planted gardens, and put the staff through an intensive training program.

Separated from the busy boulevard by a parklike garden, its facade has contemporary lines. In contrast, its interior recaptures the style of Carlos IV, with paneled walls, marble floors, and bouquets of fresh flowers. Through the lobby and drawing rooms passes almost every film star shooting on location in Spain.

This luxury palace has plush but dignified bedrooms decorated in Louis XVI, English Regency, or Italian provincial style. Each comes with fresh flowers and a TV with video movies and satellite reception (including news broadcasts beamed in from the United States).

Dining/Entertainment: A pianist provides entertainment in the lobby-level champagne bar. The in-house restaurant, the Berceo, serves international food in a glamorous setting. The hotel is known for its summer terraces, Calalú and Berceo, set in gardens. One of them, Calalú, is the only terrace in Madrid where you can enjoy live jazz, performed Tuesday to Saturday.

Services: Concierge, room service (24 hours), same-day laundry and dry cleaning, limousine service, baby-sitting.

Facilities: Business center, car rentals, barber and beauty shop, the boutique "Villa Magna," availability of both tennis and golf (15 and 25 minutes from the hotel, respectively).

✪ **Ritz.** Plaza de la Lealtad, 5, 28014 Madrid. ☎ **800/225-5843** in the U.S. and Canada, or 91/521-28-57. Fax 91/532-87-76. 154 rms, 29 suites. A/C MINIBAR TV TEL. 52,000–63,500 ptas. ($416–$508) double; 92,500–185,000 ptas. ($740–$1,480) suite. AE, DC, MC, V. Parking 2,000 ptas. ($16). Metro: Banco de España.

An international rendezvous point of legendary renown, the Ritz is the most famous hotel in Spain and the most prestigious address in Madrid. Its name has appeared countless times in the Spanish-language tabloids that document the comings and goings of its glamorous guests. Encased in a turn-of-the-century shell of soaring ceilings and graceful columns, it contains all the luxuries and special attentions that world travelers have come to expect of a grand hotel. Billions of pesetas have been spent on renovations since its acquisition in the 1980s by the British-based Forte chain. The result is a bastion of glamour where, despite modernization, great effort was expended to retain the hotel's belle époque character and architectural details.

No other Madrid hotel, except for the Palace, has a more varied history. One of Les Grands Hôtels Européens, the Ritz was built at the command of Alfonso XIII, with the aid of César Ritz, in 1908. It looks out onto the circular Plaza de la Lealtad in the center of town, near the 300-acre Retiro Park, facing the Prado, the adjacent Palacio de Villahermosa, and the Stock Exchange. The Ritz was constructed when costs were relatively low and when spaciousness, luxury, and comfort were the standard. Its facade has been designated a historic monument.

The bedrooms contain fresh flowers, well-accessorized marble bathrooms, and TVs with video movies and satellite reception.

Dining/Entertainment: The hotel maintains a formal dining room decorated in shades of cream, blue, and gold, which is lined with mirrors and 16th-century Flemish tapestries. Chefs present an international menu featuring a paella that's the most elaborate in Madrid. In time-honored Spanish tradition, guests tend to dress up here, sometimes even for breakfast. (Management stresses that this is not a resort hotel.) Guests looking for a more casual eatery usually head for the Jardín Ritz.

Services: Room service (24 hours) with everything from good nutty Jabugo ham to fresh hake, laundry/valet, express checkout.

Facilities: Fitness center, car-rental kiosk, business center, foreign currency exchange.

Wellington. Velázquez, 8, 28001 Madrid. ☎ **91/575-44-00.** Fax 91/576-41-64. 280 rms, 10 suites. A/C MINIBAR TV TEL. 33,250 ptas. ($266) double; from 48,500 ptas. ($388) suite. AE, DC, MC, V. Parking 2,200 ptas. ($17.60). Metro: Retiro or Velázquez.

The Wellington, with its somber antique-tapestried entrance, is one of Madrid's more sedate deluxe hotels, built in the mid-1950s but substantially remodeled since, although the atmosphere remains heavy. Set in the Salamanca residential area near Retiro Park, the Wellington offers redecorated but rather staid guest rooms, each with cable TV and movie channels, music, two phones (one in the bathroom), and a guest-operated combination safe. Units are furnished in English-inspired mahogany reproductions, and the bathrooms (one per accommodation) are modern and immaculate, with marble sheathing and fixtures. Doubles with private terraces (at no extra charge) are the most sought-after accommodations. This is the major bullfighter hotel of Madrid. On bullfight days camp followers show up.

Dining/Entertainment: An added bonus here is the El Fogón grill room, styled like a 19th-century tavern, where many of the provisions for the typically Spanish dishes are shipped in from the hotel's own ranch. The pub-style Bar Inglés is a hospitable rendezvous. Lighter meals are served in the Las Llaves de Oro (Golden Keys) cafeteria.

Services: Room service (24 hours), same-day dry cleaning and laundry.

Facilities: Outdoor swimming pool in summer, garage, beauty parlor.

EXPENSIVE

Emperatriz. López de Hoyos, 4, 28006 Madrid. ☎ **91/563-80-88.** Fax 91/563-98-04. 153 rms, 5 suites. A/C MINIBAR TV TEL. 24,000 ptas. ($192) double; 60,000 ptas. ($480) suite. AE, DC, MC, V. Parking 1,500 ptas. ($12) nearby. Metro: Rubén Darío.

This hotel lies just off the wide Paseo de Castellana, only a short walk from some of Madrid's most deluxe hotels, but it charges relatively reasonable rates. Built in the 1970s, it was last renovated in 1995, although the bedrooms remain much finer than the rather dowdy public rooms. The guest rooms are comfortable and classically styled, with TVs that receive many different European channels. If one is available, ask for a room on the seventh floor, where you'll get a private terrace at no extra charge. On the premises are a beauty salon, a barbershop, and well-upholstered lounges, where you're likely to meet fellow globe-trotting Americans. Laundry and valet service are provided.

Grand Hotel Velázquez. Calle de Velázquez, 62, 28001 Madrid. ☎ **91/575-28-00.** Fax 91/575-28-09. 71 rms, 75 suites. A/C MINIBAR TV TEL. 21,970 ptas. ($175.75) double; from 29,160 ptas. ($233.30) suite. AE, DC, MC, V. Parking 1,700 ptas. ($13.60). Metro: Retiro.

Opened in 1947 on an affluent residential street near the center of town, this hotel has a 1930s-style art deco facade and a 1940s interior filled with well-upholstered furniture and richly grained paneling. Several public rooms lead off a central oval area; one of them includes a bar. As in many hotels of its era, the bedrooms vary; some are large enough for entertaining, with a small but separate sitting area for reading or watching TV. All contain piped-in music. This is one of the most attractive medium-size hotels in Madrid, with plenty of comfort and convenience. The in-house restaurant, Las Lanzas, features both international and Spanish cuisine. Parking is available on the premises.

Novotel Madrid. Calle Albacete, 1 (at Avenida Badajos), 28027 Madrid. ☎ **800/221-4542** in the U.S. and Canada, or 91/405-46-00. Fax 91/404-11-05. 236 rms. A/C MINIBAR TV TEL. 17,500 ptas. ($140) double. Special weekend rate of 13,800 ptas. ($110.40) double. Children 15 and under stay free in parents' room. AE, DC, MC, V. Free parking. Metro: Concepción. Exit from M-30 at Barrio de la Concepción / Parque de las Avenidas, just before reaching the city limits of central Madrid, then look for the chain's trademark electric-blue signs.

This Novotel was originally intended to serve the hotel needs of a cluster of multinational corporations with headquarters $1\frac{1}{2}$ miles east of the center of Madrid, but its guest rooms are so comfortable and its prices so reasonable that tourists have begun using it as well. Opened in 1986, it's located on the highway, away from

👫 Family-Friendly Hotels

Meliá Castilla *(see p. 149)*   Children can spend hours and all that extra energy in the hotel's swimming pool and gymnasium. On the grounds is a showroom exhibiting the latest European automobiles. Hotel services include baby-sitting, providing fun for kids and parents too.

Novotel Madrid *(see p. 145)*   Children 15 and under stay free in their parents' room, where the sofa converts into a comfortable bed. Kids delight in the open-air swimming pool and the offerings of the bountiful breakfast buffet.

Tirol *(see p. 151)*   This centrally located three-star hotel is a favorite of families seeking good comfort at moderate price. It also has a cafeteria.

the maze of sometimes-confusing inner-city streets, which makes it attractive to motorists.

The bedrooms are laid out in a standardized format whose popularity in Europe has made it one of the hotel industry's most notable success stories. Each contains a well-designed bathroom, in-house movies, a radio, a TV, and soundproofing. The sofas, once their bolster pillows are removed, can be transformed into comfortable beds where children can sleep. The English-speaking staff is well versed in both sightseeing attractions and solutions to most business-related problems.

MODERATE

Gran Hotel Colón. Pez Volador, 11, 28007 Madrid. ☎ **91/573-59-00.** Fax 91/573-08-09. 380 rms. A/C MINIBAR TV TEL. 17,600 ptas. ($140.80) double. AE, DC, MC, V. Parking 1,500 ptas. ($12). Metro: Sainz de Baranda.

East of Retiro Park, the Gran Hotel Colón is a few minutes from the city center by subway. Built in 1966, it offers comfortable yet moderately priced accommodations in one of Madrid's modern hotel structures. More than half the accommodations have private balconies, and all contain comfortably traditional furniture, much of it built-in.

Other assets include two dining rooms, a covered garage, and Bingo games. One of the Colón's founders was an accomplished interior designer, which accounts for the unusual stained-glass windows and murals in the public rooms and the paintings by Spanish artists in the lounge.

Hotel Claridge. Plaza Conde de Casal, 6, 28007 Madrid. ☎ **91/551-94-00.** Fax 91/501-03-85. 148 rms, 2 suites. A/C TV TEL. 14,950 ptas. ($119.60) double; 19,000 ptas. ($152) suite. AE, MC, V. Free parking. Metro: Conde Casal.

This contemporary building, last renovated in 1994, is beyond Retiro Park, about 5 minutes from the Prado by taxi or subway. The bedrooms are well organized and pleasantly styled: small and compact, with coordinated furnishings and colors. You can take your meals in the hotel's cafeteria and also relax in the modern lounge.

CHAMBERÍ
VERY EXPENSIVE

Castellana Inter-Continental Hotel. Paseo de la Castellana, 49, 28046 Madrid. ☎ **800/327-0200** in the U.S., or 91/310-02-00. Fax 91/319-58-53. 270 rms, 35 suites. A/C MINIBAR TV TEL. 41,000–47,000 ptas. ($328–$376) double; from 76,500 ptas. ($612) suite. AE, DC, MC, V. Parking 2,100 ptas. ($16.80). Metro: Rubén Darío.

Solid, spacious, and conservatively modern, this is one of Madrid's more reliable hotels. Originally built in 1963 as the (then) most prestigious hotel on this famous boulevard, the Castellana Inter-Continental lies behind a barrier of trees in a neighborhood of apartment houses and luxury hotels. Its high-ceilinged public rooms provide a welcome refuge from the Madrileño heat. They're a tribute to the art of Spanish masonry, with terrazzo floors and a large-scale collection of angular abstract murals pieced together from multicolored stones and tiles. Most of the accommodations have private balconies and traditional furniture, each with a color TV with in-house videos and many channels beamed in from across Europe. Some rooms are in need of rejuvenation.

Dining/Entertainment: The La Ronda Bar offers drinks near the elegant Los Continentes Restaurant, serving both a creative and Mediterranean cuisine. In addition, El Jardín is a retreat in summer, with candlelit dinners and live soft background music. Good cookery and low prices are found at El Sarracín, yet another restaurant.

Services: Concierge and travel agent (who will book theater tickets, rental cars, and airline connections), room service (24 hours), laundry, baby-sitting.

Facilities: Kiosks and boutiques, hairdresser/barbershop, business center, top-floor gym with sauna and outdoor solarium.

Miguel Angel. Miguel Angel, 29–31, 28010 Madrid. ☎ **91/442-81-99.** Fax 91/442-53-20. 278 rms, 26 suites. A/C MINIBAR TV TEL. 35,700–42,500 ptas. ($285.60–$340) double; 42,400–105,000 ptas. ($339.20–$840) suite. AE, DC, MC, V. Parking 1,800 ptas. ($14.40). Metro: Rubén Darío.

Just off Paseo de la Castellana, the Miguel Angel, sleekly modern, opened its doors in 1975 and has been renovated and kept up-to-date periodically ever since. It has much going for it—ideal location, contemporary styling, good furnishings and art objects, an efficient staff, and plenty of comfort. Behind its facade is an expansive sun terrace on several levels, with clusters of garden furniture surrounded by paintings of semitropical scenes.

The soundproof bedrooms contain radios, TVs, color-coordinated fabrics and carpets, and in many cases reproductions of classic Iberian furniture.

Dining/Entertainment: The Farnesio bar is decorated in a Spanish Victorian style, and piano music is played beginning at 8pm. A well-managed restaurant on the premises is the Florencia. Dinner is also served until around 3am in the Zacarias boîte restaurant, where you can dine while watching an occasional cabaret or musical performance.

Services: Room service (24 hours), same-day laundry/valet.

Facilities: Indoor heated swimming pool, saunas, hairdressers, drugstore; art exhibitions are sponsored in the arcade of boutiques.

۞ Santo Mauro Hotel. Calle Zurbano, 36, 28010 Madrid. ☎ **91/319-6900.** Fax 91/308-54-17. 31 rms, 6 suites. A/C MINIBAR TV TEL. 44,000 ptas. ($352) double; from 49,000 ptas. ($392) suite. AE, DC, MC, V. Parking 1,950 ptas. ($15.60). Metro: Rubén Darío or Alonso Martínez.

This hotel opened in 1991 within the once-decrepit neoclassical walls of a villa that was originally built in 1894 for the duke of Santo Mauro. Set in a garden and reminiscent of the kind of architecture you'd expect to find in France, it contains a mixture of rich fabrics and art deco art and furnishings. Staff members outnumber rooms by two to one. Each of the bedrooms contains an audio system with a wide choice of tapes and CDs as well as many coordinated decor notes, which may include curtains of raw silk, Persian carpets, and jewel-toned colors.

Dining/Entertainment: The Belagua Restaurant is reviewed separately (see "Dining," later in this chapter). An elegant bar is located off the main lobby, and tables are set up beneath the garden's large trees for drinks and snacks.

Services: Room service (24 hours), laundry/valet, reception staff trained in the pro-curement of practically anything.

Facilities: Indoor swimming pool, health club with sauna and massage.

MODERATE

Conde Duque. Plaza Conde Valle de Súchil, 5, 28015 Madrid. ☎ **91/447-70-00.** Fax 91/448-35-69. 136 rms, 7 suites. A/C MINIBAR TV TEL. 18,200–22,850 ptas. ($145.60–$182.80) double; from 30,600 ptas. ($244.80) suite. Rates include breakfast. AE, DC, MC, V. Metro: San Bernardo.

The modern three-star Conde Duque, near a branch of the Galerías Preciados de-partment store, opens onto a tree-filled plaza in a residential neighborhood that's near the Glorieta Quevado. The hotel is 12 blocks north of Plaza de España, off Calle de San Bernardo, which starts at the Gran Vía. The walk to the plaza is too long, but a subway stop is nearby. Guest-room furnishings include built-in modern headboards and reproductions of 19th-century English pieces, plus bedside lights and telephones. Room service is provided 24 hours.

Hotel Escultor. Miguel Angel, 3, 28010 Madrid. ☎ **91/310-42-03.** Fax 91/319-25-84. 17 rms, 38 suites. A/C MINIBAR TV TEL. From 12,000 ptas. ($96) double; from 21,000 ptas. ($168) suite. AE, DC, MC, V. Parking 2,300 ptas. ($18.40) nearby. Metro: Rubén Darío.

Originally built in 1975, this comfortably furnished hotel provides fewer services and offers fewer facilities than others in its category, but it compensates with larger accommodations. Each guest unit has its own charm and contemporary styling—with video films, a private bathroom, and an efficient, logical layout. The hotel is fully air-conditioned, and the staff provides information about facilities in the neighborhood.

Dining/Entertainment: The hotel has a small but comfortable bar that's open nightly, and a traditional restaurant, the Señorio de Erazu, which is closed Saturday for lunch and all day Sunday.

Services: Room service (7 to 11am).

Residencia Bréton. Bréton de los Herreros, 29, 28003 Madrid. ☎ **91/442-83-00.** Fax 91/441-38-16. 55 rms, 2 suites. A/C MINIBAR TV TEL. 13,000 ptas. ($104) double; 20,000 ptas. ($160) suite. AE, DC, MC, V. Parking 1,500 ptas. ($12) nearby. Metro: Ríos Rosas.

You'll find this modern hotel, well furnished with reproductions of Iberian pieces, on a side street several blocks from Paseo de la Castellana. As a residencia, it doesn't offer a major dining room, but it does have a little bar and breakfast room adjoin-ing the reception lounge. All the guest rooms have wood-frame beds, wrought-iron electrical fixtures, wall-to-wall curtains, comfortable chairs, and ornate tilework in the bathrooms.

INEXPENSIVE

Hostal Residencia Don Diego. Calle de Velázquez, 45, 28001 Madrid. ☎ **91/435-07-60.** Fax 91/431-42-63. 58 rms. A/C TV TEL. 8,500 ptas. ($68) double; 11,475 ptas. ($91.80) triple. MC, V. Metro: Velázquez.

On the fifth floor of a building with an elevator, the Don Diego is in a combination residential/commercial neighborhood that's relatively convenient to many of the city monuments. The vestibule contains an elegant winding staircase accented with iron griffin heads supporting its balustrade. The hotel is warm and inviting, filled with leather couches and comfortable, no-nonsense angular but attractive furniture. A bar stands at the far end of the main sitting room. The hotel's cafeteria serves breakfast from 7:45 to 11am. From 7 to 11pm daily, you can also order drinks and snacks, especially sandwiches and omelets. Laundry service is provided, and room service is available daily from 8am to midnight.

CHAMARTÍN
EXPENSIVE

Cuzco. Paseo de la Castellana, 133, 28046 Madrid. ☎ **91/556-06-00.** Fax 91/556-03-72. 320 rms, 8 suites. A/C MINIBAR TV TEL. 21,600 ptas. ($172.80) double; from 28,000 ptas. ($224) suite. AE, DC, MC, V. Parking 1,800 ptas. ($14.40). Metro: Cuzco.

Popular with businesspeople and tour groups, the Cuzco lies in a commercial neighborhood of big buildings, government ministries, spacious avenues, and the main Congress Hall. The Chamartín railway station is a 10-minute walk north, so it's a popular and convenient address.

This 15-floor structure, set back from Madrid's longest boulevard, has been redecorated and modernized many times since it was completed in 1967. The architect of the Cuzco allowed for spacious bedrooms, each with a separate sitting area, video movies, and a private bathroom. The decorator provided modern furnishings and patterned rugs.

There's a bilevel snack bar and cafeteria. The lounge is a forest of marble pillars and leather armchairs, its ambience enhanced by contemporary oil paintings and tapestries. Facilities include free parking, a beauty parlor, a sauna, massage, a gymnasium, and a cocktail bar.

Eurobuilding. Calle Padre Damián, 23, 28036 Madrid. ☎ **91/345-45-00.** Fax 91/345-45-76. 420 rms, 100 suites. A/C MINIBAR TV TEL. 29,500 ptas. ($236) double; from 34,700 ptas. ($277.60) suite. AE, DC, MC, V. Parking 2,500 ptas. ($20). Metro: Cuzco.

Even while the Eurobuilding was on the drawing boards, the rumor was that this five-star sensation of white marble would provide, in the architect's words, "a new concept in deluxe hotels." It's actually two hotels linked by a courtyard, away from the city center but right in the midst of apartment houses, boutiques, nightclubs, first-class restaurants, tree-shaded squares, and the modern Madrid business world.

The more glamorous of the twin buildings is the main one, named Las Estancias de Eurobuilding; it contains only suites, all of which were recently renovated in luxurious pastel shades. Here, drinks await you in your refrigerator. Ornately carved gold-and-white beds, background music, roomwide terraces for breakfast and cocktail entertaining—all are tastefully coordinated. Across the courtyard, the neighbor Eurobuilding contains less impressive, but still very comfortable, double rooms, many with views from private balconies of the formal garden and swimming pool below. All the accommodations have TVs with video movies and satellite reception, security doors, and individual safes.

Dining/Entertainment: Le Relais Coffee Shop is suitable for a quick bite, and Le Relais Restaurant offers buffets at both breakfast and lunch. For more formal dining, La Taberna at both lunch and dinner features a selection of Spanish and international cuisine, specializing in seafood and various paella dishes.

Services: Concierge, room service (24 hours), laundry/valet, baby-sitting.

Facilities: Health club with sauna, outdoor swimming pool.

Meliá Castilla. Calle Capitán Haya, 43, 28020 Madrid. ☎ **800/336-3542** in the U.S., or 91/567-50-00. Fax 91/571-22-10. 896 rms, 14 suites. A/C MINIBAR TV TEL. 29,900 ptas. ($239.20) double; from 55,000 ptas. ($440) suite. AE, DC, MC, V. Parking 6,240 ptas. ($49.90). Metro: Cuzco.

Along with the above-recommended Palace, this mammoth hotel qualifies as one of the largest in Europe. Loaded with facilities and built primarily to accommodate huge conventions, the Meliá Castilla also caters to the needs of the individual traveler. Everything is larger than life here: You need a floor plan to direct yourself around its precincts. The lounges and pristine marble corridors are vast—there's even a landscaped garden as well as a showroom full of the latest-model cars.

Each twin-bedded room comes with a private bath, a radio, a color TV, and modern furniture. Some lower rooms are quite noisy. The Meliá Castilla is in the north of Madrid, about a block west of Paseo de la Castellana, a short drive from the Chamartín railway station.

Dining/Entertainment: The hotel has a coffee shop, a seafood restaurant, a restaurant specializing in paella and other rice dishes, cocktail lounges, and the Trinidad nightclub. In addition, there's the restaurant/show Scala Meliá Castilla.

Services: Concierge, room service (24 hours), hairdresser/barbershop, baby-sitting, laundry/valet.

Facilities: Swimming pool, shopping arcade with souvenir shops and bookstore, saunas, gymnasium, parking garage.

MODERATE

Aristos. Avenida Pío XII, 34, 28016 Madrid. ☎ **91/345-04-50.** Fax 91/345-10-23. 24 rms. A/C TV TEL. 18,000–20,500 ptas. ($144–$164) double. AE, DC, MC, V. Parking 1,500 ptas. ($12). Metro: Pío XII.

This three-star hotel is in an up-and-coming residential area of Madrid, not far from the Eurobuilding (see above). Its main advantage is a front garden where you can lounge, have a drink, or order a complete meal. The hotel's restaurant, El Chaflán, is popular with neighborhood residents. Each of the bedrooms has a small terrace and an uncomplicated collection of modern furniture.

Hotel Chamartín. Estacíon de Chamartín, 28036 Madrid. ☎ **91/323-30-87.** Fax 91/733-02-14. 378 rms, 18 suites. A/C MINIBAR TV TEL. 13,800 ptas. ($110.40) double; from 25,000 ptas. ($200) suite. AE, DC, MC, V. Parking 2,000 ptas. ($16) in nearby garage. Metro: Chamartín. Bus: 5.

This brick-sided hotel soars nine stories above the northern periphery of Madrid. It's part of the massive modern shopping complex attached to the Chamartín railway station, although once you're inside your soundproofed room, the noise of the railway station will seem far away. The owner of the building is RENFE, Spain's government railway system, but the nationwide chain that administers it is HUSA Hotels. The hotel lies 15 minutes by taxi from both the airport and the historic core of Madrid and is conveniently close to one of the capital's busiest metro stops. Especially oriented to the business traveler, the Chamartín offers a currency-exchange kiosk, a travel agency, a car-rental office, and a lobby video screen that posts the arrivals and departures of all of Chamartín's trains.

A coffee bar serves breakfast daily, and room service is available from 7am to midnight. The hotel restaurant, Cota 13, serves an international cuisine. A short walk from the hotel lobby, in the railway-station complex, are a handful of shops and movie theaters, a roller-skating rink, a disco, and ample parking.

ARGÜELLES/MONCLOA
VERY EXPENSIVE

Husa Princesa. Serrano Jover, 3, 28015 Madrid. ☎ **91/542-35-00.** Fax. 91/559-46-65. 275 rms, 12 suites. A/C TV TEL. 31,200 ptas. ($249.60) double; from 61,500 ptas. ($492) suite. AE, DC, MC, V. Parking 3,000 ptas. ($24). Metro: Argüelles.

Originally built during the mid-1970s and radically renovated after its takeover in 1991 by the nationwide chain HUSA, the Princesa is a sprawling hotel designed with a series of massive rectangular sections clustered into an angular whole. The concrete-and-glass facade overlooks busy boulevards in the center of Madrid.

The hotel is patronized by both businesspeople and groups of visiting tourists; each of the bedrooms contains comfortable, contemporary furniture and a modernized bathroom.

Dining/Entertainment: The hotel's restaurant is called Ricón de Argüelles. There's also a bar, the Bar Royal.

Services: Concierge, room service (24 hours), baby-sitting.

Facilities: Conference rooms, underground garage, hairdressing salon.

EXPENSIVE

Meliá Madrid. Princesa, 17, 28008 Madrid. ☎ **800/336-3542** in the U.S., or 91/541-82-00. Fax 91/541-19-05. 260 rms, 5 suites. A/C MINIBAR TV TEL. 29,800 ptas. ($238.40) double; from 58,000 ptas. ($464) suite. AE, DC, MC, V. Parking 1,600 ptas. ($12.80). Metro: Rodríguez.

Here you'll find one of the most modern yet uniquely Spanish hotels in the country. Its 23 floors of wide picture windows have taken a permanent position in the capital's skyline. Each of the bedrooms is comfortable, spacious, and filled with contemporary furnishings plus a TV with video movies and many channels from across Europe. Most offer views over the skyline of Madrid. The chalk-white walls dramatize the flamboyant use of color accents; the bathrooms are sheathed in marble.

Dining/Entertainment: The Restaurante Princesa is elegant and restful; equally popular is the Don Pepe Grill. The cuisine in both restaurants is international and includes an array of Japanese and Indian dishes. There are also three bars and a coffee shop.

Services: Concierge, room service (24 hours), baby-sitting, hairdresser/barber, laundry.

Facilities: Gallery (includes souvenir shops and bookstores), health club with sauna and massage.

MODERATE

Tirol. Marqués de Urquijo, 4, 28008 Madrid. ☎ **91/548-19-00.** Fax 91/541-39-58. 97 rms, 4 suites. A/C TEL. 10,850 ptas. ($86.80) double; 14,750 ptas. ($118) suite. MC, V. Parking 1,975 ptas. ($15.80). Metro: Argüelles. Bus: 2 or 21.

A short walk from Plaza de España and the swank Meliá Madrid hotel (see above), the Tirol is a good choice for clean, unpretentious comfort. Furnishings in this three-star hotel are simple and functional. Eight of the guest rooms have private terraces. A cafeteria and a parking garage are in the hotel.

5 Best Restaurant Bets

- **Best Spot for a Romantic Dinner: El Amparo** (☎ **91/431-64-56**) sits in one of Madrid's most elegant enclaves, with cascading vines on its facade. You can dine grandly, enjoying not only the romantic ambience but some of the finest food in the city. A sloping skylight bathes the interior with sunlight during the day, and at night lanterns cast soft, flattering glows, making you and your date look luscious.

- **Best Spot for a Business Lunch:** For decades the movers and shakers of Madrid have come to **Jockey** (☎ **91/319-24-35**) to combine power lunches with one of the true gastronomic experiences in Madrid. In spite of increased competition, Jockey is still listed among the favorite rendezvous sites for heads of state, international celebrities, and diplomats. It's the perfect place to close that business deal with your Spanish partner. He or she will be impressed with your selection of Jockey as the venue for dining and business.

- **Best Spot for a Celebration:** At night the whole area around Plaza Mayor becomes one giant Spanish fiesta, with singers, guitar players, and bands of roving students serenading for their sangría and tapas money. Since 1884 it has always been party night at **Los Galayos** (☎ **91/366-30-28**) too, with tables and chairs set out on the sidewalk for people watching. The food's good as well—everything from suckling pig to roast lamb.

- **Best Decor: Las Cuatro Estaciones** (☎ 91/553-63-05) has the most spectacu-lar floral displays in Madrid. These flowers, naturally, change with the seasons, so you never know what you'll see when you arrive to dine. The entrance might be filled with hydrangeas, chrysanthemums, or poinsettias. The food is equally superb, but it's the stunningly modern and inviting decor that makes Las Cuatro Estaciones the perfect place for a lavish dinner on the town.
- **Best View:** From the café tables on the terrace of the **Café de Oriente** (☎ 91/541-39-74) is one of the most panoramic views in Madrid—a view that takes in everything from the Palacio Real (Royal Palace) to the Teatro Real. Diplomats, even royalty, have patronized this place, known for its good food and attractive belle époque decor, which includes banquettes and regal paneling.
- **Best Wine List:** Although it may no longer be considered the finest restaurant in Madrid, as it once was, **Horcher** (☎ 91/532-35-96) has one of the city's most laudable wine lists. The cuisine is also just as good as it ever was, but there's so much competition these days that other shining stars have toppled Horcher from its throne. Nevertheless, its wine cellars have won praise from kings and gourmands throughout Europe. It offers not only Spain's best vintages but those from the rest of the continent as well. The sommelier is one of the best in the business. His ad-vice is virtually always spot-on; trust him.
- **Best for Kids: Foster's Hollywood** (☎ 91/448-91-65) wins almost with-out competition. Since 1971 it has lured kids with Tex-Mex selections, one of the juiciest hamburgers in town, and what a *New York Times* reporter found to be "probably the best onion rings in the world." The atmosphere is fun too, evoking a movie studio with props.
- **Best American Cuisine:** Not everything on the menu at **La Gamella** (☎ 91/532-45-09) is American, but what there is is choice, inspired by California. Owner Dick Stephens, a former choreographer, now runs one of Madrid's most presti-gious restaurants, in the house where the Spanish philosopher Ortega y Gasset was born. Even the king and queen of Spain have tasted the savory viands here—everything from an all-American cheesecake to a Caesar salad with strips of mari-nated anchovies. It's also known for serving what one food critic called "the only edible hamburger in Madrid," and that palate had tasted the hamburger at Foster's Hollywood (see above).
- **Best Continental Cuisine:** Although the chef at **El Mentidero de la Villa** (☎ 91/308-12-85) roams the world for culinary inspirations, much of the cookery is firmly rooted in French cuisine perfection. Continental favorites are updated here and given new twists and flavors, sometimes betraying the influence of Japan. From France come the most perfect noisettes of veal (flavored with fresh tarragon) that you're likely to be served in Spain. Even the Spanish dishes have been brought up-to-date and are lighter and more subtle in flavor.
- **Best Seafood:** On the northern edges of Madrid, **El Cabo Mayor** (☎ 91/350-87-76) consistently serves the finest and freshest seafood in the country. Even the king and queen of Spain are likely to come here for their favorite seafood treats, which might be a savory kettle of fish soup from Cantabria (a province between the Basque country and Asturias). Another specialty worth the trip here is stewed sea bream flavored with thyme. Even the atmosphere is nautically inspired.
- **Best Basque Cuisine:** Some food critics regard **Zalacaín** (☎ 91/561-48-40) as the best restaurant in Madrid. Its name comes from Pio Baroja's 1909 novel, *Zalacaín El Aventuero,* but its cuisine comes straight from heaven. When the maître d' suggests a main dish of cheeks of hake, you might turn away in horror until you try it. Whatever is served here is sure to be among the finest food you'll taste in

Spain—all the foie gras and truffles you desire, but many innovative dishes to tempt the palate as well.

- **Best Steakhouse:** Spanish steaks at their finest are offered at **Casa Paco** (☎ 91/366-31-66). Señor Paco was the first in Madrid to sear steaks in boiling oil before serving, so that the almost-raw meat continues to cook on the plate, preserving the natural juices. This Old Town favorite also has plenty of atmosphere, and has long been a celebrity favorite as well.
- **Best Roast Suckling Pig:** Even hard-to-please Hemingway agreed: The roast suckling pig served at **Sobrino de Botín** (☎ 91/366-42-17) since 1725 is the best and most aromatic dish in the Old Town. You'd have to travel to Segovia (home of the specialty) for better fare than this. Under time-aged beams, you can wash down your meal with Valdepeñas or Aragón wine.

6 Restaurants by Cuisine

AMERICAN
Alfredo's Barbacoa (Chamartín, *I*)
Foster's Hollywood (Chamberí, *I*)

BASQUE
Alkalde (Retiro/Salamanca, *E*)
Amparo, El (Retiro/Salamanca, *E*)
Arce (Gran Vía, *M*)
Asador Errota-Zar (Chamartín, *E*)
Bodegón, El (Chamartín, *E*)
Gure-Etxea (Restaurant Vasco)
    (Plaza Mayor, *M*)
Restaurant Belagua (Chamberí, *VE*)
Taberna Carmencita (Chueca, *I*)
Taberna del Alabardero
    (Puerta del Sol, I)

CALIFORNIAN
Gamella, La
    (Retiro/Salamanca, *VE*)

CASTILIAN
Casa Alberto (Puerto del Sol, *I*)
Casa Lucio (Plaza Mayor, *E*)
Gamella, La (Retiro/Salamanca, *VE*)

FAST FOOD
V.I.P. (Gran Vía, *I*)

FRENCH
Café de Oriente
    (Puerta del Sol, *M*)
Chez Lou Crêperie
    (Plaza de Cuzco, *I*)
Mentidero de la Villa, El
    (Gran Vía, *M*)

GALICIAN
O'Pazo (Chamartín, *M*)

GERMAN
Edelweiss (Plaza de las
    Cortes, *M*)
Horcher (Retiro/Salamanca, *VE*)

INTERNATIONAL
Alkalde (Retiro/Salamanca, *E*)
Argentina, La (Chueca, *I*)
Bodegón, El (Chamartín, *E*)
Cenador del Prado, El
    (Puerta del Sol, *M*)
Cuevas de Luís Candelas, Las
    (Plaza Mayor, *E*)
Espejo, El (Plaza de las Cortes, *E*)
Galette, La (Recoletos, *I*)
Horcher (Retiro/Salamanca, *VE*)
Jockey (Chamberí, *VE*)
Lhardy (Puerta del Sol, *E*)
Ríofrío (Chamberí, *I*)
Viridiana (Retiro/Salamanca, *E*)
Zalacaín (Chamartín, *VE*)

ITALIAN
Nabucco (Chueca, *I*)

MADRILEÑA
La Bola (Chamberí, *I*)

MEDITERRANEAN
Cuatro Estaciones, Las
    (Chamberí, *VE*)
Olivo Restaurant, El
    (Chamartín, *E*)

Key to abbreviations: *VE* = Very Expensive; *E* = Expensive; *M* = Moderate; *I* = Inexpensive

MEXICAN
Cuchi, El (Plaza Mayor, *I*)

PERUVIAN
Inca, El (Chueca, *I*)

SEAFOOD
Bajamar (Plaza de España, *E*)
Cabo Mayor, El (Chamartín, *E*)
O'Pazo (Chamartín, *M*)
Pescador, El (Retiro/Salamanca, *E*)
Trucha, La (Plaza de las Cortes, *I*)

SPANISH
Bodegón, El (Chamartín, *E*)
Café de Oriente (Puerta del Sol, *M*)
Chata, La (Plaza Mayor, *I*)
Cuchi, El (Plaza Mayor, *I*)
Cuevas del Duque, Las
   (Plaza de España, *M*)
Cuevas de Luís Candelas, Las
   (Plaza Mayor, *E*)
Galayos, Los (Plaza Mayor, *M*)
Gran Café de Gijón
   (Retiro/Salamanca, *I*)
Hylogui (Puerta del Sol, *I*)
Lhardy (Puerta del Sol, *E*)
Mentidero de la Villa, El
   (Gran Vía, *M*)
Mesón las Descalzas
   (Puerta del Sol, *I*)

Paellería Valenciana (Gran Vía, *I*)
Platerías Comedor (Puerta del Sol, *E*)
Plaza, La (Puerta del Sol, *I*)
Schotis, El (Plaza Mayor, *E*)
Sobrino de Botín (Plaza Mayor, *M*)
Taberna Carmencita (Chueca, *I*)
Taberna del Alabardero
   (Puerta del Sol, *I*)
Tienda de Vinos (Chueca, *I*)
Trucha, La
   (Plaza de las Cortes, *I*)
Vera Cruz (Plaza de España, *I*)

STEAK
Casa Paco (Puerta del Sol, *M*)

TASCAS
Antonio Sánchez
   (Tirso de Molina)
Casa Mingo (Norte)
Cervecería Alemania
   (Plaza de Santa Ana)
Cervecería Santa Bárbara
   (Plaza de Santa Bárbara)
Taberna Toscana (Ventura de la Vega)

VALENCIAN
Barraca, La (Gran Vía, *M*)

VEGETARIAN
Galette, La (Recoletos, *I*)

7 Dining

Even more than Barcelona, Madrid boasts the most varied cuisine and the widest choice of dining opportunities in Spain. A post-1992 recession forced many neighborhood restaurants to lower their prices, meaning there's more bang for your dining buck. At the fancy tourist restaurants, however, prices are still comparable to those in New York, London, or Paris.

It's the custom in Madrid to consume the big meal of the day from 2 to 4pm. After a recuperative siesta, Madrileños then enjoy tapas—and indeed, no culinary experience would be complete without a tour of the city's many tapas bars (see "An Early-Evening Tapeo," below, and "The Best of the Tascas," at the end of this chapter). All this nibbling is followed by dinner—more likely a light supper—in a restaurant, usually from 9:30pm to as late as midnight. Many restaurants, however, start serving dinner at 8pm to accommodate visitors from other countries who don't like to dine late.

Many of Spain's greatest chefs have opened restaurants in Madrid, energizing the city's culinary scene. Gone are the days when mainly Madrileño food was featured, which meant Castilian specialties such as *cocido* (a chickpea-and-sausage stew) or roasts of suckling pig or lamb. Now you can take a culinary tour of the country while remaining in Madrid—from Andalusia with its gazpacho and braised bull's tails to Asturias with its *fabada* (a rich pork stew) and *sidra* (cider) to the Basque country, which has the most sophisticated cuisine in Spain. There are also a host of Galician and Mediterranean restaurants in Madrid. Amazingly, though Madrid is a landlocked city surrounded by a vast arid plain, you can order some of the freshest seafood in the country here.

Meals include service and tax (ranging from 7% to 12%, depending on the restaurant) but not drinks, which add to the tab considerably. The restaurants listed below that are categorized as "Very Expensive" charge 6,000 ptas. ($48) and up per person for a meal. The restaurants that are rated "Expensive" ask 4,000 to 6,000 ptas. ($32 to $48) per person for a meal; "Moderate," 2,000 to 4,000 ptas. ($16 to $32); and "Inexpensive," less than 2,000 ptas. ($16) per person.

Don't overtip; follow the local custom. Theoretically, service is included in the price of the meal, but it's customary to leave an additional 10%.

MENÚ DEL DÍA & CUBIERTO   Order the *menú del día* (menu of the day) or *cubierto*—both fixed-price menus based on what's fresh at the market that day. They're the dining bargains in Madrid, although often lacking the quality of more expensive à la carte dining. Usually each will include a first course, such as fish soup or hors d'oeuvres, followed by a main dish, plus bread, dessert, and the wine of the house. You won't have a large choice. The *menú turístico* is a similar fixed-price menu, but for many it's too large, especially at lunch. Only those with large appetites will find it the best bargain.

CAFETERIAS   These are not self-service establishments but restaurants serving light, often American, cuisine. Go for breakfast instead of dining at your hotel, unless it's included in the room price. Some cafeterias offer no hot meals, but many feature combined plates of fried eggs, french fries, veal, and lettuce-and-tomato salad, which make adequate fare, or snacks like hot dogs and hamburgers.

NEAR PLAZA DE LAS CORTÉS
EXPENSIVE

El Espejo. Paseo de Recoletos, 31. ☎ **91/308-23-47.** Reservations required. *Menú del día* 2,750 ptas. ($22). AE, DC, MC, V. Sun–Fri 1–4pm and 9pm–1am, Sat 9pm–1am. Metro: Colón. Bus: 27. INTERNATIONAL.

Here you'll find good-tasting food and one of the most perfectly crafted art nouveau decors in Madrid. If the weather is good, you can choose one of the outdoor tables, served by a battery of uniformed waiters who carry food across the busy street to a green area flanked with trees and strolling pedestrians. We prefer a table inside, within view of the tile maidens with vines and flowers entwined in their hair. After entering, you'll find yourself in a charming café/bar, where many visitors linger before walking down a hallway toward the spacious dining room. Dishes include grouper ragoût with clams, steak tartare, guinea fowl with Armagnac, and lean duck meat with pineapple. Profiteroles with cream and chocolate sauce make a delectable dessert.

MODERATE

⑤ Edelweiss. Jovelianos, T. ☎ **91/521-03-26.** Reservations recommended. Main courses 1,200–2,600 ptas. ($9.60–$20.80); fixed-price menu 1,900 ptas. ($15.20). AE, MC, V. Mon–Sat 1–4pm and 8pm–midnight, Sun 1–4pm. Closed Aug. Metro: Sevilla. Bus: 5. GERMAN.

Edelweiss is a German standby that has provided good-quality food and service at moderate prices since World War II. You're served hearty portions of food, mugs of

Dining in Central Madrid

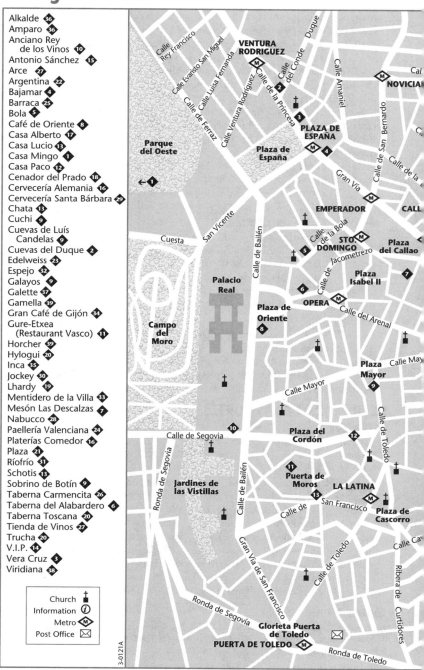

Alkalde **36**
Amparo **36**
Anciano Rey
  de los Vinos **10**
Antonio Sánchez **15**
Arce **27**
Argentina **22**
Bajamar **4**
Barraca **25**
Bola **5**
Café de Oriente **8**
Casa Alberto **17**
Casa Lucio **13**
Casa Mingo **1**
Casa Paco **12**
Cenador del Prado **18**
Cervecería Alemania **16**
Cervecería Santa Bárbara **29**
Chata **13**
Cuchi **9**
Cuevas de Luís
  Candelas **9**
Cuevas del Duque **2**
Edelweiss **23**
Espejo **32**
Galayos **9**
Galette **37**
Gamella **39**
Gran Café de Gijón **34**
Gure-Etxea
  (Restaurant Vasco) **11**
Horcher **39**
Hylogui **20**
Inca **35**
Jockey **30**
Lhardy **19**
Mentidero de la Villa **33**
Mesón Las Descalzas **7**
Nabucco **28**
Paellería Valenciana **24**
Platerías Comedor **16**
Plaza **21**
Ríofrío **31**
Schotis **13**
Sobrino de Botín **9**
Taberna Carmencita **26**
Taberna del Alabardero **6**
Taberna Toscana **20**
Tienda de Vinos **27**
Trucha **20**
V.I.P. **14**
Vera Cruz **3**
Viridiana **38**

Church   †
Information   *(i)*
Metro   **M**
Post Office   ⊠

3-0121A

draft beer, and fluffy pastries—that's why there's always a wait. *Tip:* To beat the crowds, go for dinner at un-Spanish hours, say around 9pm, when tables are not at a premium. But even when it's jammed, service is almost always courteous.

Start with Bismarck herring, then dive into goulash with spaetzle or Eisbein (pigs' knuckles) with sauerkraut and mashed potatoes, the most popular dish at the restaurant. Finish with the homemade apple tart. The decor is vaguely German, with travel posters and wood-paneled walls. Edelweiss is air-conditioned in summer.

INEXPENSIVE

La Trucha. Manuel Fernandez Gonzalez, 3. ☎ **91/429-58-33.** Reservations recommended. Main courses 1,200–3,200 ptas. ($9.60–$25.60); *menú del día* 2,800 ptas. ($22.40). AE, MC, V. Mon–Sat 2:30–4pm and 7:30pm–midnight. Metro: Sevilla. SPANISH/SEAFOOD.

With its Andalusian tavern ambience, La Trucha boasts a street-level bar and small dining room—the arched ceiling and whitewashed walls festive with hanging braids of garlic, dried peppers, and onions. On the lower level the walls of a second bustling area are covered with eye-catching antiques, bullfight notices, and other bric-a-brac. The specialty is fish; there's a complete à la carte menu including trucha (trout), verbenas de abumados (a "street party" of smoked delicacies), a stew called fabada ("glorious"; made with beans, Galician ham, black sausage, and smoked bacon), and a comida casera rabo de toro (home-style oxtail). No one should miss nibbling on the tapas variadas in the bar. If this Trucha turns out to be too crowded, there's another La Trucha at Núñez de Arce, 6 (☎ 91/532-08-82).

NEAR PLAZA DE ESPAÑA
EXPENSIVE

Bajamar. Gran Vía, 78. ☎ **91/559-59-03.** Reservations recommended. Main courses 1,850–4,500 ptas. ($14.80–$36). AE, DC, MC, V. Daily 1–4pm and 8pm–midnight. Metro: Plaza de España. SEAFOOD.

Bajamar, one of the best fish houses in Spain, is right in the heart of the city. Both fish and shellfish are flown in fresh daily, the prices depending on what the market charges. Lobster, king crab, prawns, and soft-shell crabs are all priced according to weight. There's a large array of reasonably priced dishes as well. The service is smooth and professional. The menu is in English. For an appetizer, order a half dozen giant oysters or rover crayfish. The special seafood soup is a most satisfying meal in itself. Try also the lobster bisque. Some of the noteworthy main courses include turbot Gallego style, seafood paella, and baby squid cooked in its ink. Desserts are simple, including the chef's custard.

MODERATE

Las Cuevas del Duque. Princesa, 16. ☎ **91/559-50-37.** Reservations required. Main courses 1,875–3,000 ptas. ($15–$24). AE, DC, MC, V. Mon–Fri 1–4pm and 8pm–midnight, Sat–Sun 8pm–midnight. Metro: Ventura Rodríguez. Bus: 1, 2, or 42. SPANISH.

In front of the duke of Alba's palace, a short walk from Plaza de España, is Las Cuevas del Duque, with an underground bar and a small, 20-table *mesón* that serves such simple Spanish fare as roast suckling pig, sirloin, tiny grilled lamb cutlets, and a few seafood dishes, including hake in garlic sauce and sole cooked in cider. In fair weather a few tables are set outside, beside a tiny triangular garden. Other tables line the Calle de la Princesa side and make an enjoyable roost for an afternoon drink.

INEXPENSIVE

🛇 **Vera Cruz.** San Leonardo, 5. ☎ **91/547-11-50.** Main courses 400–950 ptas. ($3.20–$7.65); fixed-price menu 950 ptas. ($7.65). No credit cards. Daily 1–5pm and 8pm–midnight. Metro: Plaza de España. SPANISH.

An Early-Evening Tapeo

What's more fun than a pub crawl in London or Dublin? In Madrid, it's a *tapeo,* and you can drink just as much or more than in those far northern climes. A *tapeo*— one of the pleasures of a visit to Madrid—is strolling from one tapas bar to another, the way to keep yourself amused and fed before the fashionable Madrileño dining hour of 10pm.

Most of the world knows that tapas are Spain's delectable appetizer foods, and hundreds of restaurants in England and the United States now serve them. In Madrid they're served in tabernas, tascas, bars, and cafés.

Although Madrid took to tapas with a passion, they may have originated in Andalusia, especially around Jerez de la Frontera, where they were traditionally served to accompany the sherry produced there. The first tapa (which means a cover or lid) was probably *chorizo* (a spicy sausage) or a slice of cured ham perched over the mouth of a glass to keep the flies out. Later, the government mandated bars to serve a "little something" in the way of food with each drink to dissipate the effects of the alcohol. This was important when drinking a fortified wine like sherry, as its alcohol content is more than 15% higher than that of normal table wines. A selection of tapas will help preserve sobriety.

Tapas can be relatively simple: toasted almonds; slices of ham, cheese, or sausage; potato omelets; or the inevitable olives. But they can also be more elaborate: a succulent veal roll; herb-flavored snails; *gambas* (fried shrimp); a saucer of peppery *pulpo* (octopus); stuffed peppers; delicious *anguila* (eel); *cangrejo* (crabmeat salad); hake salad flavored with sweet red peppers, garlic, and cumin—and even bull testicles. Each bar in Madrid gains a reputation for its rendition of certain favorite foods.

Louis Armstrong, Manolete, Ava Gardner, or even Orson Welles may no longer be around Madrid to accompany you on a tapeo, but the tradition lives on. For a selection of our favorite bars, see "The Best of the Tascas," later in this chapter.

Behind the landmark Edificio España, you'll find this old standby for hungry budget-minded visitors. It's a simple *económico,* but the food is acceptable and the service polite. The *menú del día* usually includes soup or appetizer, followed by a meat or fish dish, then cheese or fruit, plus bread and wine. The Vera Cruz also has daily specials like paella and cocido, a typical Madrid dish made of chickpeas, sausage, cabbage, and potatoes.

ON OR NEAR THE GRAN VÍA
MODERATE

Arce. Augusto Figueroa, 32. ☎ **91/522-59-13.** Reservations recommended. Main courses 2,500–3,500 ptas. ($20–$28). AE, DC, MC, V. Mon–Fri 1:30–4pm and 9pm–midnight, Sat 9pm–midnight. Closed the week before Easter and Aug 15–31. Metro: Colón. BASQUE.

Arce has brought some of the best modern interpretations of Basque cuisine to the palates of Madrid, thanks to the enthusiasm of owner/chef Iñaki Camba and his wife, Theresa. In a comfortably decorated dining room, you can enjoy simple dishes made of the finest ingredients; natural flavors are designed to dominate your taste buds. Examples include a salad of fresh scallops and an oven-baked casserole of fresh boletus mushrooms, seasoned lightly so the woodsy vegetable taste shines through. Look for unusual preparations of hake and seasonal variations of such game dishes as pheasant and woodcock.

La Barraca. Reina, 29–31. ☎ **91/532-71-54.** Reservations recommended. Main courses 1,800–3,000 ptas. ($14.40–$24); fixed-price menu 3,500 ptas. ($28). AE, DC, MC, V. Daily 1–4pm and 8:30pm–midnight. Metro: Gran Vía or Sevilla. Bus: 1, 2, or 74. VALENCIAN.

La Barraca is like a country inn right off the Gran Vía, and it has been a longtime local favorite. The food, frankly, used to be better, but perhaps our tastes have changed since our student days. This Valencian-style restaurant is a well-managed establishment recommendable for its tasty Levante cooking. There are four different dining rooms, three of which lie one flight above street level; they're colorfully cluttered with ceramics, paintings, photographs, Spanish lanterns, flowers, and local artifacts. The house specialty, paella à la Barraca, is made with pork and chicken. House specialties in the appetizer category include desgarrat (a salad made with codfish and red peppers), mussels in a white-wine sauce, and shrimp sautéed with garlic. In addition to the recommended paella, you can select at least 16 rice dishes, including black rice and queen paella. Main-dish specialties include brochette of angler fish and prawns and rabbit with fines herbes. Lemon-and-vodka sorbet brings the meal to a fitting finish.

El Mentidero de la Villa. Santo Tomé, 6. ☎ **91/308-12-85.** Reservations required. Main courses 1,950–2,400 ptas. ($15.60–$19.20). AE, DC, MC, V. Mon–Fri 1:30–4pm and 9pm–midnight, Sat 9pm–midnight. Closed the last 2 weeks of Aug. Metro: Alonso Martínez, Colón, or Gran Vía. Bus: 37. SPANISH/FRENCH.

This "Gossip Shop" (its name in English) is certainly a multicultural experience. The owner describes the cuisine as "modern Spanish with Japanese influence and a French cooking technique." That may sound confusing, but the end result is an achievement; each ingredient in every dish manages to retain its distinct flavor. The kitchen plays with such adventuresome combinations as veal liver in sage sauce, a type of spring roll filled with fresh shrimp and leeks, noisettes of veal with tarragon, filet steak with a sauce of mustard and brown sugar, and médaillons of venison with purées of chestnut and celery. Sherry trifle is but one of the notable desserts. The postmodern decor includes softly trimmed trompe l'oeil ceilings, exposed wine racks, ornate columns with unusual lighting, and a handful of antique carved horses from long-defunct merry-go-rounds.

INEXPENSIVE

Ⓢ **Paellería Valenciana.** Caballero de Gracia, 12. ☎ **91/531-17-85.** Reservations recommended. Main courses 1,250–2,500 ptas.($10–$20); fixed-price menus 1,250–1,600 ptas. ($10–$12.80). AE, MC, V. Mon–Sat 1:30–4:30pm. Metro: Gran Vía. SPANISH.

This lunch-only restaurant ranks as one of the best values in the city. The specialty is paella, which you must order by phone in advance. Once you arrive, you might begin with a homemade soup or the house salad, then follow with the paella, served in an iron skillet. At least two must order this rib-sticking fare. Among the desserts, the chef's special pride is razor-thin orange slices flavored with rum, coconut, sugar, honey, and raspberry sauce. A carafe of house wine comes with the set menu, and after lunch the owner comes around dispensing free cognac.

V.I.P. Gran Vía, 43. ☎ **91/559-64-57.** Main courses 750–1,400 ptas. ($6–$11.20). AE, DC, MC, V. Daily 9am–3am. Metro: Callao. FAST FOOD.

This place looks like a bookstore emporium from the outside, but in back it's a cafeteria serving fast food. You might begin with a cup of soothing gazpacho. There are more than a dozen V.I.P.s scattered throughout Madrid, but this is the most central one. Hamburgers are the rage here. Service leaves a lot to be desired.

NEAR THE PUERTA DEL SOL
EXPENSIVE

Lhardy. Carrera de San Jéronimo, 8. ☎ **91/521-33-85.** Reservations recommended in the upstairs dining room. Main dishes 1,900–5,000 ptas. ($15.20–$40). AE, DC, MC, V. Mon–Sat 1–3:30pm and 9–11:30pm. Closed Aug. Metro: Puerta del Sol. SPANISH/INTERNATIONAL.

Lhardy has been a Madrileño legend since it opened in 1839 as a gathering place for the city's literati and political leaders. In 1846 it entertained Dumas. On the street level is what might be the most elegant snack bar in Spain. In a dignified and antique setting of marble and varnished hardwoods, cups of steaming consommé are dispensed from silver samovars into delicate porcelain cups, and rows of croquettes, tapas, and sandwiches are served to stand-up clients who pay for their food at a cashier's kiosk near the entrance. Virtually anything you select (tapas, sandwiches, pastries, whatever) will cost around 90 ptas. (70¢). The ground-floor deli and takeaway service is open daily from 9am to 3pm and 5 to 9:30pm.

The real culinary skill of the place, however, is found on Lhardy's second floor, where you'll find a formal restaurant decorated in the ornate belle époque style of Isabel Segunda. Specialties of the house include fish, pork and veal, tripe in a garlicky tomato-and-onion/wine sauce, and cocido, the celebrated chickpea stew of Madrid. Soufflé sorpresa (baked Alaska) is the dessert specialty.

Platerías Comedor. Plaza de Santa Ana, 11. ☎ **91/429-70-48.** Reservations recommended. Main courses 1,000–5,000 ptas. ($8–$40). AE, DC, MC, V. Mon–Fri 2:30–4pm and 9pm–midnight, Sat 9pm–midnight. Metro: Puerta del Sol. SPANISH.

One of the most charming dining rooms in Madrid, Platerías Comedor has richly brocaded walls evocative of 19th-century Spain. Busy socializing may take place on the plaza outside, but this serene oasis makes few concessions to the new generation in its food, decor, or formally attired waiters. Specialties include beans with clams, stuffed partridge with cabbage and sausage, duck liver with white grapes, tripe à la Madrid, veal stew with snails and mushrooms, and guinea hen with figs and plums. Follow up any of these with the passionfruit sorbet. Many restaurants have sprouted up in recent years that serve better food, but Platerías Comedor continues to thrive as a culinary tradition; its old-fashioned atmosphere is hard to come by.

MODERATE

Café de Oriente. Plaza de Oriente, 2. ☎ **91/541-39-74.** Reservations recommended in restaurant only. Restaurant, main courses 1,700–3,950 ptas. ($13.60–$31.60). Café, tapas 850 ptas. ($6.80); coffee 650 ptas. ($5.20). AE, DC, MC, V. Daily 1–4pm and 9pm–1:30am. Metro: Ópera. FRENCH/SPANISH.

The Oriente is a café-and-restaurant complex, the former being one of the most popular in Madrid. From the café tables on its terrace there's a spectacular view of the Palacio Real (Royal Palace) and the Teatro Real. The dining rooms—Castilian upstairs, French Basque downstairs—are frequented by royalty and diplomats. Typical of the refined cuisine are vichyssoise, fresh vegetable flan, and many savory meat and fresh-fish offerings; service is excellent. Most visitors, however, patronize the café, trying if possible to get an outdoor table. The café is decorated in turn-of-the-century style, with banquettes and regal paneling, as befits its location. Pizza, tapas, and drinks (including Irish, Viennese, Russian, and Jamaican coffees) are served.

Casa Paco. Plaza Puerta Cerrada, 11. ☎ **91/366-31-66.** Reservations required. Main courses 1,100–3,800 ptas. ($8.80–$30.40); fixed-price menu 3,300 ptas. ($26.40). DC. Mon–Sat 1:30–4pm and 8:30pm–midnight. Closed Aug. Metro: Puerta del Sol, Ópera, or La Latina. Bus: 3, 21, or 65. STEAK.

Madrileños defiantly name Casa Paco, just beside Plaza Mayor, when someone has the "nerve" to denigrate Spanish steaks. They know that here you can get the thickest, juiciest, tastiest steaks in Spain, which are priced according to weight. Señor Paco was the first in Madrid to sear steaks in boiling oil before serving them on plates so hot that the almost-raw meat continues to cook, preserving the natural juices. Located in the Old Town, this two-story restaurant has three dining rooms—but reservations are imperative. If you face a long wait, while away the time sampling the tapas at the tasca in front. Around the walls are autographed photographs of such notables as Frank Sinatra.

Casa Paco isn't just a steakhouse. You can start with a fish soup and proceed to grilled sole, baby lamb, or Casa Paco cocido, Madrid's famous chickpea-and-pork soup. You might top it off with one of the luscious desserts, but know that Paco no longer serves coffee. It made customers linger, keeping tables occupied while potential patrons had to be turned away.

✪ **El Cenador del Prado.** Prado, 4. ☎ **91/429-15-61.** Reservations recommended. Jackets and ties recommended for men. Main courses 850–1,950 ptas. ($6.80–$15.60); fixed-price menu 3,200 ptas. ($25.60). AE, DC, MC, V. Mon–Fri 1:45–4pm and 9pm–midnight, Sat 9pm–midnight. Closed Aug 12–19. Metro: Puerta del Sol. INTERNATIONAL.

This restaurant is deceptively elegant. In the simple anteroom an attendant will check your coat and packages in an elaborately carved armoire and the maître d' will usher you into one of a trio of rooms. Two of the rooms, done in tones of peach and sepia, have cove moldings and English furniture, as well as floor-to-ceiling gilded mirrors. A third room, the most popular, is ringed with lattices and flooded with sun from a skylight.

The food reflects a basically French influence, with the occasional Asian flourish. Many of the Spanish dishes are innovative. You can enjoy such well-flavored specialties as crêpes with salmon and Iranian caviar, a salad of crimson peppers and salted anchovies, a casserole of snails and oysters with mushrooms, a ceviche of salmon and shellfish, potato-leek soup studded with tidbits of hake and clams, sea bass with candied lemons, veal scaloppine stuffed with asparagus and garlic sprouts, and médallions of venison served with pepper-and-fig chutney.

INEXPENSIVE

Casa Alberto. Huertas, 18. ☎ **91/429-93-56.** Reservations recommended. Main courses 650–2,250 ptas. ($5.20–$18). AE, V. Tues–Sat 1–4pm and 8:30pm–midnight, Sun 1–4pm. Metro: Antón Martín. CASTILIAN.

One of the oldest tascas in the neighborhood, Casa Alberto was originally established in 1827 and has thrived ever since. It lies on the street level of the house where Miguel de Cervantes lived briefly in 1614, and contains an appealing mixture of bullfighting memorabilia, engravings, and reproductions of old master paintings. Many visitors opt only for the tapas, which are continually replenished from platters on the bartop, but there's also a sit-down dining area for more substantial meals. Specialties include fried squid, shellfish in vinaigrette sauce, chorizo (sausage) in cider sauce, and several versions of baked or roasted lamb.

Hylogui. Ventura de la Vega, 3. ☎ **91/429-73-57.** Reservations recommended. Main courses 1,000–2,200 ptas. ($8–$17.60); fixed-price menus 1,400–1,700 ptas. ($11.20–$13.60). AE, MC, V. Mon–Sat 1–4:30pm and 9pm–midnight, Sun 1–4:30pm. Metro: Sevilla. SPANISH.

Hylogui, a local legend, is one of the largest dining rooms along Ventura de la Vega, but there are many arches and nooks for privacy. One globe-trotting American wrote enthusiastically that he took all his Madrid meals here, finding the soup pleasant and

🙂 Family-Friendly Restaurants

Children visiting Spain will delight in patronizing any of the restaurants at the Parque de Atracciones in the **Casa de Campo** (see "Especially for Kids" in Chapter 6). Another good idea is to go on a picnic (see "Picnic Fare & Where to Eat It," later in this chapter).

For a taste of home, there are always the fast-food chains: McDonald's, Burger King, and Kentucky Fried Chicken. Remember, however, that the burgers and chicken will have a slightly different taste from those served back home.

Try taking the family to a local tasca, where children are bound to find something they like from the wide selection of tapas.

Foster's Hollywood *(see p. 167)* This restaurant has juicy hamburgers, plus lots of fare familiar to American kids.

V.I.P. *(see p. 160)* This chain spread across Madrid serves fast food, hamburgers, and other foodstuffs that kids go for in a big way, especially the ice cream concoctions.

rich, the flan soothing, and the regional wine dry. The food is old-fashioned Spanish home-style cooking.

Mesón las Descalzas. Postigo San Martín, 3. ☎ **91/522-72-17.** Reservations recommended. Main courses 1,600–1,800 ptas. ($12.80–$14.40); fixed-price menu 1,200 ptas. ($9.60). AE, DC, MC, V. Daily noon–4pm and 8pm–midnight. Metro: Callao. SPANISH.

Las Descalzas, a recommended tavern-style restaurant, has a massive tapas bar that's often crowded at night. Behind a glass-and-wood screen is the restaurant section, its specialties including kidneys with sherry, sopa castellana, seafood soup, Basque-style hake, crayfish, shrimp, oysters, clams, and paella with shellfish—in other words, all that good food beloved during the Franco era. For entertainment, there's folk music.

✪ La Plaza. La Galería del Prado, Plaza de las Cortes, 7. ☎ **91/429-65-37.** Buffet 1,200–1,500 ptas. ($9.60–$12). Metro: Sevilla. SPANISH.

This restaurant serves as the underground centerpiece of one of Madrid's shopping complexes, La Galería del Prado. Surrounded by thick marble-sheathed walls, its bunker-style position eliminates the possibility of natural sunlight streaming through windows. Still, it's an attractive option for light, refreshing buffet meals in the expensive neighborhood near the Prado. Some of the tables overflow into the rotunda of the shopping mall, but most diners sit in a glossy series of lattices that form a garden-inspired enclave near a well-stocked salad bar (visits here are priced according to the portions you take). You might begin with Serrano ham or a mountain-fermented goat cheese, perhaps a homemade pâté. Daily specials include such dishes as ragoût of veal. Platters of pasta are another zesty way to fill up.

Taberna del Alabardero. Felipe V, 6. ☎ **91/547-25-77.** Reservations required for restaurant only. Restaurant, main courses 800–2,900 ptas. ($6.40–$23.20). Bar, tapas 450–1,200 ptas. ($3.60–$9.60); glass of house wine 200 ptas. ($1.60). AE, DC, V. Daily 1–4pm and 9pm–midnight. Metro: Ópera. BASQUE/SPANISH.

Because of its proximity to the Royal Palace, this little Spanish classic is usually visited for its selection of tasty tapas, ranging from squid cooked in wine to fried potatoes dipped in hot sauce. Photographs of former patrons, including Nelson Rockefeller and the race-car driver Jackie Stewart, line the walls. The restaurant in the rear is said to be one of the city's best-kept secrets. Decorated in typical tavern style, it serves a savory Spanish and Basque cuisine with market-fresh ingredients.

RETIRO/SALAMANCA
VERY EXPENSIVE

✪ **La Gamella.** Alfonso XII, 4. ☎ **91/532-45-09.** Reservations required. Main courses 2,300–4,200 ptas. ($18.40–$33.60). AE, DC, MC, V. Mon–Fri 1:30–4pm and 9pm–midnight, Sat 9pm–midnight. Closed 2 weeks around Easter and 2 weeks in Aug. Metro: Retiro. Bus: 19. CALIFORNIAN/CASTILIAN.

La Gamella established its gastronomic reputation shortly after it opened, several years ago, in less imposing quarters in another part of town. In 1988 its Illinois-born owner, former choreographer Dick Stephens, moved his restaurant into the 19th-century building where the Spanish philosopher Ortega y Gasset was born. The prestigious Horcher, one of the capital's legendary restaurants (see below), is just across the street—but the food at La Gamella is better. The russet-colored, high-ceilinged design invites customers to relax. Mr. Stephens has prepared his delicate and light-textured specialties for the king and queen of Spain, as well as for Madrid's most talked-about artists and merchants, many of whom he knows and greets personally between sessions in his kitchen.

Typical menu items include a ceviche of Mediterranean fish, sliced duck liver in truffle sauce, a dollop of goat cheese served over caramelized endives, duck breast with peppers, and an array of well-prepared desserts, among which is an all-American cheesecake. Traditional Spanish dishes such as chicken with garlic have been added to the menu, plus what has been called "the only edible hamburger in Madrid." Because of the intimacy and the small dimensions of the restaurant, reservations are important.

Horcher. Alfonso XII, 6. ☎ **91/532-35-96.** Reservations required. Jackets and ties required for men. Main courses 3,400–8,000 ptas. ($27.20–$64). AE, DC, MC, V. Mon–Fri 1:30–4pm and 8:30pm–midnight, Sat 8:30pm–midnight. Metro: Retiro. GERMAN/INTERNATIONAL.

Horcher originated in Berlin in 1904. In 1943, prompted by a tip from a high-ranking German officer that Germany was losing the war, Herr Horcher moved his restaurant to Madrid. For years it was known as the best dining room in the city, until culinary competition overtook that stellar position. Nevertheless, the restaurant has continued its grand European traditions, including excellent service.

Where to start? You might try the skate or shrimp tartare or the distinctive warm hake salad. Both the venison stew with green pepper and orange peel and the crayfish with parsley and cucumber are typical of the elegant fare served with impeccable style. Spanish aristocrats often come here in autumn to sample game dishes, including venison, wild boar, or roast wild duck. Other main courses include veal scaloppine in tarragon and sea bass with saffron. For dessert, the house specialty is crêpes Sir Holden, prepared at your table, with fresh raspberries, cream, and nuts.

EXPENSIVE

Alkalde. Jorge Juan, 10. ☎ **91/576-33-59.** Reservations required. Main courses 1,550–5,600 ptas. ($12.40–$44.80); fixed-price menu from 4,750 ptas. ($38). AE, DC, MC, V. Daily 1–4:30pm and 8:30pm–midnight. Closed Sat–Sun July–Aug. Metro: Retiro or Serrano. Bus: 8, 20, 21, or 53. BASQUE/INTERNATIONAL.

For decades Alkalde has been known for serving top-quality Spanish food in an old tavern setting. Decorated like a Basque inn, it has beamed ceilings and hams hanging from the rafters. Upstairs is a large *típico* tavern; downstairs is a maze of stone-sided cellars that are pleasantly cool in summer (though the whole place is air-conditioned).

Basque cookery is the best in Spain, and Alkalde honors that noble tradition. Begin with the cream of crabmeat soup, followed by gambas a la plancha (grilled shrimp) or cigalas (crayfish). Other well-recommended dishes include mero salsa verde (brill in a green sauce), trout Alkalde, stuffed peppers, and chicken steak. The dessert specialty is copa Cardinal (ice cream topped with fruit).

✪ El Amparo. Callejón de Puígcerdá, 8 (at corner of Jorge Juan). ☎ **91/431-64-56.** Reservations required. Main courses 3,000–4,000 ptas. ($24–$32); fixed-price menu 9,500 ptas. ($76). AE, MC, V. Mon–Fri 1:30–3:30pm and 9:30–11:30pm, Sat 9:30–11:30pm. Closed the week before Easter and in Aug. Metro: Goya. Bus: 21 or 53. BASQUE.

Behind the cascading vines on El Amparo's facade is one of Madrid's most elegant gastronomic enclaves. Inside, three tiers of roughly hewn wooden beams surround tables set with pink napery and glistening silver for a touch of cosmopolitan glamour. A sloping skylight floods the interior with sun by day; at night, pinpoints of light from the high-tech hanging lanterns create intimate shadows. Polite, uniformed waiters serve well-prepared nouvelle cuisine versions of cold marinated salmon with a tomato sorbet, cold cream of vegetable and shrimp soup, bisque of shellfish with Armagnac, ravioli stuffed with seafood, roast lamb chops with garlic purée, breast of duck, ragoût of sole, a platter of steamed fish of the day, roulades of lobster with soy sauce, and steamed hake with pepper sauce.

El Pescador. Calle José Ortega y Gasset, 75. ☎ **91/402-12-90.** Reservations required. Main courses 5,000–15,000 ptas. ($40–$120); fixed-price menu 6,250 ptas. ($50). MC, V. Mon–Sat 1:30–4pm and 8:30pm–midnight. Closed Aug. Metro: Lista. SEAFOOD.

El Pescador is a well-patronized fish restaurant that has become a favorite of Madrileños who appreciate the more than 30 kinds of fish prominently displayed in a glass case. Many of these are unknown in North America, and some originate off the coast of Galicia. The management air-freights them in and prefers to serve them grilled (a la plancha).

You might precede your main course with a spicy fish soup and accompany it with one of the many good wines from northeastern Spain. If you're not sure what to order (even the English translations might sound unfamiliar), try one of the many varieties and sizes of shrimp. These go under the names langostinos, cigalas, santiaguinos, and carabineros. Many of them are expensive and priced by the gram, so be careful when you order.

✪ Viridiana. Juan de Mena 14. ☎ **91/523-44-78.** Reservations recommended. Main courses 3,000–4,000 ptas. ($24–$32). AE, MC, V. Mon–Sat 1:30–4pm and 9pm–midnight. Closed 1 week at Easter and in Aug. Metro: Banco. INTERNATIONAL.

Viridiana is praised as one of the up-and-coming restaurants of Madrid, known for the creative imagination of its chef and part-owner, Abraham García. Menu specialties are usually contemporary adaptations of traditional recipes, and they change frequently according to the availability of the ingredients. Examples include a salad of exotic lettuces served with smoked salmon, guinea fowl stuffed with herbs and wild mushrooms, baby squid with curry served on a bed of lentils, roast lamb served in puff pastry with fresh basil, and carpaccio of beef with a mousseline of white truffles.

INEXPENSIVE

Gran Café de Gijón. Paseo de Recoletos, 21. ☎ **91/521-54-25.** Reservations needed for the restaurant. Main courses 3,000–5,000 ptas. ($24–$40); fixed-price menu 1,500 ptas. ($12). MC, V. Sun–Fri 9am–1:30am, Sat 9am–2am. Metro: Banco de España, Colón, or Recoletos. SPANISH.

Each of the old European capitals has a coffeehouse that traditionally attracts the literati—in Madrid it's the Gijón, which opened in 1888 in the heyday of the city's belle époque. Artists and writers still patronize this venerated old café, many of them spending hours over one cup of coffee. Ernest Hemingway made the place famous for Americans, and such notables as Ava Gardner and Truman Capote followed in his footsteps in the 1950s. Open windows look out onto the wide paseo; the large terrace is perfect for sun worshippers and birdwatchers. Along one side of the café is a stand-up bar, and on the lower level is a restaurant. The food is prepared the "way it used to be" in Madrid. Patrons liked it then, and they come back for the same dishes they enjoyed in their youth. In summer you can sit in the garden to enjoy a blanco y negro (black coffee with ice cream) or a mixed drink.

CHAMBERÍ
VERY EXPENSIVE

✪ **Las Cuatro Estaciones.** General Ibéñez Ibero, 5. ☎ **91/553-63-05.** Reservations required. Main courses 1,500–5,000 ptas. ($12–$40); fixed-price dinner 4,500 ptas. ($36). AE, DC, MC, V. Mon–Fri 1:30–4pm and 9pm–midnight, Sat 9–11:30pm. Closed Aug. Metro: Guzmán el Bueno. MEDITERRANEAN.

Las Cuatro Estaciones is placed by gastronomes and horticulturists alike among their favorite Madrid dining spots, and it has become a neck-and-neck rival with the prestigious Jockey (see below). In addition to superb food, the establishment prides itself on the masses of flowers that change with the season. Depending on the time of year, the mirrors surrounding the multilevel bar near the entrance reflect thousands of hydrangeas, chrysanthemums, or poinsettias. Even the napery matches whichever colors the resident botanist has chosen as the seasonal motif. Each person involved in food preparation spends a prolonged apprenticeship at restaurants in France before returning home to try his or her talents on the tastebuds of aristocratic Madrid.

Representative specialties include crab bisque, a petite marmite of fish and shellfish, a salad of eels, fresh asparagus and mushrooms in puff pastry with parsley-butter sauce, and a nouvelle cuisine version of blanquette of monkfish so tender that it melts in your mouth. The "festival of desserts" includes the specials the chef has concocted that day, a selection of which is brought temptingly to your table.

✪ **Jockey.** Amador de los Ríos, 6. ☎ **91/319-24-35.** Reservations required. Main courses 2,000–5,000 ptas. ($16–$40). AE, DC, MC, V. Mon–Sat 1–4pm and 9–11:30pm. Closed Aug. Metro: Colón. INTERNATIONAL.

For decades this was the premier restaurant of Spain, though that title is hotly contested today. The favorite of international celebrities, diplomats, and heads of state, it was once known as the "Jockey Club," although "Club" was eventually dropped because it suggested exclusivity. The restaurant, with tables on two levels, isn't large. Wood-paneled walls and colored linen provide warmth. Against the paneling are a dozen prints of jockeys mounted on horses—hence the name of the place.

Since Jockey's establishment shortly after World War II, the chef has prided himself on coming up with new and creative dishes. Sheiks can still order Beluga caviar from Iran, but others might settle happily for the goose-liver terrine or slices of Jabugo ham. Cold melon soup with shrimp is soothing on a hot day, especially when followed by grill-roasted young pigeon from Talavera or sole filets with figs in chardonnay. Stuffed small chicken Jockey style is a specialty, as is tripe Madrileña, a local dish. The desserts are sumptuous.

✪ **Restaurante Belagua.** In the Hotel Palacio Santo Mauro, Calle Zurbano, 36. ☎ **91/319-69-00.** Reservations recommended. Main courses 2,300–3,900 ptas. ($18.40–$31.20). AE, DC, MC, V. Mon–Sat 1–4pm and 8:30–11:30pm. Closed national holidays. Metro: Rubén Darío or Alonso Martínez. BASQUE.

This glamorous restaurant was originally built in 1894 as a small palace in the French neoclassical style. In 1991 Catalán designer Josep Joanpere helped transform the building into a carefully detailed hotel (the Santo Mauro), which we've recommended separately (see "Accommodations," earlier in this chapter). On the hotel premises is this highly appealing postmodern restaurant, today one of the capital's finest.

Assisted by the well-mannered staff, you'll select from a menu whose inspiration and ingredients change with the seasons. Examples include watermelon-and-prawn salad, light cream of cold ginger soup, haddock baked in a crust of potatoes tinted with squid ink, filet of monkfish with prawn-and-zucchini sauce, and duck with honey and black cherries. Depending on the efforts of the chef, dessert might include miniature portions of flan with strawberry sauce plus an array of the day's pastries. The restaurant's name, incidentally, derives from a village in Navarre known for its natural beauty.

INEXPENSIVE

La Bola. Calle de la Bola, 5. ☎ **91/547-69-30.** Reservations required. Main courses 1,400–2,200 ptas. ($11.20–$17.60); fixed-price menu 2,125 ptas. ($17). No credit cards. Mon–Sat 1–4pm and 9pm–midnight. Metro: Plaza de España or Ópera. Bus: 1 or 2. MADRILEÑA.

This is just the taberna in which to savor the 19th century. Just north of the Teatro Real, it's one of the few restaurants (if not the only one) left in Madrid with a blood-red facade; at one time nearly all fashionable restaurants were so coated. La Bola hangs on to tradition like a tenacious bull. Time has passed, but not inside this restaurant: The soft, traditional atmosphere; the gentle and polite waiters; the Venetian crystal; the Carmen-red draperies; and the aging velvet preserve the 1870 ambience. Ava Gardner, with her entourage of bullfighters, used to patronize this establishment, but that was long before La Bola became so well known to tourists. Grilled sole, filet of veal, and roast veal are regularly featured. Basque-style hake and grilled salmon also are well recommended. A host of refreshing dishes to begin your meal include grilled shrimp, red-pepper salad, and lobster cocktail.

Foster's Hollywood. Magallanes, 1. ☎ **91/448-91-65.** Main courses 600–1,000 ptas. ($4.80–$8). AE, DC, MC, V. Sun–Thurs 1pm–midnight, Fri–Sat 1pm–2am. Metro: Quevedo. AMERICAN.

When Foster's opened its doors in 1971, it was not only the first American restaurant in Spain, it was one of the first in Europe. Since those early days it has grown to 15 restaurants in Madrid, and has even opened restaurants in Florida. A popular hangout for both locals and visiting Yanks, it offers a choice of dining venues, ranging from "classical club American" to studios, the latter evoking a working movie studio with props. Its varied menu includes Tex-Mex selections, ribs, steaks, sandwiches, freshly made salads, and, as its signature product, hamburgers grilled over natural charcoal in many variations. The *New York Times* once claimed that it had "probably the best onion rings in the world."

Locations where you can have a direct hook-up to the U.S.A. in Madrid are: Paseo de la Castellana, 116–118 (☎ 91/564-63-08); Padre Damián, 38 (☎ 91/457-36-42), next to the Eurobuilding hotel; Apolonio Morales, 3 (☎ 91/345-10-36), in the Castellana area; Avenida de Brasil, 14 (☎ 91/597-16-74), near the Meliá Castilla hotel; Princesa, 13 (☎ 91/559-19-14), near Plaza de España; Velázquez, 80 (☎ 91/435-61-28), in the Serrano shopping area; Tamayo y Baus, 1 (☎ 91/531-51-15), close to Plaza de la Cibeles and the Prado; Plaza Sagrado Corazón de Jesús, 2 (☎ 91/564-66-50), next to the National Music Auditorium; Centro Comercial Arturo Soria (☎ 91/759-73-42); and Centro Comercial La Vaguada (☎ 91/738-12-67).

Ríofrío. Centro Colón; Plaza de Colón, 1. ☎ **91/319-29-77.** Main courses 700–3,200 ptas. ($5.60–$25.60); fixed-price menu 2,500 ptas. ($20); sandwiches 525–900 ptas. ($4.20–$7.20). AE, DC, MC, V. Daily 7:30am–2am. Metro: Colón. Bus: 5, 14, 21, 27, or 45. INTERNATIONAL.

Overlooking Madrid's version of New York's Columbus Circle, this is a sort of all-purpose place for drinking, eating, dining, and nightclubbing. The least expensive way to eat here is to patronize one of two self-service cafeterias, where average meals run 1,000 to 1,500 ptas. ($8 to $12). There's also a large restaurant with an international cuisine, serving meals averaging 3,500 ptas. ($28), plus yet another dining room for informal lunches, dinners, snacks, or apéritifs. The spacious glassed-in terrace, open year round, is known for serving some of the best paella in Madrid. Finally, there's even a nightclub, El Descubrimiento, should you desire to make an evening of it. The club serves dinner costing from 4,500 pesetas ($36), which includes not only the meal but a show to follow. Sandwiches are also available throughout the day if you'd like just a light bite in the hot Madrid sun.

CHAMARTÍN
VERY EXPENSIVE

✪ **Zalacaín.** Alvarez de Baena, 4. ☎ **91/561-48-40.** Reservations required. Jackets and ties required for men. Main courses 3,500–5,000 ptas. ($28–$40). AE, DC, MC, V. Mon–Fri 1:30–3:30pm and 9–11:30pm, Sat 9–11:30pm. Closed the week before Easter and in Aug. Metro: Rubén Darío. INTERNATIONAL.

Outstanding in both food and decor, Zalacaín opened in 1973 and introduced nouvelle cuisine to Spain. It's reached by an illuminated walk from Paseo de la Castellana and housed at the garden end of a modern apartment complex. In fact, it's within an easy walk of such deluxe hotels as the Castellana and the Miguel Angel. The name of the restaurant comes from the intrepid hero of Basque author Pío Baroja's 1909 novel *Zalacaín El Aventurero*. Zalacaín is small, exclusive, and expensive. It has the atmosphere of an elegant old mansion: The walls are covered with textiles, and some are decorated with Audubon-type paintings.

The menu features many Basque and French specialties, often with nouvelle cuisine touches. It might offer a superb sole in a green sauce, but it also knows the glory of grilled pig's feet. Among the most recommendable main dishes are a stew of scampi in cider sauce; crêpes stuffed with smoked fish; ravioli stuffed with mushrooms, foie gras, and truffles; Spanish bouillabaisse; and veal escalopes in orange sauce. For dessert, we'd suggest baked apples stuffed with cinnamon-flavored custard.

EXPENSIVE

Asador Errota-Zar. Corazón de María, 32. ☎ **91/413-52-24.** Reservations required. Main courses 1,500–3,000 ptas. ($12–$24). AE, DC, MC, V. Mon–Sat 1–4pm and 9pm–midnight. Closed Jan 1, Easter, in Aug, and Dec 24–25 and 31. Metro: Alfonso XIII or Cartagena. Bus: 43. BASQUE.

An *asador* is a kind of Spanish restaurant that typically roasts meat on racks or spits over an open fire, and the Errota-Zar is one of Madrid's best. (The technique is said to have been brought to the Basque country by repatriated émigrés who learned it in Argentina and Uruguay a century ago. Since then, the Basques have claimed it as their own, and presumably do it better than anyone else.) Asador Errota-Zar, contained behind the stucco-and-stone walls of an antique mill, is managed by Basque-born Segundo Olano and his wife, Eugenia.

You might begin your meal with slices of pork loin, grilled spicy sausage, scrambled eggs with boletus mushrooms, a savory soup made from Basque kidney beans, or red peppers stuffed with codfish. The real specialties of the house are the succulent cuts of beef, fish, or pork—first gently warmed, then seared, then cooked by the expert hand of Señor Olano himself. The restaurant is at its most interesting when groups of friends arrive, sharing portions of several different appetizers among themselves before concentrating on a main course. The offerings of meat tend to be very fresh but rather limited. The culinary variety here lies in the appetizers.

El Bodegón. Pinar, 15. ☎ **91/562-31-37.** Reservations required. Main courses 3,400–4,000 ptas. ($27.20–$32); fixed-price dinner 4,900 ptas. ($39.20). AE, DC, MC, V. Mon–Fri 1:30–4pm and 9pm–midnight, Sat 9pm–midnight. Closed holidays and Aug. Metro: Rubén Darío. INTERNATIONAL/BASQUE/SPANISH.

El Bodegón is imbued with the atmosphere of a gentleman's club for hunting enthusiasts. International globe-trotters are attracted here, especially in the evening, as the restaurant is near such deluxe hotels as the Castellana and the Miguel Angel. King Juan Carlos and Queen Sofía have dined here.

Waiters in black and white, with gold braid and buttons, bring dignity to the food service. Even bottled water is served champagne style, chilled in a silver floor stand. There are two main dining rooms—both conservative and oak-beamed in the country-inn style.

We recommend cream-of-crayfish bisque or velvety vichyssoise to launch your meal. Main-course selections include grilled filet mignon with classic béarnaise sauce and venison bourguignon. Other main-course selections include shellfish au gratin Escoffier, quails Fernand Point, tartare of raw fish marinated in parsley-enriched vinaigrette, and smoked salmon.

✪ El Cabo Mayor. Juan Ramón Jiménez, 37. ☎ **91/350-87-76.** Reservations recommended. Main courses 2,000–3,400 ptas. ($16–$27.20). AE, DC, MC, V. Mon–Fri 1:30–5pm and 9pm–1:30am, Sat 9pm–1:30am. Closed 1 week at Easter and in Aug. Metro: Cuzco. SEAFOOD.

In the prosperous northern edges of Madrid, El Cabo Mayor is not far from the city-within-a-city of Chamartín Station. This is one of the best, most popular, and most stylish restaurants in Madrid, attracting on occasion the king and queen of Spain. The open-air staircase leading to the entranceway descends from a manicured garden on a quiet side street. A battalion of uniformed doormen stand ready to greet arriving taxis. The restaurant's decor is a nautically inspired mass of hardwood panels, brass trim, old-fashioned pulleys and ropes, a tile floor custom-painted with sea-green and blue replicas of waves, and hand-carved models of fishing boats. In brass replicas of portholes, some dozen bronze statues honoring fishers and their craft are displayed in illuminated positions of honor.

Menu choices include paprika-laden peppers stuffed with fish, a salad composed of Jabugo ham and foie gras of duckling, fish soup from Cantabria, stewed sea bream with thyme, asparagus mousse, salmon in sherry sauce, and loin of veal in cassis sauce. Desserts include such selections as a mousse of rice with pine-nut sauce.

✪ El Olivo Restaurant. General Gallegos, 1. ☎ **91/359-15-35.** Reservations recommended. Main courses 2,950–3,500 ptas. ($23.60–$28); fixed-price meals 3,850–5,600 ptas. ($30.80–$44.80). AE, DC, MC, V. Tues–Sat 1–4pm and 9pm–midnight. Closed Aug 15–31 and 4 days around Easter. Metro: Plaza de Castilla. MEDITERRANEAN.

Locals praise the success of a non-Spaniard (in this case, French-born Jean Pierre Vandelle) in recognizing the international appeal of two of Spain's most valuable culinary resources, olive oil and sherry. His likable restaurant, located in northern Madrid, pays homage to the glories of the Spanish olive. Designed in tones of green and amber, it's the only restaurant in Spain that wheels a trolley stocked with 40 regional olive oils from table to table. From the trolley, diners select a variety to soak up with chunks of rough-textured bread that is, according to your taste, seasoned with a dash of salt.

Menu specialties include grilled filet of monkfish marinated in herbs and olive oil, then served with black-olive sauce over a compote of fresh tomatoes, and four preparations of codfish arranged on a single platter and served with a pil-pil sauce. (Named after the sizzling noise it makes as it bubbles on a stove, pil-pil sauce is composed of codfish gelatin and herbs that are whipped into a mayonnaiselike consistency with olive oil.) Desserts might be one of several different chocolate pastries. A wide array of reasonably priced bordeaux and Spanish wines can accompany your meal.

A final note: Many clients deliberately arrive early as an excuse to linger in El Olivo's one-of-a-kind sherry bar. Although other drinks are offered, the bar features more than a hundred brands of vino de Jerez, more than practically any other establishment in Madrid. Priced at 300 to 800 ptas. ($2.40 to $6.40) per glass, they make the perfect apéritif.

MODERATE

O'Pazo. Calle Reina Mercedes, 20. ☎ **91/553-23-33.** Reservations required. Main courses 2,000–3,000 ptas. ($16–$24). MC, V. Mon–Sat 1–4pm and 8:30pm–midnight. Closed Aug. Metro: Nuevos Ministerios or Alvarado. Bus: 3 or 5. GALICIAN/SEAFOOD.

O'Pazo is a deluxe Galician restaurant, viewed by local cognoscenti as one of the top seafood places in the country. The fish is flown in daily from Galicia and much of it is priced by weight, depending on market rates. In front is a cocktail lounge and bar, all in polished brass, with low sofas and paintings. Carpeted floors, cushioned Castilian furniture, soft lighting, and colored-glass windows complete the picture. O'Pazo lies north of the center of Madrid, near the Chamartín Station.

The fish and shellfish soup is delectable, although others gravitate to the seaman's broth as a beginning course. Natural clams are succulent, as are cigalas (a kind of crayfish), spider crabs, and Jabugo ham. Main dishes range from baby eels to sea snails, from scallops Galician style to zarzuela (a seafood casserole).

INEXPENSIVE

Alfredo's Barbacoa. Juan Hurtado de Mendoza, 11. ☎ **91/345-16-39.** Reservations recommended. Main courses 700–2,000 ptas. ($5.60–$16). AE, DC, MC, V. Mon–Sat 1–5pm and 8:30pm–midnight. Metro: Cuzco. AMERICAN.

Alfredo's is a popular rendezvous for Americans longing for home-style food. Al arrives at his bar/restaurant wearing boots, blue jeans, and a 10-gallon hat; his friendly welcome has made the place a center for both his friends and newcomers to Madrid. You *can* have hamburgers here, but they're of the barbecued variety, and you might prefer the barbecued spareribs or chicken. The salad bar is an attraction. And it's a rare treat to be able to have corn on the cob in Spain.

The original Alfredo's Barbacoa, Lagasca, 5 (☎ 91/576-62-71; metro: Retiro), is still in business, and also under Al's auspices.

CHUECA
INEXPENSIVE

🄢 **La Argentina.** Gravina, 19. ☎ **91/531-91-17.** Main courses 800–1,250 ptas. ($6.40–$10); fixed-price menu 1,200 ptas. ($9.60). No credit cards. Tues–Sat noon–4pm and 9pm–midnight, Sun noon–4pm. Closed July 25–Aug. Metro: Chueca. INTERNATIONAL.

La Argentina is run under the watchful eye of the owner, Andres Rodríguez. The restaurant has only 16 tables, but the food is well prepared, sort of Spanish family style. The best bets are cannelloni Rossini, noodle soup, creamed spinach, and meat dishes, including entrecôte and roast veal. All dishes are served with mashed or french-fried potatoes. For dessert, have a baked apple or rice pudding. The decor is simple and clean, and you're usually served by one of the two waitresses who have been here for years.

❺ El Inca. Gravina, 23. ☎ **91/532-77-45.** Reservations required on weekends. Main courses 1,800–3,500 ptas. ($14.40–$28); fixed-price menu (lunch only) 1,800 ptas. ($14.40). AE, DC, V. Tues–Sat 1:30–5pm and 9pm–1am, Sun 1:30–5pm. Closed Aug. Metro: Chueca. PERUVIAN.

For a taste of South America, try El Inca, decorated with Incan motifs and artifacts. Since it opened in the early 1970s it has hosted its share of diplomats and celebrities, although you're more likely to see families and local office workers. The house cocktail is a deceptively potent pisco sour—the recipe comes straight from the Andes. Many of the dishes contain potatoes, the national staple of Peru. The salad of potatoes and black olives is given unusual zest with a white-cheese sauce. Other specialties are the ceviche de merluza (raw hake marinated with onions) and aji de gallina (a chicken-and-rice dish made with peanut sauce), a Peruvian favorite.

Nabucco. Calle Hortaleza, 108. ☎ **91/310-06-11.** Reservations recommended. Pizza 595–825 ptas. ($4.75–$6.60); main courses 720–1,380 ptas. ($5.75–$11.05). AE, DC, MC, V. Mon–Thurs 1:30–4pm and 8:45pm–midnight, Fri–Sat 1:30–4pm and 9pm–1am. Metro: Alonso Martínez. Bus: 7 or 36. ITALIAN.

In a neighborhood of Spanish restaurants, the Italian format here comes as a welcome change. The decor resembles a postmodern update of an Italian ruin, complete with trompe l'oeil walls painted like marble. Roman portrait busts and a prominent bar lend a dignified air. Menu choices include cannelloni, a good selection of veal dishes, and such main courses as osso buco. You might begin your meal with a selection of antipasti.

❺ Taberna Carmencita. Libertad, 16. ☎ **91/531-66-12.** Reservations recommended. Main courses 900–2,500 ptas. ($7.20–$20); fixed-price menu (lunch only) 1,200 ptas. ($9.60). AE, DC, MC, V. Mon–Fri 1–4pm and 9pm–midnight, Sat 9pm–midnight. Metro: Chueca. SPANISH/BASQUE.

Carmencita, founded in 1840 and exquisitely restored, is a street-corner enclave of old Spanish charm, filled with 19th-century detailing and tilework. It was a favorite hangout for the poet Federico García Lorca, as well as a meeting place for intelligentsia in the pre–Civil War days. Meals might include entrecôte with green-pepper sauce, escalope of veal, braised mollusks with port, filet of pork, codfish with garlic, and Bilbao-style hake. Every Thursday the special dish is a complicated version of Madrid's famous cocido. Patrons wax lyrical over this regional stew; at least the chefs have had decades to get it right.

Tienda de Vinos. Augusto Figueroa, 35. ☎ **91/521-70-12.** Main courses 600–2,000 ptas. ($4.80–$16); fixed-price menu 1,100 ptas. ($8.80). No credit cards. Mon–Sat 9am–4:30pm and 8:30pm–midnight. Metro: Chueca. SPANISH.

Officially this restaurant is known as the "Wine Store," but ever since the 1930s Madrileños have called it "El Comunista." Its now-deceased owner was a fervent Communist, and many locals who shared his political beliefs patronized the establishment. This rickety old wine shop with a few tables in the back is quite fashionable with actors and journalists looking for Spanish fare without frills. There is a menu, but no one ever looks at it—just ask what's available. Nor do you get a bill—you're just told how much to pay. You sit at simple wooden tables with wooden chairs and benches; the walls are decorated with old posters, calendars, pennants, and clocks. Start with garlic or vegetable soup or lentils, followed by lamb chops, tripe in a spicy sauce, or meatballs and soft-set eggs with asparagus.

OFF PLAZA MAYOR
EXPENSIVE

Casa Lucio. Cava Baja 35. ☎ **91/365-32-52.** Reservations recommended. Main courses 2,000–3,500 ptas. ($16–$28). AE, DC, MC, V. Sun–Fri 1–4pm and 9pm–midnight, Sat 9pm–midnight. Closed Aug. Metro: La Latina. CASTILIAN.

Set on a historic street whose edges once marked the perimeter of Old Madrid, this is a venerable tasca with all the requisite antique accessories. Dozens of cured hams hang from hand-hewn beams above the well-oiled bar. Among the clientele is a stable of sometimes surprisingly well-placed public figures—even perhaps, the king of Spain. The two dining rooms, each on a different floor, have whitewashed walls, tile floors, and exposed brick. A well-trained staff offers classic Castilian food, which might include Jabugo ham with broad beans, shrimp in garlic sauce, hake with green sauce, several types of roasted lamb, and a thick steak served sizzling hot on a heated platter, churrasco de la casa.

Las Cuevas de Luís Candelas. Calle de Cuchilleros, 1. ☎ **91/366-54-28.** Reservations required. Main courses 1,400–3,400 ptas. ($11.20–$27.20). DC, MC, V. Daily 1–4pm and 8pm–midnight. Metro: Puerta del Sol. SPANISH/INTERNATIONAL.

Right down the steps from the popular but very touristy Mesón del Corregidor, a competitor restaurant, is the even-better-known Las Cuevas de Luís Candelas, housed in a building dating from 1616. The restaurant opened its doors at the turn of the century. Enter through a doorway under an arcade, on steps leading to Calle de Cuchilleros—the nightlife center of Madrid that teems with restaurants, flamenco clubs, and rustic taverns. The restaurant is named after Luís Candelas, an 18th-century bandit who's sometimes known as the "Spanish Robin Hood." He's said to have hidden out in this maze of *cuevas* (dens). Although the menu is in English, the cuisine is authentically Spanish. Specialties include the chef's own style of hake. To begin your meal, you might try another house dish, sopa de ajo Candelas (garlic soup). Roast suckling pig and roast lamb, as in the other restaurants on Plaza Mayor, are featured, but we prefer these two dishes at Botín (see below).

El Schotis. Cava Baja, 11. ☎ **91/365-32-30.** Reservations recommended. Main courses 1,000–2,550 ptas. ($8–$20.40); fixed-price menu 3,150 ptas. ($25.20). AE, DC, MC, V. Tues–Sat 1–4pm and 9pm–midnight, Sun 1–4pm. Closed 2 weeks in Aug. Metro: Puerta del Sol or La Latina. SPANISH.

El Schotis was established in 1962 in a solid stone building on one of Madrid's oldest and most historic streets. A series of large and pleasingly old-fashioned dining rooms is the setting for an animated crowd of Madrileños and foreign visitors, who receive ample portions of conservative, well-prepared vegetables, salads, soups, fish, and above all, meat. Specialties of the house include roast baby lamb, grilled steaks and veal chops, shrimp with garlic, fried hake in green sauce, and traditional desserts. Although one reader found everything but the gazpacho "ho-hum," this local favorite pleases thousands of diners annually. There's a bar near the entrance for tapas and before- or after-dinner drinks.

MODERATE

Los Galayos. Calle Botoneras, 5. ☎ **91/366-30-28.** Reservations recommended. Main courses 1,160–3,875 ptas. ($9.30–$31). AE, MC, V. Daily 12:30pm–12:45am. Metro: Puerta del Sol. SPANISH.

Its location is among the most desirable in the city, on a narrow side street about three steps from the arcades of Plaza Mayor. Set in two separate houses, the restaurant has flourished on this site since 1894. In summer, cascades of vines accent a series of tables and chairs on the cobblestones outside, perfect for tapas sampling and people watching. Some visitors consider an evening here among the highlights of their trip to Spain.

The ambience inside evokes Old Castile; the several dining rooms sport vaulted or beamed ceilings. The Grande family, your multilingual hosts, prepare traditional versions of fish, shellfish, pork, veal, and beef in time-tested ways. Suckling pig, baby goat, and roast lamb are almost always featured.

Gure-Etxea (Restaurante Vasco). Plaza de la Paja, 12. ☎ **91/365-61-49.** Reservations recommended. Main courses 1,425–3,000 ptas. ($11.40–$24); fixed-price menu 3,500 ptas. ($28). AE, DC, MC, V. Mon 9pm–midnight, Tues–Sat 1:30–4pm and 9pm–midnight. Closed Aug. Metro: La Latina. BASQUE.

This restaurant is housed in a stone-walled building that was the convent for the nearby Church of San Andres before the Renaissance. Today, amid a decor enhanced by Romanesque arches, vaulted tunnels, and dark-grained paneling, you can enjoy selections from a small but choice menu. Specialties include lomo de merluza (hake), calamares en su tinta (squid in its own ink), Gure-Etxea's special filet of sole, and bacalau al pil-pil (codfish in a fiery sauce).

✪ Sobrino de Botín. Calle de Cuchilleros, 17. ☎ **91/366-42-17.** Reservations required. Main courses 800–3,000 ptas. ($6.40–$24); fixed-price menu 3,700 ptas. ($29.60). AE, DC, MC, V. Daily 1–4pm and 8pm–midnight. Metro: La Latina or Ópera. SPANISH.

Ernest Hemingway made this restaurant famous. In the final two pages of his novel *The Sun Also Rises,* Jake invites Brett to Botín for the Segovian specialty of roast suckling pig, washed down with Rioja Alta.

By merely entering its portals, you step back to 1725, the year the restaurant was founded. You'll see an open kitchen, with a charcoal hearth, hanging copper pots, an 18th-century tile oven for roasting the suckling pig, and a big pot of regional soup whose aroma wafts across the tables. Your host, Don Antonio, never loses his cool—even when he has 18 guests standing in line waiting for tables.

The two house specialties are roast suckling pig and roast Segovian lamb. From the à la carte menu, you might try the fish-based "quarter-of-an-hour" soup. Good main dishes include baked Cantabrian hake and filet mignon with potatoes. The dessert list features strawberries (in season) with whipped cream. You can wash down your meal with Valdepeñas or Aragón wine, although most guests order sangría.

INEXPENSIVE

La Chata. Cava Baja, 24. ☎ **91/366-14-58.** Reservations recommended. Main dishes 1,500–2,300 ptas. ($12–$18.40). AE, MC, V. Mon–Sat 12:30–5pm and 7pm–midnight or 2am, Sun 12:30–5pm and 7pm–midnight. Metro: La Latina. SPANISH.

The cuisine here is Castilian, Galician, and northern Spanish. Set behind a heavily ornamented tile facade, the place has a stand-up tapas bar at the entrance and a formal restaurant in a side room. Many locals linger at the darkly paneled bar, which is framed by hanging Serrano hams, cloves of garlic, and photographs of bullfighters. Full meals might include such dishes as roast suckling pig, roast lamb, calamares en su tinta (squid in its own ink), grilled filet of steak with peppercorns, and omelets flavored with strips of eel.

El Cuchi. Calle de Cuchilleros, 3. ☎ **91/366-44-24.** Reservations required. Main courses 1,500–3,000 ptas. ($12–$24). AE, DC, MC, V. Mon 8pm–midnight, Tues–Sun 1–4pm and 8pm–midnight. Metro: Puerta del Sol. MEXICAN/SPANISH.

A few doors down from Botín (see above), El Cuchi defiantly claims that "Hemingway never ate here." However, just about everybody else has, attracted by both its low prices and its labyrinth of dining rooms. A European link in Mexico's famous Carlos 'n' Charlie's chain, the Madrid restaurant stands off a corner of Plaza Mayor. Ceiling beams and artifacts suggest rusticity. Menu specialties include black-bean soup, ceviche, guacamole, stuffed trout, and roast suckling pig (much cheaper than that served at Botín).

NEAR PLAZA DE CUZCO

Chez Lou Crêperie. Pedro Munguruza, 6. ☎ **91/350-34-16.** Reservations required on weekends. Crêpes 800–1,800 ptas. ($6.40–$14.40). No credit cards. Mon–Fri 1:30–4pm and 8pm–midnight. Metro: Plaza de Castilla. Bus: 27 or 147. FRENCH.

Near the Eurobuilding in the northern sector of Madrid, Chez Lou stands near the huge mural by Joan Miró, which would be worth the trek up here alone. Come here if you're seeking a light supper when it's too hot for one of those table-groaning Spanish meals. In this intimate setting, you get well-prepared and reasonably priced French food. The restaurant serves pâté as an appetizer, then a large range of crêpes with many different fillings. Folded envelope style, the crêpes are not tearoom size, and they're perfectly adequate as a main course. We've sampled several variations, finding the ingredients nicely blended yet distinct enough to retain their identity. A favorite is the large crêpe stuffed with minced onions, cream, and smoked salmon. The ham-and-cheese crêpe is also tasty.

NEAR RECOLETOS

La Galette. Conde de Aranda, 11. ☎ **91/576-06-41.** Reservations recommended. Main courses 1,100–1,700 ptas. ($8.80–$13.60); fixed-price menu 2,500 ptas. ($20). AE, DC, MC, V. Mon–Sat 2–4pm and 9pm–midnight. Metro: Retiro. VEGETARIAN/INTERNATIONAL.

La Galette was one of Madrid's first vegetarian restaurants, and it remains one of the best. Small and charming, it lies in a residential and shopping area in the exclusive Salamanca district, near Plaza de la Independencia and the northern edge of Retiro Park. There's a limited selection of meat dishes, but the true allure lies in this establishment's imaginative preparation of vegetables. Examples include baked stuffed peppers, omelets, eggplant croquettes, and even vegetarian "hamburgers." Some of the dishes are macrobiotic. The place is also noted for its mouth-watering pastries. The same owners also operate La Galette II, in the same complex.

THE BEST OF THE TASCAS

Don't starve waiting around for Madrid's fashionable 9:30 or 10pm dinner hour. Throughout the city you'll find *tascas,* bars that serve wine and platters of tempting hot and cold hors d'oeuvres known as tapas: mushrooms, salads, baby eels, shrimp, lobster, mussels, sausage, ham—and, in one establishment at least, bull testicles. Below we've listed our favorite tapas bars. Keep in mind that you can often save pesetas by ordering at the bar rather than occupying a table.

Antonio Sánchez. Mesón de Parades, 13. ☎ **91/539-78-26.** Tapas (in the bar) 200–600 ptas. ($1.60–$4.80); main courses 1,200–2,500 ptas. ($9.60–$20); fixed-price menu (Mon–Fri lunch only) 1,200 ptas. ($9.60). MC, V. Mon–Sat noon–4pm and 8pm–midnight, Sun noon–4pm. Metro: Tirso de Molina. SPANISH.

Named in 1850 after the founder's son, who was killed in the bullring, Antonio Sánchez is full of bullfighting memorabilia, including the stuffed head of the animal that gored young Sánchez. Also featured on the dark paneled walls are three works by the Spanish artist Zuloaga, who had his last public exhibition in this restaurant near Plaza Tirso de Molina. A limited array of tapas, including garlic soup, are served with Valdepeñas wine drawn from a barrel—though many guests ignore the edibles

Picnic Fare & Where to Eat It

On a hot day, do as the Madrileños do: Secure the makings of a picnic lunch and head for Casa de Campo (metro: El Batán), those once-royal hunting grounds in the west of Madrid across the Manzanares River. Children delight in this adventure, as they can also visit a boating lake, the Parque de Atracciones, and the Madrid zoo.

Your best choice for picnic fare is **Mallorca,** Velázquez, 59 (☎ **91/431-99-00;** metro: Velázquez). This place has all the makings for a deluxe picnic. It's open daily from 9am to 9pm.

Another good bet is **Rodilla,** Preciados, 25 (☎ **91/522-57-01;** metro: Callao), where you can find sandwiches, pastries, and takeaway tapas. Sandwiches, including vegetarian, meat, and fish, begin at 80 ptas. (65¢). It's open daily from 8:30am to 10:30pm.

---

in favor of smoking cigarettes and arguing the merits of this or that bullfighter. A restaurant in the back serves Spanish food with a vaguely French influence.

Ⓢ Casa Mingo. Paseo de la Florida, 2. ☎ **91/547-79-18.** Main courses 550–1,200 ptas. ($4.40–$9.60). No credit cards. Daily 11am–midnight. Metro: Norte; then a 15-minute walk. SPANISH.

Casa Mingo has been known for decades for its Asturian cider, both still and bubbly. The perfect accompanying tidbit is a piece of the local Asturian cabrales (goat cheese), but the roast chicken is the specialty of the house, with an unbelievable number of helpings served daily. There's no formality here, since customers share big tables under the vaulted ceiling in the dining room. In summer the staff sets up tables and wooden chairs out on the sidewalk. This is not so much a restaurant as a bodega/ taverna that serves food.

Cervecería Alemania. Plaza de Santa Ana, 6. ☎ **91/429-70-33.** Beer 100–200 ptas. (80¢– $1.60); tapas 200–1,800 ptas. ($1.60–$14.40). No credit cards. Wed–Thurs and Sun–Mon 10am–12:30am, Fri–Sat 10am–2am. Metro: Alonso Martín or Sevilla. TAPAS.

Hemingway used to frequent this casual spot with the celebrated bullfighter Luís Miguel Dominguín—ask the waiter to point out "Hemingway's table." However, it earned its name because of its long-ago German clients. Opening directly onto one of the liveliest little plazas in Madrid, it clings to its turn-of-the-century traditions. Young Madrileños are fond of stopping in for a mug of draft beer. You can sit at one of the tables, leisurely sipping beer or wine, since the waiters make no attempt to hurry you along. To accompany your beverage, try the fried sardines or a Spanish omelet.

Cervecería Santa Bárbara. Plaza de Santa Bárbara, 8. ☎ **91/319-04-049.** Beer 150–290 ptas. ($1.20–$2.30); tapas 1,000–3,750 ptas. ($8–$30). No credit cards. Daily 11am–11:30pm. Metro: Alonzo or Martínez. Bus: 3, 7, or 21. TAPAS.

Unique in Madrid, the Cervecería Santa Bárbara is an outlet for a beer factory, and the management has spent a lot to make it modern and inviting. Hanging globe lights and spinning ceiling fans create an attractive ambience, as does the black-and-white checkerboard marble floor. You go here for beer, of course: cerveza negra (black beer) or cerveza dorada (golden beer). The local brew is best accompanied by homemade potato chips or by fresh shrimp, lobster, crabmeat, or barnacles. You can either stand at the counter or go directly to one of the wooden tables for waiter service.

Taberna Toscana. Ventura de la Vega, 22. ☎ **91/429-60-31.** Beer 120 ptas. (95¢); glass of wine 90 ptas. (70¢); tapas 200–4,000 ptas. ($1.60–$32). V. Mon 8pm–midnight, Tues noon–4pm, Wed–Sat noon–4pm and 8pm–midnight. Closed Aug. Metro: Puerta del Sol or Sevilla. TAPAS.

Many Madrileños begin their nightly tasca crawl here. The aura is that of a village inn that's far removed from 20th-century Madrid. You sit on crude country stools, under sausages, pimientos, and sheaves of golden wheat that hang from the age-darkened beams. The long, tiled tasca bar is loaded with tasty tidbits, including the house specialties: lacón y cecina (boiled ham), habas (broad beans) with Spanish ham, and chorizo (a sausage of red peppers and pork)—all are almost meals in themselves. Especially delectable are the kidneys in sherry sauce and the snails in hot sauce.

Madrid Attractions | 6

Madrid has changed drastically in recent years. No longer is it fair to say that it has only the Prado, and after you see that you should head for Toledo or El Escorial. As you'll discover, Madrid has something to amuse and delight everyone.

SUGGESTED ITINERARIES

If You Have 1 Day

If you've just arrived in Spain after a long flight, don't tackle too much on your first day. Spend the morning at the Prado, one of the world's great art museums, arriving when it opens at 9am (remember, it's closed Monday). Have lunch and then visit the Palacio Real (Royal Palace). Have an early dinner near Plaza Mayor.

If You Have 2 Days

Spend Day 1 as described above. On Day 2, take a trip to Toledo, where you can visit El Greco's House and Museum, the Santa Cruz Museum, the Church of Santo Tomé, and the Alcázar. Return to Madrid in the evening.

If You Have 3 Days

Follow the suggestions for Days 1 and 2. On Day 3, take a 1-hour train ride to the Monastery of San Lorenzo de El Escorial, in the foothills of the Sierra de Guadarrama. Return to Madrid in the evening.

If You Have 5 Days

Follow the suggestions for Days 1 to 3. Day 4 would be a very busy day indeed if you visited the Thyssen-Bornemisza Museum in the morning (it opens at 10am) and toured the Museo Nacional Centro de Arte Reina Sofía in the late afternoon or early evening (it closes at 9pm on most nights). Here you can see Picasso's *Guernica,* as well as other great 20th-century art. Have dinner once again at one of the many restaurants off Plaza Mayor. On Day 5, take a trip to Segovia, in Old Castile. Its Alcázar, Roman aqueduct, and cathedral are the major attractions. Sample regional specialties at lunch and return to Madrid for dinner in the old town.

1 The Major Museums

✪ **Museo del Prado.** Paseo del Prado. ☎ **91/420-28-36.** Admission 450 ptas. ($3.60). Tues–Sat 9am–7pm, Sun and holidays 9am–2pm. Closed Jan 1, Good Friday, May 1, and Dec 25. Metro: Banco de España or Atocha. Bus: 10, 14, 27, 34, 37, or 45.

With more than 7,000 paintings, the Prado is one of the most important repositories of art in the world. It began as a royal collection and was enhanced by the Hapsburgs, especially Charles V, and later the Bourbons. In paintings of the Spanish school the Prado has no equal; on your first visit, concentrate on the Spanish masters (Velázquez, Goya, El Greco, and Murillo).

Most major works are exhibited on the first floor. You'll see art by Italian masters—Raphael, Botticelli, Mantegna, Andrea del Sarto, Fra Angelico, and Correggio. The most celebrated Italian painting here is Titian's voluptuous Venus being watched by a musician who can't keep his eyes on his work.

The Prado is a trove of the work of El Greco (c. 1541–1614), the Crete-born artist who lived much of his life in Toledo. You can see a parade of "The Greek's" saints, Madonnas, and Holy Families—even a ghostly *John the Baptist*.

You'll find a splendid array of works by the incomparable Diego Velázquez (1599–1660). The museum's most famous painting, in fact, is his *Las Meninas,* a triumph in the use of light effects. The faces of the queen and king are reflected in the mirror in the painting itself. The artist in the foreground is Velázquez, of course.

The Flemish painter Peter Paul Rubens (1577–1640), who met Velázquez while in Spain, is represented by the peacock-blue *Garden of Love* and by the *Three Graces.* Also worthy is the work of José Ribera (1591–1652), a Valencia-born artist and contemporary of Velázquez whose best painting is the *Martyrdom of St. Philip.* The Seville-born Bartolomé Murillo (1617–82)—often referred to as the "painter of Madonnas"—has three versions of *The Immaculate Conception* on display.

The Prado has one of the world's outstanding collections of the work of Hieronymus Bosch (1450?–1516), the Flemish genius. *The Garden of Earthly Delights,* the best-known work of "El Bosco," is here. You'll also see his *Seven Deadly Sins* and his triptych *The Hay Wagon. The Triumph of Death* is by another Flemish painter, Pieter Breughel the Elder (1525?–69), who carried on Bosch's ghoulish vision.

Francisco de Goya (1746–1828) ranks along with Velázquez and El Greco in the trio of great Spanish artists. Hanging here are his unflattering portraits of his patron, Charles IV, and his family, as well as the *Clothed Maja* and the *Naked Maja.* You can also see the much-reproduced *Third of May* (1808), plus a series of Goya sketches (some of which, depicting the decay of 18th-century Spain, brought the Inquisition down on the artist) and his expressionistic "black paintings."

✪ **Thyssen-Bornemisza Museum.** Palacio de Villahermosa, Paseo del Prado, 8. ☎ **91/369-01-51.** Admission 650 ptas. ($5.20). Tues–Sun 10am–7pm. Metro: Banco de España. Bus: 1, 2, 5, 9, 10, 14, 15, 20, 27, 34, 45, 51, 52, 53, 74, 146, or 150.

Until around 1985 the contents of this museum virtually overflowed the premises of a legendary villa near Lugano, Switzerland. One of the most frequently visited sites of Switzerland, the collection had been laboriously amassed over a period of about 60 years by the Thyssen-Bornemisza family, scions of a shipping, banking, mining, and chemical fortune whose roots began around 1905 in Holland, Germany, and Hungary. Experts had proclaimed it one of the world's most extensive and valuable privately owned collections of paintings, rivaled only by the legendary holdings of Elizabeth II.

For tax and insurance reasons, and because the collection had outgrown the boundaries of the lakeside villa that housed it, the collection was discreetly marketed in the early 1980s to the world's major museums. Amid endless intrigue, a litany of glamorous supplicants from eight different nations came calling. Among them were Margaret Thatcher and Prince Charles; trustees of the Getty Museum in Malibu, California; the president of West Germany; the duke of Badajoz, brother-in-law of Carlos II; even emissaries from Walt Disney World in Orlando, Florida—all hoping to acquire the collection for their respective countries or entities.

Eventually, thanks partly to the lobbying by Baron Hans Heinrich Thyssen-Bornemisza's fifth wife, a Spanish-born beauty (and former Miss Spain) named Tita, the collection was awarded to Spain for $350 million. Controversies over the public cost of the acquisition raged for months. Despite the brouhaha, various estimates have placed the value of this collection at anywhere between $1 billion and $3 billion.

To house the collection, an 18th-century building adjacent to the Prado, the Villahermosa Palace, was retrofitted with the appropriate lighting and security devices, and renovated at a cost of $45 million. The rooms are arranged numerically so that by following the order of the various rooms (numbers 1 to 48, spread out over three floors), a logical sequence of European painting can be traced from the 13th through the 20th century. The nucleus of the collection consists of 700 world-class paintings. They include works by, among others, El Greco, Velázquez, Dürer, Rembrandt, Watteau, Canaletto, Caravaggio, Hals, Memling, and Goya.

Unusual among the world's great art collections because of its eclecticism, the Thyssen group also contains goodly numbers of 19th- and 20th-century paintings by many of the notable French impressionists, as well as works by Picasso, John Singer Sargent, Kirchner, Nolde, and Kandinsky—artists whose previous absence from Spanish museums had become increasingly obvious. This museum has attracted many millions of visitors since its long-awaited opening; be prepared for magnificent art but long lines.

○ **Museo Nacional Centro de Arte Reina Sofía.** Santa Isabel, 52. ☎ **91/467-50-62.** Admission 450 ptas. ($3.60). Mon and Wed–Sat 10am–9pm, Sun 10am–2:30pm. Metro: Atocha. Bus: 6, 14, 26, 27, 32, 45, 57, or C.

Filling for the world of modern art the role that the Prado has filled for traditional art, the "MOMA" of Madrid (its nickname) is the greatest repository of 20th-century art in Spain. Set in the echoing, futuristically renovated walls of the former General Hospital, originally built between 1776 and 1781, the museum is a sprawling, high-ceilinged showplace named after the Greek-born wife of Spain's present king. Once designated as "the ugliest building in Spain" by Catalán architect Oriol Bohigas, the Reina Sofía has a design that hangs in limbo somewhere between the 18th and the 21st centuries. It incorporates a 50,000-volume art library and database, a café, a theater, a bookstore, Plexiglas-sided elevators, and systems that calibrate security, temperature, humidity, and the quality of light surrounding the exhibits.

Special emphasis is paid to the great artists of 20th-century Spain: Juan Gris, Salvador Dalí, Joan Miró, and Pablo Picasso (the museum has been able to acquire a handful of his works). What many critics claim as Picasso's masterpiece, *Guernica*, now rests at this museum after a long and troubling history of traveling. Banned in Spain during Franco's era (Picasso refused to have it displayed here anyway), it hung until 1980 at New York's Museum of Modern Art. The fiercely antiwar painting immortalizes the town's shameful blanket bombing by the German Luftwaffe, who were fighting for Franco during the Spanish Civil War. Guernica was the cradle of the Basque nation, and Picasso's canvas made it a household name around the world.

Madrid Attractions

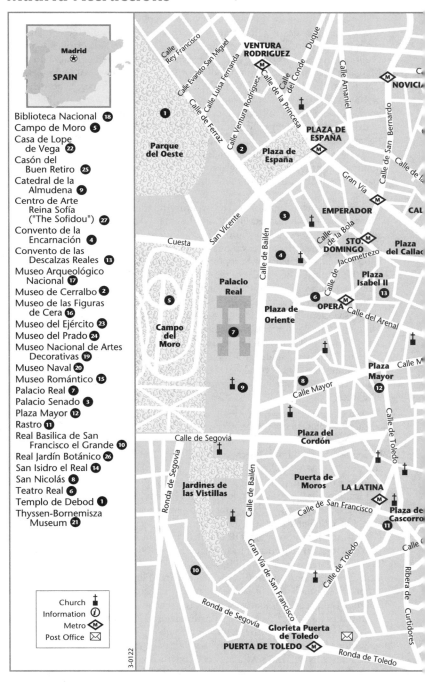

Church †
Information ⓘ
Metro Ⓜ
Post Office ✉

3-0122

2 Near Plaza Mayor / Puerta del Sol

Museo de la Real Academia de Bellas Artes de San Fernando (Fine Arts Museum). Alcalá, 13. ☎ **91/522-14-91.** Admission 200 ptas. ($1.60) adults, free for children and seniors 60 and over, free for everyone Sat–Sun. Tues–Fri 9am–7pm, Sat–Mon 9am–2:30pm. Metro: Puerta del Sol or Sevilla. Bus: 15, 20, 51, 52, 53, or 150.

An easy stroll from the Puerta del Sol, the Fine Arts Museum is located in the restored and remodeled 17th-century baroque palace of Juan de Goyeneche. The collection—more than 1,500 paintings and 570 sculptures, ranging from the 16th century to the present—was started in 1752 during the reign of Fernando VI (1746–59). It emphasizes works by Spanish, Flemish, and Italian artists. You can see masterpieces by El Greco, Rubens, Velázquez, Zurbarán, Ribera, Cano, Coello, Murillo, Goya, and Sorolla.

✪ **Palacio Real (Royal Palace).** Plaza de Oriente, Calle de Bailén, 2. ☎ **91/542-00-59.** Admission 900 ptas. ($7.20); Museo de las Carruajes (Carriage Museum), 200 ptas. ($1.60). Mon–Sat 9am–6pm, Sun 9am–3pm. Metro: Ópera or Plaza de España.

This huge palace was begun in 1738 on the site of the Madrid Alcázar, which burned to the ground in 1734. Some of its 2,000 rooms—which that "enlightened despot" Charles III called home—are open to the public; others are still used for state business. The palace was last used as a royal residence in 1931, before Alfonzo XIII and his wife, Victoria Eugénie, fled Spain.

You'll be taken on a guided tour that includes the Reception Room, the State Apartments, the Armory, and the Royal Pharmacy. To get an English-speaking guide, say "*Inglés*" to the person who takes your ticket.

The Reception Room and State Apartments should get priority here if you're rushed. They embrace a rococo room with a diamond clock; a porcelain salon; the Royal Chapel; the Banquet Room, where receptions for heads of state are still held; and the Throne Room.

The rooms are literally stuffed with art treasures and antiques—salon after salon of monumental grandeur, with no apologies for the damask, mosaics, stucco, Tiepolo ceilings, gilt and bronze, chandeliers, and paintings.

If your visit falls on the first Wednesday of the month, look for the changing of the guard ceremony, which occurs at noon and is free to the public.

In the Armory you'll see the finest collection of weaponry in Spain. Many of the items—powder flasks, shields, lances, helmets, and saddles—are from the collection of Charles V (Charles of Spain). From here, the comprehensive tour takes you into the Pharmacy.

You may also want to visit the **Museo de las Carruajes (Carriage Museum),** also at the Royal Palace, to see some of the grand old relics used by Spanish aristocrats. Afterward, stroll through the **Campo del Moro,** the gardens of the palace.

Real Basilica de San Francisco el Grande. Plaza de San Francisco el Grande, San Buenaventura, 1. ☎ **91/365-38-00.** Admission 50 ptas. (40¢). Tues–Sat 10am–1pm and 4–6pm. Metro: La Latina or Puerta del Toledo. Bus: 3, 60, C, or M4.

Ironically, Madrid, the capital of cathedral-rich Spain, does not itself possess a famous cathedral—but it does have an important church, with a dome larger than that of St. Paul's in London. This 18th-century church is filled with a number of ecclesiastical works, notably a Goya painting of St. Bernardinus of Siena. A guide will show you through.

3 Along Paseo del Prado

Museo Arqueológico Nacional. Serrano, 13. ☎ **91/577-79-12.** Admission 400 ptas. ($3.20), free for children and seniors 60 and over, free for everyone Sat 2:30–8:30pm and Sun. Tues–Sat 9:30am–8:30pm, Sun 9:30am–2:30pm. Metro: Serrano or Retiro. Bus: 1, 9, 19, 51, 74, or M2.

This stately mansion is a storehouse of artifacts from the prehistoric to the baroque. One of the prime exhibits here is the Iberian statue *The Lady of Elche,* a piece of primitive carving (from the 4th century B.C.), discovered on the southeastern coast of Spain. Finds from Ibiza, Paestum, and Rome are on display, including statues of Tiberius and his mother, Livia. The Islamic collection from Spain is outstanding. There are also collections of Spanish Renaissance lusterware, Talavera pottery, Retiro porcelain, and some rare 16th- and 17th-century Andalusian glassware.

Many of the exhibits are treasures that were removed from churches and monasteries. A much-photographed choir stall from the palace of Palencia dates from the 14th century. Also worth a look are the reproductions of the Altamira cave paintings (chiefly of bison, horses, and boars), discovered near Santander in northern Spain in 1868.

Museo del Ejército (Army Museum). Méndez Núñez, 1. ☎ **91/522-89-77.** Admission 100 ptas. (80¢) adults, free for children 17 and under and for seniors 65 and over. Tues–Sun 10am–2pm. Metro: Banco de España.

This museum, in the Buen Retiro Palace, houses outstanding exhibits from military history, including El Cid's original sword. In addition, you can see the tent used by Charles V in Tunisia, relics of Pizarro and Cortes, and an exceptional collection of armor. Look for the piece of the cross that Columbus carried when he landed in the New World. The museum had a notorious founder: Manuel Godoy, who rose from relative poverty to become the lover of Maria Luisa of Parma, wife of Carlos IV.

Museo Nacional de Artes Decorativas. Calle de Montalbán, 12. ☎ **91/532-64-99.** Admission 400 ptas. ($3.20). Tues–Fri 9:30am–3pm, Sat–Sun 10am–2pm. Metro: Banco de España. Bus: 14, 27, 34, 37, 45, or M6.

In 62 rooms spread over several floors, this museum, near Plaza de la Cibeles, displays a rich collection of furniture, ceramics, and decorative pieces. Emphasizing the 16th and 17th centuries, the eclectic collection includes Gothic carvings, alabaster figurines, festival crosses, elaborate dollhouses, elegant baroque four-poster beds, a chapel covered with leather tapestries, and even kitchens from the 18th century. Two new floors focusing on the 18th and 19th centuries have recently been added to the museum.

Museo Naval. Paseo del Prado. 5. ☎ **91/379-52-99.** Free admission. Tues–Sun 10:30am–1:30pm. Closed Aug. Metro: Banco de España. Bus: 10, 14, 27, 34, 37, 45, or M6.

The history of nautical science and the Spanish navy, from the time of Isabella and Ferdinand until today, comes alive at the Museo Naval. The most fascinating exhibit is the map made by the *Santa María's* first mate to show the Spanish monarchs the new discoveries. There are also souvenirs of the Battle of Trafalgar.

4 Near Gran Vía / Plaza de España

✪ **Monasterio de las Descalzas Reales.** Plaza de las Descalzas Reales, s/n. ☎ **91/542-00-59.** Admission 650 ptas. ($5.20) adults, 350 ptas. ($2.80) children. Tues–Thurs and Sat 10:30am–12:30pm and 4–5:30pm, Fri 10:30am–12:30pm, Sun 11am–1:30pm. Bus: 1, 2, 5, 20,

46, 52, 53, 74, M1, M2, M3, or M5. From Plaza del Callao, off the Gran Vía, walk down Postigo de San Martín to Plaza de las Descalzas Reales; the convent is on the left.

In the mid–16th century, aristocratic women—either disappointed in love or "wanting to be the bride of Christ"—stole away to this convent to take the veil. Each brought a dowry, making this one of the richest convents in the land. By the mid–20th century the convent sheltered mostly poor women. True, it still contained a priceless collection of art treasures, but the sisters were forbidden to auction anything; in fact, they were literally starving. The state intervened and the pope granted special dispensation to open the convent as a museum. Today the public can look behind the walls of what was once a mysterious edifice on one of the most beautiful squares in Old Madrid.

An English-speaking guide will show you through. In the Reliquary are the noblewomen's dowries, one of which is said to contain bits of wood from Christ's Cross; another, some of the bones of St. Sebastian. The most valuable painting is Titian's *Caesar's Money*. The Flemish Hall shelters other fine works, including paintings by Hans de Beken and Pieter Breughel the Elder. All the tapestries were based on Rubens's cartoons, displaying his chubby matrons.

Templo de Debod. Paseo de Rosales. No phone. Admission 300 ptas. ($2.40) adults, 150 ptas. ($1.20) children 15 and under; free for everyone Wed and Sun. Tues–Fri 10am–1pm and 4–7pm, Sat–Sun 10am–1pm. Metro: Plaza de España or Ventura Rodríguez. Bus: 25, 33, 39, 46, or 74.

This Egyptian temple near Plaza de España once stood in the Valley of the Nile, 19 miles from Aswan. When the new dam threatened the temple, the Egyptian government dismantled it and presented it to Spain. Taken down stone by stone in 1969 and 1970, it was shipped to Valencia and taken by rail to Madrid, where it was reconstructed and opened to the public in 1971. Photos upstairs depict the temple's long history.

5 Chamartín / Chueca / Salamanca

✪ **Museo Lázaro Galdiano.** Serrano, 122. ☎ **91/561-60-84.** Admission 300 ptas. ($2.40). Tues–Sun 10am–2pm. Closed holidays and Aug. Metro: Avenida de América. Bus: 9, 16, 19, 51, or 89.

Imagine 37 rooms in a well-preserved 19th-century mansion bulging with artworks—including many by the most famous old masters of Europe. Most visitors take the elevator to the top floor and work their way down, lingering over such artifacts as 15th-century hand-woven vestments, swords and daggers, royal seals, 16th-century crystal from Limoges, Byzantine jewelry, Italian bronzes from ancient times to the Renaissance, and medieval armor.

❓ Did You Know ?

- Sobrino de Botín, a Hemingway favorite founded in 1725, claims to be the world's oldest restaurant.
- The only public statue anywhere dedicated to the Devil stands in Madrid's Retiro Park.
- A Mexican composer wrote the unofficial anthem "Madrid, Madrid, Madrid"— and he had never been to Madrid.

One painting by Bosch evokes his own peculiar brand of horror, his canvases peopled with creepy fiends devouring human flesh. The Spanish masters are the best represented—El Greco, Velázquez, Zurbarán, Ribera, Murillo, and Valdés-Leal.

One section is devoted to works by the English portrait and landscape artists Reynolds, Gainsborough, and Constable. Italian artists exhibited include Tiepolo and Guardi. Salon 30—for many, the most interesting—is devoted to Goya and includes paintings from his "black period."

Museo Municipal. Fuencarral, 78. ☎ **91/588-86-72.** Admission 300 ptas. ($2.40). Tues–Fri 9:30am–8pm, Sat–Sun 10am–2pm. Metro: Bilbao or Tribunal. Bus: 3, 7, 40, 147, or 149.

After years of restoration, the Museo Municipal displays collections on local history, archeology, and art, with an emphasis on the Bourbon Madrid of the 18th century. Paseos with strolling couples are shown on huge tapestry cartoons. Paintings from the royal collections are here, plus period models of the best-known city squares and a Goya that was painted for the Town Hall.

Museo Romántico. San Mateo, 13. ☎ **91/448-10-71.** Admission 400 ptas. ($3.20) adults, 200 ptas. ($1.60) children. Tues–Sat 9am–3pm, Sun 10am–2pm. Closed Aug. Metro: Alonso Martínez.

Geared toward those seeking the romanticism of the 19th century, the museum is housed in a mansion decorated with numerous period pieces—crystal chandeliers, faded portraits, oils from Goya to Sorolla, opulent furnishings, and porcelain. Many exhibits date from the days of Isabella II, the high-living, fun-loving queen who was forced into exile and eventual abdication.

Museo Sorolla. General Martínez Campos, 37. ☎ **91/310-15-84.** Admission 400 ptas. ($3.20). Tues–Sat 10am–3pm, Sun 10am–2pm. Metro: Iglesia or Rubén Darío. Bus: 5, 16, 61, 40, or M3.

From 1912 the painter Joaquín Sorolla and his family occupied this elegant Madrileño town house off Paseo de la Castellana. His widow turned it over to the government, and it's now maintained as a memorial. Much of the house remains as Sorolla left it, right down to his stained paintbrushes and pipes. In the museum wing a representative collection of his works is displayed.

Although Sorolla painted portraits of Spanish aristocrats, he was essentially interested in the common people, often depicting them in their native dress. On view are the artist's self-portrait and the paintings of his wife and their son. Sorolla was especially fond of painting beach scenes of the Costa Blanca.

6 Outside the City Center

Museo de América (Museum of the Americas). Avenida de los Reyes Católicos, 6. ☎ **91/549-26-41.** Admission 400 ptas. ($3.20) adults, 200 ptas. ($1.60) children. Tues–Sat 10am–3pm, Sat–Sun 10am–2:30pm. Metro: Moncloa.

This museum, situated near the university campus, houses an outstanding collection of pre-Columbian, Spanish-American, and Native American art and artifacts. Various exhibits chronicle the progress of the inhabitants of the New World, from the Paleolithic period to the present day. One exhibit, "Groups, Tribes, Chiefdoms, and States," focuses on the social structure of the various peoples of the Americas. Another display outlines the various religions and deities associated with them. Also included in the museum is an entire exhibit dedicated to communication, highlighting written as well as nonverbal expressions of art.

Museo Taurino (Bullfighting Museum). Plaza de Toros de las Ventas, Alcalá, 237. ☎ **91/ 725-18-57.** Free admission. Mar–Oct, Tues–Fri and Sun 9:30am–2:30pm; Nov–Feb, Mon–Fri 9:30am–2:30pm. Bus: 12, 21, 38, 53, 146, M1, or M8.

This museum might serve as a good introduction to bullfighting for those who want to see the real event. Here you'll see the death costume of Manolete, the *traje de luces* (suit of lights) that he wore when he was gored to death at age 30 in Linares's bullring.

Other memorabilia evoke the heyday of Juan Belmonte, the Andalusian who revolutionized bullfighting in 1914 by performing close to the horns. Other exhibits include a Goya painting of a matador, as well as photographs and relics that trace the history of bullfighting in Spain from its ancient origins to the present day.

Panteón de Goya (Goya's Tomb). Glorieta de San Antonio de la Florida. ☎ **91/ 542-07-22.** Admission 300 ptas. ($2.40). Tues–Fri 10am–2pm and 4–8pm, Sat–Sun 10am–2pm. Metro: Norte. Bus: 41, 46, 75, or C.

In a remote part of town beyond the North Station lies Goya's tomb, containing one of his masterpieces—an elaborately beautiful fresco depicting the miracles of St. Anthony on the dome and cupola of the little hermitage of San Antonio de la Florida. This has been called Goya's Sistine Chapel. Already deaf when he began the painting, Goya labored from dawn to dusk for 16 weeks, painting with sponges rather than brushes. By depicting common street life—stone masons, prostitutes, and beggars—Goya raised the ire of the nobility who held judgment until the patron, Carlos IV, viewed it. When the monarch approved, the formerly "outrageous" painting was deemed acceptable.

The tomb and fresco are in one of the twin chapels (visit the one on the right) that were built in the latter part of the 18th century. Discreetly placed mirrors will help you see the ceiling better.

Real Fábrica de Tapices (Royal Tapestry Factory). Fuenterrabía, 2. ☎ **91/551-34-00.** Admission 250 ptas. ($2). Mon–Fri 9am–12:30pm. Closed Aug and holidays. Metro: Menéndez Pelayo. Bus: 10, 14, 26, 32, 37, C, or M9.

At this factory, the age-old process of making exquisite (and very expensive) tapestries is still carried on with consummate skill. Nearly every tapestry is based on a cartoon of Goya, who was the factory's most famous employee. Many of these patterns—such as *The Pottery Salesman*—are still in production today. (Goya's original cartoons are in the Prado.) Many of the other designs are based on cartoons by Francisco Bayeu, Goya's brother-in-law.

Museo Tiflológico. La Coruña, 18. ☎ **91/571-12-36.** Free admission. Tues–Fri 11am–2pm and 5–8pm, Sat 11am–2pm. Metro: Estrecho. Bus: 3, 42, 43, 64, or 124.

This museum is designed for sightless and sight-impaired visitors. Maintained by Spain's National Organization for the Blind, it's one of the few museums in the world that emphasizes tactile appeal. All the exhibits are meant to be touched and felt; to that end, the museum provides audiotapes, in English and Spanish, to guide visitors as they move their hands over the object on display. It also offers pamphlets in large type and Braille.

One section of the museum features small-scale replicas of such architectural wonders as the Mayan and Aztec pyramids of Central America, the Eiffel Tower, and the Statue of Liberty. Another section contains paintings and sculptures created by blind artists, such as Miguel Detrel and José António Braña. A third section outlines the status of blind people throughout history, with a focus on the sociology and technology that led to the development of Braille during the 19th century.

7 Parks & Gardens

For a touch of green in Madrid's sprawling gray urban expanse, visit one of the following:

The **Casa de Campo** (metro: Lago or Batán) is the former royal hunting grounds—miles of parkland lying south of the Royal Palace across the Manzanares River. You can see the gate through which the kings rode out of the palace grounds, either on horseback or in carriages, on their way to the tree-lined park. A lake in the Casa de Campo is usually filled with rowers. You can have drinks and light refreshments around the water or go swimming in a municipally operated pool. Children will love both the zoo and the Parque de Atracciones (see "Especially for Kids," below). The Casa de Campo can be visited daily from 8am to 9pm.

The **Parque de Retiro** (metro: Retiro), originally a royal playground for the Spanish monarchs and their guests, extends over 350 acres. The huge palaces that once stood here were destroyed in the early 19th century; only the former dance hall, the **Cáson del Buen Retiro** (housing the modern works of the Prado), and the building containing the Army Museum remain. The park boasts numerous fountains and statues, plus a large lake. There are also two exposition centers, the Velásquez and Crystal palaces (built to honor the Philippines in 1887), and a lakeside monument, erected in 1922 in honor of Alfonso XII. In summer the rose gardens are worth a visit, and you'll find several places for inexpensive snacks and drinks. The park is open daily 24 hours, but it's safest from 7am to 8:30pm.

Across Calle de Alfonso XII, at the southwest corner of the Parque de Retiro, is the **Real Jardín Botánico (Botanical Garden)** (metro: Atocha; bus: 10, 14, 19, 32, or 45). Founded in the 18th century, the garden contains more than 104 species of trees and 3,000 types of plants. Also on the premises are an exhibition hall and a library specializing in botany. The park is open daily from 10am to 8pm; admission is 200 ptas. ($1.60).

8 Especially for Kids

Aquápolis. Villanueva de la Canada, Carretera de El Escorial. ☎ **91/815-69-11.** Admission 3,500 ptas. ($28) adults, 1,500 ptas. ($12) children. Daily 10am–8pm. Closed Oct–Apr. Free bus at 10am, 11am, and noon, leaving Madrid from Calle de los Reyes, next to the Coliseum Cinema, on the eastern edge of Plaza de España.

Some 16 miles northwest of Madrid lies a watery attraction where the kids can cool off. Scattered amid shops, a picnic area, and a barbecue restaurant are water slides, wave-making machines, and tall slides that spiral children into a swimming pool below.

Museo de Cera de Madrid (Wax Museum). Paseo de Recoletas, 41. ☎ **91/319-26-49.** Admission 900 ptas. ($7.20) adults, 600 ptas. ($4.80) children. Daily 10:30am–1:30pm and 4–8pm. Metro: Colón. Bus: 27, 45, or 53.

The kids will enjoy seeing a lifelike wax Columbus calling on Ferdinand and Isabella, as well as Jackie Onassis having champagne at a supper club. The 450 wax figures also include heroes and villains of World War II. Two galleries display Romans and Arabs from the ancient days of the Iberian Peninsula; a show in multivision gives a 30-minute recap of Spanish history from the Phoenicians to the present.

Parque de Atracciones. Casa de Campo. ☎ **91/463-29-00.** Admission 450 ptas. ($3.60); an all-inclusive ticket (good for all rides), 9,000 ptas. ($72). Apr–June, Tues–Fri noon–9pm, Sat–Sun noon–1am; July–Aug, Tues–Fri 6pm–1am, Sat 6pm–2am, Sun noon–1am; Sept, Tues–Sun hours vary (call to check before going there); Oct–Mar, Sat noon–8pm (sometimes 9pm), Sun 11am–8pm (sometimes 9pm). Take the Teleférico cable car (see below); at end of this ride, "microbuses" take you the rest of the way. Alternatively, take a suburban train from Plaza de España to the stop near the entrance to park (Entrada de Batán).

The park was created in 1969 to amuse the young at heart with an array of rides and concessions. The former include a toboggan slide, a carousel, pony rides, an adventure into "outer space," a walk through a transparent maze, a visit to "jungleland," a motor-propelled series of cars disguised as a tail-wagging dachshund puppy, and a gyrating whirligig clutched in the tentacles of an octopus named El Pulpo. The most popular rides are a pair of roller coasters named "7 Picos" and "Jet Star."

The park also has many diversions for adults. See "Madrid After Dark," later in this chapter, for details.

Planetarium. Parque Tierno Galván, Méndez Alvaro. ☎ **91/467-34-61.** Admission 450 ptas. ($3.60) adults, 250 ptas. ($2) children 13 and under. Tues–Sun shows at 11:30am and 12:45, 5:30, 6:45, and 8pm. Closed 2 weeks in Jan. Metro: Méndez Alvaro. Bus: 148.

This planetarium has a projection room with optical and electronic equipment—including a multivision system—designed to reproduce outer space.

Teleférico. Paseo del Pintor Rosales, s/n. ☎ **91/541-74-40.** Fare 354 ptas. ($2.85) one-way, 500 ptas. ($4) round-trip. Mar–Oct, daily noon–9pm; Nov–Feb, Sat–Sun noon–9pm. Metro: Plaza de España or Argüelles. Bus: 74.

Strung high above several of Madrid's verdant parks, this cable car was originally built in 1969 as part of a public fairgrounds (Parque de Atracciones) modeled vaguely along the lines of Disneyland. Today, even for visitors not interested in visiting the park, the *teleférico* retains an allure of its own as a high-altitude method of admiring the cityscape of Madrid. The cable car departs from Paseo Pintor Rosales at the eastern edge of the Parque del Oeste (at the corner of Calle Marqués de Urquijo) and carries you high above two parks, railway tracks, and over the Manzanares River to a spot near a picnic ground and restaurant in the Casa de Campo. Weather permitting, there are good views of the Royal Palace along the way. The ride takes 11 minutes.

Zoo Aquarium de la Casa de Campo. Casa de Campo. ☎ **91/711-99-50.** Admission 1,500 ptas. ($12) adults, 1,210 ptas. ($9.70) children 3–8, free for children 2 and under. Daily 10am–sunset. Metro: Batán. Bus: 33.

This modern, well-organized facility allows you to see wildlife from five continents, with about 3,000 animals on display. Most are in simulated natural habitats, with moats separating them from the public. There's a petting zoo for the kids and a show presented by the Chu-Lin band. The zoo/aquarium complex includes a 520,000-gallon tropical marine aquarium, a dolphinarium, and a parrot club.

9 Special-Interest Sightseeing

FOR THE LITERARY ENTHUSIAST

Casa de Lope de Vega. Cervantes, 11. ☎ **91/429-92-16.** Admission 200 ptas. ($1.60). Tues–Thurs 9:30am–2pm, Sat 10am–1:30pm. Closed Aug. Metro: Antón Martín.

Felix Lope de Vega, a prolific Madrid-born author, dramatized Hapsburg Spain as no one had before, earning a lasting position in Spanish letters. A reconstruction of his medieval house stands on a narrow street—ironically named for Cervantes, his competitor for the title of the greatest writer of the golden age of Spain. The dank, dark house is furnished with relics of the period, although one can't be sure that any of the furnishings or possessions actually belonged to this 16th-century genius.

Chicote. Gran Vía, 12. ☎ **91/532-67-37.** Beer 550 ptas. ($4.40), whiskey and soda 1,000 ptas. ($8). Mon–Sat 5pm–2am. Metro: Gran Vía.

Ernest Hemingway used Chicote as a setting for his only play, *The Fifth Column.* He would sit here night after night, gazing at the *putas* (it was a famed hooker bar back then) as he entertained friends with such remarks as "Spain is a country for living and not for dying." The bar still draws a lively crowd.

Museo del Prado. Paseo del Prado. ☎ **91/420-28-36.**

Of the Prado, A. E. Hotchner wrote in his *Papa Hemingway:* "Ernest loved the Prado. He entered it as he entered cathedrals." More than any other, one picture held him transfixed, Andrea del Sarto's *Portrait of a Woman.* (For further details about the Prado, see "The Major Museums," earlier in this chapter.)

Sobrino de Botín. Cuchilleros, 17. ☎ **91/366-42-17.**

In the final two pages of Hemingway's novel *The Sun Also Rises,* Jake invites Brett here for roast suckling pig and red wine. In another book, *Death in the Afternoon,* Hemingway told his mythical "Old Lady": "I would rather dine on suckling pig at Botín's than sit and think of casualties my friends have suffered." Since that time, thousands upon thousands of Americans have eaten at Botín (see "Dining" in Chapter 5 for details), a perennial favorite of all visiting Yankees.

FOR THE ARCHITECTURE ENTHUSIAST

In the heart of Madrid, the famous ✪ **Plaza Mayor** (metro: Puerta del Sol) was known as the Plaza de Arrabal in medieval times, when it stood outside the city wall. The original architect of the square itself was Juan Gómez de Mora, who worked during the reign of Philip III. Under the Hapsburgs the square rose in importance as the site of public spectacles, including the abominable autos-da-fé, in which "heretics" were burned. Bullfights, knightly tournaments, and festivals were also staged here.

Three times the buildings on the square burned—in 1631, 1672, and 1790—but each time the plaza bounced back. After the last big fire, it was completely redesigned by Juan de Villanueva.

Nowadays a Christmas fair is held around the equestrian statue of Philip III (dating from 1616) in the center of the square. On summer nights Plaza Mayor becomes the virtual living room of Madrid, as tourists sip sangría at the numerous cafés and listen to the music performances, many of which are spontaneous.

The **Puerta de Toledo** (metro: Puerta de Toledo) is one of the two surviving town gates (the other is the Puerta de Alcalá). Constructed during the brief and unpopular rule of Joseph I Bonaparte, this one marks the spot where citizens used to set out for the former imperial capital of Toledo. On an irregularly shaped square, it stands at the intersection of the Ronda de Toledo and Calle de Toledo. Its original purpose was a triumphal arch to honor Napoléon Bonaparte. In 1813 it became a symbol of Madrid's fierce independence and the loyalty of its citizens to their Bourbon rulers, who had been restored to the throne in the wake of the Napoleonic invasion.

WALKING TOUR
The Prado in Two Hours

Start: The Velázquez door (western entrance).
Finish: Room 57A.
Time: 2 hours.

Best Times: At the 9am opening.
Worst Times: From 12:30 to 3pm (too crowded); Monday, when it's closed.

The greatest cultural institution in all of Spain and the root of a deep-seated pride in the country's artistic heritage, the Prado places Madrid firmly on the artistic map of Europe. It's also one of the capital's most consistently reliable tourist attractions, as witnessed by the more than two million visitors who shuffle through its corridors every year.

But because of the Prado's *embarras de richesses* (only a third of the collection can be displayed at any given time), you may need some guidance to see at least some of the world-acclaimed masterpieces. You could devote weeks to the Prado, but regrettably many visitors have only 2 hours. Here's how to make the most of that limited time.

Because the lines there tend to be shorter, we usually prefer to enter via the:

1. **Velázquez door,** the Prado's western (central) entrance, near the larger-than-life bronze statue of the seated artist, one of Spain's most famous painters. Ignoring (for the time being) the riches of the museum's street level, climb to the upper floor, using the building's central (western) staircase, which lies a short distance to the right of the entrance turnstile. At the top of the stairs, walk down the short hall that will deposit you in the museum's famous:

2. **Long Gallery.** Although referred to as a gallery, it's more technically the connected series of Rooms 24 to 32. Echoing, marble-sheathed, and often very crowded, these rooms are the main traffic artery of the Prado's second showcase floor. Walk south through Rooms 28 and 29, admiring the large-scale works mainly by Italian Renaissance painters as you go. Specific artworks will include representations by Raphael, Titian, Tintoretto, and Fra Angelico. The gallery will eventually funnel into an octagonal room (no. 32), which contains:

3. **paintings by Goya,** including his most famous portraits: the cruel depictions of the family of Carlos IV. You're standing amid the museum's densest concentration of oils by Goya. The best of these lie a few steps to the east. With your back to the Long Gallery, turn left into the long and narrow Room 31. At the end of Room 31, turn left into Room 22. This and four of its neighbors (specifically, Rooms 19 to 23, which lie in a straight, uninterrupted line) contain many of the cartoons (sketches for tapestries) Goya designed for eventual execution by teams of weavers. Walk southward into Room 18 to see:

4. **paintings by Murillo, Ribera, and Zurbarán.** This room, along with its immediate neighbors, Rooms 18A and 17A, contains works by Murillo, Ribera, and Zurbarán (1598–1664). Each of these artists produced works that are worthy contemporaries of the most-acclaimed artwork ever to emerge from Spain, the:

5. **paintings by Velázquez.** These lie ahead of you, in about half a dozen rooms whose contents are the centerpiece of the Prado. Wander through Rooms 16A, 15A, 14, 16, and 13—in any order that appeals to your roving eye. You'll intuitively gravitate to the Prado's architectural and artistic centerpiece, Room 12. Although masterpieces await you on all sides, note in particular *Las Meninas* (The Maids of Honor), whose enigmatic grouping has intrigued observers for centuries.

Now exit through Room 12's northern door into Room 11, turn left into Room 11A, then turn immediately right into Rooms 10B and 9B. This series of rooms contains one of Europe's most important collections of:

6. **paintings by El Greco.** Famous for his nervous depictions of mystical ecstasy, his dramatically lurid colors, and the elongated limbs of his characters (who seem to be physically rising upward to heaven), El Greco was the premier exponent of the late baroque school of mannerism.

Walking Tour—The Prado in Two Hours

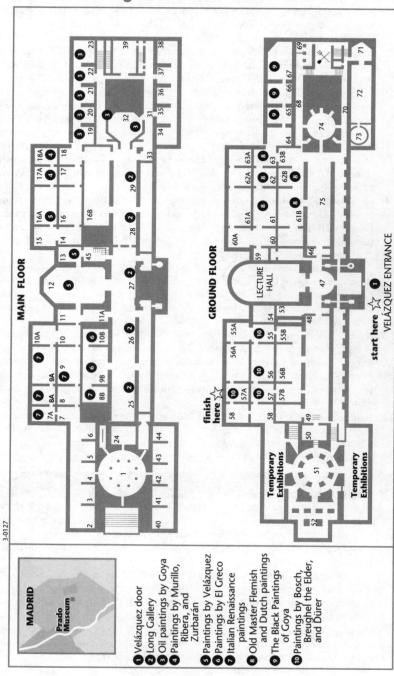

MAIN FLOOR

GROUND FLOOR

VELÁZQUEZ ENTRANCE

start here

finish here

LECTURE HALL

Temporary Exhibitions

Temporary Exhibitions

3-0127

MADRID

Prado Museum

1 Velázquez door
2 Long Gallery
3 Oil paintings by Goya
4 Paintings by Murillo, Ribera, and Zurbarán
5 Paintings by Velázquez
6 Paintings by El Greco
7 Italian Renaissance paintings
8 Old Master Flemish and Dutch paintings
9 The Black Paintings of Goya
10 Paintings by Bosch, Breughel the Elder, and Dürer

191

Time will by now be rushing by. If you choose to prolong your visit, you might want to gaze briefly into Rooms 8B, 9, 8, 7, 7A, 8A, and 9A, all of which contain an array of:

7. **Italian Renaissance paintings.** These connected rooms are within a few steps of one another, and each contains more world-class examples of works by such Italian masters as Tintoretto, Titian, and Paolo Veronese.

Know at this point that by now you've seen—albeit briefly—many of the grandest artworks of the Prado's upper floor. Head for the nearest staircase. (You might prefer to ask a guard at this point, but in any event, the museum's most important staircases lie off the previously visited Long Gallery—comprised of Rooms 24 to 32.) Midway along the Long Gallery's length, look for the staircase and descend to the museum's ground floor. When you reach it, head south through the very long Room 75. Midway down its length, turn left into Room 61B, the beginning of the Prado's superb collection of:

8. **old master Flemish and Dutch paintings.** These are in Room 61B (famous for Rubens's *Martyrdom of St. Andrew*) and continue in a cluster of rooms that include Rooms 62B, 63B, 63, 62, and 61. Room 61 contains some of the most famous paintings in history: Rubens's *The Three Graces* and the somewhat less well known *Judgment of Paris.*

Your tour is nearing an end, but if time remains, a final excursion back into the artistic vision of Goya would not be amiss. For views of some of the most depressing paintings in the history of Spain, brilliant for their evocation of neurotic emotional pain and anguish, leave the Flemish section by walking to the ground floor's southeastern corner. There, in Rooms 65, 66, and 67, you'll find:

9. **the black paintings of Goya.** Refresh yourself, if time remains, at the nearby cafeteria. (Signs are prominently posted.) Before concluding your tour, however, you might be tempted to view the weird, hallucinogenic paintings of the Dutch artist Hieronymus Bosch ("El Bosco"). To reach them, walk to the northeastern corner of the museum's ground floor, where the artist's works lie scattered among Rooms 55 to 57A, featuring:

10. **paintings by Bosch, Breughel the Elder, and Dürer.** The most important of these works is Bosch's *The Garden of Earthly Delights,* whose convoluted and bizarre images have provided fodder for the nightmares of generations of children. Also nearby are works by the Flemish painter Rogier van der Weyden.

10 Organized Tours

A large number of agencies in Madrid book organized tours and excursions to sights and attractions both within and outside the city limits. Although their mobility and freedom might be somewhat hampered, some visitors appreciate the ease, convenience, and efficiency of being able to visit so many sights in a single efficiently organized day.

Many of the city's hotel concierges, and all the city's travel agents, will book anyone who asks for a guided tour of Madrid or its environs with one of Spain's largest tour operators, **Pullmantours,** Plaza de Oriente, 8 (☎ **91/541-18-07**). Regardless of their destination and duration, virtually every tour departs from the Pullmantour terminal, at that address. Among the half-day tours of Madrid are an artistic tour priced at 4,950 ptas. ($39.60) per person, which includes entrance to a selection of the city's museums, and a panoramic half-day tour for 2,750 ptas. ($22).

Southward treks to Toledo are the most popular full-day excursions outside the city limits. They cost 7,650 ptas. ($61.20). These tours (including lunch) depart daily at 8:30am from the above-mentioned departure point, last all day, and include ample opportunities for wandering at will through the city's narrow streets. You can, if you wish, take an abbreviated morning tour of Toledo, without stopping for lunch, for 5,000 ptas. ($40).

Another popular tour stops briefly in Toledo and continues on to visit both the monastery at El Escorial and the Valley of the Fallen (Valle de los Caídos) before returning the same day to Madrid. With lunch included, this all-day excursion costs 10,700 ptas. ($85.60).

Other worthwhile full-day tours include visits to Segovia and the Bourbon dynasty's 18th-century palace of La Granja costing 6,200 ptas. ($49.60) without lunch and 9,400 ptas. ($75.20) with lunch. A half-day tour of Aranjuez and Chinchón, without lunch, costs 5,900 ptas. ($47.20).

The hop-off, hop-on **Madrid Vision Bus** lets you set your own pace and itinerary. A scheduled panoramic tour lasts a half hour, providing you don't get off the bus. Otherwise, you can opt for an unlimited number of stops, exploring at your leisure. The Madrid Vision makes four complete tours daily, two in the morning and two in the afternoon; on Sunday and Monday buses depart only in the morning. Check with Trapsa Tours (☎ **91/542-66-66**) for times of your departure, which are variable. The panoramic tour (without your getting off the bus) costs 600 ptas. ($4.80); the full-day tour with unlimited stops, 1,200 ptas. ($9.60). You can board the bus at the Madrid tourist office.

11 Outdoor Activities

SPECTATOR SPORTS

THE BULLFIGHT   Madrid draws the finest matadors in Spain. If a matador hasn't proved his worth in the **Plaza Monumental de Toros de las Ventas,** Alcalá, 237 (☎ **91/356-22-00;** metro: Ventas), he just hasn't been recognized as a top-flight artist. The major season begins during the Fiestas de San Isidro, patron saint of Madrid, on May 15. This is the occasion for a series of fights, during which talent scouts are in the audience. Matadors who distinguish themselves in the ring are signed up for Majorca, Málaga, and other places.

For tickets to this biggest bullfight stadium in Madrid, go to its box office (open Friday to Sunday from 10am to 2pm and 5 to 8pm). Admission usually ranges between 400 and 15,000 ptas. ($3.20 and $120). Many hotels also have good seats that you can buy. Front-row seats are known as *barreras. Delanteras*—third-row seats—are available in both the *alta* (high) and the *baja* (low) sections. The cheapest seats sold, *filas,* afford the worst view and are in the sun (*sol*) during the entire performance. The best seats are in the shade (*sombra*). Bullfights are held on Sunday and holidays throughout most of the year, and every day during certain festivals, which tend to last around 3 weeks, usually in the late springtime. Starting times are adjusted according to the anticipated hour of sundown on the day of a performance, usually 7pm from March to October, and at 5pm during late autumn and early spring. Late-night fights by neophyte matadors are sometimes staged under spotlights on Saturday around 11pm.

HORSE RACING   There are two seasons—spring (February to June) and fall (mid-September to early December). Races, often six or seven, are generally held on Sunday and holidays (11am), with a series of night races (11pm) held on weekends in July and August. A restaurant and bar are at the **Hipódromo de la Zarzuela,** Carretera de la Coruña, Kilometer 7.8 (☎ **91/207-01-40;** take the free bus that leaves from Moncloa, across from the Air Ministry). The hippodrome is 11 miles (18km) from the center of Madrid (N-VI). Admission is 500 ptas. ($4).

SOCCER Futbol is played with a passion all year in Madrid. League matches, on Saturday or Sunday, run from September to May, culminating in the annual summer tournaments. Madrid has two teams in the top division.

The team Real Madrid plays home games at the Estadio Santiago Bernabéu, Concha Espina, 1 (☎ **91/344-00-52;** metro: Lima). Tickets, which run 1,500 to 15,000 ptas. ($12 to $120), can be obtained at the stadium. The Club Atlético de Madrid plays at the Estadio Vicente Calderón, Paseo de la Virgen del Puerto, 67 (☎ **91/366-47-07;** metro: Pirámides). Tickets are sold at the stadium, costing 1,500 to 15,000 ptas. ($12 to $120). Both box offices are open daily from noon to 1:30pm and 5 to 7pm.

RECREATION

FITNESS CENTERS Although Madrid has scores of gyms, bodybuilding studios, and aerobic-exercise centers, many of them are private. For one open to the public, try **Atenas,** Victor de la Serna, 37 (☎ **91/345-16-75;** metro: Colombia). This facility for men and women has an indoor swimming pool, workout equipment, a sauna, and such personal services as massage. It's open Monday to Friday from 7:30am to 10pm and on Saturday from 9am to 2pm.

JOGGING Both the Parque del Retiro and the Casa de Campo have jogging tracks. For details on how to get there, see below and also refer to "Parks & Gardens," earlier in this chapter.

SWIMMING & TENNIS The best swimming and tennis facilities are found at the **Casa de Campo,** Avenida del Angel (☎ **91/463-00-50;** metro: Lago or Batán), a 4,300-acre former royal hunting preserve that lies on the right bank of the Manzanares River. Today it's a public park, serving as a playground for Madrileños.

12 Shopping

The 17th-century playwright Tirso de Molina called Madrid "a shop stocked with every kind of merchandise," and it's true—an estimated 50,000 stores sell everything from high-fashion clothing to flamenco guitars to art and ceramics.

If your time is limited, go to one of the big department stores (see below). They all carry a "bit of everything."

THE SHOPPING SCENE

SHOPPING AREAS   The Center The sheer diversity of shops in Madrid's center is staggering. Their densest concentration lies immediately north of the Puerta del Sol, radiating out from Calle del Carmen, Calle Montera, and Calle Preciados.

Calle Mayor & Calle del Arenal Unlike their more stylish neighbors to the north of the Puerta del Sol, shops in this district to the west tend toward the small, slightly dusty enclaves of coin and stamp dealers, family-owned souvenir shops, clockmakers, sellers of military paraphernalia, and an abundance of stores selling musical scores.

Gran Vía Conceived, designed, and built in the 1910s and 1920s as a showcase for the city's best shops, hotels, and restaurants, the Gran Vía has since been eclipsed by other shopping districts. Its art nouveau / art deco glamour still survives in the hearts of most Madrileños, however. The bookshops here are among the best in the city, as are outlets for fashion, shoes, jewelry, furs, and handcrafted accessories from all regions of Spain.

El Rastro   It's the biggest flea market in Spain, drawing collectors, dealers, buyers, and hopefuls from throughout Madrid and its suburbs. The makeshift stalls are at their most frenetic on Sunday morning. For more information, refer to the "Flea Markets" section under "Shopping A to Z," below.

Plaza Mayor   Under the arcades of the square itself are exhibitions of lithographs and oil paintings, and every weekend there's a loosely organized market for stamp and coin collectors. Within 3 or 4 blocks in every direction you'll find more than the average number of souvenir shops.

On Calle Marqués Viudo de Pontejos, which runs east from Plaza Mayor, is one of the city's headquarters for the sale of cloth, thread, and buttons. Also running east, on Calle de Zaragoza, are silversmiths and jewelers. On Calle Postas you'll find housewares, underwear, soap powders, and other household items.

Near the Carrera de San Jerónimo   Several blocks east of the Puerta del Sol is Madrid's densest concentration of gift shops, crafts shops, and antiques dealers— a decorator's delight. Its most interesting streets include Calle del Prado, Calle de las Huertas, and Plaza de las Cortes. The neighborhood is pricey—so don't expect bargains here.

Northwest Madrid   A few blocks east of the Parque del Oeste is an upscale neighborhood that's well stocked with luxury goods and household staples. Calle de la Princesa, its main thoroughfare, has shops selling shoes, handbags, fashion, gifts, and children's clothing. Thanks to the presence of the university nearby, there's also a dense concentration of bookstores, especially on Calle Isaac Peral and Calle Fernando el Católico, several blocks north and northwest, respectively, from the subway stop of Argüelles.

Salamanca District   It's known throughout Spain as the quintessential upper-bourgeois neighborhood, uniformly prosperous, and its shops are correspondingly exclusive. They include outlets run by interior decorators, furniture shops, fur and jewelry shops, several department stores, and design headquarters whose output ranges from the solidly conservative to the high-tech. The main streets of this district are Calle de Serrano and Calle de Velázquez. The district lies northeast of the center of Madrid, a few blocks north of Retiro Park. Its most central metro stops are Serrano and Velázquez.

HOURS & SHIPPING   Major stores are open (in most cases) Monday to Saturday from 9:30am to 8pm. Many small stores take a siesta between 1:30 and 4:30pm. Of course, there's never any set formula, and hours can vary greatly from store to store, depending on the idiosyncracies and schedules of the owner.

Many art and antiques dealers will crate and ship bulky objects for an additional fee. Any especially large or heavy item, such as a piece of furniture, should be sent by ship. Every antiques dealer in Spain maintains lists of reputable maritime shippers. One reliable option is **Emery Ocean Freight** (☎ **91/747-55-33**), which maintains branch offices in Barcelona, Alicante, Madrid, Málaga, Bilbao, and Valencia. For more information, either before your departure, or when checking the whereabouts of your shipment in transit from Spain, call Emery in the United States at 800/488-9451.

For most small and medium-size shipments, air freight isn't much more expensive than shipping. **Iberia's Air Cargo Division** (☎ **91/587-33-07** at Madrid's Barajas airport, 93/401-34-26 at Barcelona's airport, or 800/221-6002 in the U.S.) offers air-freight service from Spain to New York, Miami, and Los Angeles. For a shipment under 300 pounds from either Barcelona or Madrid to New York, the cost is 333 ptas. ($2.65) per pound. The price per pound goes down as the weight increases, reaching 269 ptas. ($2.15) per pound for shipments weighing more than 1,000 pounds. Regardless of what you ship, there's a minimum charge of 8,500 ptas. ($68). For an additional fee, Iberia or one of its representatives will pick up your package. For a truly precious cargo, ask the seller to build a crate for it.

Remember that your air-cargo shipment will need to clear Customs after it's brought into the United States. This involves some additional paperwork, costly delays, and in some cases a trip to the airport where the shipment first entered the country. It's usually easier (and in some cases, much easier) to hire a commercial Customs broker to do the work for you. **Emery Worldwide** (☎ **800/323-4685** in the U.S.), a division of CF Freightways, can clear your goods for around $125 for most shipments, which you'll pay in addition to any applicable duty you owe your home government.

TAX & HOW TO RECOVER IT If you're not a European Union resident and make purchases in Spain worth more than 86,520 ptas. ($692.15), you can get a tax refund. (The internal tax, known as VAT in most of Europe, is called IVA in Spain.) Depending on the goods, the rate usually ranges from 7% to 12% of the total worth of your merchandise. Luxury items are taxed at 33%.

To get this refund, you must complete three copies of a form that the store will give you, detailing the nature of your purchase and its value. Citizens of non-EU countries show the purchase and the form to the Spanish Customs Office. The shop is supposed to refund the amount due you. Inquire at the time of purchase how they will do so and discuss in what currency your refund will arrive.

TRADITIONAL SALES The best sales are usually in summer. Called *rebajas,* they start in July and go through August. As a general rule, merchandise is marked down even more in August to make way for the new fall wares in most stores.

DUTY-FREE—WORTH IT OR NOT? Before you leave home, check the regular retail price of items that you're most likely to buy. Duty-free prices vary from one country to another and from item to item. Sometimes you're better off purchasing an item in a discount store at home. If you don't remember the prices back home, you can't tell when you're getting a good deal.

BARGAINING The days of bargaining are, for the most part, long gone. Most stores have what is called *precio de venta al público* (PVP), a firm retail price not subject to negotiation. With street vendors and flea markets, it's a different story because haggling *a la española* is expected. However, you'll have to be very skilled to get the price reduced a lot, as most of these street-smart vendors know exactly what their merchandise is worth and are old hands at getting that price.

SHOPPING A TO Z

Spain has always been known for its craftspeople, many of whom still work in the time-honored and labor-intensive traditions of their grandparents. It's hard to go wrong if you stick to the beautiful handcrafted Spanish objects—hand-painted tiles, ceramics, and porcelain; hand-woven rugs; handmade sweaters; and intricate embroideries. And, of course, Spain produces some of the world's finest leather. Jewelry, especially gold set with Majorca pearls, represents good value and unquestioned luxury.

Some of Madrid's art galleries are known throughout Europe for discovering and encouraging new talent. Antiques are sold in highly sophisticated retail outlets. Better suited to the budgets of many travelers are the weekly flea markets.

Spain continues to make inroads into the fashion world. Its young designers are regularly featured in the fashion magazines of Europe. Excellent shoes are available, some highly fashionable. But be advised that prices of shoes and quality clothing are generally higher in Madrid than in the United States.

ANTIQUES

In addition to the shops listed below, these are sold at the flea market (see El Rastro, below).

Centro de Anticuarios Lagasca. Lagasca, 36. No phone. Metro: Serrano or Velázquez.

You'll find about a dozen antiques shops here, clustered into one covered arcade. They operate as individual businesses, although by browsing through each you'll find an impressive assemblage of antique furniture, porcelain, and whatnots. Open Monday to Saturday from 10am to 1:30pm and 5 to 8pm.

Centro de Arte y Antigüedades. Serrano, 5. ☎ **91/576-96-82.** Metro: Retiro. Bus: 9 or 15.

Housed in a mid–19th-century building are several unusual antiques dealers (and a large carpet emporium as well). Each establishment maintains its own schedule, although the center itself has overall hours. Open Monday to Saturday from 11am to 2pm and 5 to 8:30pm.

ART GALLERIES

Galería Kreisler. Hermosilla, 6. ☎ **91/431-42-64.** Metro: Serrano. Bus: 27, 45, or 150.

One successful entrepreneur on Madrid's art scene is Ohio-born Edward Kreisler, whose gallery, now run by his son Juan, specializes in figurative and contemporary paintings, sculptures, and graphics. The gallery prides itself on occasionally displaying and selling the works of artists who are critically acclaimed in and displayed in museums in Spain. Open Monday to Saturday from 10:30am to 2pm and 5 to 9pm; closed Saturday afternoon July 15 to September 15 and closed in August.

CAPES

Capas Seseña. Cruz, 23. ☎ **91/531-68-40.** Metro: Sevilla or Puerta del Sol. Bus: 5, 51, or 52.

Founded shortly after the turn of the century, this shop manufactures and sells wool capes for both women and men. The wool comes from the mountain town of Béjar, near Salamanca. Celebrities who have been spotted donning Seseña capes include Picasso, Hemingway, Miró, and recently, First Lady Hillary Clinton and daughter Chelsea. Open Monday to Friday from 10am to 1:30pm and 5 to 8pm and on Saturday from 10am to 1:30pm.

CARPETS

Ispahan. Serrano, 5. ☎ **91/575-20-12.** Metro: Retiro. Bus: 1, 2, 9, and 15.

In this 19th-century building, behind bronze handmade doors, are three floors devoted to carpets from around the world, notably Afghanistan, India, Nepal, Iran, Turkey, and the Caucasus. One section features silk carpets. In addition, the Art Gallery of the Louvre, Ispahan II, displays both old masters and contemporary art. Open Monday to Saturday from 10am to 2pm and 4:30 to 8:30pm.

CERAMICS

Antigua Casa Talavera. Isabel la Católica, 2. ☎ **91/547-34-17.** Metro: Santo Domingo. Bus: 1, 2, 46, 70, 75, or 148.

"The first house of Spanish ceramics" has wares that include a sampling of regional styles from every major area of Spain, including Talavera, Toledo, Manises, Valencia, Puente del Arzobispa, Alcora, Granada, and Seville. Sangría pitchers, dinnerware, tea sets, plates, and vases are all handmade. Inside one of the showrooms is an interesting selection of tiles, painted with reproductions of scenes from bullfights, dances, and folklore. There's also a series of tiles depicting famous paintings in the Prado. At its present location since 1904, the shop is only a short walk from Plaza de Santo Domingo. Open Monday to Friday from 10am to 1:30pm and 5 to 8pm and on Saturday from 10am to 1:30pm.

CRAFTS

El Arco de los Cuchilleros Artesania de Hoy. Plaza Mayor, 9 (basement level). ☎ **91/365-26-80.** Metro: Puerta del Sol.

Set in one of the 17th-century vaulted cellars of Plaza Mayor, this shop is entirely devoted to unusual craft items derived from throughout Spain. The merchandise is unusual, one of a kind, and in most cases contemporary; it includes a changing array of pottery, leather, textiles, wood carvings, glassware, wickerwork, papier-mâché, and silver jewelry. The hardworking owners deal directly with the artisans who produce each item, ensuring a wide inventory of handcrafts. The staff here is familiar with the rituals of applying for tax-free status of purchases, and speaks several different languages. It's open January to September, Monday to Saturday from 11am to 8pm; October to December, Monday to Saturday from 11am to 9pm.

DEPARTMENT STORES

El Corte Inglés. Preciados, 3. ☎ **91/532-18-00.** Metro: Puerta del Sol.

This flagship of the largest department-store chain in Madrid sells hundreds of souvenirs and Spanish handcrafts—damascene steelwork from Toledo, flamenco dolls, and embroidered shawls. Some astute buyers report that it also sells glamorous fashion articles, such as Pierre Balmain designs, for about a third less than equivalent items in most European capitals. Services include interpreters, currency-exchange windows, and parcel delivery either to a local hotel or overseas. Open Monday to Saturday from 10am to 9pm.

EMBROIDERIES

Casa Bonet. Núñez de Balboa, 76. ☎ **91/575-09-12.** Metro: Núñez de Balboa.

The intricately detailed embroideries produced in Spain's Balearic Islands (especially Majorca) are avidly sought for bridal chests and elegant dinner settings. A few examples of the store's extensive inventory are displayed on the walls. Open Monday to Friday from 9:45am to 2pm and 5 to 8pm and on Saturday from 10:15am to 2pm.

ESPADRILLES

Casa Hernanz. Toledo, 18. ☎ **91/366-54-50.** Metro: Puerta del Sol, Ópera, or La Latina.

A brisk walk south of Plaza Mayor delivers you to this store, in business since the 1840s. In addition to espadrilles, it sells shoes in other styles, as well as hats. Open Monday to Friday 9am to 1:30pm and 4:30 to 8pm and on Saturday from 10am to 2pm.

FANS & UMBRELLAS

Casa de Diego. Puerta del Sol, 12. ☎ **91/522-66-43.** Metro: Puerta del Sol.

Here you'll find a wide inventory of fans, ranging from plain to fancy, from plastic to exotic hardwood, from cost-conscious to lavish. Some fans tend to be a bit overpriced; shopping around may increase your chances of finding a real bargain. In summer Casa de Diego is open Monday to Saturday from 9:30am to 8pm; in winter, Monday to Saturday from 9:30am to 1:30pm and 5 to 8pm.

FASHIONS
For Men

For the man on a budget who wants to dress reasonably well, the best outlet for off-the-rack men's clothing is one of the branches of the Corte Inglés department-store chain (see above). Most men's boutiques in Madrid are very expensive and may not be worth the investment.

For Women

Don Carlos. Serrano, 92. ☎ **91/575-75-07.** Metro: Núñez de Balboa.

This boutique has a limited but tasteful array of clothing for women (and a somewhat smaller selection for men). Open Monday to Saturday from 10am to 2pm and 5 to 8:30pm.

Herrero. Preciados, 7. ☎ **91/521-29-90.** Metro: Puerta del Sol or Callao.

The sheer size and buying power of this popular retail outlet for women's clothing make it a reasonably priced emporium for all kinds of feminine garb as well as various articles for gentlemen. It's open Monday to Saturday from 10:30am to 8pm, and on some Sundays from noon to 8pm. Additional outlets are on the same street at no. 16 and at Calle de Carrestas, 10. Both these stores are open Monday to Saturday from 10:30am to 2pm and 4:30 to 8pm.

Modas Gonzalo. Gran Vía, 43. ☎ **91/547-12-39.** Metro: Callao or Puerta del Sol.

This boutique's baroque, gilded atmosphere evokes the 1940s, but its fashions are strictly up-to-date, well made, and intended for stylish adult women. No children's garments are sold. Open Monday to Saturday from 10am to 1:30pm and 4:30 to 8pm.

FLEA MARKETS

El Rastro. Plaza Cascorro and Ribera de Curtidores. Metro: La Latina. Bus: 3 or 17.

Foremost among markets is El Rastro (translated as either flea market or thieves' market), occupying a roughly triangular district of streets and plazas a few minutes' walk south of Plaza Mayor. Its center is Plaza Cascorro and Ribera de Curtidores. This market will delight anyone attracted to a mishmash of fascinating junk interspersed with bric-a-brac and paintings. *Note:* Thieves are rampant here (hustling more than just antiques), so secure your wallet carefully, be alert, and proceed with caution. Open Tuesday to Sunday from 9:30am to 1:30pm and 5 to 8pm.

FOOD & WINE

Mallorca. Velázquez, 59. ☎ **91/431-99-09.** Metro: Velázquez.

Madrid's best-established gourmet shop opened in 1931 as an outlet selling a pastry called ensaimada, and this is still one of the store's most famous products. Tempting arrays of cheeses, canapés, roasted and marinated meats, sausages, and about a dozen kinds of pâté—these accompany a spread of tiny pastries, tarts, and chocolates. Don't overlook the displays of Spanish wines and brandies. A stand-up tapas bar is always clogged with clients three deep, sampling the wares before they buy larger portions to take home. Tapas cost from 250 to 300 ptas. ($2 to $2.40) per *ración* (portion). Open daily from 9am to 9pm.

HATS & HEADGEAR

Casa Yustas. Plaza Mayor, 30. ☎ **91/366-50-84.** Metro: Puerta del Sol.

Founded in 1894, this extraordinary hat emporium is very popular. Want to see yourself as a Congo explorer, a Spanish sailor, an officer in the kaiser's army, or even

Napoleon? Open Monday to Friday from 9:45am to 1:30pm and 4:30 to 8pm and on Saturday from 9:45am to 1:30pm.

LEATHER

Loewe. Gran Vía, 8. ☎ **91/522-68-15.** Metro: Banco de España.

Since 1846 this has been the most elegant leather store in Spain. Its gold medal–winning designers have always kept abreast of changing tastes and styles, but the inventory still retains a timeless chic. The store sells luggage, handbags, and jackets for men and women (in leather or suede). Open Monday to Saturday from 9:30am to 8pm.

MUSICAL INSTRUMENTS

Real Musical. Carlos III, no. 1. ☎ **91/541-30-07.** Metro: Ópera.

You'll find the best selection here—everything from a Spanish guitar to a piano, along with string and wind instruments. The place also has excellent Spanish records and sheet music. Open Monday to Friday from 9:30am to 2pm and 5 to 8pm and on Saturday from 10am to 2pm.

PERFUMES

Perfumería Padilla. Preciados, 17. ☎ **91/522-66-83.** Metro: Puerta del Sol.

This store sells a large and competitively priced assortment of Spanish and international scents for women. They also maintain a branch at Calle del Carmen, 78 (same phone). Both branches are open Monday to Saturday from 10am to 8:30pm.

Urguiola. Mayor, 1. ☎ **91/521-59-05.** Metro: Puerta del Sol.

Located at the western edge of the Puerta del Sol, this time-tested shop carries one of the most complete stocks of perfume in Madrid—both national and international brands. It also sells gifts, souvenirs, and costume jewelry. Open Monday to Saturday from 10am to 8pm.

PORCELAIN

Lasarte. Gran Vía, 44. ☎ **91/521-49-22.** Metro: Callao.

This store is an imposing outlet for Lladró porcelain, devoted almost exclusively to its distribution. The staff can usually tell you about new designs and releases the Lladró company is planning for the near future. Open Monday to Friday from 9:30 to 8pm and on Saturday from 10am to 8pm.

SHOPPING MALLS

Galería del Prado. Plaza de las Cortes, 7. Metro: Banco de España or Atocha.

Spain's top designers are represented in this marble-sheathed concourse below the Palace Hotel. It opened in 1989 with 47 different shops, many featuring *moda joven* (fashions for the young). Merchandise changes with the season, but you'll always find a good assortment of fashions, Spanish leather goods, cosmetics, perfumes, and jewelry. You can also eat and drink in the complex. The entrance to the gallery is in front of the hotel, facing the broad tree-lined Paseo del Prado across from the Prado itself. Open Monday to Saturday from 10am to 9pm.

13 Madrid After Dark

Madrid abounds in dance halls, tascas, cafés, theaters, movie houses, music halls, and nightclubs. You'll have to proceed carefully through this maze, as many of these offerings are strictly for the residents or for Spanish-speakers.

Because dinner is served late in Spain, nightlife doesn't really get under way until after 11pm, and it generally lasts until around 3am—Madrileños are so fond of prowling around at night that they're known around Spain as *gatos* (cats). If you arrive at a club at 9:30pm, you'll have the place all to yourself.

In most clubs a one-drink minimum is the rule: Feel free to nurse one drink through the entire evening's entertainment.

In summer Madrid becomes a virtual free festival because the city sponsors a series of plays, concerts, and films. Pick up a copy of the *Guía del Ocio* (available at most newsstands) for listings of these events. This guide also provides information about occasional discounts for commercial events, such as the concerts that are given in Madrid's parks. Also check the program of *Fundación Juan March*, Calle Castello, 77 (☎ **91/435-42-40;** metro: Núñez de Balboa), which frequently stages free concerts.

Flamenco in Madrid is geared mainly to tourists with fat wallets, and nightclubs are expensive. But since Madrid is preeminently a city of song and dance, you can often be entertained at very little cost—in fact, for the price of a glass of wine or beer, if you sit at a bar with live entertainment.

Like flamenco clubs, discos tend to be expensive, but they often open for what is erroneously called "afternoon" sessions (from 7 to 10pm). Although discos charge entry fees, at an "afternoon" session the cost might be as low as 300 ptas. ($2.40), rising to 2,000 ptas. ($16) and beyond for a "night" session—that is, beginning at 11:30pm and lasting until the early-morning hours. Therefore, go early, dance until 10pm, then proceed to dinner (you'll be eating at the fashionable hour).

Nightlife is so plentiful in Madrid that the city can be roughly divided into the following "night zones":

Plaza Mayor / Puerta del Sol   The most popular areas from the standpoint of both tradition and tourist interest, they can also be dangerous, so explore them with caution, especially late at night. They're filled with tapas bars and *cuevas* (drinking "caves"). Here it's customary to begin a tasca crawl, going to tavern after tavern, sampling the wine in each, along with a selection of tapas. The major streets for such a crawl are Cava de San Miguel, Cava Alta, and Cava Baja. You can order pinchos y raciones (tasty snacks and tidbits).

Gran Vía   This area contains mainly cinemas and theaters. Most of the after-dark action takes place on little streets branching off the Gran Vía.

Plaza de Isabel II / Plaza de Oriente   This is another area much frequented by tourists. Many restaurants and cafés flourish here, including the famous Café de Oriente.

Chueca   Embracing such streets as Hortaleza, Infantas, Barquillo, and San Lucas, this is the gay nightlife district, with many clubs. Cheap restaurants, along with a few female striptease joints, are also found here. This area can also be dangerous at night, so watch for pickpockets and muggers. As of late, there has been greater police presence at night.

Argüelles/Moncloa   For university students, this part of town sees most of the action. Many dance clubs are found here, along with ale houses and fast-food joints. The area is bounded by Pintor Rosales, Cea Bermúdez, Bravo Murillo, San Bernardo, and Conde Duque.

THE PERFORMING ARTS

There are within Madrid a number of theaters, opera companies, and dance companies. To discover where and when specific cultural events are being performed, pick up a copy of *Guía del Ocio* at any city newsstand. The sheer volume of cultural offerings might stagger you; for a concise summary of the highlights, see below.

Tickets to dramatic and musical events usually range in price from 700 to 3,000 ptas. ($5.60 to $24), with discounts of up to 50% granted on certain days of the week (usually Wednesday and early performances on Sunday).

The concierges at most major hotels can usually get you tickets to specific concerts, if you're clear about your wishes and needs. They, of course, charge a considerable markup, part of which is passed along to whichever agency originally booked the tickets. You'll save money if you go directly to the box office to buy tickets. In the event your choice is sold out, you may be able to get tickets (with a considerable markup) at **Localidades Galicia,** at Plaza del Carmen (☎ **91/531-27-32;** metro: Puerta del Sol). This agency also markets tickets to bullfights and sports events. It's open Tuesday to Saturday from 9:30am to 1:30pm and 4:30 to 7:30pm and on Sunday from 9:30am to 1:30pm.

Here follows a grab bag of nighttime diversions that might amuse and entertain you. First, the cultural offerings:

MAJOR PERFORMING ARTS COMPANIES

For those who speak Spanish, the **Compañía Nacional de Nuevas Tendencias Escénicas** is an avant-garde troupe that performs new (often controversial) works by undiscovered writers. On the other hand, the **Compañía Nacional de Teatro Clásico,** as its name suggests, is devoted to the Spanish classics, including works by the ever-popular Lope de Vega and Tirso de Molina.

Among dance companies, the national ballet of Spain—devoted exclusively to Spanish dance—is the **Ballet Nacional de España.** Its performances are always well attended. The national lyrical ballet company of the country is the **Ballet Lírico Nacional.**

World-renowned flamenco sensation Antonio Canales and his troup, **Ballet Flamenco Antonio Canales,** offer high-energy, spirited performances. Productions are centered around Canales's impassioned *Torero,* his interpretation of a bullfighter and the physical and emotional struggles within the man. For tickets and information, call 91/401-28-25.

Madrid's opera company is the **Teatro de la Ópera,** and its symphony orchestra is the outstanding **Orquesta Sinfónica de Madrid.** The national orchestra of Spain—widely acclaimed on the continent—is the **Orquesta Nacional de España,** which pays particular homage to Spanish composers.

CLASSICAL MUSIC

Auditorio del Parque de Atracciones. Casa de Campo. Metro: Lago or Batán.

The schedule of this 3,500-seat facility might include everything from punk-rock musical groups to the more high-brow warm-weather performances of visiting symphony orchestras. Check with Localidades Galicia to see what's on at the time of your visit (see "The Performing Arts," above).

Auditorio del Real Conservatorio de Música. Plaza de Isabel II. ☎ **91/337-01-00.** Tickets 1,500–7,500 ptas. ($12–$60). Metro: Ópera.

This is one of the home bases of the Spanish Philharmonic Orchestra, which presents its concerts between September and May. When it's not performing, the space is sometimes lent to relatively unknown musical newcomers, who perform at admission-free concerts. The auditorium also presents concerts by chamber music ensembles visiting from abroad. Containing only about 400 seats, the hall is sometimes sold out long in advance, especially for such famous names as Plácido Domingo.

Auditorio Nacional de Música. Príncipe de Vergara, 146. ☎ **91/337-01-00.** Tickets 1,000–6,000 ptas. ($8–$48). Metro: Cruz del Rayo.

Sheathed in slabs of Spanish granite, marble, and limestone and capped with Iberian tiles, this hall is the ultramodern home of both the National Orchestra of Spain and the National Chorus of Spain. Standing just north of Madrid's Salamanca district, it ranks as a major addition to the competitive circles of classical music in Europe. Inaugurated in 1988, it's devoted exclusively to the performances of symphonic, choral, and chamber music. In addition to the Auditorio Principal (Hall A), whose capacity is almost 2,300, there's a hall for chamber music (Hall B), as well as a small auditorium (seating 250) for intimate concerts.

Fundación Juan March. Castelló, 77. ☎ **91/435-42-40.** Metro: Núñez de Balboa.

This foundation sometimes holds free concerts at lunchtime. The advance schedule is difficult to predict, so call for information.

BALLET

Centro Cultural de la Villa. Plaza de Colón. ☎ **91/575-60-80.** Tickets (depending on the event) 1,200–4,000 ptas. ($9.60–$32). Metro: Serrano or Colón.

Spanish-style ballet is presented at this cultural center. Tickets go on sale 5 days before the event of your choice, and performances are usually presented at two evening shows (8 and 10:30pm).

FLAMENCO

Café de Chinitas. Torija, 7. ☎ **91/559-51-35.** Dinner and show, 8,500 ptas. ($68); show and one drink, 3,900 ptas. ($31.20). Metro: Santo Domingo. Bus: 1 or 2.

One of the best flamenco clubs in town, the Café de Chinitas is set one floor above street level in a 19th-century building midway between the Ópera and the Gran Vía. It features an array of (usually) Gypsy-born flamenco artists from Madrid, Barcelona, and Andalusia, with acts and performers changing about once a month. You can arrange for dinner before the show, although many Madrileños opt for dinner somewhere else and then arrive just for drinks and the flamenco. Open Monday to Saturday, with dinner served from 9 to 11pm and the show lasting from 10:30pm to 2am. Reservations are recommended.

Casa Patas. Calle Cañizares 10. ☎ **91/369-04-96.** Admission 1,500–2,000 ptas. ($12–$16). Metro: Tirso de Molina.

This club is now one of the best places to see "true" flamenco as opposed to the more tourist-oriented version presented at Corral de la Morería (see below). It's also a bar and restaurant, with space reserved in the rear for flamenco. Shows are presented at midnight on Thursday, Friday, and Saturday and during Madrid's major fiesta month of May. The best flamenco in Madrid (on occasions) is presented here. Proof of the pudding is that flamenco singers and dancers often hang out here after hours. Tapas—rather pricey—are available at the bar. The club is open daily from 9pm to 5am.

Corral de la Morería. Morería, 17. ☎ **91/365-84-46.** Dinner and show, 9,500 ptas. ($76); show and one drink, 4,000 ptas. ($32). Metro: La Latina or Puerta del Sol.

In the old town, the Morería—meaning "where the Moors reside"—sizzles with flamenco. Strolling performers, colorfully costumed, warm up the audience around 11pm; a flamenco show follows, with at least 10 dancers. It's much cheaper to eat somewhere else first, paying only the one-drink minimum. Open daily from 9pm to 3am.

The Sultry Sound of Flamenco

The lights dim and the flamenco stars clatter rhythmically across the dance floor. Their lean bodies and hips shake and sway to the music. The word *flamenco* has various translations, meaning everything from "gypsified Andalusian" to "knife," from "blowhard" to "tough guy."

Accompanied by stylized guitar music, castanets, and the fervent clapping of the crowd, the dancers are filled with tension and emotion. Flamenco dancing, with its flash, color, and ritual, is evocative of Spanish culture.

Its origins remain mysterious, however. Experts disagree as to where it came from, but most seem to claim Andalusia as its seat of origin. Although its influences were both Jewish and Islamic, it was the Gypsy artist who perfected both the song and the dance. Gypsies took to flamenco like "rice to paella," in the words of the historian Fernando Quiñones.

The deep song of flamenco represents a fatalistic attitude to life. Marxists used to say that it was a deeply felt protest of the lower classes against their oppressors, but this seems unfounded. Protest or not, rich patrons—often young, brash young men—over the centuries liked the sound of flamenco and booked artists to stage *juergas* or fiestas. Dancer-prostitutes became the "erotic extras." The style had reached its present format by the early 17th century. Flamenco was linked with pimping, prostitution, and lots and lots of drinking, by both the audience and the artists.

By the mid–19th century flamenco had gone legitimate and was heard in theaters and *cafés cantantes.* By the 1920s even the pre-Franco Spanish dictator, Primo de Rivera, was singing the flamenco tunes of his native Cádiz. The poet Federico García Lorca and the composer Manuel de Falla preferred a purer form, attacking what they viewed as the degenerate and "ridiculous" burlesque of *flamenquismo,* the jazzed-up, audience-pleasing form of flamenco. The two artists launched a Flamenco Festival in Grenada in 1922. Of course, in the decades since, their voices have been drowned out and flamenco is more *flamenquismo* than ever.

In his 1995 book *Flamenco Deep Song,* Thomas Mitchell draws a parallel to flamenco's "lowlife roots" and the "orgiastic origins" of jazz. He notes that early jazz, like flamenco, was "associated with despised ethnic groups, gangsters, brothels, free-spending bluebloods, and whoopee hedonism." By disguising their origins, Mitchell notes, both jazz and flamenco have entered the musical mainstream.

THEATER

Madrid offers many different theater performances, useful to you only if your Spanish is very fluent. If it isn't, check the *Guía del Ocio* for performances by English-speaking companies on tour from Britain or select a concert or subtitled movie instead.

In addition to the major ones listed below, there are at least 30 other theaters, including one devoted almost entirely to children's plays, the **Sala la Bicicleta,** in the Ciudad de los Niños at Casa de Campo. Dozens of other plays are staged by non-professional groups in such places as churches.

Teatro Calderón. Atocha, 18. ☎ **91/369-14-34.** Tickets 2,000–3,500 ptas. ($16–$28). Metro: Tirso de Molina.

This is the largest theater in Madrid, with a seating capacity of 1,700. It's known for its popular revues, performances of popular Spanish plays, and flamenco.

Teatro de la Comedia. Príncipe, 14. ☎ **91/521-49-31.** Tickets 1,500–2,600 ptas. ($12–$20.80); 50% discount on Thurs. Metro: Sevilla. Bus: 15, 20, or 150.

This is the home of the Compañía Nacional de Teatro Clásico. Here, more than anywhere else in Madrid, you're likely to see performances from the classic repertoire of great Spanish drama. Closed on Thursday and in July and August. The box office is open daily from 11:30am to 1:30pm and 5 to 6pm.

Teatro Español. Príncipe, 25. ☎ **91/429-62-97.** Tickets 200–2,000 ptas. ($1.60–$16); 50% discount on Wed. Metro: Sevilla.

The company is funded by Madrid's municipal government, its repertoire a time-tested assortment of great and/or favorite Spanish plays. The box office is open daily from 11:30am to 1:30pm and 5 to 6pm.

Teatro Lírico Nacional de la Zarzuela. Jovellanos, 4. ☎ **91/524-54-00.** Tickets 1,800–13,200 ptas. ($14.40–$105.60). Metro: Sevilla.

Near Plaza de la Cibeles, this theater of potent nostalgia produces ballet and an occasional opera in addition to zarzuela. Show times vary. The box office is open daily from noon to 5pm.

Teatro María Guerrero. Tamayo y Baus, 4. ☎ **91/319-47-69.** Tickets 1,600–2,600 ptas. ($12.80–$20.80); 50% discount on Wed. Metro: Banco de España or Colón.

Also funded by the government, it works in cooperation with the Teatro Español (see above) for performances of works by such classic Spanish playwrights as Lope de Vega and García Lorca. The theater was named after a much-loved Spanish actress. The box office is open daily from 11:30am to 1:30pm and 5 to 6pm.

Teatro Nuevo Apolo. Plaza de Tirso de Molina, 1. ☎ **91/369-14-67.** Cover usually 2,800 ptas. ($22.40). Metro: Tirso de Molina.

The Nuevo Apolo is the permanent home of the renowned Antología de la Zarzuela company. It's on the restored site of the old Teatro Apolo, where these musical variety shows have been performed since the 1930s. Prices and times depend on the show. The box office is open daily from 11:30am to 1:30pm and 5 to 6pm; show times vary.

THE CLUB & MUSIC SCENE
CABARET

Madrid's nightlife is no longer steeped in prudishness, as it was (at least officially) during the Franco era. You can now see glossy cabarets and shows with lots of nudity.

Café del Foro. Calle San Andres, 38. ☎ **91/445-37-52.** No cover (but may be imposed for a specially booked act). Metro: Bilbao. Bus: 40, 147, 149, or N19.

This old-time favorite in the Malasaña district has suddenly in the mid-1990s become one of the most fashionable places in Madrid to hang out after dark. Patronizing the club are members of the literati along with a large student clientele. You never know exactly what the offering will be on any given evening, although live music of some sort generally starts at 11:30pm. Cabaret is often featured, along with live merengue and salsa. There's a *faux* starry sky above the stage arena. Open daily from 7pm to 2am.

China Club. Calle Amor de Dios, 13. ☎ **91/429-74-24.** Cover (including the first drink) 1,000 ptas. ($8). Metro: Antón Martín.

The most outrageous cabaret acts in Madrid are performed here, with the performers often in drag. These acts don't start until 12:30am, however. Follow the dark passage into a spacious main arena. Tubes and pipes form part of the modernist architecture. In the words of the club manager, this place attracts "all kinds—everybody is welcome." Those "all kinds" get up to dance to a wide variety of sounds after the show is over. The club is open daily from 10:30pm to 3am.

Las Noches de Cuple. La Palma, 51. ☎ **91/533-71-15.** Cover (including the first drink) 3,000 ptas. ($24). Metro: Noviciado.

If you don't mind going to bed at sunrise, you might enjoy this updated version of a once-celebrated Madrileño cabaret. Its entrance is on a narrow, crowded street. Inside, in a long room with a vaulted ceiling and a tiny stage, Señora Olga Ramos conducts an evening of Iberian song. The charm of her all-Spanish act is increased by the discreet humor of an octogenarian accompanist with an ostrich-feather tiara and a fuchsia-colored boa. Open Monday to Saturday from 9:30pm to 2am; shows are at midnight. Dinner is also served, beginning at 7,500 ptas. ($60).

Scala Meliá Castilla. Calle Capitán Haya, 43 (entrance at Rosario Pino, 7). ☎ **91/571-44-11.** Dinner and show, 9,550 ptas. ($76.40); show and one drink, 5,100 ptas. ($40.80). Metro: Cuzco.

Madrid's most famous dinner show is a major Las Vegas–style spectacle, with music, water, light, and color. The program is varied—you might see international or Spanish ballet, magic acts, ice skaters, whatever. Most definitely you'll be entertained by a live orchestra. It's open Monday to Saturday from 8:30pm to 3am. Dinner is served beginning at 9pm; the show is presented at 10:30pm. Reservations are needed.

JAZZ

Café Central. Plaza del Angel, 10. ☎ **91/369-41-43.** Cover 800 ptas. ($6.40) Mon, 1,000 ptas. ($8) Tues–Sun—but prices vary depending on the show. Metro: Antón Martín.

Off Plaza de Santa Ana, beside the famed Gran Hotel Victoria, the Café Central has a vaguely art deco interior with an unusual series of stained-glass windows. Many of the customers read newspapers and talk at the marble-topped tables during the day, but the ambience is far more animated during the nightly jazz sessions. Open Sunday to Thursday from 1:30pm to 2:30am and on Friday and Saturday from 1:30pm to 3:30am; live jazz is offered daily from 10pm to midnight.

Café Populart. Calle Huertas, 22. ☎ **91/429-84-07.** Metro: Antón Martín or Sevilla. Bus: 6 or 60.

This club is known for its exciting jazz groups, who encourage the audience to dance. It specializes in Brazilian, Afro-bass, reggae, and "new African wave" music. When the music starts, the drink prices are nearly doubled. Open daily from 6pm to 2 or 3am.

Clamores. Albuquerque, 14. ☎ **91/445-79-38.** No cover. Sun–Mon, usually 500–800 ptas. ($4–$6.40) Tues–Sat, but it varies with the act. Metro: Bilbao.

With dozens of small tables and a huge bar in its dark and smoky interior, Clamores is the largest and one of the most popular jazz clubs in Madrid. Established in the early 1980s, it has thrived because of the diverse roster of American and Spanish jazz bands who have appeared here. The place is open daily from 6pm to around 3am, but jazz is presented only Tuesday to Saturday. Tuesday to Thursday, performances are at 11pm and again at 1am; on Saturday the performance begins at 11:30pm, with an additional show at 1:30am. There are no live performances on Sunday or Monday nights, when the format is recorded disco music.

DANCE CLUBS

The Spanish dance club takes its inspiration from those of other Western capitals. In Madrid most clubs are open from around 6 to 9pm, reopening around 11pm. They generally start rocking at midnight or thereabouts.

Aqualung. Paseo de la Ermita del Santo. ☎ **91/526-59-04.** Cover (including the first drink) 1,200 ptas. ($9.60). Metro: Puerto de Toledo.

This is one of the new, relatively ephemeral clubs of the sort that tend to open, thrive briefly, then disappear into the mists of forgotten Madrileño nightclubs. The entrance is behind a tawdry pizza and hamburger complex, all part of an indoor water park and leisure center. Able to hold 2,000 patrons, it's the hottest spot in town for live music. If the scene heats up too much, you can always jump into the pool. Currently, the venue is youthful, high energy, and late night in this concert hall–cum–disco. Clients have a good time enjoying the funky music, acid rock, and cool jazz. Open Monday to Thursday from 11pm to 3am and Friday to Sunday from 11:30pm to 5:30am.

Archy. Calle Marqués de Riscal. ☎ **91/308-31-62.** No cover. Metro: Colón.

In the cellar of an old apartment building, this art deco–style dance club manages to remain fashionable despite several years in that difficult role. Many of the women might remind you of Cher in her more youthful days, and virtually everyone seems to make some effort to dress the part of the young, the beautiful, and the restless. Open Thursday to Sunday from 10pm to 5am.

Joy Eslava. Arenal, 1. ☎ **91/366-37-33.** Cover (including the first drink) 1,500 ptas. ($12). Metro: Puerta del Sol.

Set near the Puerto del Sol, this place has survived the passing fashions of Madrileño nightlife with more style than many of its (now-defunct) competitors. Virtually everyone in Madrid is likely to show up here, ranging from traveling sales reps in town from Düsseldorf to the youthful members of the Madrileño *movida*. Open nightly from 11:30pm to dawn.

Kapital. Atocha, 125. ☎ **91/420-29-06.** Cover (including the first drink) 1,000–1,500 ptas. ($8–$12). Metro: Antón Martín.

This is the most sprawling, labyrinthine, and multicultural disco in Madrid at the moment. In what was originally conceived as a theater, it contains seven different levels, each of which sports at least one bar and an ambience that's often radically different from the one you just left on a previous floor. Voyeurs of any age, take heart—there's a lot to see at the Kapital, with a mixed crowd that pursues whatever form of sexuality seems appropriate at the moment. Open Thursday to Sunday from 11:30pm to 5:30am.

Ku Madrid. Princesa, 1 (Plaza de España). No phone. Cover 1,400 ptas. ($11.20). Metro: Argüelles.

The decor is showplace modern, obviously the result of a cadre of decorators hired to make an important decorative statement. Its reputation is as a hip but potentially fleeting late-night venue for young and not-so-young night owls who enjoy a permissive and sophisticated ambience. Open Tuesday to Sunday from midnight to 5am.

Long Play. Plaza Vasquez de Mella, 2. ☎ **91/531-01-11.** Cover (including the first drink) 1,000 ptas. ($8). Metro: Gran Vía.

Catering to crowds of all ages, it manages to combine disco music with long stretches of bars, comfortable tables and chairs, and a crowd with seemingly nothing to do but dance, dance, dance. Recorded music is sometimes interspersed with live bands. Open Tuesday to Sunday from 7pm to 3am.

Pachá. Calle Barcelo, 11. ☎ **91/446-01-37.** Cover (including the first drink) 1,200 ptas. ($9.60). Metro: Tribunal.

The carefully contrived setting is pseudo-opulent, and the drinks sometimes hard to get because of the milling crowds. Despite that, the place thrives as one of the late-night staples in Madrid for the mid-20s to late-40s clientele (a crowd who often segregate themselves by age into distinctly different areas of the place). More than other nightclubs in Madrid, this has been the subject of complaints from neighbors about late-night noise. It's open Tuesday to Sunday from 11pm to 5am.

THE BAR SCENE
PUBS & BARS

Balmoral. Hermosilia, 10. ☎ **91/431-41-33.** Metro: Serrano.

Its exposed wood and comfortable chairs evoke a London club. The clientele tends toward journalists, politicians, army brass, owners of large estates, bankers, diplomats, and the occasional literary star. *Newsweek* magazine once dubbed it one of the "best bars in the world." No food other than tapas is served. Open Monday to Saturday from noon to midnight or 1am.

Balneario. Juan Ramón Jiménez, 37. ☎ **91/350-87-76.** Metro: Cuzco.

Clients enjoy potent drinks in a setting with fresh flowers, white marble, and a stone bathtub that might have been used by Josephine Bonaparte. Near Chamartín Station on the northern edge of Madrid, Balneario is one of the most stylish and upscale bars in the city. It's adjacent to and managed by one of Madrid's most elegant and prestigious restaurants, El Cabo Mayor, and often attracts that dining room's clients for apéritifs or after-dinner drinks. Tapas include endive with smoked salmon, asparagus mousse, and anchovies with avocado. Open Monday to Saturday from noon to 2:30am. Tapas cost 550 to 1,750 ptas. ($4.40 to $14).

Bar Cock. De la Reina, 16. ☎ **91/532-28-26.** Metro: Gran Vía.

This bar attracts some of the most visible artists, actors, models, and filmmakers in Madrid. The name comes from the word *cocktail,* or so they say. The decoration is elaborately unique, in contrast to the hip clientele. Open daily from 7pm to 3am; closed December 24 to 31.

Chicote. Gran Vía, 12. ☎ **91/532-67-37.** Metro: Gran Vía.

Beloved by Hemingway, who had quite a few drinks here, this is Madrid's most famous cocktail bar. It's a classic, with the same 1930s interior design it had when the foreign press came to sit out the civil war, although the sound of artillery shells along the Gran Vía could be heard at the time. Even the seats are the same ones that held such luminaries as Don Ernesto, Grace Kelly, and Ava Gardner. Long a favorite of artists and writers, the bar became a haven for prostitutes in the late Franco era. No more. It's back in the limelight again, a sophisticated and much-frequented rendezvous. Open daily from 11am to 3am. Drink prices can be high, but the waiters serve them with such grace you don't mind.

Los Gabrieles. Echegaray, 17. ☎ **91/429-62-61.** Metro: Tirso de Molina.

Located in the heart of one of Madrid's most visible warrens of narrow streets, in a district that pulsates with after-dark nightlife options, this historic bar served throughout most of the 19th century as the sales outlet for a Spanish wine merchant.

In the 1980s its two rooms were transformed into a bar and café, where you can admire lavishly tiled walls with detailed scenes of courtiers, dancers, and Andalusian maidens peering from behind mantillas and fans. Open Monday to Friday from noon to 2am and on Saturday and Sunday from noon to 3am.

Hanoi. Hortaleza, 81. ☎ **91/319-66-72.** Cover (including the first drink) 1,200 ptas. ($9.60). Metro: Alonso Martínez.

Its setting is stylish and minimalist—stainless steel, curving lines, and sharp angles—and its clients are youthful, attractive, and warmly sentimental about the memories that remain from the heady, early days of Madrid's *movida*. They include a bevy of male and female models who seem as mobile and changeable as the *movida* itself. The atmosphere is comfortable for attendees of any conceivable form of sexuality. At least a half-dozen video screens show films from long-defunct TV series, and the music reflects what's happening in London, Los Angeles, and New York. It's open Wednesday to Saturday from 9pm to 4am.

Hispano Bar/Buffet. Paseo de la Castellana, 78. ☎ **91/411-48-76.** Metro: Nuevos Ministerios.

This establishment does a respectable lunch trade every day for members of the local business community, who crowd in to enjoy the amply portioned *platos del día*. These might include a platter of roast duck with figs or orange sauce, or a suprême of hake. After around 5pm, however, the ambience becomes that of a busy after-office bar, patronized by stylishly dressed women and many local entrepreneurs. The hubbub continues on into the night. Open daily from 1:30pm to 1:30am. Full meals at lunchtime cost from around 4,000 pesetas ($32).

Mr. Pickwick's. Marqués de Urquijo, 44 (at corner of Paseo del Pintor Rosales). ☎ **91/559-51-85.** Metro: Argüelles.

For homesick English expatriates, no other establishment in Madrid better captures the pub atmosphere than Mr. Pickwick's, a 10-minute walk from Plaza de España. Although only a few of the staff speak fluent English, the decor includes everything you'd expect in London: framed prints of Dickens characters, brass hunting horns, and pewter and ceramic beer mugs. Loners can drink at the bar, or you can sit at one of the small tables, sinking into the soft sofas and armchairs. Open daily from 6pm to 1am.

Oliver Piano Bar. Almirante, 12. ☎ **91/521-73-79.** Metro: Chueca. Bus: 70.

The Oliver Piano Bar, off Paseo de la Castellana, is a pub-style hangout for show-biz people, with a good sprinkling of foreign personalities. The bar feels like a drawing room or library, and there are two club rooms, each with its own personality. The first floor has sofas and comfortable armchairs arranged for conversational gatherings. Reached by a curving stairway, the downstairs room is more secluded. On either side of the fireplace are shelves with an eclectic collection of records (you can pick the ones you want played) and books on theater, movies, and painting. Open Monday to Friday from 4pm to 3:30am and on Saturday from 6pm to 3:30am.

Palacio Gaviria. Calle del Arenal, 9. ☎ **91/526-60-69.** Cover (including the first drink) 1,500 ptas. ($12). Metro: Puerta del Sol or Ópera.

Its construction in 1847 was heralded as the architectural triumph of one of the era's most flamboyant aristocrats, the marqués de Gaviria. Famous as one of the paramours of Isabella II, he outfitted his palace with the ornate jumble of neoclassical and baroque styles that later became known as *Isabelino*. In 1993, after extensive renovations, the building was opened to the public as a concert hall for the occasional presentation of classical music and as a late-night cocktail bar. Ten high-ceilinged rooms now function as richly decorated, multipurpose areas for guests to wander in, drinks in hand, reacting to whatever, or whomever, happens to be there at the time. (One room is discreetly referred to as the bedroom-away-from-home of the queen herself.) No food is served, but the libations include a stylish list of cocktails and wines. The often-dull music doesn't match the elegance of the decor. Thursday, Friday, and Saturday are usually dance nights, everything from the tango to the waltz. Cabaret is usually featured most other nights. Open Monday to Friday from 10:30pm to 3am and on Saturday and Sunday from 10:30pm to 5am.

Viva Madrid. Manuel Fernández y González, 7. ☎ **91/410-55-35.** Metro: Antón Martín.

A congenial and sudsy mix of students, artists, foreign tourists, and visiting Yanks cram into its turn-of-the-century interior, where antique tile murals and blatant belle époque nostalgia contribute to an undeniable charm. Crowded and noisy, it's a place where lots of beer is swilled and spilled. It's set in a neighborhood of antique houses and narrow streets near Plaza de Santa Ana. Open on Friday from noon to lam and on Saturday from noon to 2am.

SUMMER TERRAZAS

At the first of the spring weather, Madrileños rush outdoors to drink, talk, and sit at a string of open-air cafés throughout the city. The best ones—and also the most expensive—are along Paseo de la Castellana between Plaza de la Cibeles and Plaza Emilio Castelar, but there are dozens more throughout the city.

You can wander up and down the boulevard, selecting one that appeals to you; if you get bored, you can go on later to another one. Sometimes these terrazas are called *chirinquitos.* You'll also find them along other paseos, the Recoletos and the Prado, both fashionable areas, although not as hip as the Castellana. For old, traditional atmosphere, the terrazas at Plaza Mayor win out. The terrazas of Plaza Santa Ana also hold several atmospheric choices in the old city. Friday and Saturday are the most popular nights for drinking; many locals sit here all night.

CAVE CRAWLING

To capture a peculiar Madrid joie de vivre of the 18th century, visit some *mesones* and *cuevas,* many found in the *barrios bajos.* From Plaza Mayor, walk down Arco de Cuchilleros until you find a Gypsy-like cave that fits your fancy. Young people love to meet in the taverns and caves of Old Madrid for communal drinking and songfests. The sangría flows freely, the atmosphere is charged, and the room usually is packed; the sounds of guitars waft into the night air. Sometimes you'll see a strolling band of singing students (*tuna*) going from bar to bar, colorfully attired, with ribbons fluttering from their outfits.

Mesón del Champiñón. Cava de San Miguel, 17. No phone. Metro: Puerta del Sol or Ópera.

The bartenders keep a brimming bucket of sangría behind the long stand-up bar as a thirst quencher for the crowd. The name of the establishment in English is Mushroom, and that's exactly what you'll see depicted in various sizes along sections of the vaulted ceilings. A more appetizing way to experience a champiñón is to order a ración of grilled, stuffed, and salted mushrooms, served with toothpicks, for 575 ptas. ($4.60). Two tiny, slightly dark rooms in the back are where Spanish families go to hear organ music performed. Unless you want to be exiled to the very back, don't expect to get a seat—practically everybody prefers to stand. Open daily from 6pm to 2am. Sangría is 1,400 ptas. ($11.20); tapas begin at 600 ptas. ($4.80).

Mesón de la Guitarra. Cava de San Miguel, 13. ☎ **91/559-95-31.** Metro: Puerta del Sol or Ópera.

Our favorite cueva in the area, the Mesón de la Guitarra is loud and exciting any night of the week, and it's as warmly earthy as anything you'll find in Madrid. The decor combines terra-cotta floors, antique brick walls, hundreds of sangría pitchers clustered above the bar, murals of gluttons, old rifles, and faded bullfighting posters. Like most things in Madrid, the place doesn't get rolling until around 10:30pm, although you can stop in for a drink and tapas earlier. Don't be afraid to start singing an American song if it has a fast rhythm—60 people will join in, even if they don't know the words. Open daily from 7pm to 1:30am. Tapas are 700 to 900 ptas. ($5.60 to $7.20).

Sesamo. Príncipe, 7. ☎ **91/429-65-24.** Metro: Sevilla or Puerta del Sol.

In a class by itself, this cueva, dating from the early 1950s, draws a clientele of young painters and writers with its bohemian ambience. Hemingway was one of those early visitors (a plaque commemorates him). At first you'll think you're walking into a tiny snack bar—and you are. But proceed down the flight of steps to the cellar. Here, the walls are covered with contemporary paintings and quotations. At squatty stools and tables, an international assortment of young people listens to piano music and sometimes folk singing or guitar playing. Open daily from 6:30pm to 2am.

GAY & LESBIAN NIGHTLIFE

Alves. Calle Veneras 2. ☎ **91/548-20-22.** Cover (including the first drink) 1,200–1,500 ptas. ($9.60–$12). Metro: Santo Domingo.

No longer Madrid's leading gay disco, Alves still attracts a widely diversified crowd of various sexual persuasions. Dance arenas are spread across three floors, and there's also a dark room for more amorous diversions. The bars offer surprisingly good food. Upstairs you can dance the sevillana, or dance to "rave" music on the lower levels. On Sunday there is sometimes a cabaret. Open daily from midnight to 6am, but at its hottest from 3 to 5am.

Black and White. Gravina (at the corner of Libertad). ☎ **91/531-11-41.** Metro: Chueca.

This is the major gay bar of Madrid, located in the center of the Chueca district. A guard will open the door to a large room—painted, as you might expect, black and white. There's a disco in the basement, but the street-level bar is the premier gathering spot, featuring drag shows Thursday to Sunday, male striptease, and videos. Old movies are shown against one wall. Open Monday to Friday from 8pm to 4am and on Saturday and Sunday from 8pm to 5am.

Café Figueroa. Augusto Figueroa, 17 (at Hortaleza). ☎ **91/521-16-73.** Metro: Chueca.

This turn-of-the-century café attracts a diverse clientele, including a large number of gay men and lesbians. It's one of the city's most popular gathering spots for drinks and conversations. Open Monday to Friday from 3pm to 1am and on Saturday and Sunday from 3pm to 2:30am.

Cruising. Perez Galdos, 5. ☎ **91/521-51-43.** Metro: Chueca.

One of the predominant gay bars of Madrid, a center for gay consciousness-raising and gay cruising (as its name suggests), this place has probably been visited at least once by virtually every gay male in Castile. It doesn't get crowded or lively until late at night. Open Monday to Friday from 8pm to 3am and on Saturday and Sunday from 8pm to 4:30am.

Refugio. Calle Doctor Cortezo, 1. ☎ **91/308-14-62.** Cover 1,200–1,500 ptas. ($9.60–$12). Metro: Tirso de Molina.

This is one of the hottest venues for gays meeting gays in Madrid. It's equivalent would be Soho in London or the Sound Factory in New York. Spacious and lively, it's often a venue for theme parties during the week. Open daily from midnight to 5am.

MORE ENTERTAINMENT

MOVIES   Cinematic releases from Paris, New York, Rome, and Hollywood come quickly to Madrid, where an avid audience often waits in long lines for tickets. Most foreign films are dubbed into Spanish, unless they're indicated as *VO* (original version).

Madrid boasts at least 90 legitimate movie houses (many of which have several theaters under one roof) and many others with adult entertainment only. The premier theaters of the city are the enormous, slightly faded movie palaces of the Gran Vía, whose huge movie marquees announce in lurid colors whichever romantic or adventure *espectáculo* happens to be playing at the moment. For listings, consult the *Guía del Ocio* or *Guía de Diario 16* (both available at newsstands), or a newspaper.

If you want to see a film while in Madrid, one of the best places is the quadruplex **Alphaville,** Martín de los Héroes, 14 (☎ **91/559-38-36;** metro: Plaza de España). It shows English-language films with Spanish subtitles as well as other foreign-language films such as French and German. If the film is not too long, there are four daily showings, at 4:30, 6:30, 8:30, and 10:30pm; on Saturday and Sunday there's a late-night show at 12:30am. Admission is 700 ptas. ($5.60). The complex also includes a bookstore and a café decorated in art deco style.

For classic revivals and foreign films, check the listings at **Filmoteca** in the Cine Doré, Santa Isabel, 3 (☎ **91/369-11-25;** metro: Antón Martín). Movies here tend to be shown in their original language. Tickets cost 225 ptas. ($1.80). There's a bar and a simple restaurant.

A CASINO   The **Casino Gran Madrid** is at km 28,300 of Carretera Nacional VI—Madrid–La Coruña (☎ **91/856-11-00**). Even nongamblers sometimes make the trek here from the capital; the casino's many entertainment facilities are considered by some to be the most exciting thing around. Its scattered attractions include two restaurants, four bars, and a nightclub. The casino is open daily from 4pm to 5am. For an entrance fee of 500 ptas. ($4), you can sample the action in the gaming rooms, including French and American roulette, blackjack, punto y banco, baccarat, and chemin de fer.

An à la carte restaurant in the French Gaming Room offers international cuisine, with dinners costing 7,000 ptas. ($56) and up. A buffet in the American Gaming Room will cost around 3,000 ptas. ($24). The restaurants are open from 9:15pm to 2am. The casino is about 18 miles (29km) northwest of Madrid, along the Madrid–La Coruña N-VI highway. If you don't feel like driving, the casino has buses that depart from Plaza de España, 6, every afternoon and evening at 4:30, 6, 7:30, and 9pm. Note that between October and June men must wear jackets and ties; T-shirts and tennis shoes are forbidden in any season. To enter, European visitors must present an identity card and non-European visitors must present a passport.

Easy Excursions from Madrid

Some of Europe's most interesting and varied scenery and attractions lie in the satellite cities and towns ringing Madrid. These include Toledo, with its El Greco masterpieces; Aranjuez, with its autumn/spring Bourbon palace; San Lorenzo with its monastery (El Escorial) that's considered the eighth wonder of the world; Segovia, with its castles that appear to "float" in the clouds, and nearby La Granja, with its summer palaces of the Bourbon dynasty; and Cuenca, the town famous for its precarious "hanging houses." If your time is short, go at least to Toledo, which captures the ages of Spain in miniature. Many tourists combine a tour of Toledo with a stopover at the royal palace in Aranjuez.

1 Toledo

42 miles (68km) SW of Madrid

The ancient capital of Spain looms on the horizon like an El Greco painting, seemingly undisturbed by the ages. The see of the primate of Spain, the ecclesiastical center of the country, Toledo is medieval but well preserved. The Tagus River loops around the granite promontory on which Toledo rests, surrounding the Imperial City on three sides like a snake.

Toledan steel, known as early as the 1st century B.C., has sliced its name down through the ages. Many a Mexican or Peruvian—if he had lived—could attest to the deadly accuracy of a Toledan sword. But except for its steel and damascene work, the lack of major industrial activity has kept Toledo a virtual museum. Many of its buildings are intact, having survived countless battles, the most recent being the bloody fighting the city witnessed in the Spanish Civil War. It's not uncommon for mansions to preserve their original coats-of-arms in their facades.

The natural fortress that is Toledo is a labyrinth of narrow and precipitous streets, decaying palaces, towers, and squares—all tourist-trodden. The Spanish government has seen fit to preserve all of Toledo as a "national monument." One critic labeled the entire city "a gallery of art," with every style represented from Romanesque to Moorish to Gothic (best exemplified by the cathedral) to Renaissance.

ESSENTIALS

GETTING THERE   By Train   RENFE trains run frequently every day. Those departing Madrid's Atocha railway station for Toledo run from 7am to 8:25pm; those leaving Toledo for Madrid run daily from 7am to 9pm. Travel time is approximately 2 hours. For train information in Madrid, call 91/468-45-11; in Toledo, call 925/22-30-99.

By Bus   Bus transit between Madrid and Toledo is faster and more convenient than travel by train. Buses, which are operated by several companies, the largest of which include Continental and Galiano, depart at 30-minute intervals from Madrid's **Estación Sur de Autobuses** (South Bus Station), Canarias, 17 (☎ **91/527-29-61** for information), every day between 6:30am and 10pm. The fastest of the lot leave Monday to Friday on the hour. Those that depart weekdays on the half hour and those that run on weekends take a bit longer. Travel time, depending on whether the bus stops at villages en route, is between 1 hour and 1 hour and 20 minutes.

Once you reach Toledo, you'll be deposited at the Estación de Autobuses, which lies beside the river, about three-quarters of a mile from the historic center. Although many visitors opt to walk, know in advance that the ascent is steep. Buses no. 5 and 6 run from the station uphill to the center; pay the driver directly.

By Car   Exit Madrid via Cibeles (Paseo del Prado) and take N-401 south.

VISITOR INFORMATION   The **tourist information office** is at the Puerta de Bisagra (☎ **925/22-08-43**). It's open Monday to Friday from 9am to 2pm and 4 to 6pm, on Saturday from 9am to 3pm and 4 to 7pm, and on Sunday from 9am to 3pm.

WHAT TO SEE & DO

You can see all the major attractions in 1 day, provided you arrive early and stay late. One of the major attractions of Toledo, the Casa y Museo de El Greco, will not reopen until 1998—if you're visiting in 1997, you'll miss out on this stellar sight.

✪ **Cathedral.** Arco de Palacio. ☎ **925/22-22-41.** Cathedral, free; Treasure Room, 500 ptas. ($4). Daily 10:30am–1pm and 3:30–6pm (until 7pm in summer). Bus: 5 or 6.

Built at the flowering peak of the Gothic era of architecture, the cathedral, which stands directly east of Plaza del Ayuntamiento in the heart of Toledo, is one of the greatest in Europe. It was erected principally between 1226 and 1493, although there have been later additions. The monument is a bastion of Christian architecture, but a great deal of the actual construction work was carried out by the Moors, master builders themselves.

The cathedral witnessed many prime moments in Spanish history—such as a proclamation naming "Juana la Loca" (the insane daughter of Isabella I) and her husband, Philip the Handsome, heirs to the throne of Spain.

Inside, the Transparente—the altar completed in 1732 by Narciso Tome—is a landmark in European architecture. Lit by a "hole" cut through the ceiling, this production includes angels on fluffy clouds, a polychrome *Last Supper,* and a Madonna winging her way to heaven.

Dating from the 16th century, the cathedral's iron gate is in the plateresque style. Works of art include *The Twelve Apostles* by El Greco and paintings by Velázquez, Goya, Morales, and van Dyck. El Greco's first painting in Toledo was commissioned by the cathedral. Called *El Expolio,* it created a furor when the devout saw the vivid coloring of Christ's garments. The artist was even hauled into the courts. Many elaborately sculpted tombs of both the nobility and the ecclesiastical hierarchy are sheltered inside.

You can also visit the Gothic cloister, the Capilla Mayor, and the Renaissance-style Choir Room (elaborate wood carvings), and you should see the rose windows, preferably near sunset. In the Treasure Room is a 500-pound monstrance, dating from the 16th century and said to have been made, in part, from gold Columbus brought back from the New World. To celebrate Corpus festivities, the monstrance is carried through the streets of Toledo. The Mozarabic Chapel dates from the 16th century and contains paintings by Juan de Borgoña (a mass using Mozarabic liturgy is still conducted here).

✪ **Museo de Santa Cruz.** Calle de Miguel Cervantes, 3. ☎ **925/22-10-36.** Admission 200 ptas. ($1.60) adults, free for children. Tues–Sat 10am–6:30pm, Sun–Mon 10am–2pm. Bus: 5 or 6. Pass beneath the granite archways piercing the eastern edge of Plaza de Zocodover and walk about 1 block.

Built in the form of a Greek cross, this 16th-century plateresque hospice has been turned into a museum of fine arts and archeology. As a hospital, it was founded by Cardinal Mendoza. The facade is almost more spectacular than any of the exhibits inside. It's a stunning architectural achievement in the classical plateresque style. The major artistic treasure inside is El Greco's *The Assumption of the Virgin,* his last known work. Paintings by Goya and Ribera are also on display, along with gold items, opulent antique furnishings, Flemish tapestries, and even Visigothic artifacts. In the patio of the museum you'll stumble across various fragments of carved stone and sarcophagus lids. One of the major exhibits is of a large Astrolablio tapestry of the zodiac from the 1400s. In the basement are shown artifacts from various archeological digs throughout the province of Toledo, including elephant tusks.

Casa y Museo de El Greco. Calle de Samuel Leví. ☎ **925/22-40-46.** Admission 400 ptas. ($3.20), free for children 9 and under. Tues–Sat 10am–2pm and 4–6pm, Sun 10am–2pm. Bus: 5 or 6. *Note:* It's currently closed for restoration, which was scheduled to be finished in 1998; check with the tourist office to see if it has reopened.

The famous painter Doménikos Theotokópoulos, called El Greco because he was born in Crete, arrived in Toledo in 1577 and lived here with Doña Jerónima, a noted beauty (either his wife or his mistress), until his death in 1614. His living quarters stood in the *antiguo barrio judío,* or the old Jewish quarter, on Calle de Samuel Leví in the heart of Toledo. It's believed the painter moved to this site in 1585.

Samuel Ha-Leví, chancellor of the exchequer to Pedro the Cruel, is said to have built a series of houses here, forming a complex in the 14th century. These little connected houses were often called "apartments." Ha-Leví had subterranean passages dug to hide his treasury; and a Don Enrique de Villena, it is said, practiced alchemy in these underground cellars.

The apartments or houses were torn down in the late 19th century, but many people in Toledo say that El Greco's house or apartment was rescued. Perhaps it was, but critics aren't sure. What emerged, nevertheless, was identified for visitors as the "Casa del Greco." Eventually a neighboring house was incorporated to shelter a museum with 19 paintings by El Greco.

Visitors are admitted into the so-called studio of El Greco, which contains a painting by the artist. Especially interesting are the garden and kitchen.

Monasterio de San Juan de los Reyes. Calle de los Reyes Católicos, 17. ☎ **925/ 22-38-02.** Admission 150 ptas. ($1.20), free for children 8 and under. Summer, daily 10am–1:45pm and 3:30–7pm; winter, daily 10am–1:45pm and 3:30–6pm. Bus: 5 or 6.

Ferdinand and Isabella founded this church to commemorate their 1476 triumph over the Portuguese at Toro. Construction began in 1477, according to the plans of the architect Juan Guas. The church and its splendid cloisters were completed in

1504, dedicated to St. John the Evangelist, and used, from the very beginning, by the Franciscan friars. It's a perfect example of Gothic-Spanish-Flemish style.

San Juan de los Reyes was restored after being damaged in the invasion of Napoleon and abandoned in 1835. Actually, the national monument has been entrusted again to the Franciscans since 1954.

✪ **Iglesía de Santo Tomé.** Plaza del Conde, 2 (at Calle de Santo Tomé). ☎ **925/ 21-02-09.** Admission 150 ptas. ($1.20). Daily 10am–1:45pm and 3:30–6:45pm (until 5:45pm in winter). Closed Jan 1 and Dec 25.

Except for its Mudéjar tower, this little 14th-century chapel is rather unprepossessing. But by some strange twist it was given the honor of exhibiting El Greco's masterpiece, *The Burial of the Conde de Orgaz.* Long acclaimed for its composition, the painting is a curious work in its blending of realism with mysticism.

El Alcázar. Calle General Moscardó 4. ☎ **925/22-30-38.** Admission 125 ptas. ($1), free for children 9 and under. Oct–June, Tues–Sun 10am–1:30pm and 4–5:30pm (until 6:30pm July–Sept). Bus: 5 or 6.

The characteristic landmark dominating the skyline of Toledo is the Alcázar, in the very center of the city. It attracted worldwide attention during the 1936 siege of the city, when Nationalists held the fortress for 70 days until relief troops could respond to their plea for help, arriving on September 27, 1936.

The Alcázar was destroyed. The one standing in its place today is a reconstruction that houses an Army Museum. A monument out front is dedicated to the heroes of that 1936 struggle.

Sinagoga del Tránsito. Calle de Samuel Leví. ☎ **925/22-36-65.** Admission 400 ptas. ($3.20). Tues–Sat 10am–1:45pm and 4–5:45pm, Sun 10am–1:45pm. Closed Jan 1, May 1, Dec 24–25, and Dec 31. Bus: 5 or 6.

Down the street from El Greco's museum is the once-important place of worship for the large Jewish population that once lived here peacefully amid both Christians and Arabs. This 14th-century building is noted for its superb stucco and its Hebrew inscriptions. There are some psalms along the top of the walls and on the east wall a poetic description of the temple. The construction of the synagogue was ordered by Don Samuel Ha-Leví, the chancellor of the exchequer to Pedro the Cruel. The name of the king appears clearly in a frame in the Hebrew inscription.

The synagogue is the most important part of the **Museo Sefardi,** which was inaugurated in 1971 and contains tombstones with Hebrew epigraphy dating from before 1492 and other artworks.

Sinagoga de Santa María la Blanca. Calle de los Reyes Católicos 2. ☎ **925/22-72-57.** Admission 150 ptas. ($1.20). Apr–Sept, daily 10am–2pm and 3:30–7pm; Oct–Mar, daily 10am–2pm and 3:30–6pm. Bus: 2.

In the late 12th century the Jews of Toledo erected an important synagogue in the almohade style, which employs graceful horseshoe arches and ornamental horizontal moldings. Although by the early 15th century it had been converted into a Christian church, much of the original remains, including the five naves and elaborate Mudéjar decorations—mosquelike in their effect. The synagogue lies on the western edge of the city, midway between the El Greco museum and San Juan de los Reyes.

Hospital de Tavera. Hospital de Tavera, 2. ☎ **925/22-04-51.** Admission 500 ptas. ($4). Daily 10:30am–1:30pm and 3:30–6pm.

This 16th-century Greco-Roman palace north of Toledo's medieval ramparts was built by Cardinal Tavera; it now houses a private art collection. Titian's portrait of

Madrid Environs

N110

Sierra de Guadarrama

Segovia

San Ildefonso
la Granja
604

Sierra de Gredos

To
Ávila
←

600

607

101

E5

Guadalajara

N320

NI M103

Colmenar
Viejo

San Lorenzo
de El Escorial

San Sebastián
de los Reyes

Galapagar

Valle de los Caídos

NVI El Pardo

A6

Aravaca

Las Rozas

E90

Barajas Airport

✈

MADRID

Alcalá de
Henares

NII

Mejorada
del Campo

404

602

600

Alcorcón

Leganés

Arganda

San Martín
de la Vega

Chinchón NIII

E901

NV

E90

Ciempozuelos

Illescas

N401

To
Cuenca
→

Aranjuez

N400

Ocaña

N301

N400

NIV

N403

E5

502

Toledo

N401

Airport ✈

La
Guardia

401

3-0312

217

The Siege of the Alcázar

Although the Alcázar of Toledo has suffered many a siege, the only time it captured world headlines was in 1936. The Republicans were fighting to gain control of conservative, staunchly Catholic Toledo. Franco's rebel troops were commanded by one tough officer, Col. José Moscardó. Not only were his troops inside the Alcázar, but women and children were holed up there as well. The Alcázar, although under heavy attack, held out for 70 days of bombardment.

On July 23, a Republican officer reached Moscardó by telephone in the Alcázar. The colonel was informed that Republican forces had kidnapped Luís, his 16-year-old son. Moscardó was told that unless he immediately surrendered the fortress, Luís would be executed.

To show that they indeed did have the child, Luís was put on the phone to his father. "Papa!" he shouted, "They say they are going to shoot me if you don't surrender."

Without hesitation, Moscardó told his son: "Then commend your soul to God, shout '¡Viva España!' and die like a hero."

The Republicans were good as their word. Luís was shot in the head. The fortress surrendered in September of that year. In the Alcázar today hangs the wall phone on which the colonel spoke to his son for the last time.

Charles V hangs in the banqueting hall, and the museum owns five paintings by El Greco: *The Holy Family, The Baptism of Christ,* and portraits of St. Francis, St. Peter, and Cardinal Tavera. Ribera's *The Bearded Woman* also attracts many. The libarary's collection of books is priceless. In the nearby church is the mausoleum of Cardinal Tavera, designed by Alonso Berruguete.

SPORTS & RECREATION

FISHING   Anglers wanting to try their luck in the Tagus River often head for Toledo, where the river forms a natural moat around the city. The Spanish government has introduced black bass at Finisterre Dam, which is some 28 miles southeast of the city. In various reservoirs, rather large pike and carp can be caught. To fish these waters, you must obtain a permit in Madrid at either **ICONA,** Gran Vía de San Francisco, 4 (☎ **91/347-60-00**), or from the **Federación Española de Pesca,** Navas de Tolosa, 3 (☎ **91/532-83-53**).

SWIMMING   The best place for swimming is the **Parador Conde de Orgaz** (see "Where to Stay," below), but the pool here is available only to hotel guests. The best outdoor pool—and a welcome relief in Toledo in July and August—is at the **Camping Circo Romano,** Calle Circo Romano, 21 (☎ **925/22-04-42**), a campground just north of the old city walls.

TENNIS   In summer this sport is best practiced either before noon or after 4pm. The **Club de Tenis de Toledo,** Calle Navalpino, km 49 (☎ **925/22-42-78**), is private but will accept guests who call to make arrangements in advance.

SHOPPING

In swashbuckling days, the swordsmiths of Toldeo were renowned. They're still around and still turning out **swords,** although Errol Flynn in green tights is long gone. Toledo is equally renowned for its *damasquinado* or **damascene work,** which was the Moorish art of inlaying gold, even copper or silver threads, against a matte black steel backdrop.

Marzipan (called *mazapán* locally) is often prepared by nuns and is a local specialty. Marzipan of course is made of sweet almond paste, and many shops in town specialize in this treat.

The province of Toledo is also renowned for its **pottery,** which is sold in so many shops at competitive prices that it's almost unnecessary to recommend specific branches hawking these wares. For the best deals, and if you're interested in buying a number of items, consider a trip to Talavera la Reina, 47 miles west of Toledo, where most of the pottery is made. Since Talavera is the largest city in the province, it's hardly a picture-postcard little potter's village. Most of the shops lie along the main street of town, where you'll find store after store selling this distinctive pottery in multicolored designs.

Casa Bermejo. Calle Airosas, 5. ☎ **925/22-03-46.**

Established in 1910, this factory and store employs almost 50 artisans whose progress you can observe as part of the drama of a visit to its premises. At the outlet is a wide array of damascene objects fashioned into Toledo's traditional Mudéjar designs. These include swords, platters, pitchers, and other accessory-type gift items. Don't think, however, that everything this place manufactures follows the inspiration of the medieval Arabs. The outfit engraves many of the ornamental swords that are awarded to graduates of West Point, USA, as well as the decorative, full-dress military accessories used by the armies of other countries of Europe, including France. Open Monday to Friday from 8am to noon and 4 to 8pm.

Casa Telesforo. Plaza de Zocodover, 17. ☎ **925/22-33-79.**

Many long-time residents of Toledo remember this place as the outfit that supplied the marzipan consumed at their childhood birthday parties and celebrations. A specialist in the almond-nut-and-sugar confection whose origins go back hundreds of years, it sells the best marzipan in town, cunningly configured into shapes that include hearts, diamonds, flowers, etc. It's open daily from 10am to 2pm and 4 to 9pm.

Felipe Suarez. Paseo de los Canónigos, 19. ☎ **925/22-56-15.**

Established in the 1920s, this outfit has manufactured damascene work in various forms that range from unpretentious souvenir items to art objects of rare museum-quality beauty that sell for as much as 2,000,000 ptas. ($16,000). The inventory includes swords, straight-edged razors, pendants, fans, and an array of pearls. The shop maintains extended hours throughout the year, daily from 9:30am to 7pm.

Santiago Sanchez Martín. Calle Río Llano, 15. ☎ **925/22-77-57.**

This is one of the most painstaking and prestigious manufacturers of damascene work in Toledo. It specializes in the elaborately detailed arabesques whose techniques are as old as the Arab conquest of Iberia. Look for everything from decorative tableware (platters, pitchers, etc.) to mirror frames, jewelry, letter openers, and ornamental swords. It's open Monday to Friday from 8am to noon and 4 to 8pm.

WHERE TO STAY
EXPENSIVE

✪ **Parador Nacional de Conde Orgaz.** Cerro del Emperador, 45002 Toledo. ☎ **925/22-18-50.** Fax 925/22-51-66. 76 rms, 2 suites. MINIBAR TV TEL. 19,500 ptas. ($156) double; 24,000 ptas. ($192) suite. AE, DC, MC, V. Free parking. Drive across Puente San Martín and head south for 2¹/₂ miles (4km).

Make reservations well in advance at this parador, built on the ridge of a rugged hill where El Greco is said to have painted *View of Toledo*. That view is still there, and without a doubt it's one of the grandest in the world. The main living room/lounge has fine furniture—old chests, brown-leather chairs, heavy tables—and leads to a sunny terrace overlooking the city. On chilly nights you can sit by the fireplace. A stairway and balcony lead to dark oak-paneled doors opening onto the guest rooms, the most luxurious in all Toledo, far superior to those at the María Cristina. Spacious and beautifully furnished, they contain reproductions of regional antique pieces.

Dining/Entertainment: See the restaurant recommendation under "Where to Dine," below.

Services: Room service, laundry/valet.

Facilities: Outdoor pool.

MODERATE

✪ **Hostal del Cardenal.** Paseo de Recaredo, 24, 45003 Toledo. ☎ **925/22-49-00.** Fax 925/22-29-91. 27 rms, 2 suites. A/C TV TEL. 10,800 ptas. ($86.40) double; 15,000 ptas. ($120) suite. AE, DC, MC, V. Bus: 2 from the train station.

The entrance to this unusual hotel is set into the stone fortifications of the ancient city walls, a few steps from the Bisagra Gate. Although long acclaimed as the best restaurant in Toledo (see "Where to Dine," below), the "secret" is that you can also find lodgings here. Of course, they're not as grand as those of the parador, but they're choice nevertheless, eagerly sought by those wanting to capture an Old Toledo atmosphere. To enter the hotel, you must climb a series of terraces to the top of the crenellated walls of the ancient fortress. There, grandly symmetrical and very imposing, is the hostal, the former residence of the 18th-century cardinal of Toledo, Señor Lorenzana. Just beyond the entrance, still atop the city wall, you'll find flagstone walkways, Moorish fountains, rose gardens, and cascading vines. The establishment has tiled walls; long, narrow salons; dignified Spanish furniture; and a smattering of antiques. Each room has a private bath, all of which were recently renovated.

Hotel Carlos V. Calle Trastamara, 1, 45001 Toledo. ☎ **925/22-21-00.** Fax 925/22-21-05. 69 rms. A/C TEL. 11,555–12,000 ptas. ($92.45–$96) double. AE, DC, MC, V. Bus: 5 or 6.

In Franco's day, this was *the* place to stay in Toledo. But increasing competition from newer hotels such as the María Cristina and the Alfonso VI have relegated it to second-tier status. It's still going strong and filling up many a night, though some readers have complained of the "unhelpful staff." The parador (see above) is remotely located, requiring frequent taxi rides, but the Carlos V is right in the center of the action, between the cathedral and the Alcázar. Inside, a strong, masculine aura prevails, with brown leather chairs in the lounges. The rooms are also decorated in a rather severe masculine style. An outdoor bar is a summer feature, and rather standard Castilian meals are served in the dining room, with its Mudéjar decorative motif.

Hotel María Cristina. Marqués de Mendigorría, 1, 45003 Toledo. ☎ **925/21-32-02.** Fax 925/21-26-50. 60 rms, 3 suites. A/C TV TEL. 10,800 ptas. ($86.40) double; 16,500 ptas. ($132) suite. AE, DC, MC, V. Parking 650 ptas. ($5.20).

Located adjacent to the historic Hospital de Tavera, near the northern perimeter of the old town, this stone-sided, awning-fronted hotel resembles a palatial country home. If you're willing to forgo the view from the parador and the Castilian charm of the Hostal del Cardenal, this hotel is generally cited as *numero segundo* in Toledo. Originally built as a convent and later used as a hospital, it was transformed into this comfortably stable hotel in the early 1980s. Sprawling, historic, and generously proportioned, it contains clean and amply sized guest rooms, each attractively but simply furnished.

On site is the very large and well-recommended restaurant, El Abside, where fixed-price lunches and dinners are offered. (The food is much better, however, at the Hostal del Cardenal.) There's also a bar. A concierge is at the ready, and 24-hour room service, laundry service, and baby-sitting are available. There are tennis courts on the premises.

Ⓢ **Hotel Pintor El Greco.** Alamillos del Tránsito, 13, 45002 Toledo. ☎ **925/21-42-50.** Fax 925/21-58-19. 33 rms. A/C TV TEL. 12,000 ptas. ($96) double. AE, DC, MC, V.

In the old Jewish quarter, one of the most tradition-laden and historic districts of Toledo, this hotel was converted from a typical *casa Toledana* that had once been used as a bakery. It's the only hotel in Toledo that matches the antique charm of the Hostal del Cardenal, although it seems relatively unknown. It's a better alternative than the landmark Carlos V (see above). With careful restoration, especially of its antique facade, it was converted into one of Toledo's best and most atmospheric small hotels. The old patio with a fountain was restored, and decoration in both the public rooms and the guest rooms is in a traditional Castilian style. Automatic phones, piped-in music, satellite TV, and individual security boxes were added to the immaculately kept guest rooms. At the hotel's doorstep are such landmarks as the Monasterio de San Juan de los Reyes, Sinagoga de Santa María la Blanca, Sinagoga del Tránsito, Casa y Museo de El Greco, and Iglesia de Santo Tomé.

Hotel Residencia Alfonso VI. Calle General Moscardó, 2, 45001 Toledo. ☎ **925/22-26-00.** Fax 925/21-44-58. 85 rms, 3 suites. A/C TV TEL. 11,990–13,000 ptas. ($95.90–$104) double; 19,185–19,500 ptas. ($153.50–$156) suite. AE, DC, MC, V. Bus: 5 or 6.

Although built in the early 1970s, this hotel has been kept up-to-date. Run by the same management as the Carlos V, it's a superior hotel with better appointments and comfort, though some of the public rooms are so *faux* Castilian they look like a movie set created by a designer. It sits near a great concentration of souvenir shops in the center of the old city, at the Alcázar's southern perimeter. Inside, you'll discover a high-ceilinged, marble-trimmed decor with a scattering of Iberian artifacts, copies of Spanish provincial furniture, and dozens of leather armchairs. You can dine in the stone-floored dining room, where standard fixed-price meals are served.

INEXPENSIVE

Hotel Maravilla. Plaza de Barrio Rey, 7, 45001 Toledo. ☎ **925/22-85-82.** Fax 925/22-81-55. 18 rms. A/C TV TEL. 6,600 ptas. ($52.80) double. AE, MC, V. Bus: 5 or 6.

If you enjoy hotels with lots of local color, then this little place might please you. It's only 1 block south of Plaza de Zocodover and opens directly onto its own cobblestone plaza. Semimodernized in 1995, the building has many bay windows; the guest rooms are modest but adequate, the furnishings so-so. You can hang your laundry on the roof and use an iron in the downstairs laundry room.

Ⓢ **Hotel Residencia Imperio.** Cadenea, 5, 45001 Toledo. ☎ **925/22-76-50.** Fax 925/25-31-83. 21 rms. A/C TV TEL. 6,000 ptas. ($48) double. MC, V. Bus: 5 or 6.

Just off Calle de la Plata, 1 block west of Plaza de Zocodover, the Imperio is the best bet for those on a tight budget. The rooms are clean and comfortable but small and lackluster, showing the wear of their years. Most overlook a little church with a wall overgrown with wisteria.

NEARBY PLACES TO STAY

For readers who have a car or don't mind one or two taxi rides a day, there are a couple of excellent accommodations across the Tagus.

La Almazara. Carretera Toledo-Argés-Cuerva, km 3400, 45080 Toledo. ☎ **925/22-38-66.** 21 rms. TEL. 5,900 ptas. ($47.20) double. AE, MC, V. Closed Dec 10–Mar 10. Free parking. Follow the road to the Parador of Ciudad Real, then take C-781 toward Cuerva.

Taking its name from an olive-oil mill that used to stand here, La Almazara offers some of the most offbeat accommodations around. Hidden away in the hills, this old-fashioned country villa, with its own courtyards and vineyards, embodies the atmosphere of Old Spain, far removed from the pace of city life. It has an exceptional view of Toledo. You may be assigned either a spacious chamber in the main house or a room in the less comfortable annex.

Hotel los Cigarrales. Carretera Circunvalación, 32, 45000 Toledo. ☎ **925/22-00-53.** Fax 925/21-55-46. 36 rms. A/C TEL. 5,980 ptas. ($47.85) double. MC, V. Free parking. Bus: Chamartín from the train station.

About a mile south of the city center, this hotel offers quiet seclusion. Built in the 1960s in traditional red brick, it looks like a private villa with a garden; the friendliness of the family owners adds to this feeling. Most of the interior is covered with blue and green tiles. The rooms are clean and sunny, decorated with heavy Spanish furniture, a bit sterile but comfortable. From the cozy bar's flower-filled terrace you can see the towers of medieval Toledo.

WHERE TO DINE
MODERATE

✪ **Asador Adolfo.** Calle La Granada, 6 (at Calle Hombre de Palo, behind a discreet sign). ☎ **925/22-73-31.** Reservations recommended. Main courses 1,850–2,500 ptas. ($14.80–$20); fixed-price menu 3,400 ptas. ($27.20). AE, DC, MC, V. Mon–Sat 1–4pm and 8pm–midnight, Sun 1–4pm. Bus: 5 or 6. SPANISH.

The Asador Adolfo is located less than a minute's walk north of the cathedral, in a warren of narrow medieval streets. Though considered by many residents the finest and most renowned restaurant in Toledo, we'd rate it under the Hostal del Cardenal. Sections of the building were constructed during the 1400s, but recent renovations in the kitchens have enabled its chefs to prepare many modern variations of traditional Toledo-derived dishes. The ceilings of the several dining rooms are supported by massive beams and occasionally contain faded frescoes dating from the year of the building's original construction.

The house specialties are different preparations of game dishes, which are among the best anywhere. These might include partridge with white beans, venison, or any of the wild game birds the region produces in such abundance. Nongame dishes include hake flavored with local saffron and any of a wide array of beef, veal, and lamb dishes. To begin, try the pimientos rellenos (red peppers stuffed with pulverized shellfish). The house dessert is marzipan; it's prepared in a wood-fired oven and is noted for its lightness.

Casa Aurelio. Calle de la Sinagoga, 6, and Calle de la Sinagoga, 1. ☎ **925/22-20-97.** Reservations recommended. Main courses 2,500–4,000 ptas. ($20–$32); fixed-price menu 3,250 ptas. ($26). AE, DC, MC, V. Daily 1–4pm and 8–11:30pm. Bus: 5 or 6. CASTILIAN.

Established in the late 1940s near the northern edge of the cathedral, Casa Aurelia occupies two separate dining rooms with two separate entrances a few feet apart. It's one of Toledo's restaurant staples, offering Castilian ambience and efficient service. Menu items include traditional versions of sopa castellana, grilled hake, lubina a la sal (whitefish cooked in salt), fresh salmon, roast lamb, and at certain times of year, Toledo partridge or roast suckling pig. Note that the main outlet of this restaurant (at Calle de la Sinagoga, 6) is usually closed every Wednesday, although the smaller of the restaurant's two dining rooms (at Calle de la Sinagoga, 1) remains open.

⭘ Hostal del Cardenal. Paseo de Recaredo, 24. ☎ **925/22-08-62.** Reservations required. Main courses 800–2,600 ptas. ($6.40–$20.80); fixed-price menu 2,550 ptas. ($20.40). AE, DC, MC, V. Daily 1–4pm and 8:30–11:30pm. Bus: 2 from the train station. SPANISH.

You may want to treat yourself to Toledo's best-known restaurant, owned by the same people who run Madrid's Casa Botín, so beloved by Hemingway. The dishes are mainly regional in origin, and the chef prepares them with flair and originality. The menu is very similar to the more fabled Madrid restaurant. You might begin with "quarter of an hour" (fish) soup or white asparagus, then move on to curried prawns, baked hake, filet mignon, or smoked salmon. Roast suckling pig is a specialty, as is partridge in casserole. Arrive early and enjoy a sherry in the bar or in the courtyard.

Parador Nacional de Conde Orgaz. Cerro del Emperador. ☎ **925/22-18-50.** Reservations not accepted. Main courses 1,000–2,500 ptas. ($8–$20); fixed-price menu 3,500 ptas. ($28). AE, DC, MC, V. Daily 1–4pm and 8:30–11pm. Drive across Puente San Martín and head south for 2¹/₂ miles (4km). CASTILIAN.

Some of the best Castilian regional cuisine is combined here with one of the most panoramic views from any European restaurant. Located in a fine parador (see "Where to Stay," above), the restaurant is on the crest of a hill—said to be the spot that El Greco selected for his *View of Toledo.* The place is a little too tourist trodden, and the food doesn't quite match the view, but it's a worthy choice nonetheless. The fixed-price meal might include tasty hake, then perhaps either veal or beef grilled on an open fire, plus dessert. If you're dining lightly, try a local specialty, tortilla española con magra (potato omelet with ham or bacon). There's a bar on the upper level.

Venta de Aires. Calle Circo Romano, 35. ☎ **925/22-05-45.** Reservations recommended. Main courses 1,500–2,500 ptas. ($12–$20); fixed-price menu 2,500 ptas. ($20). AE, DC, MC, V. Mon–Sat 1–4pm and 8–11pm, Sun 1–4pm. SPANISH/INTERNATIONAL.

Just outside the city gates, directly southwest of the Circo Romano (Roman Circus), this restaurant has served Toledo's pièce de résistance—perdiz (partridge)—since 1891, when the place was a roadside inn. On the à la carte menu, this dish is best eaten with the red wine of Méntrida, but if you want to keep your tab low, you'd better stick to the fixed-price menu. For dessert, try the marzipan, an institution in Toledo. On your way out, take note of former President Nixon's entry in the guest book (he dined here in 1963 and they're still talking about the visit).

INEXPENSIVE

Ⓢ El Emperador. Carretera del Valle, 1. ☎ **925/22-46-91.** Reservations recommended. Main courses 1,200–1,800 ptas. ($9.60–$14.40); fixed-price menu 1,400 ptas. ($11.20). V. Tues–Sun 2–4:30pm and 8–11pm. Bus: Carretera del Valle. SPANISH.

A modern restaurant on the outskirts of Toledo, southwest of the town's historic core, El Emperador is reached via an arched bridge. Its terraces overlook the river and the towers of Toledo. Inside, the look is tavern style, with leather-and-wood chairs, heavy beams, and wrought-iron chandeliers. The fixed-price menu might include a choice of soup (beef, vegetable, or noodle), followed by a small steak with french fries, then fresh fruit, plus wine. Although the food is decently prepared and concocted from fresh ingredients, it's the economical prices that make this such an appealing choice.

Ⓢ Maravilla. Plaza de Barrio Rey, 7. ☎ **925/22-83-17.** Reservations not accepted. Main courses 1,200–1,600 ptas. ($9.60–$12.80); fixed-price menus 1,075–1,800 ptas. ($8.60–$14.40). AE, MC, V. Tues–Sun 1–4pm and 8–11pm. Bus: 5 or 6. SPANISH.

Maravilla is located in the Barrio Rey, a small square off the historic Plaza de Zocodover, filled with budget restaurants and cafés that change their names so often it's virtually impossible to keep track. This unassuming eatery offers the best all-around dining bargain of the lot. Its kitchen serves a typically Castilian menu, specializing in the famous perdiz (partridge), but also preparing cordero asado (roast lamb).

La Parilla. Horno de los Bizcochos, 8. ☎ **925/21-22-45.** Main courses 1,100–1,775 ptas. ($8.80–$14.20); fixed-price menu 1,400 ptas. ($11.20). AE, DC, MC, V. Daily 1–4pm and 8–11pm. Bus: 5 or 6. SPANISH.

This classic Spanish restaurant, in a thick-walled medieval building, stands on a cobblestone street near the Hotel Alfonso VI, just east of the cathedral. The menu offers no surprises, but it's reliable. Likely inclusions on the bill of fare are roast suckling pig, spider crabs, Castilian baked trout, stewed quail, baked kidneys, and La Mancha rabbit. This is the type of heavy fare so beloved by Castilians, who still frequent the place in great numbers. Go here for some real Franco-era dishes.

A TAPAS BAR

Bar Ludeña. Plaza de la Horn Madelena, 13, Corral de Don Diego, 10. ☎ **925/22-33-84.** Reservations not accepted. Tapas 250–800 ptas. ($2–$6.40). No credit cards. Thurs–Tues 10am–midnight. TAPAS.

Tapas are passed through a window to clients standing outside enjoying the view of the square. The bar is little more than a narrow corridor, serving raciones of tapas that are so generous they make little meals, especially when eaten with bread. The roasted red peppers in olive oil are especially tasty, along with the stuffed crabs and calimares (squid). Huge dishes of pickled cucumbers, onions, and olives are available. A tiny dining room behind a curtain at the end of the bar serves inexpensive fare.

2 Aranjuez

29 miles (47km) S of Madrid, 30 miles (48km) NE of Toledo

On the Tagus River, Aranjuez strikes visitors as a virtual garden. It was mapped out in the 18th century by the royal architects and landscapers of Ferdinand VI. The natural setting has been blended with wide boulevards and fountain- and statuary-filled gardens.

Surrounded in late spring by beds of asparagus and heavily laden strawberry plants, Aranjuez exudes the spirit of May. But for some visitors, autumn best reveals the royal town. It's then that the golden cypress trees cast lingering shadows in countless ponds, evoking a painting by Santiago Rusiñol Prats.

ESSENTIALS

GETTING THERE   By Train   Trains run about every 20 minutes to and from Madrid's Atocha station (50 minutes). Trains run less often along the east-west route to and from Toledo (40 minutes). The Aranjuez station lies about a mile outside town. You can walk it in about 15 minutes, but taxis and buses line up on Calle Stuart (2 blocks from the tourist office). The bus that makes the run from the center of Aranjuez to the railway station is marked "NZ."

By Bus   Buses bound for Aranjuez depart from Madrid's **Estación Sur de Autobuses,** Canarias, 17 (call **91/468-45-11** in Madrid for information). Buses depart every 30 minutes from 7:30am to 10pm. They arrive at and depart from the **City Bus Terminal,** Calle Infantas, 8 (☎ **91/891-01-83**), in Aranjuez.

By Car   Driving is easy and takes about 30 minutes once you reach the southern city limits of Madrid. To reach Aranjuez, follow the signs to Aranjuez and Granada, taking the N-IV highway.

VISITOR INFORMATION   The **tourist information office** is on Plaza Puente de San Antonio (☎ **91/891-04-27**), open Monday to Friday from 10am to 2pm and 3 to 5pm and on Saturday from 10am to 2pm.

WHAT TO SEE & DO

✪ **Palacio Real.** Plaza del Palacio. ☎ **925/891-07-40.** Admission 500 ptas. ($4) adults, 250 ptas. ($2) students and children. Apr–Sept, Tues–Sun 10am–6:30pm; Oct–Mar, Tues–Sun 10am–5:30pm. Bus: Routes from the rail station converge at the square and gardens at the westernmost edge of the palace.

Since the beginning of a united Spain, the climate and natural beauty of Aranjuez have attracted Spanish monarchs, notably Ferdinand and Isabella and Philip II, who managed to tear himself away from El Escorial. But the Palacio Real, lying immediately west of the center, in its present form dates primarily from the days of the Bourbons, who used to come here mainly in the autumn and spring, reserving La Granja, near Segovia, for their summer romps. The palace was also favored by Philip V and Charles III.

Fires have swept over the structure numerous times, but most of the present building dates from 1778. William Lyon, writing in the Madrid weekly, the *Guidepost,* called its dominant note one of "deception: in almost each of its widely varying rooms there is at least one thing that isn't what it first appears." Mr. Lyon cites assemblages of mosaics that look like oil paintings, a trompe l'oeil ceiling that seems three-dimensional although it's flat, and a copy of a salon at Granada's Alhambra Palace.

In spite of these eye-fooling tricks, the palace is lavishly and elegantly decorated. Especially notable are the dancing salon, the throne room, the ceremonial dining hall, the bedrooms of the king and queen, and a remarkable Salon de Porcelana (Porcelain Room). Paintings include works by Lucas Jordan and José Ribera.

Jardín de la Isla. Palacio Real. No phone. Free admission. Apr–Sept, daily 8am–8:30pm; Oct–Mar, daily 8am–6:30pm. Bus: See the Palacio Real entry, above.

These gardens appear somehow forgotten, their mood melancholic. They lie to the east of the Palacio Real, adjoining a royal ornamental garden called the Parterre. From the Parterre, two bridges lead to the "garden of the island." The Non Plus Ultra fountain is dazzling. Under linden trees, the fountain of Apollo is romantic, and others honor Neptune, king of the sea, and Cybele, goddess of agriculture. The most delightful stroll is along an avenue of trees, called the Salón de los Reyes Católicos, which lies along the river.

Casita del Labrador. Calle de la Reina. ☎ **91/891-13-44.** Admission 425 ptas. ($3.40). Apr–Sept, Tues–Sun 10am–6:30pm; Oct–Mar, Tues–Sun 10am–5:30pm. Bus: See the Palacio Real entry, above.

"The little house of the worker" is a classic example of understatement. Actually, it was modeled after the Petit Trianon at Versailles. If you visit the Royal Palace in the morning, you can spend the afternoon here in the northeastern part of town. Those with a car can motor to it through the tranquil **Jardín del Príncipe,** with its black poplars.

The little palace was built in 1803 by Charles IV, who later abdicated in Aranjuez. The queen came here with her youthful lover, Godoy (whom she had elevated to the position of prime minister), and the feebleminded Charles didn't seem to care a bit. Surrounded by beautiful gardens, the "bedless" palace is lavishly furnished in grand 18th- and 19th-century style. The marble floors represent some of the finest workmanship of that day. The brocaded walls emphasize luxurious living—and the royal bathroom is a sight to behold (in those days, royalty preferred an audience). The clock here is one of the treasures of the house.

WHERE TO STAY

Hostal Castilla. Carretera Andalucía, 98, 28300 Aranjuez. ☎ **91/891-26-27.** 17 rms. MINIBAR TV TEL. 5,600 ptas. ($44.80) double. AE, DC, MC, V.

On one of the town's main streets north of the Royal Palace and gardens, the Castilla consists of the ground floor and part of the first floor of a well-preserved early 18th-century house. Most accommodations overlook a courtyard with a fountain and flowers. The owner, Joaquin Suárez, speaks English fluently, and suggests that reservations be made at least a month in advance. There are excellent restaurants nearby, and the hostal has an arrangement with a neighboring bar that provides guests here with an inexpensive lunch. The Castilla is a good location from which to explore either Madrid or Toledo on a day trip.

WHERE TO DINE

Casa Pablo. Almibar, 42. ☎ **91/891-14-51.** Reservations recommended. Main courses 1,900–2,500 ptas. ($15.20–$20); four-course fixed-price menu 3,000 ptas. ($24). AE, MC, V. Daily 1–4:30pm and 8pm–midnight. Closed Aug. SPANISH.

An unpretentious and well-managed restaurant near the bus station in the town center, Casa Pablo was established in 1941. At tables set outside under a canopy, you can dine while enjoying the tree- and geranium-lined street; in cooler weather you can eat either upstairs or in the cozy rear dining room. The fixed-price menu includes four courses, a carafe of wine, bread, and service. If it's hot and you don't want a heavy dinner, try a shrimp omelet or half a roast chicken; once we ordered just a plate of asparagus in season, accompanied by white wine. If you want a superb dish, try a fish called mero (Mediterranean pollack, of delicate flavor), grilled over an open fire.

La Rana Verde. Calle de la Reina, 1. ☎ **91/891-32-38.** Reservations recommended. Main courses 900–2,200 ptas. ($7.20–$17.60); fixed-price menu 2,200 ptas. ($17.60). MC, V. Daily 6–11pm. SPANISH.

"The Green Frog," just east of the Royal Palace and next to a small bridge spanning the Tagus, is still the traditional choice for many. It was opened in 1905 by Tomás Díaz Heredero, and is still owned and run by a third-generation member of the family, who has decorated it in 1920s style. The restaurant looks like a summer house with its high-beamed ceiling and soft ferns drooping from hanging baskets. The preferred tables are in the nooks overlooking the river. As in all the restaurants of Aranjuez, asparagus is a special feature. Game, particularly partridge, quail, and pigeon, can be recommended in season; fish, too, including fried hake and fried sole, makes a good choice. Strawberries are served with sugar, orange juice, or ice cream.

3 San Lorenzo de El Escorial

30 miles (48km) W of Madrid, 32 miles (52km) SE of Segovia

Next to Toledo, the most important excursion from Madrid is to the austere Royal Monastery of San Lorenzo de El Escorial. Philip II ordered the construction of this granite-and-slate structure in 1563, 2 years after he moved his capital to Madrid. Once the haunt of aristocratic Spaniards, El Escorial is now a resort where hotels and restaurants flourish in summer. Despite the appeal of its climate, the town of San Lorenzo itself is not very noteworthy. But because of the monastery's size, you might decide to spend a night or two at San Lorenzo—or more if you have the time.

San Lorenzo makes an ideal base for visiting nearby Segovia, the royal palace of La Granja, and the Valley of the Fallen.

ESSENTIALS

GETTING THERE   By Train   More than two dozen trains depart daily from Madrid's Atocha, Nuevos Ministerios, and Chamartín railway stations. During the summer extra coaches are added. The railway station for San Lorenzo de El Escorial is located about a mile outside town. The Herranz bus company meets all arriving trains with a shuttle bus that ferries passengers to and from the Plaza Virgen de Gracia, about a block east of the entrance to the monastery.

By Bus   The office of **Empresa Herranz,** Calle Reina Victoria, 3, in El Escorial (☎ 91/890-41-22 or 91/890-41-25) runs some 40 buses per day back and forth between Madrid and El Escorial. On Sunday, service is curtailed to 10 buses. Trip time is 1 hour. The same company also runs three buses a day to El Valle de los Caídos. They leave El Escorial at 11:15am, 1:15pm, and 3:15pm with returns at 2:15, 4:15, and 6:15pm. The ride takes only 15 minutes.

By Car   Follow the N-VI highway (on some maps marked as A-6) from the north-western perimeter of Madrid toward Lugo, La Coruña, and San Lorenzo de El Escorial. After about half an hour, turn left onto C-505 toward San Lorenzo de El Escorial. Driving time is about an hour.

VISITOR INFORMATION   The **tourist information office,** at Floridablanca, 10 (☎ 91/890-15-54), is open Monday to Friday from 10am to 2pm and 3 to 5pm and on Saturday from 10am to 2pm.

WHAT TO SEE & DO

✪ **Real Monasterio de San Lorenzo de El Escorial.** Calle San Lorenzo de El Escorial, 1. ☎ **91/890-59-02.** Comprehensive ticket 850 ptas. ($6.80) adults, 350 ptas. ($2.80) children. Apr–Sept, Tues–Sun 10am–6pm; Oct–Mar, Tues–Sun 10am–5pm.

In the Guadarrama mountain resort of El Escorial stands this imposing monastery, which many refer to as the eighth wonder of the world. Both a palace and a monastery, it was ordered built south of the town by Philip II to commemorate the 1557 triumph of his forces at the Battle of San Quentin. Escorial was dedicated to St. Lawrence, the martyred saint who was burned to death.

The original architect of El Escorial in 1563 was Juan Bautista de Toledo. After his death the monumental task was assumed by the greatest architect of Renaissance Spain, Juan de Herrera, who completed it in the shape of a gridiron in 1584.

The severe lines of the great pile of granite strike many as being as austere as the pious Philip himself. The architectural critic Nikolaus Pevsner called it "overwhelming, moving no doubt, but frightening."

In the **Charter Hall** is one of the greatest art collections in Spain outside the Prado, the canvases dating primarily from the 15th to the 17th century. Among the most outstanding are El Greco's *The Martyrdom of St. Maurice,* Titian's *Last Supper,* Velázquez's *The Tunic of Joseph,* van der Weyden's *Crucifixion,* and another version of Bosch's *The Hay Wagon* (see also a remarkable tapestry based on a painting by "El Bosco," as the Spanish call this artist). There are also works by Ribera, Tintoretto, and Veronese.

The **Biblioteca**—one of the most important libraries in the world—is estimated to contain in excess of 50,000 volumes. The collection, started by Philip II, ranges far and wide: Muslim codices; a Gothic 13th-century "Cántigas" from the reign of Alfonso X (known as "The Wise King"); and signatures from the Carmelite nun

St. Teresa of Jesús, who conjured up visions of the devil and of angels sticking burning-hot lances into her heart.

For many sightseers, the tour's highlight is a visit to the **Apartments of Philip II,** which contain many of the original furnishings. He died in 1598, in the "cell for my humble self" that he ordered built. He desired quarters that were spartan, and so they remain today—graced by a painting by Bosch, a copy he made of his *The Seven Capital Sins,* now at the Prado.

The **Apartments of the Bourbons** reflect a different style—a complete break from the asceticism imposed by the Hapsburg king. They're closed at present for restoration; check to see if they're open when you visit.

From a window in his bedroom, a weak and dying Philip II could look down at the services being conducted in the **basilica.** As the dome clearly indicates, the church was modeled after Michelangelo's drawings of St. Peter's in Rome. Works of art include a crucifix by Benvenuto Cellini, choir stalls by Herrera, and sculpted groups of father and son (Charles V and Philip II), along with their wives, flanking the altar.

Casa del Príncipe (Prince's Cottage). Calle de la Reina. ☎ **91/891-03-05.** Admission included in the comprehensive ticket, mentioned above. Apr–July and Sept, Sat–Sun and holidays 10am–5:45pm; Aug, Tues–Sun 10am–5:45pm; Oct–Mar, Sat–Sun and holidays 10am–6:45pm.

This small but elaborately decorated 18th-century palace near the railway station was originally a hunting lodge built for Charles III by Juan de Villanueva. Most visitors stay in El Escorial for lunch, visiting the cottage in the afternoon.

El Valle de los Caídos (Valley of the Fallen). ☎ **91/890-56-11.** Admission 650 ptas. ($5.20). Apr–Sept, Tues–Sun 9:30am–7pm; Oct–Mar, Tues–Sun 10am–6pm. Drive to the valley entrance, about 5 miles (8km) north of El Escorial in the heart of the Guadarrama Mountains; once there, drive 3¹/₂ miles (6km) along a woody road west to the underground basilica. Bus: See "Getting There," above. Tour buses from Madrid usually include an excursion to the Valley of the Fallen on their 1-day trips to El Escorial. Funicular: From near the entrance of the basilica to the base of the gigantic cross erected on the mountaintop above (where there's a superb view); the fare is 300 ptas. ($2.40), and the funicular runs daily from 10:30am to 1:15pm and 4 to 6pm.

This architectural marvel took two decades to complete and is dedicated to those who died in the Spanish Civil War. Its detractors say that it represents the worst of Neo-Fascist design; its admirers say that they have found renewed inspiration by coming here.

A gargantuan cross, nearly 500 feet high, dominates the Rock of Nava, a peak of the Guadarrama mountains. Directly under the cross is a basilica with a vault in mosaic, completed in 1959. Here José Antonio Primo de Rivera, the founder of the Falange party, is buried. When this Nationalist hero was buried at El Escorial, many, especially influential monarchists, protested that he was not a royal. Infuriated, Franco decided to erect another monument. Originally it was slated to honor the dead on the Nationalist side only, but the intervention of several parties led to a decision to include all the *caídos* (fallen). In time the mausoleum claimed Franco as well; his body was interred behind the high altar.

On the other side of the mountain is a Benedictine monastery that has sometimes been dubbed "the Hilton of monasteries" because of its seeming luxury.

WHERE TO STAY

Ⓢ Hostal Cristina. Juan de Toledo, 6, 28200 San Lorenzo de El Escorial. ☎ **91/890-19-61.** 16 rms. 6,000 ptas. ($48) double. MC, V.

One of the best choices for those on a budget, this hotel is run by the Delgado family, who opened it in the mid-1980s. It doesn't pretend to compete with the comfort and amenities of the Victoria Palace or even the Miranda & Suizo (see below), but has its devotees nonetheless. About 50 yards from the monastery, it stands in the town center, offering clean and comfortable but simply furnished rooms. The helpful staff will direct you to their small garden. Since the food in the restaurant is both good and plentiful, many Spanish visitors prefer to book here for a summer holiday.

Hotel Victoria Palace. Calle Juan de Toledo, 4, 28200 San Lorenzo de El Escorial. ☎ **91/890-15-11.** Fax 91/890-12-48. 90 rms. TV TEL. 13,500–15,800 ptas. ($108–$126.40) double. AE, DC, MC, V. Free parking.

The Victoria Palace, with its view of El Escorial, is the finest hotel in town—a traditional establishment that has been modernized without losing its special aura of style and comfort. It's surrounded by beautiful gardens and has an outdoor pool. The rooms, some with private terrace, are well furnished and maintained. The rates are reasonable enough, and a bargain for a four-star hotel. The dining room serves some of the best food in town. Laundry and room service are provided.

Miranda & Suizo. Calle Floridablanca, 20, 28200 San Lorenzo de El Escorial. ☎ **91/890-47-11.** Fax 91/890-43-58. 50 rms, 2 suites. TV. 9,000 ptas. ($72) double; 12,000 ptas. ($96) suite. AE, DC, MC, V.

On a tree-lined street in the heart of town, within easy walking distance of the monastery, this excellent middle-class establishment ranks as a leading two-star hotel. It's the "second choice" in town, with rooms not quite as comfortable as those at the Victoria Palace. The Victorian-style building, nevertheless, has good guest rooms, some with terraces. The furnishings are comfortable, the beds often have brass frames, and sometimes you'll find fresh flowers on the table. In summer there's outside dining.

WHERE TO DINE

Charolés. Calle Floridablanca, 24. ☎ **91/890-59-75.** Reservations required. Main courses 2,650–3,650 ptas. ($21.20–$29.20). AE, DC, MC, V. Daily 1–4pm and 9pm–midnight. SPANISH/INTERNATIONAL.

The thick and solid walls of this establishment date, according to its managers, "from the monastic age" and probably predate the town's larger and better-known monastery of El Escorial. The restaurant here was established around 1980 and has been known ever since as the best dining room in town. It has a flower-ringed outdoor terrace, for use during clement weather, and a wide choice of menu items based entirely on fresh seafood and meats. These include such dishes as grilled hake with green or hollandaise sauce, shellfish soup, monkfish in butter-and-herb sauce, pepper steak, pastel of fresh vegetables with crayfish, and herb-flavored baby lamb chops. A strawberry or kiwi tart is a good dessert choice.

Mesón la Cueva (The Cave). San Antón, 4. ☎ **91/890-15-16.** Reservations recommended. Main courses 850–2,500 ptas. ($6.80–$20); menu del día 1,800 ptas. ($14.40). No credit cards. Tues–Sun 1–4pm and 8:30–11:30pm. CASTILIAN.

Founded in 1768, this restaurant captures the world of Old Castile, and it lies only a short walk from the monastery. A *mesón típico,* built around an enclosed courtyard, it boasts such nostalgic accents as stained-glass windows, antique chests, faded engravings, paneled doors, and iron balconies. The cooking is on target, the portions generous. Regional specialties include Valencian paella and fabada asturiana (pork sausage and beans), but fresh trout broiled in butter is the best of all. The menu's most expensive items are Segovian roast suckling pig and roast lamb (tender inside, crisp outside). Off the courtyard through a separate doorway is La Cueva's tasca, filled with Castilians quaffing their favorite before-dinner drinks.

NEAR THE VALLEY OF THE FALLEN

Hostelerie Valle de los Caídos. Valle de los Caídos. ☎ **91/890-55-11.** Reservations not accepted. Main courses 600–1,300 ptas. ($4.80–$10.40); fixed-price menu 1,250 ptas. ($10). No credit cards. Daily 9–10am, 2–3:30pm, and 9–10pm. Closed Dec 15–Jan 15. SPANISH.

This restaurant is the most likely bet for those heading up into the Valley of the Fallen. Set amid an arid but dramatic landscape halfway along the inclined access road leading to Franco's monuments, and reachable only by car or bus, it's a mammoth modern structure with wide terraces, floor-to-ceiling windows, and a well-established pattern of feeding busloads of foreign tourists, mainly from tour groups. The *menu del día* usually includes such dishes as cannelloni Rossini, pork chops with potatoes, a dessert choice of flan or fruit, and wine. The typical fare of roast chicken, roast lamb, shellfish, and paella is somewhat cafeteria style in nature. View it mainly as a "feeding station" for the hundreds flocking to this attraction.

4 Segovia

54 miles (91km) NW of Madrid, 42 miles (68km) NE of Ávila

In Old Castile, Segovia is one of the most romantic of Spanish cities, its glory of another era. Isabella I was proclaimed queen of Castile here in 1474. Segovians live with the memory of the time when their star was ascendant.

The capital of a province of the same name, it lies on a slope of the snow-capped Sierra de Guadarrama mountains, between two ravine-studded valleys and the Eresma and Clamores rivers (actually streams). As it appears on the horizon, dominated by its Alcázar and its Gothic cathedral, Segovia is decidedly of the Middle Ages.

The city was of strategic importance to the Roman troops, and one of its greatest monuments, the Aqueduct, dates from those times. The skyline is characterized by the Romanesque belfries of the churches and the towers of its old and decaying palaces.

The Upper Town is mainly encased by its old walls; but the part outside the walls is of interest too, especially for views of the Alcázar.

ESSENTIALS

GETTING THERE   By Train   Nine trains leave Madrid's Chamartín station every day and arrive 2 hours later in Segovia, where you can board bus no. 3, which departs every quarter of an hour for Plaza Mayor. The **train station** is on Paseo Obispo Quesada (☎ **921/42-07-74**), a 20-minute walk southeast of the town center.

By Bus   Buses arrive and depart from the **Estacionamiento Municipal de Autobuses,** Paseo de Ezequiel González, 10 (☎ **921/43-30-10**), near the corner of Avenida Fernández Ladreda and the steeply sloping Paseo Conde de Sepulveda. There are 10 to 15 buses a day to and from Madrid (which depart from Paseo de la Florida, 11; metro: Norte), and about four a day traveling between Ávila, Segovia, and Valladolid.

By Car   Take N-VI (on some maps it's known as A-6) or the Autopista del Nordeste northwest from Madrid, toward León and Lugo. At the junction with Route 110 (signposted to Segovia), turn northeast.

VISITOR INFORMATION   The **tourist information office** is at Plaza Mayor,10 (☎ **921/46-03-34**). It's open daily from 10am to 2pm and 5 to 8pm.

WHAT TO SEE & DO

✪ **El Alcázar.** Plaza de la Reina Victoria Eugenia. ☎ **921/43-01-76.** Admission 375 ptas. ($3) adults, 175 ptas. ($1.40) children 8–14, free for children 7 and under. Apr–Sept, daily 10am–7pm; Oct–Mar, daily 10am–6pm. Take either Calle Vallejo, Calle de Velarde, Calle de Daoiz, or Paseo de Ronda. Bus: 3.

If you've ever dreamed of castles in the air, then all the fairy-tale romance of childhood will return when you view the Alcázar. Many have waxed poetic about it, comparing it to a giant boat sailing through the clouds. See it first from down below, at the junction of the Clamores and Eresma rivers. It's on the west side of Segovia, and you may not spot it when you first enter the city, but that's part of the surprise.

The castle dates back many hundreds of years—perhaps to the 12th century. But a large segment of it—notably its Moorish ceilings—was destroyed by fire in 1862. Over the years, under an ambitious plan, the Alcázar has been restored.

Inside you'll discover a facsimile of Isabella's dank bedroom. It was at the Alcázar that she first met Ferdinand, preferring him to the more "fatherly" king of Portugal. But she wasn't foolish enough to surrender her "equal rights" after marriage. In the Throne Room, with its replica chairs, you'll note that the seats are equally proportioned. Royal romance continued to flower at the Alcázar. Philip II married his fourth wife, Anne of Austria, here.

After you inspect the polish on some medieval armor inside, you may want to walk the battlements of this once-impregnable castle, whose former occupants poured boiling oil over the ramparts onto their uninvited guests below. Or you can climb the tower, originally built by Isabella's father as a prison, for a panoramic view of Segovia. (In particular, note the so-called pregnant-woman mountain.)

✪ **Roman Aqueduct.** Plaza del Azoguejo.

The aqueduct, an architectural marvel, is still used to carry water, though it was constructed by the Romans almost 2,000 years ago. It's not only the most colossal reminder of Roman glory in Spain, but also one of the best-preserved Roman architectural achievements in the world. It consists of 118 arches, and in one two-tiered section—its highest point—it soars 95 feet. You'll find no mortar in these granite blocks brought from the Guadarrama mountains. The Spanish call it El Puente, and it spans Plaza del Azoguejo, the old market square, stretching a distance of nearly 800 yards. When the Moors took Segovia in 1072, they destroyed 36 arches. However, Ferdinand and Isabella ordered that they be rebuilt in 1484. You can see it any time night or day since it's an integral landmark of Segovia.

✪ **Cabildo Catedral de Segovia.** Plaza Mayor, Calle Marqués del Arco. ☎ **921/43-53-25.** Admission: Cathedral, free; cloisters, museum, and chapel room, 250 ptas. ($2) adults, 50 ptas. (40¢) children. Spring and summer, daily 9am–7pm; fall and winter, daily 9:30am–noon and 3–6pm. Bus: 3.

Constructed between 1515 and 1558, this structure lays claim to being the last Gothic cathedral built in Spain. Fronting the historic Plaza Mayor, the cathedral of Segovia stands on the spot where Isabella I was proclaimed queen of Castile. It's affectionately called *la dama de las catedrales*. Inside, it contains numerous treasures, such as the Blessed Sacrament Chapel (created by the flamboyant Churriguera), stained-glass windows, elaborately carved choir stalls, and 16th- and 17th-century paintings, including a reredos portraying the deposition of Christ from the cross by Juan de Juni. Even older than the cathedral are the cloisters, which belonged to a former church destroyed in the War of the Communeros. The cathedral's museum exhibits jewelry, paintings, and a rare collection of antique manuscripts, along with the inevitable vestments.

Iglesia de la Vera Cruz. Carretera de Zamarramala. ☎ **921/43-14-75.** Admission 175 ptas. ($1.40). Apr–Sept, Tues–Sun 10:30am–1:30pm and 3:30–7pm; Oct–Mar, Tues–Sun 10:30am–1:30pm and 3:30–6pm.

Built in either the 11th or 12th century by the Knights Templar, this is the most fascinating Romanesque church in Segovia. It stands in isolation outside the old town's walls, overlooking the Alcázar. Its unusual 12-sided design is believed to have been copied from the Church of the Holy Sepulchre in Jerusalem. Inside you'll find an inner temple, rising two floors, where the knights conducted night-long vigils as part of their initiation rites.

Monasterio del Parral. Calle del Marqués de Villena (across the Eresma River). ☎ **921/43-23-98.** Free admission. Daily 10am–2:30pm and 4–6:30pm. Take Ronda de Sant Lucía, cross the Erma River, and head down Alle del Marqués de Villena.

The restored Monastery of the Grape was established for the Hironymites by Henry IV, a Castilian king (1425–74) known as "The Impotent." The monastery lies across the Eresma River about half a mile north of the city. The church is a medley of styles and decoration—mainly Gothic, Renaissance, and plateresque. The facade was never completed, and the monastery itself was abandoned when religious orders were suppressed in 1835. Today it has been restored and is once again the domain of the *jerónimos*, Hieronymus priests and brothers. Inside, a robed monk will show you the various treasures of the order, including a polychrome altarpiece and the alabaster tombs of the marquis of Villena and his wife—all the work of Juan Rodríguez.

WHERE TO STAY

Los Arcos. Paseo de Ezequiel González, 26, 40002 Segovia. ☎ **800/528-1234** in the U.S., or 921/43-74-62. Fax 921/42-81-61. 59 rms. A/C MINIBAR TV TEL. 12,350 ptas. ($98.80) double. AE, DC, MC, V. Parking 900 ptas. ($7.20).

This five-story concrete-and-glass structure opened in 1987 and is generally cited as the best in town, although you may prefer Los Linajes instead (see below). Well run and modern, it attracts the business traveler, although tourists frequent the place in droves as well. The rooms are generally spacious, although furnished in a standard bland international way, except for the beautiful rug-dotted parquet floors. Built-in furnishings and tiny combination baths are part of the offering, along with private safes. The rooms are well kept, although some furnishings look worn.

Even if you don't stay here, consider dining at the hotel's La Cocina de Segovia, which is the only hotel dining room that competes successfully with the Mesón de Candido (see "Where to Dine," below). Like the nearby leading competitors, roast suckling pig and roast Segovia lamb perfectly cooked in custom-made ovens are the specialties. There's also a tavernlike café and a bar. In all, it's a smart, efficiently run, and pleasant, though not exciting choice.

Hotel Los Linajes. Dr. Velasco, 9, 40003 Segovia. ☎ **921/46-04-75.** Fax 921/46-04-79. 55 rms, 10 suites. TV TEL. 10,500 ptas. ($84) double; from 13,200 ptas. ($105.60) suite. AE, DC, MC, V. Parking 800 ptas. ($6.40). Bus: 1.

In the historic district of St. Stephen, at the northern edge of the old town, stands this hotel, the former home of a Segovian noble family. While the outside facade dates from the 11th century, the interior is modern except for some Castilian decorations. Following a 1996 renovation, the hotel looks brighter and fresher than Los Arcos. One of the best hotels in town, Los Linajes offers gardens and patios where guests can enjoy a panoramic view over the city. The hotel also has a bar/lounge, coffee shop, disco, and garage.

⊙ **Parador de Segovia.** Carretera Valladolid (N-601), 40003 Segovia. ☎ **921/44-37-37.**
Fax 921/43-73-62. 113 rms, 7 suites. A/C MINIBAR TV TEL. 16,500 ptas. ($132) double; from
25,000 ptas. ($200) suite. AE, DC, MC, V. Parking 900 ptas. ($7.20).

This 20th-century tile-roofed parador sits on a hill 2 miles northeast of Segovia (take
N-601). It stands on an estate called El Terminillo, which used to be famous for its
vines and almond trees, a few of which still survive. If you have a car and can get a
reservation, book in here, as its physical plant, luxury, and comfort will dwarf that
found at either Los Arcos and Los Linajes. The guest rooms are deluxe, containing
such extras as private safes and tiled combination baths. The furnishings are tasteful
(often in "blond" pieces), and large windows open onto panoramic views of the
countryside. Some of the older rooms here are a bit dated, however, with a lackluster decor. The vast lawns and gardens contain two lakelike pools, and there's also an
indoor pool. Other facilities include saunas and tennis courts.

WHERE TO DINE

⑤ **El Bernardino.** Calle Cervantes, 2. ☎ **921/43-32-25.** Reservations recommended. Main
courses 1,300–2,350 ptas. ($10.40–$18.80); fixed-price menu 2,750 ptas. ($22). AE, DC,
MC, V. Daily 1–4pm and 7:30–11:30pm. CASTILIAN.

El Bernardino, a 3-minute walk west of the Roman aqueduct, is built like an old tavern. Lanterns hang from beamed ceilings, and the view over the red-tile rooftops of
the city is delightful. The *menu del día* might include a huge paella, roast veal with
potatoes, flan or ice cream, plus bread and wine. You might begin your meal with
sopa castellana (made with ham, sausage, bread, egg, and garlic). The roast dishes are
exceptional here, including roast suckling pig from a special oven and roast baby
lamb. You can also order grilled rib steak or stewed partridge.

Casa Duque. Calle Cervantes, 12. ☎ **921/43-05-37.** Reservations recommended. Main
courses 600–2,500 ptas. ($4.80–$20); fixed-price menu 1,875 ptas. ($15). AE, DC, MC, V. Daily
12:30–5pm and 8–11:30pm. CASTILIAN.

Duque—the *maestro asador,* as he calls himself—supervises the roasting of the pig,
the house specialty, in this *mesón típico* founded in 1895. Waitresses wearing the
traditional garb of the mayoress of Zamarramala will serve you other Segovian
gastronomic specialties, such as sopa castellana or a cake known as ponche alcázar.
There's a tavern below so you may enjoy a before-dinner drink.

José María. Cronista Lecea, 11. ☎ **921/46-11-11.** Reservations recommended. Main dishes
1,200–2,800 ptas. ($9.60–$22.40); fixed-price menu 3,800 ptas. ($30.40). AE, DC, MC, V. Daily
1–4pm and 8–11:30pm. SEGOVIAN.

This centrally located bar/restaurant, a block east of Plaza Mayor, serves quality
regional cuisine in a rustic stucco-and-brick dining room. Before dinner, locals crowd
in for tapas at the bar, then move into the dining room for such Castilian specialties as roast suckling pig, rural-style conger eel, and freshly caught sea bream. Try the
cream-of-crabmeat soup, roasted peppers, salmon with scrambled eggs, grilled veal
steak, or house-style hake. For dessert, try the ice-cream tart with whiskey sauce.

⊙ **Mesón de Candido.** Plaza del Azoguejo, 5. ☎ **921/42-59-11.** Reservations recommended. Main courses 1,300–2,500 ptas. ($10.40–$20); fixed-price menu 2,500 ptas. ($20).
AE, DC, MC, V. Daily 12:30–4:30pm and 8–11:30pm or midnight. CASTILIAN.

For years this beautiful old Spanish inn, standing on the old town's eastern edge, has
maintained a monopoly on the tourist trade. Outside the hotels (specifically La
Cocina de Segovia at the Los Arcos), it's the town's finest dining choice, only slightly
better and more traditional than José María or Duque. The Candido family took it
over in 1905 and the fourth- and fifth-generation members of that family still run

it, having fed, over the years, everybody from Nixon to Hemingway. The oldest part of the building housing the restaurant dates from 1822, and the restaurant has gradually been enlarged since then. The proprietor of the House of Candido is known as *mesonero mayor de Castilla* (the major innkeeper of Castile). He has been decorated with more medals and honors than paella has grains of rice. The restaurant's popularity can be judged by the crowd of hungry diners who fill every seat in the six dining rooms. Specialties include cordero asado (roast baby lamb) and cochinillo asado (roast suckling pig).

Mesón el Cordero. Calle de Carmen, 4. ☎ **921/43-51-96.** Reservations recommended. Main courses 1,000–1,800 ptas. ($8–$14.40); fixed-price menus 2,200–3,500 ptas. ($17.60–$28). AE, DC, MC, V. Daily 12:30–4:30pm and 8–11:30pm. CASTILIAN/IBERIAN.

This restaurant is known throughout the town for the flavorful roasted meats it serves. It was built in the 1800s as a Carmelite convent, near the base of the town's Roman aqueduct; in the 1970s a pair of hardworking partners added dozens of rustic artifacts and enlarged its premises to create the charming restaurant you see today. One noteworthy specialty is roast suckling lamb (cordero lechal), served on the bone and seasoned with fresh herbs that include ample amounts of rosemary and thyme. The wine list includes an array of suitably robust reds from Rioja, Rivera, and southern France.

La Oficina. Cronista Lecea, 10. ☎ **921/46-02-83.** Reservations not required. Main courses 600–1,700 ptas. ($4.80–$13.60); fixed-price menu 1,200 ptas. ($9.60). AE, DC, MC, V. Wed–Mon 1–4:30pm and 7–11:30pm. Closed 3 weeks in Nov. CASTILIAN.

A meal here provides many insights into the traditions and aesthetics of Old Spain. Established in 1893, Oficina has been maintained ever since by three subsequent generations of the original owners. As such, it has virtually welcomed every resident of Segovia inside the thick brick-and-stone walls that give it a distinctive Castilian flavor. Few changes, other than repairs, seem to have been made to the decor since its founding, a fact that contributes significantly to its charm. Set adjacent to Plaza Mayor, a short walk east of the cathedral, it offers a stand-up bar accessible through a separate entrance, where locals usually opt for a wine or sherry apéritif. The owners have won various awards for the quality of their roast suckling pig, prepared and served with suitable pomp and ceremony by the well-trained staff.

AN EASY EXCURSION TO LA GRANJA

To reach La Granja, 7 miles (11km) southeast of Segovia, you can take a 20-minute bus ride from the city center. About 12 buses a day leave from Paseo Conde de Sepulveda at Venida Fernández Ladreda.

✪ **Palacio Real de la Granja.** Plaza de España, 17, San Ildefonso (Segovia). ☎ **921/47-00-19.** Admission 650 ptas. ($5.20) adults, 250 ptas. ($2) children 5–14, children 4 and under free. Apr–May, Mon–Fri 10am–1:30pm and 3–5pm, Sat–Sun 10am–6pm; June–Sept, daily 10am–6pm; Oct–Mar, Mon–Sat 10am–1:30pm and 3–5pm, Sun 10am–2pm.

San Ildefonso de la Granja was the summer palace of the Bourbon kings of Spain, who imitated the grandeur of Versailles here in this Segovia province. Set against the snow-capped Sierra de Guadarrama, the slate-roofed palace dominates the village (nowadays a summer resort) that grew up around it.

The founder of La Granja was Philip V, grandson of Louis XIV and the first Bourbon king of Spain (his body, along with that of his second queen, Isabel de Fernesio, is interred in a mausoleum in the Collegiate Church). Philip V was born at Versailles in 1683, which may explain why he wanted to re-create that atmosphere at Segovia.

Before the palace was built in the early 18th century, a farm stood here—hence the totally inappropriate name *granja*, meaning "farm" in Spanish. Inside you'll find valuable antiques (many in the Empire style), paintings, and a remarkable collection of tapestries based on Goya cartoons from the Royal Factory in Madrid.

Most visitors, however, seem to find a stroll through the gardens more to their liking, so allow adequate time for it. The fountain statuary is a riot of cavorting gods and nymphs, hiding indiscretions behind jets of water. The gardens are studded with chestnuts and elms.

5 Cuenca

100 miles (161km) E of Madrid, 202 miles (325km) SW of Zaragoza

This medieval town, once dominated by the Arabs, is a spectacular sight with its *casas colgadas*, the cliff-hanging houses set on multiple terraces that climb up the impossibly steep sides of a ravine. The Júcar and Huécar rivers meet at the bottom.

ESSENTIALS

GETTING THERE   By Train   Trains for Cuenca leave Madrid's Atocha Railway Station about eight times throughout the day, and arrive in Cuenca at **Po. del Ferrocarril** in the new city (☎ **969/22-07-20**), after a journey lasting anywhere from 2¹/₂ to 3 hours.

By Bus   There are about eight buses from Madrid every day. Buses arrive at Calle Fermín Caballero; call 969/22-70-87 for information and schedules.

By Car   Cuenca is the junction for several highways and about a dozen lesser roads that connect it to towns within its region. From Madrid, take N-III to Tarancon, then N-400, which leads directly into Cuenca.

VISITOR INFORMATION   The **tourist information office** is at San Pedro, 6 (☎ **969/23-21-19**), open Monday to Friday from 9am to 2pm and 4 to 7pm and on Saturday and Sunday from 9am to 2pm and 4 to 8pm.

WHAT TO SEE & DO

The chief sight of Cuenca is the town itself. Isolated from the rest of Spain, it requires a northern detour from the heavily traveled Valencia–Madrid road. Deep gorges give it an unreal quality, and eight old bridges spanning two rivers connect the ancient parts of town with the growing new sections. One of the bridges is suspended over a 200-foot drop.

Cuenca's streets are narrow and steep, often cobblestoned, and even the most athletic tire quickly. But you shouldn't miss it, even if you have to stop and rest periodically. At night you're in for a special treat when the *casas colgadas* are illuminated. Also, try to drive almost to the top of the castle-dominated hill. The road gets rough as you approach the end, but the view makes the effort worthwhile.

Cathedral. Plaza Pío XII. Free admission. Daily 8:45am–2pm and 4–7pm (closes at 6pm in winter). Bus: 1 or 2.

Begun in the 12th century, the Gothic cathedral was influenced by England's Norman style, becoming the only Anglo-Norman cathedral in Spain. Part of it collapsed in this century, but it has been restored. A national monument filled with religious art treasures, the cathedral is a 10-minute walk from Plaza Mayor, up Calle Palafox. The cathedral's *museo diocesano* exhibits two canvases by El Greco, a collection of Flemish tapestries (some beautifully designed), and a statue of the Virgin del Sagrario from the 1100s.

✪ **Museo de Arte Abstracto Español.** Calle los Canónigos, s/n. ☎ **969/21-29-83.** Admission 300 ptas. ($2.40). Tues–Sat 11am–2pm and 4–8pm, Sun 11am–2:30pm. Bus: 1 or 2.

North of Plaza Mayor, housed in a cliff-hanging dwelling, this ranks as one of the finest museums of its kind in Spain. It was conceived by the painter Fernando Zóbel, who donated it in 1980 to the Juan March Foundation. The most outstanding abstract Spanish painters are represented, including Rafael Canogar (especially his *Toledo*), Luís Feito, Zóbel himself, Tàpies, Eduardo Chillida, Gustavo Torner, Gerardo Rueda, Millares, Sempere, Cuixart, and Antonio Saura (see his grotesque Geraldine Chaplin and his study of Brigitte Bardot, a vision of horror, making the French actress look like an escapee from Picasso's *Guernica*).

WHERE TO STAY

💲 **Hotel Avenida.** Carretería, 39, 16004 Cuenca. ☎ **969/21-43-43.** Fax 969/21-23-35. 49 rms. TEL. 4,500 ptas. ($36) double. MC, V. Parking 900 ptas. ($7.20).

A good value for the money, this hotel lies in Cuenca's modern commercial center, about a block southwest of the Parque de San Julian. Built in 1971 and renovated in 1991, it offers tidy rooms with simple amenities, and access to a helpful staff. Only a handful of rooms have air-conditioning; the rest are on the shaded side of the building and—at least according to management—don't seem to get very hot. No meals are served other than breakfast, but the staff can direct guests to the nearby Calle Colón, where many different restaurants in various price ranges are ready, willing, and able to feed foreign visitors. Parking, incidentally, is in a nearby parking lot maintained by Cuenca's municipal government.

Hotel Figón de Pedro. Calle Cervantes, 15, 16004 Cuenca. ☎ **969/22-45-11.** Fax 969/23-11-92. 28 rms. TEL. 6,000 ptas. ($48) double. AE, DC, MC, V.

The Figón de Pedro lies south of the old city, a short walk north of the bus and rail stations. The hotel (with elevator) is immaculate but not stuffy, since the staff keeps the atmosphere pleasantly informal. On the second floor you'll find a lounge with a TV, and the hotel boasts a country-style dining room with a tasca in front. Wood beams, fresh linens on the tables, and personal service all make this an inviting place for meals.

✪ **Parador de Turismo de Cuenca.** Convento de San Pablo, Paseo de la Hoz del Huécar, 16001 Cuenca. ☎ **969/23-23-20.** Fax 969/23-25-84. 62 rms, 1 suite. A/C MINIBAR TV TEL. 16,500 ptas. ($132) double; 26,000 ptas. ($208) suite. AE, DC, MC, V. Parking 805 ptas. ($6.45).

This government-sponsored hotel occupies the dignified premises of what was originally built, in 1523, as a Dominican monastery. A noteworthy example of late Gothic architecture, it lies on a hillside above Cuenca, about half a mile northwest of the town's historic center. It's clearly the town's prestige address. Opened for business after extensive renovations in 1992, its three stories contain masses of intricately chiseled 16th-century stonework (some enhanced with glass panels overlooking the river), a church, a severely beautiful cloister, a sense of timeless solidity, and a swimming pool. There's a bar, a high-ceilinged restaurant, and two floors of bedrooms which, despite comfortably traditional furniture and modern bathrooms, richly convey their ecclesiastical origins.

💲 **Posada de San José.** Julián Romero, 4, 16001 Cuenca. ☎ **969/21-13-00.** Fax 969/23-03-65. 30 rms, 16 with bath. 3,800–4,600 ptas. ($30.40–$36.80) double without bath, 6,600–8,900 ptas. ($52.80–$71.20) double with bath. AE, DC, MC, V. Bus: 1 or 2.

The Posada de San José stands in the oldest part of Cuenca, a short walk north of the cathedral. The 17th-century cells that used to shelter the sisters of this former convent now house overnight guests who consider its views of the old city the best in town. It sits atop a cliff, overlooking the forbidding depths of a gorge. Owners Antonio and Jennifer Cortinas renovated this place into one of the most alluring hotels of the region, with the bar perhaps the most charming of its well-decorated public rooms.

WHERE TO DINE

Mesón Casa Colgadas. Canónigos, 3. ☎ **969/22-35-09.** Reservations recommended. Main courses 1,750–2,800 ptas. ($14–$22.40); fixed-price menus 3,300–3,800 ptas. ($26.40–$30.40). AE, DC, MC, V. Tues 1:30–4pm, Wed–Mon 1:30–4pm and 9–11pm. SPANISH/INTERNATIONAL.

One of the most spectacular dining rooms in Spain stands on one of the most precarious precipices in Cuenca. Established in the late 1960s, it occupies a 19th-century house, five stories high, with sturdy supporting walls and beams. Pine balconies and windows overlook the ravine below and the hills beyond. In fact, it's the most photographed "suspended house" in town, and dinner here is worth every peseta. The menu includes regional dishes and a wide variety of well-prepared international cuisine. Drinks are served in the tavern room on the street level, so even if you're not dining here, you may want to drop in for a drink and the view. You'll find the Mesón Casa Colgadas just south of the cathedral and near the Museum of Spanish Abstract Art.

Togar. Avenida República Argentina, 3. ☎ **969/22-01-62.** Reservations required. Main courses 900–1,950 ptas. ($7.20–$15.60); fixed-price menu 1,500 ptas. ($12). AE, MC, V. Mon–Sat 1–4pm and 8–11pm, Sun 1–4pm. Closed 1 week in July (dates vary). Bus: 1 or 6. SPANISH.

Rich with local flavor, and aggressively cost-conscious, this is a simple but likable tasca on the southwestern periphery of town. Established in 1955 in an angular building erected the same year, it offers homemade cookery whose inspiration derives from the various regions of Spain. One of the specialties is revuelto Togar, an egg, ham, and shrimp dish served with herbs and crusty bread. Also available are well-peppered versions of pork, several kinds of rich soups, and various beef and fish dishes.

8 Seville

Sometimes a city becomes famous for its beauty and romance—Seville, the capital of Andalusia, is such a place. In spite of its sultry heat in summer and its many problems, such as rising unemployment and street crime, it remains one of the most charming of Spanish cities.

Don Juan and Carmen—aided by Mozart and Bizet—have given Seville a romantic reputation. Because of the acclaim of *Don Giovanni* and *Carmen,* not to mention *The Barber of Seville,* debunkers have risen to challenge this reputation. But if a visitor can see only two Spanish cities in a lifetime, they should be Seville and Toledo.

All the images associated with Andalusia—orange trees, mantillas, lovesick toreros, flower-filled patios, and castanet-rattling Gypsies—come to life in Seville. But it's not just a tourist city: It's a substantial river port, and it contains some of the most important artistic works and architectural monuments in Spain.

Unlike most Spanish cities, Seville has fared rather well under most of its conquerors—the Romans, Arabs, and Christians. Pedro the Cruel and Ferdinand and Isabella held court here. When Spain entered its 16th-century golden age, Seville funneled gold from the New World into the rest of the country. Columbus docked here after his journey to America.

Be warned, however, that driving here is a nightmare: Seville was planned for the horse and buggy rather than for the car, and nearly all the streets run one-way toward the Guadalquivir River. Locating a hard-to-find restaurant or a hidden little square might require patience and even a little luck.

1 Orientation

GETTING THERE

BY PLANE   Iberia flies several times a day between Madrid (and elsewhere via Madrid) and Seville's **San Pablo Airport,** Calle Almirante Lobo (☎ 95/451-53-20). It also flies several times a week from/to Alicante, Grand Canary Island, Lisbon, Barcelona, Palma de Majorca, Tenerife, Santiago de Compostela, and (once a week) Zaragoza. The airport lies about 6 miles (9.6km) from the center of the city, along the highway leading to Carmona.

BY TRAIN   Train service into Seville is now centralized in the **Estación Santa Justa,** Avenida Kansas City, s/n (☎ **95/454-02-02** for information and reservations). Bus nos. C1 and C2 from the train station take you to the bus station at Prado de San Sebastián, and bus no. EA runs to and from the airport. The high-speed AVE train has reduced travel time from Madrid to Seville to 2¹/₂ hours. The train makes 12 trips daily, with a stop in Córdoba. Ten trains a day connect Seville and Córdoba; the AVE train takes 50 minutes and a TALGO takes 1¹/₂ hours. Three trains a day run from Málaga, taking 3 to 4 hours, depending on the train; there are also three trains per day from Granada (4 to 5 hours).

BY BUS   Although Seville confusingly has several satellite bus stations servicing small towns and nearby villages of Andalusia, most buses arrive and depart from the city's largest **bus terminal,** on the southeast edge of the old city, at Prado de San Sebastián, Calle José María Osborne, 11 (☎ **95/441-71-11**). Many lines also converge on Plaza de la Encarnación, Plaza Nueva, in front of the cathedral on Avenida de la Constitución, and at Plaza de Armas (across the street from the old train station, Estación de Córdoba). From there, buses from several different companies make frequent runs to and from Córdoba (2¹/₂ hours), Málaga (3¹/₂ hours), Granada (4 hours), and Madrid (8 hours). For **information and ticket prices,** call Alsina (☎ **95/441-88-11**).

BY CAR   Seville lies 341 miles (540 km) southwest of Madrid and 135 miles (217 km) northwest of Malága. Several major highways converge on Seville, connecting it with all the rest of Spain and Portugal. During periods of heavy holiday traffic, the N-V (E90) from Madrid through Extremadura which, at Mérida, connects with the southbound N630 (E-803) is usually less congested than the N-IV (E5) through eastern Andalusia.

VISITOR INFORMATION

The tourist office, **Oficina de Información del Turismo,** at Avenida de la Constitución, 21B (☎ **95/422-14-04**), is open Monday to Saturday from 9am to 7pm and on Sunday and holidays from 10am to 2pm.

CITY LAYOUT

The heart of Seville lies along the east bank of the Guadalquivir River. This **old town** or *centro histórico* is a fairly compact area and can be explored on foot—the only real way to see it. Once this part of Seville was enclosed by walls. Today nearly all the sights lie between two of the major bridges of Seville: the Puente de San Telmo to the south and the Puente de Isabel II (also known as the Puente de Triana), an Eiffel Tower–like structure from the mid-1800s. Near the Puente de San Telmo are found such sights as the Torre del Oro, the University of Seville, and the Parque de María Luisa. Near the Puente de Isabel II are the Maestranza bullring, the major shopping streets, and the Museo de Bellas Artes. In the middle of the centro histórico rises the cathedral and its adjoining Giralda tower, the Alcázar, and the colorful streets of the old Jewish quarter, the Barrio de Santa Cruz.

MAIN STREETS & ARTERIES   The old **Paseo de Colón** is that part of Seville's historic core that opens onto the Guadalquivir River. Any number of streets, including Santander, lead to **Avenida de la Constitución** where you'll find the major attractions of Seville, including the Alcázar and the cathedral. To the east of both the Alcázar and the cathedral lies the Barrio de Santa Cruz. Major historic squares include Plaza Nueva, Plaza de El Salvador, Plaza de Jerez, and Plaza de Triunto. From Plaza del Duque, the Museo de Bellas Artes is reached by heading west toward the river along Calle Alfonso XII. The best place to start your exploration of Seville is Plaza Virgen de los Reyes. From here many of the major attractions, including the Giralda, the Patio de los Naranjos, and the Archivo de Indias, are all close at hand. Directly south of the plaza is the Alcázar—the whole area, in fact, is historic Seville in a nutshell.

FINDING AN ADDRESS   Most of Seville's streets run one-way, usually toward the Guadalquivir River. Individual buildings are numbered with odd addresses on one side of the street and even numbers on the opposite side, so no. 14 would likely fall opposite nos. 13 and 15. Many addresses are marked *s/n*, without a number. When this occurs, be sure that you're given the name of a cross street as a reference point.

STREET MAPS   Arm yourself with a detailed street map, not the general overview often handed out free at tourist offices. Even if you're in Seville only for a day or two, you'll still need a detailed street map to find such attractions as the Museo de Bellas Artes. The best street maps of Seville are those published by **Euro City**—available at local newsstands and in bookstores. These maps contain not only a detailed street index, but provide tourist information, places of interest, and even locations of vital SOS services (such as the police station) on the map. Regrettably, no one seems to have come up with an adequate map to get you through the intricate maze of the Barrio de Santa Cruz—so you can more or less count on getting lost there. There is, however, a sketch map provided by the tourist office to help get you around the area.

NEIGHBORHOODS IN BRIEF

Centro Histórico   This is the heart of historic Seville, with its most imposing sights, of which the massive cathedral is the most dominant attraction. This is the area where you'll want to spend the most time, and it's also the center of the finest hotels and restaurants.

Barrio de Santa Cruz   This is an area of wrought-iron *cancelas* (gates), courtyards with Andalusian tiled fountains, art galleries, restaurants, cafés, tabernas, flower pots of geraniums, and winding narrow alleyways. The former ghetto of Seville's Jews, it's today named after a Christian saint, and is the single most colorful part of the city for exploring—which is best done during the day (at night, muggings might be a danger). Filled with interesting sights, such as Casa Murillo and some fascinating churches, it's one of the architectural highlights of Andalusia.

La Macarena   Thought to be named for a Roman, Macarios, and the site of his former estate, this is a famous quarter of Seville that seems sadly neglected by visitors, who spend most of their time in the two previous quarters (see above). The name also describes a popular rumba. It's filled with interesting attractions such as the Convento de Santa Inés (reached along Calle María Coronel). According to legend, King Pedro the Cruel was so taken with Inés's beauty that he pursued her constantly until she poured boiling oil over her face to disfigure herself.

Triana & El Arenal   These two districts were immortalized by Cervantes, Quevedo, and Lope de Vega, the fabled writers of Spain's golden age. It was the rough-and-tough seafaring quarters when Seville was a thriving port in the 1600s. In El Arenal, the 12-sided Torre del Oro, or "gold tower," built by the Almohads in 1220, overlooks the river on Paseo Cristobal Colón. You can take the riverside esplanade, Marqués de Contadero, which stretches along the banks of the river from the tower. The Museo Provincial de Bellas Artes is also found here, containing Spain's best collection of Seville's painters, notably Murillo. Across the river, Triana was once the Gypsy quarter but has now been gentrified.

Seville Orientation

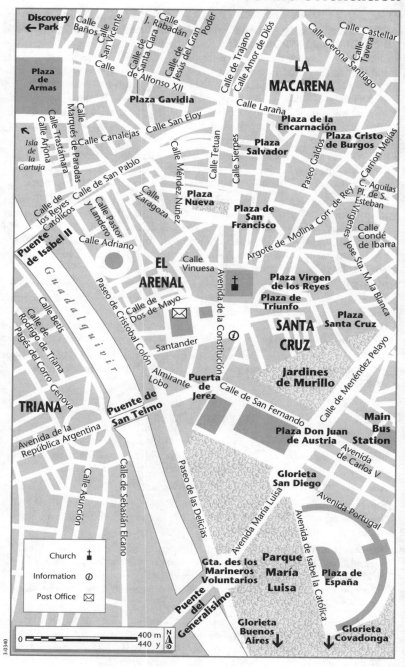

2 Getting Around

BY PUBLIC TRANSPORTATION   Actually, you walk in Seville, although there are buses. But most of these are used for visiting the environs, which have no touristic interest. If you use a bus for getting around the city, you'll find that most lines converge at Plaza de la Encarnación, Plaza Nueva, or in front of the cathedral on Avenida de la Constitución. Bus service is daily from 6am to 11:15pm. The city tourist office will furnish you a booklet outlining bus routes. You can purchase a 10-trip *bonobús* to save money. The best buses for circling through the center of town include C1 and C2 (*circulares interiores*).

BY TAXI   This is quite a viable means of getting around, especially at night when streets are dangerous because of frequent muggings. Call Tele Taxi at 95/462-22-22 or Radio Taxi at 95/458-00-00. Cabs are metered and charge by the kilometer.

BY CAR   Chances are you arranged to rent a car before you came to Seville (rates are lower that way). However, if you didn't, you'll find offices of Avis and Hertz at the airport as well as in the city: **Avis** at Avenida de la Constitución, 15B (☎ **95/ 421-65-49**), and **Hertz** at Avenida de la República Argentina, 3 (☎ **95/427-88-87**). Both offices are open Monday to Friday from 9am to 1:30pm and 4 to 7pm and on Saturday from 9am to 1pm.

BY BIKE   Although Seville is intensely hot in summer, bike rentals are possible, even though spring and autumn are better times—at least cooler—for cycling around. Rentals are available at **El Ciclismo,** Paseo Catalina de Ribera 2 (☎ **95/441-19-59**), in Puerta de la Carne, at the northern end of the Jardines de Murillo. It's open Monday to Friday from 10am to 2pm and 6 to 8pm and on Saturday from 10am to 2pm.

ON FOOT   This is virtually the only way to explore the heart of Old Seville. Wear sturdy, strong walking shoes, and also some protection from the intense heat if you're strolling about in summer.

FAST FACTS: Seville

American Express   The American Express office in Seville is in the Hotel Inglaterra, Plaza Nueva, 7 (☎ 95/421-16-17), open Monday to Friday from 9:30am to 1:30pm and 4:30 to 7:30pm and on Saturday from 10am to 1pm.

Area Code   The telephone area code for Seville is **95.**

Bus Information   The Central Bus Station, Prado de San Sebastián, Calle José María Osborne, 11 (☎ 95/441-71-11), is the place to go for bus information, or you can call daily from 7am to 9pm.

Business Hours   Most **banks** in Seville are open Monday to Friday from 9am to 2pm and on Saturday from 9am to noon. (Always conceal your money before walking out of a bank in Seville.) **Shops** are generally open Monday to Saturday from 9:30am to 1:30pm and 4:30 to 8pm. Most department stores are open Monday to Saturday from 10am to 8pm.

Consulates   The consulate of the **United States** is at Paseo de las Delicias, 7 (☎ 95/423-18-83), open Monday to Friday from 10am to 1pm and 2 to 4:30pm. The consulate of **Canada** is on the second floor at Avenida de la Constitución, 30 (☎ 95/422-94-13), open Monday to Friday from 9:30am to 1pm. The consulate of the **United Kingdom** is at Plaza Nueva, 8 (☎ 95/422-88-75), open Monday to Friday from 8am to 3pm.

Hospital   For medical emergencies, go to the Hospital Universitario y Provincial, Avenida Doctor Fedriani, s/n (☎ 95/455-74-00).

Laundry   Lavandería Robledo, Calle Sánchez Bedoya, 18 (☎ 95/421-81-32), is open Monday to Friday from 10am to 2pm and 5 to 8pm and on Saturday from 10am to 2pm.

Police   The police station is located on Paseo de las Delicias (☎ 95/461-54-50).

Post Office   The post office is at Avenida de la Constitución, 32 (☎ 95/421-95-85). It's open Monday to Friday from 8:30am to 8:30pm and on Saturday from 9:30am to 2pm.

Safety   With massive unemployment, the city has been hit by a crime wave in recent years. María Luisa Park is especially dangerous, as is the highway leading to Jerez de la Frontera and Cádiz. Dangling cameras and purses are especially vulnerable. Don't leave cars unguarded with your luggage inside. Regrettably, some daring attacks are made—as they are in U.S. cities—when passengers stop for traffic signals.

Telephone/Telex   The telephone office is at Plaza Gavidia, 7 (for telephone service information, call 003). To send wires by phone, call 95/422-20-00.

3 Best Hotel Bets

- **Best Historic Hotel:** The **Hotel Alfonso XIII** (☎ 800/221-2340 in the U.S. and Canada, or 95/422-28-50), a reproduction of a Spanish palace, opened originally in 1929 for the Iberoamerican Exposition and was completely remodeled for Expo '92. It has hosted all the leading stars, politicians, and luminaries who have come through Seville over the years—everyone from Jackie Onassis to Grace Kelly to Spain's most famous matadors. It remains the grandest period piece in Andalusia, with an ornate lobby filled with pillars and coffered ceilings.
- **Best for Business Travelers:** In the unlikely event that you're in Seville strictly for business, the **Hotel Inglaterra** (☎ 800/528-1234 in the U.S. and Canada, or 95/422-49-70), on a busy square in the heart of town, has the best and most efficient business center. The center is new, with all the latest equipment, and the staff is helpful and particularly adept at taking messages or locating some hard-to-find outlet that you need for your business.
- **Best for a Romantic Getaway:** On a hillside in the hamlet of Sanlúcar, 12 miles south of Seville, is the **Hacienda Benazuza** (☎ 95/570-33-44). This manor house, set on 40 acres, boasts one of the most romantic and tranquil settings in all of Andalusia. Operated since 1992 by Basque entrepreneurs, this delightful retreat, with elegant rooms, reflecting pools, and landscaped gardens, is welcome relief after hot, dusty Seville.
- **Best Trendy Hotel:** Named for the son and designated heir of Juan Carlos I, the **Radisson Príncipe de Asturias Plaza Hotel Sevilla** (☎ 800/333-3333 in the U.S., or 95/446-22-22) opened just in time for Seville's Expo '92. Its design consists of a trio of ultramodern ring-shaped modules, each rising four floors and connected by passageways leading to the public rooms. Many dignitaries—even heads of state—who visit Seville have rejected the AlfonsoXIII in favor of this newer contemporary selection.
- **Best Lobby for Pretending You're Rich:** The **Alfonso XIII** (☎ 800/221-2340 in the U.S. and Canada, or 95/422-28-50) is the only choice here. It's an architectural monument, the grandest hotel lobby in all of Andalusia. Acres of marble,

mahogany, antiques, and *azulejos* (hand-painted tiles) make it a stellar example of Mudéjar/Andalusian style. Although you can't sit and watch Grace Kelly parade through the lobby anymore, you can be sure that the current media headliner will appear here at some time during a visit to Seville, if only to walk through the lobby on the way to a splendid and elegant dinner.

- **Best for Families:** The **Hotel Doña María** (☎ 95/422-49-90), just steps from the cathedral, is best for families who want a central location so they can walk to all of Seville's major attractions. The hotel is a winner in its own right, with a swimming pool on the upper floor. Many of the rooms are large enough to accommodate families traveling together. Overall, it's a gracious choice with a helpful staff.
- **Best Moderately Priced Hotel:** The **Residencia y Restaurant Fernando III** (☎ 95/421-77-08) lies in Barrio de Santa Cruz, the old Jewish ghetto, reached along a maze of narrow streets. Although the four-story hotel is modern and commercial, its many Andalusian touches convey a cozy atmosphere. The English-speaking staff is helpful and efficient, making this a winning choice.
- **Best Budget Hotel:** The **Residencia Murillo** (☎ 95/421-60-95), in the heart of the Barrio de Santa Cruz, is named after the artist, who used to live in the district. It's virtually next to the gardens of the Alcázar, within walking distance of all of Seville's major attractions (which saves on taxi costs). The functional rooms offer good value. A few are a little too dark, but most are quite good. This has been the old-quarter favorite of budgeteers for decades.
- **Best Service:** Seville's most efficient staff—each member polite, professional, and helpful—operate in the **Hotel Inglaterra** (☎ 800/528-1234 in the U.S., or 95/422-49-70), in the heart of town 3 blocks north of the bullring. Employees welcome guests (most often in English) with friendly smiles; there's 24-hour room service, and every wish—within reason—is fulfilled speedily and efficiently.
- **Best Location:** The **Bécquer** (☎ 95/422-89-00) enjoys an excellent location, 3 blocks west of the bullring and 2 blocks north of the river—in the heart of Seville. Many of the city's best restaurants and attractions can be reached by foot, and numerous tapas bars line the streets surrounding the hotel. The Museo de Bellas Artes is also nearby.
- **Best Health Club:** Although Seville's hoteliers were late in discovering the world demand for health clubs in hotels, the **Hotel Meliá Sevilla** (☎ 800/336-3542 in the U.S., or 95/442-26-11) responded to the challenge and opened the most professional facility. The staff employed is very skilled, guiding you through and showing the hotel's array of facilities, ranging from the best sauna and Jacuzzi in town to a gym and squash courts. There's also a pool.
- **Best Hotel Pool:** On the Isla de la Cartuja, accessible by the Puerta Itálica, **Radisson Príncipe de Asturias Plaza Hotel** (☎ 800/333-3333 in the U.S., or 95/446-22-22) was built on the site where Expo '92 stood. Its well-maintained, state-of-the-art outdoor swimming pool is the best in town. Gardens surround the pool—an inviting oasis in the often sweltering heat of Seville.

4 Accommodations

During Holy Week and the Seville Fair, hotels often double, even triple, their rates. Price increases are often not announced until the last minute. If you're going to be in Seville at these times, arrive with an iron-clad reservation and an agreement about the price before checking in.

VERY EXPENSIVE

✪ **Hotel Alfonso XIII.** San Fernando, 2, 41004 Sevilla. ☎ **800/221-2340** in the U.S. and Canada, or 95/422-28-50. Fax 95/421-60-33. 130 rms, 18 suites. A/C MINIBAR TV TEL. 38,000-56,000 ptas. ($304-$448) double; from 82,000 ptas. ($656) suite. AE, DC, MC, V. Parking 4,800 ptas. ($38.40).

Set at the southwestern corner of the gardens that front Seville's famous Alcázar, in the historic heart of town, this five-story rococo building is one of the three or four most legendary hotels in Spain. As such, it is obviously the premier address in Seville. Built as an aristocratic shelter for patrons of the Iberoamerican Exposition of 1929 and named after the then-king of Spain, it reigns as a superornate and superexpensive bastion of glamour. Built in the Mudéjar/Andalusian revival style, it contains hallways that glitter with handpainted tiles, acres of marble and mahogany, antique furniture embellished with intricately embossed leather, and a floor plan and spaciousness that are nothing short of majestic.

Dining/Entertainment: The San Fernando restaurant offers a refined Italian and continental cuisine. A lobby bar features midday coffee amid potted palms and memorials to another age, its blue, white, and yellow tiles reflecting the colors of Seville.

Services: 24-hour room service, laundry/valet, concierge, car rentals with or without drivers, baby-sitting.

Facilities: Spectacular garden, designed in the Andalusian style; outdoor pool; tennis courts; shops; arcade-enclosed courtyard with potted flowers and splashing fountain.

EXPENSIVE

Hotel Inglaterra. Plaza Nueva, 7, 41001 Sevilla. ☎ **800/528-1234** in the U.S., or 95/422-49-70. Fax 95/456-13-36. 116 rms. A/C TV TEL. Apr, 21,000–25,000 ptas. ($168–$200) double. May–Mar, 17,000–22,000 ptas. ($136–$176) double. AE, DC, MC, V. Parking 1,500 ptas. ($12).

Established in 1857 and since modernized into a comfortably glossy seven-story contemporary design, this eminently respectable and rather staid hotel lies a 5-minute walk southwest of the cathedral, occupying one entire side of a palm-fringed plaza. Much of its interior is sheathed with acres of white or gray marble, and the furnishings include ample use of Spanish leather and floral-patterned fabrics. Despite their modernity, the bedrooms nonetheless evoke old-fashioned touches of Iberian gentility. The best rooms are on the fifth floor.

Dining/Entertainment: One floor above street level, overlooking the mosaic pavements of Plaza Nueva, the hotel's sunny restaurant serves well-prepared fixed-price meals from a frequently changing international menu. There's also an in-house cocktail lounge that seems favored by local businesspeople.

Services: Concierge, room service (24 hours), laundry/valet service, baby-sitting.
Facilities: Car-rental facilities, business center.

Hotel Meliá Sevilla. Doctor Pedro de Castro, 1, 41004 Sevilla. ☎ **800/336-3542** in the U.S., or 95/442-26-11. Fax 95/442-16-08. 361 rms, 5 suites. A/C MINIBAR TV TEL. 17,750 ptas. ($142) double; from 26,500 ptas. ($212) suite. AE, DC, MC, V. Parking 1,350 ptas. ($10.80).

Located a short walk east of Plaza de España, near the Parque María Luisa, this is the most elegant, tasteful, and international of the modern skyscraper hotels of Seville. It opened in 1987, rising 11 floors. A member of the Meliá chain, it incorporates acres of white marble as well as several dozen shopping boutiques and private apartments into its L-shaped floor plan. The guest-room decor is contemporary and comfortable, and each unit offers a private bath. Rooms at the back lack views. The Meliá was a favorite of the planners of the massive Expo '92 fair, which transformed the face of both Seville and Andalusia. The hotel lacks the personal touch provided by the staff at the Alfonso XIII, but its rooms are superior to those at the Inglaterra.

Dining/Entertainment: The Giralda Restaurant serves three-course fixed-price lunches and dinners. There's also a large and stylish piano bar, Corona, plus an informal coffee shop, Las Salinas.

Services: Room service (24 hours), laundry, baby-sitting on request.

Facilities: Business center, car rentals, outdoor swimming pool (with a section reserved for children), sauna, arcade of shops and boutiques, several flowering outdoor terraces.

Hotel Tryp Colón. Canalejas 1, 41001 Sevilla. ☎ **800/387-8842** in the U.S., or 95/422-29-00. Fax 95/422-09-38. 204 rms, 14 suites. A/C MINIBAR TV TEL. 24,200–38,200 ptas. ($193.60–$305.60) double; 82,050–117,200 ptas. ($656.40–$937.60) suite. AE, DC, MC, V. Parking 2,200 ptas. ($17.60).

Set about a quarter of a mile northwest of the Giralda and about 2 blocks southeast of the Fine Arts Museum (Museo Provincial de Bellas Artes), this hotel is Seville's closest rival—in prestige and architectural allure—to the legendary Alfonso XIII. Originally built around the turn of the century and renovated in 1988, it retains such features as a massive stained-glass dome stretching over the lobby, staircases worthy of a Spanish baron, formal service, and all the niceties of a good expensive hotel. The bedrooms, all with private baths, are conservative and traditional, although some are in need of an overhaul.

Dining/Entertainment: El Burladero restaurant serves lunches and dinners (see our recommendation in "Dining," later in this chapter). There's also a bar luring self-styled Hemingways that seems to be favored by visiting bullfighters, journalists, and politicians.

Services: Concierge, room service (24 hours), baby-sitting, laundry/valet.

Facilities: Sauna, car-rental facilities, shopping boutiques.

☼ Radisson Príncipe de Asturias Plaza Hotel Sevilla. Isla de la Cartuja, 41018 Sevilla. ☎ **800/333-3333** in the U.S., or 95/446-22-22. Fax 95/446-04-28. 285 rms, 18 suites. A/C MINIBAR TV TEL. Mon–Thurs, 21,000 ptas. ($168) double; 65,000 ptas. ($520) suite. Fri–Sun, 14,000 ptas. ($112) double; 35,000 ptas. ($280) suite. Rates include breakfast. AE, DC, MC, V. Free parking.

Named after the son and designated heir of Juan Carlos I, Don Felipe de Borbón, príncipe de Asturias (his title is something akin to Britain's prince of Wales), this hotel was expressly built to house the surge of visitors at Seville's Expo '92. The only hotel located at the former site of Expo itself, facing the Guadalquivir River, it lies a 5-minute taxi ride from the center of Seville. It was designed in three hypermodern ring-shaped modules, each four stories tall and connected to the public rooms by passageways. Designated as a five-star luxury hotel, this Radisson was reserved during Expo for visiting dignitaries and heads of state. Its designers intended its perpetual use, at the end of the party, as one of the city's most visible hotels—sort of a modern-day counterpart to the Alfonso XIII (which was designed for use by dignitaries during Seville's International Exposition of 1929).

Dining/Entertainment: The Restaurant Colón serves gourmet versions of regional cuisine. The lobby bar and the Cartura Bar offer soothing libations, sometimes to live piano music.

Services: Concierge, room service (24 hours), laundry/valet, limousine pickups, baby-sitting.

Facilities: Business center, conference facilities, outdoor swimming pool, in-house florist, shops, currency exchange, car rentals, trilingual TV channels, health club with sauna, massage, gymnasium, squash courts.

MODERATE

Ⓢ **Bécquer.** Calle de los Reyes Católicos, 4, 41001 Sevilla. ☎ **95/422-89-00.** Fax 95/421-44-00. 120 rms. A/C TV TEL. 11,000 ptas. ($88) double. AE, DC, MC, V. Parking 1,200 ptas. ($9.60). Bus: 21, 24, 30, or 31.

A short walk from the action of the Seville bullring (Maestranza) and only 2 blocks from the river, the Bécquer lies on a street of cafés where you can order tapas and drink Andalusian wine. The Museo de Bellas Artes also lies nearby. Built in the 1970s, the hotel was enlarged and much renovated in the late 1980s. It occupies the site of a mansion and retains many objets d'art rescued before the building was demolished. Guests register in a wood-paneled lobby before being shown to one of the bedrooms, which are functionally furnished, well kept, and reasonably comfortable—in all, a good value in a pricey city. All have private baths. Only breakfast is served, but you'll find a bar and lounge, as well as a garage nearby.

Hotel Alcázar. Menéndez y Pelayo, 10, 41004 Sevilla. ☎ **95/441-20-11.** Fax 95/442-16-59. 100 rms. A/C TV TEL. 13,000 ptas. ($104) double. Rates include breakfast. AE, DC, MC, V. Parking 1,000 ptas. ($8).

On the wide and busy Boulevard Menéndez y Pelayo, across from the Jardines de Alcázon, this pleasantly contemporary hotel is sheltered behind a facade of brown brick. Built in 1964, the hotel was last renovated in 1991, but even with improvements it's still no match for the Doña María (see below). Slabs of striated gray marble cool the reception area in the lobby, next to which you'll find a Spanish restaurant and bar. Above, three latticed structures resemble a trio of *miradores* (bay windows). The medium-size guest rooms have functional modern furniture and private baths.

Hotel Doña María. Don Remondo, 19, 41004 Sevilla. ☎ **95/422-49-90.** Fax 95/421-95-46. 60 rms. A/C TV TEL. Jan–Feb and July–Aug, 12,000 ptas. ($96) double. Mar–June and Sept–Dec, 16,500 ptas. ($132) double. AE, DC, MC, V. Parking 1,200 ptas. ($9.60).

Its location a few steps from the cathedral creates a dramatic view from the Doña María's rooftop terrace. Staying at this four-star, four-story hotel represents a worthwhile investment, partly because of the tasteful Iberian antiques in the stone lobby and upper hallways. The ornate neoclassical entryway is offset with a pure-white facade and iron balconies, which hint at the building's origin in the 1840s as a private villa. Amid the flowering plants on the upper floor, you'll find a swimming pool ringed with garden-style lattices and antique wrought-iron railings. Each of the one-of-a-kind bedrooms offers a private bath and is well furnished and comfortable, although some are rather small. A few have four-poster beds; others, a handful of antique reproductions. Light sleepers might find the noise of the church bells jarring. Breakfast is the only meal served. The sleepy staff, however, needs to perk up.

Residencia y Restaurant Fernando III. San José, 21, 41001 Sevilla. ☎ **95/421-77-08.** Fax 95/422-02-46. 157 rms. A/C TV TEL. 16,000 ptas. ($128) double. AE, DC, MC, V. Parking 1,000 ptas. ($8).

You'll find the Fernando III on a narrow, quiet street at the edge of the Barrio de Santa Cruz, near the northern periphery of the Murillo Gardens. Its vast lobby and baronial dining hall are reminiscent of a luxurious South American hacienda. The building is modern, constructed around 1970 with marble and hardwood detailing; it's coolly and sparsely furnished with leather chairs, plants, and wrought-iron accents.

👪 Family-Friendly Hotels

Hotel Doña María *(see p. 247)*   Behind the cathedral and the Giralda, this is one of the most gracious places for a family seeking lodgings in the old quarter of Seville. There's also a pool on the roof to delight adults and children. The hotel also rings a garden courtyard. Some of the rooms are large enough for families, and there are wide beds and baths with dual sinks.

Hotel Meliá Sevilla *(see p. 245)*   On the outskirts, this is an 11-story structure with a lot of facilities appreciated by families, including a pool, fitness center, squash court, and a garage. Families enjoy dining on a terrace alfresco, and there's also a snack bar on the grounds. Housekeeping in the bedrooms is good.

Residencia y Restaurant Fernando III *(see p. 247)*   This hotel lies in the medieval Barrio de Santa Cruz, the old Jewish quarter. The helpful and polite staff speak English and are welcoming to families, offering some guest rooms large enough to accommodate those traveling with children.

Many of the accommodations—medium in size, comfortably furnished, and well maintained—offer balconies filled with cascading plants; all have private baths. There is a TV salon and a paneled bar. The hotel's restaurant features a regional Andalusian cuisine on its set menu.

INEXPENSIVE

Hostal Ducal. Plaza de la Encarnación, 19, 41003 Sevilla. ☎ **95/421-51-07.** Fax 95/422-89-99. 51 rms. A/C TEL. 6,250–10,500 ptas. ($50–$84) double. AE, DC, MC, V.

In this fairly modern hotel the guest rooms are modest but comfortable, with provincial and utilitarian furnishings and central heating for those Sevillian winters. A continental breakfast can be brought to your room, but no other meals are served. The location, near El Corte Inglés department store, is handy to many specialty shops.

☉ Hostal Goya. Mateus Gago, 31, 41004 Sevilla. ☎ **95/421-11-70.** Fax 95/456-02-88. 20 rms, 10 with bath. May–Mar, 5,500 ptas. ($44) double without bath, 6,200 ptas. ($49.60) double with bath. Apr, 6,200 ptas. ($49.60) double without bath, 7,000 ptas. ($56) double with bath. No credit cards. Parking 1,500 ptas. ($12).

Its location in a narrow-fronted town house in the oldest part of the barrio is one of the Goya's strongest virtues. The building's gold-and-white facade, ornate iron railings, and picture-postcard demeanor are all noteworthy. The bedrooms are cozy and simple, without phones or TVs. Guests congregate in the marble-floored ground-level salon, where a skylight floods the couches and comfortable chairs with sunlight. No meals are served. Reserve well in advance.

Hotel América. Jesús del Gran Poder, 2, 41002 Sevilla. ☎ **95/422-09-51.** Fax 95/421-06-26. 100 rms. A/C MINIBAR TV TEL. 11,000 ptas. ($88) double; 15,000 ptas. ($120) triple. AE, DC, MC, V. Parking 2,000 ptas. ($16) nearby.

Built in 1976 and partially renovated in 1994, this hotel contains rather small bedrooms but keeps the place spick-and-span. Superior features include wall-to-wall carpeting and, in winter, an individual heat control that *works*. Relax in the TV lounge or order a drink in the Duque Bar. Near the hotel is a parking garage for 600 cars. There isn't a major restaurant, but the América does offer a tearoom, snack bar, and cafeteria that serves regional and international cuisine. The hotel is set on the northern side of Plaza del Duque. One of Spain's major department stores, El Corte Inglés, opens onto the same square.

Accommodations in Seville

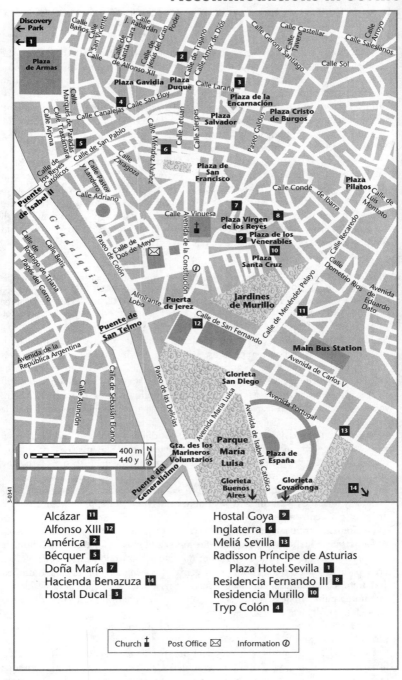

Alcázar **11**
Alfonso XIII **12**
América **2**
Bécquer **5**
Doña María **7**
Hacienda Benazuza **14**
Hostal Ducal **3**

Hostal Goya **9**
Inglaterra **6**
Meliá Sevilla **13**
Radisson Príncipe de Asturias
    Plaza Hotel Sevilla **1**
Residencia Fernando III **8**
Residencia Murillo **10**
Tryp Colón **4**

Church †   Post Office ✉   Information ℹ

Residencia Murillo. Calle Lope de Rueda, 7–9, 41004 Sevilla. ☎ **95/421-60-95.** Fax 95/421-96-16. 57 rms. TEL. 7,000 ptas. ($56) double; 8,500 ptas. ($68) triple. AE, DC, MC, V. Parking 1,000 ptas. ($8) nearby.

Tucked away on a narrow street in the heart of Santa Cruz, the old quarter, the Residencia Murillo (named after the artist who used to live in this district) is almost next to the gardens of the Alcázar. Inside, the lounges harbor some fine architectural characteristics and antique reproductions; behind a grilled screen is a retreat for drinks. Some of the rooms we inspected were cheerless and gloomy, so have a look before checking in. Most of them, however, are quite good and inviting, making the Murillo the favorite budgeteers' choice in the old quarter for decades. Like all of Seville's hotels, the Murillo is in a noisy area.

You can reach this residencia from Menéndez y Pelayo, a wide avenue west of the Parque María Luisa, where a sign will take you through the Murillo Gardens on the left. Motorists should try to park in Plaza de Santa Cruz. Then walk 2 blocks to the hotel, which will send a bellhop back to the car to pick up your suitcases. If there are two in your party, station a guard at the car, and if you're going out at night, call for an inexpensive taxi to take you instead of strolling through the streets of the old quarter—it's less romantic but a lot safer.

NEARBY

✪ **Hacienda Benazuza.** Calle Virgen de las Nieves, s/n, 41800 Sanlúcar la Major, Seville. ☎ **95/570-33-44.** Fax 95/570-34-10. 26 rms, 18 suites. A/C MINIBAR TV TEL. 33,000–40,000 ptas. ($264–$320) double. Fri–Sun, free breakfast. Suite 40,000–90,000 ptas. ($284–$639) seven days a week, plus breakfast. AE, DC, MC, V. Closed July 15–Aug. Free parking. From Seville, follow the signs for Huelva, and head south on the A49 Hwy., turning off it at Exit 6.

Set on a hillside above the agrarian hamlet of Sanlúcar la Mayor, 12 miles south of Seville, this legendary manor house is surrounded by 40 acres of olive groves and its own farmland. Its ownership has been a cross-section of every major cultural influence that has swept through Andalusia since its foundations were laid in the 10th century by the Moors. After the Catholic conquest of southern Spain, the site became a much-feared stronghold of the fanatically religious Caballeros de Santiago.

In 1992 the property was bought by Basque-born entrepreneur Rafael Elejabeitia, who, after spending many millions of pesetas, transformed the premises into one of Andalusia's most charming hotels. Careful attention was paid to preserving the ancient Moorish irrigation system whose many reflecting pools nourish the gardens. All but a few of the bedrooms are within the estate's main building, and each is individually furnished with Andalusian antiques and Moorish trappings, representative of the original construction.

Dining/Entertainment: The most formal of the hotel's three restaurants is La Alquería, where first-class service and Andalusian and international cuisine culminate in "surprise menus." El Patio is an indoor-outdoor affair overlooking the estate's red-brick patio and palm trees. (Both of the above are open daily for lunch and dinner, and are open to nonresidents who reserve in advance.) A lunch buffet beside the swimming pool, where everyone seems to show up in bathing suits and jewelry, is offered in La Alberca.

Services: Concierge well trained to procure almost anything, room service (24 hours), laundry.

Facilities: Tennis courts with a resident pro, paddle tennis courts, golf range, billiards room, outdoor pool. A mini-museum of Andalusian agriculture is in an antique building originally designed as an olive press. Many other sporting options lie within driving distance, and can be arranged by the concierge staff.

5 Best Restaurant Bets

- **Best View:** The **Río Grande** (☎ 95/427-39-56) is a classic Sevillian restaurant with large terraces that open onto the Guadalquivir River. Near Plaza de Cuba in front of the Torre del Oro, it has the most panoramic view in town. Although many diners find the view absorbing, the restaurant's Andalusian cuisine is also delightful, prepared with old-fashioned care. Here are all the matador favorites— everything from bull tail Andalusian to garlic-chicken Giralda, the latter dish dedicated to the tower adjoining the cathedral.
- **Best Value:** In the heart of the Barrio de Santa Cruz, the **Mesón Don Raimundo** (☎ 95/421-29-25) is housed in a former 17th-century convent. Considering the size of the portions, the restaurant offers very good value if you'd like to sample an array of tasty Spanish dishes such as fish soup or partridge casserole in sherry sauce. However, its special delight is that it prepares many recipes from ancient Arab-Hispanic cookbooks. An exceptional treat.
- **Best for Kids:** Next door to the more fabled Río Grande, the multilevel **El Puerto** (☎ 95/427-17-25) also has an alfresco terrace opening onto the river. It features the most reasonably priced cubiertos (fixed-price menus) in town. Fresh seafood is a special treat here. There's also a cafeteria bar.
- **Best Andalusian:** A small, cozy restaurant, close to the cathedral, **Enrique Becerra** (☎ 95/421-30-49) is a whitewashed house with wrought-iron window grilles that offers the city's best array of traditional Andalusian home-cooked dishes. Other restaurants are more innovative, but Enrique Becerra sticks fast to Sevillian tradition, both in decor and in menu offerings. Try, for example, jarrete de ternera a la cazuela (a regional veal stew). Every time-tested favorite is launched by a soothing bowl of gazpacho, and washed down with sangría.
- **Best Continental Cuisine:** Seville has no finer dining selection than **Egaña Oriza** (☎ 95/422-72-11), located in a restored mansion adjacent to Murillo Park. A chic Basque enclave of nouvelle cuisine, Egaña Oriza features a few Basque specialties, but most of the dishes are rooted in the continental style. The food is innovative and beautifully prepared: Instead of the typical gazpacho with vegetables and olive oil, the preparation here includes succulent Sanlúcar prawns. And steak, for example, comes with foie gras in a grape sauce.
- **Best Italian Cuisine:** In spite of the name, the **Pizzería San Marco** (☎ 95/421-43-90) serves not just pizza, but a wide array of delectable Italian specialties as well: among them, chicken parmesan, various forms of scaloppine, and some savory pastas. The cookery has flavor and flair.
- **Best Seafood:** La Isla (☎ 95/421-26-31), in the Arenal district, is the place to go for the freshest fish. Though Seville is inland, fish is rushed to the restaurant from the Huelva or Cádiz coasts, and more exotic catches are flown in from Galicia, in the northwest. Many of the fish dishes are based on traditional Galician cooking methods. The parrillada de mariscos y pescados, a fish and seafood grill for two people, is the best dish on the menu.
- **Best Pizza:** The **Pizzería San Marco** (see "Best Italian Cuisine," above).
- **Best Outdoor Dining:** See the **Río Grande** ("Best View," above) and **Hostería del Laurel** ("Best Local Favorite," below).
- **Best Fast Food:** The **Cervecería Giralda** (☎ 95/422-74-35) serves not only the best fast food in town, it's also the most conveniently located eatery, lying near such attractions as the cathedral, the Alcázar, and Giralda Tower. If you're in a hurry, ask for one of the *platos combinados* (combination plates), which are most filling and are served quickly without a long wait.

- **Best Local Favorite:** In the heart of the Barrio de Santa Cruz, the **Hostería del Laurel** (☎ 95/422-02-95) is one of the most enduring restaurants in town, long popular with visitors and locals alike. In summer patrons can dine on an outdoor terrace on the square. The decor is old-school—white walls, leather-backed chairs, and heavy wooden tables. The food is traditional Spanish fare, with many Andalusian specialties.
- **Best Spot to Meet a Matador:** El Burladero, in the Hotel Tryp Colón (☎ 95/422-29-00), is the local favorite of visiting matadors. The bullring in Seville often draws the country's biggest stars. They like to relax and unwind here in a setting devoted to the memorabilia of their trade. Photographs adorning the walls trace the history of bullfighting. Even the name of the restaurant comes from the wooden barricades in the ring where bullfighters can escape the charge of an enraged bull.

6 Dining

VERY EXPENSIVE

✪ **Egaña Oriza.** San Fernando, 41. ☎ **95/422-72-11.** Reservations required. Main courses 2,150–3,800 ptas. ($17.20–$30.40); three-course fixed-price menu 5,000 ptas. ($40). AE, DC, MC, V. Mon–Fri 1:30–3:30pm and 9–11:30pm, Sat 9–11:30pm. (Bar, daily 9am–midnight.) Closed Aug. BASQUE/INTERNATIONAL.

Set in the conservatory of a restored mansion adjacent to Murillo Park is Seville's best, most stylish restaurant. Its reputation stems primarily from its role as one of the few game specialists in Andalusia—a province that's otherwise devoted to seafood. The restaurant was established by Basque-born owner and chef José Mari Egaña, who managed to combine his passion for hunting with his flair for cooking his catch. Many of the raw ingredients that go into the dishes presented on the menu were trapped or shot in Andalusia, a region whose potential for sports shooting is underutilized, according to Sr. Egaña. The view from the dining room encompasses a garden and a wall that formed part of the fortifications of Muslim Seville.

The availability of many specialties depends on the season, but might include fresh vegetable soup studded with morsels of confit of duck, gazpacho with prawns, steak with foie gras in grape sauce, casserole of wild boar with cherries and raisins, quenelles of duck in a potato nest with apple purée, stewed mountain sheep cooked with figs, rice with stewed thrush, and woodcock flamed in Spanish brandy. The wine list provides an ample supply of hearty Spanish reds to accompany any of these dishes. Dessert might feature a chocolate tart slathered with freshly whipped cream. Señor Egaña's wife, Mercedes, runs the establishment's two-story dining room.

EXPENSIVE

El Burladero. In the Hotel Tryp Colón, Canalejas, 1. ☎ **95/422-29-00.** Reservations recommended. Main courses 2,000–4,000 ptas. ($16–$32); fixed-price menus 4,100–4,500 ptas. ($32.80–$36). AE, DC, MC, V. Daily 1:30–4:30pm and 9pm–midnight. Closed Aug. CONTINENTAL.

Set in one of Seville's most prominent hotels, this restaurant is chock full of memorabilia and paraphernalia from the bullfighting trade. The wall tiles that decorate parts of the interior were removed from one of the pavilions at the 1929 Seville World's Fair, and the photographs adorning the walls are a veritable history of bullfighting. (The restaurant, incidentally, is named after the arena's wooden barricade—*el burladero*—which bullfighters use to escape from the charge of an enraged bull.) The restaurant boasts a popular bar where a wide assortment of Sevillanos meet and mingle before their meals.

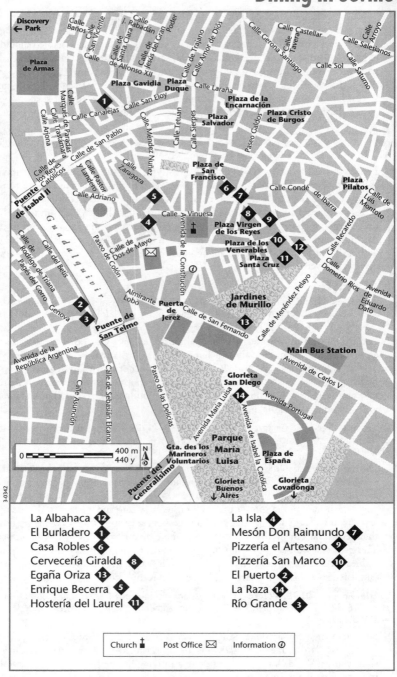

Dining in Seville

Discovery ← Park

Plaza de Armas

Calle Baños
Calle San Vicente
Calle Santa Clara
Calle de Jesús del Gran Poder
Calle de Alfonso XII
Calle J. Rabadán
Calle de Trajano
Calle Amor de Diós
Calle Gerona Santiago
Calle Castellar
Calle Tavera
Calle Salesianos
Calle Arroyo
Calle Sol
Calle Saturno

Plaza Gavidia
Plaza Duque
Calle San Eloy
Calle San Pablo
Calle Canalejas
Calle Marqués de Paradas
Calle Trastámara
Calle Arjona

Plaza de la Encarnación
Plaza Cristo de Burgos
Plaza Salvador
Calle Laraña
Calle Tetuán
Calle Sierpes
Calle Méndez Núñez
Paseo Caldos

Plaza de San Francisco

Plaza Pilatos
Calle de Luis Montoto

Calle de los Reyes Católicos
Calle Pastor y Landero
Calle Zaragoza
Calle Adriano
Calle de Vinuesa
Calle Condé de Ibarra
Calle Recaredo

Puente de Isabel II

Guadalquivir

Calle de Betis
Calle del Betis
Calle de Rodrigo de Triana
Pagés del Corro Genova

Paseo de Colón
Calle de Dos de Mayo
Avenida de la Constitución

Plaza Virgen de los Reyes
Plaza de los Venerables
Plaza Santa Cruz
Calle Dometrio Rios
Avenida de Eduardo Dato

Almirante Lobo
Puerta de Jerez
Calle de San Fernando
Jardines de Murillo
Calle de Menéndez Pelayo

Puente de San Telmo

Avenida de la República Argentina
Calle de Sebastián Elcano
Calle Asunción

Main Bus Station
Avenida de Carlos V

Glorieta San Diego
Avenida Portugal

Paseo de las Delicias
Avenida María Luisa
Avenida de Isabel la Católica

Parque María Luisa
Plaza de España

Gta. des los Marineros Voluntarios
Glorieta Buenos ↓ Aires
Glorieta Covadonga

Puente del Generalismo

0 — 400 m / 440 y N

3-0342

La Albahaca **12**	La Isla **4**
El Burladero **1**	Mesón Don Raimundo **7**
Casa Robles **6**	Pizzería el Artesano **9**
Cervecería Giralda **8**	Pizzería San Marco **10**
Egaña Oriza **13**	El Puerto **2**
Enrique Becerra **5**	La Raza **14**
Hostería del Laurel **11**	Río Grande **3**

Church ✝ Post Office ✉ Information ℹ

253

Menu specialties include upscale interpretations of local country dishes, with an attractive mix of items from other regions of Spain as well. Examples include bacalao al horno con patatas (baked salt cod with potatoes and saffron sauce), roasted shoulder of lamb stuffed with a deboned bull's tail and served in a richly aromatic sauce, clams with white kidney beans, a local version of cocido (a boiled amalgam of sausages, meats, chickpeas, and vegetables), and a stew of eel meat heavily laced with garlic and spices. Dishes from other parts of Europe might include truffled filet steak in puff pastry, duck liver, and salmon cooked in lemon-flavored dill sauce.

Casa Robles. Calle Alvarez Quintero, 58. ☎ **95/456-32-72.** Reservations recommended. Main courses 1,200–2,200 ptas. ($9.60–$17.60); fixed-price menus 4,800–10,500 ptas. ($38.40–$84). AE, DC, MC, V. Daily 1–4:30pm and 8pm–1am. ANDALUSIAN.

Praised by local residents as well as by temporary visitors, this restaurant began its life as an unpretentious bar and bodega in 1954. Over the years, thanks to a staff directed by owner-chef Juan Robles and his children, it developed into a courteous but bustling restaurant scattered over two floors of a building a short walk from the cathedral. Amid an all-Andalusian decor, you can enjoy such dishes as fish soup in the Andalusian style, lubina con naranjas (whitefish with Sevillana oranges), hake baked with strips of Serrano ham, and many kinds of fresh fish. The dessert list is long, diverse, and very tempting.

MODERATE

La Albahaca. Plaza de Santa Cruz, 12. ☎ **95/422-07-14.** Reservations recommended. Main courses 1,800–3,000 ptas. ($14.40–$24); fixed-price menus 4,500–5,500 ptas. ($36–$44). AE, DC, MC, V. Mon–Sat noon–4pm and 8pm–midnight. BASQUE/FRENCH.

Located on a prominent square in the old Barrio de Santa Cruz, this restaurant with an open-air terrace offers a limited but savory menu that has become a favorite of Sevillians. Specialties include a salad of carpaccio of codfish with fresh asparagus and herbs, seafood soup, shellfish bisque, grilled lamb chops, partridge braised in sherry, salmon in papillote (parchment), and chocolate pudding for dessert. The restaurant is in an antique seignorial home built in 1929.

Ⓢ Enrique Becerra. Gamazo, 2. ☎ **95/421-30-49.** Reservations recommended. Main courses 1,600–2,000 ptas. ($12.80–$16). AE, DC, MC, V. Mon–Sat 1–5pm and 8pm–midnight. ANDALUSIAN.

During our latest rounds, this restaurant, off Plaza Nueva and near the cathedral, provided one of our best meals. The restaurant takes its name from its owner, a smart and helpful host, who installed it in a late 19th-century building. A popular tapas bar and Andalusian dining spot, it offers an intimate setting and a hearty welcome that leaves you with the feeling that your business is really appreciated. While perusing the menu, you can sip dry Tío Pepe and nibble herb-cured olives with lemon peel. The gazpacho here is among the city's best, and the sangría is served ice cold. Specialties include hake real (royal), sea bream Bilbaon style, and a wide range of meat and fish dishes. Many vegetarian dishes are also featured.

La Isla. Arfe, 25. ☎ **95/421-26-31.** Reservations recommended. Main courses 2,000–3,000 ptas. ($16–$24). AE, DC, MC, V. Tues–Sun 1–5pm and 8pm–midnight. Closed Aug. SPANISH/ANDALUSIAN.

Set in two large dining rooms designed in Andalusian fashion (thick plaster walls, tile floors, and taurine memorabilia), this air-conditioned restaurant was established shortly after World War II and has done a thriving business ever since. Its seafood is trucked or flown in from either Galicia, in northern Spain, or Huelva, one of Andalusia's major ports, and is almost always extremely fresh. Menu items include

🌀 Family-Friendly Restaurants

El Puerto *(see p. 256)* Down by the river, onto which its terraces open, this is a good and inexpensive family seafood restaurant, offering one of the most reasonably priced cubiertos (fixed-price menus) in Seville. It's ideal for the family on a tight budget.

Pizzería El Artesano *(see p. 256)* Near the cathedral, this is an ideal place for lunch when you're touring the heart of Seville, viewing the Alcázar and other attractions. The pizzas are good here, and the staff starts serving them at 12:30pm so you don't have to wait around with hungry children until many restaurants open at 1:30pm.

Río Grande *(see p. 255)* This is the best place to go for a classic Sevillian meal. It can turn into a real family affair if you order a big platter of paella, studded with chicken and shellfish. The restaurant sits against the bank of the Guadalquivir River, and there's also a snack bar if you're lunching light.

merluza à la primavera (hake with young vegetables), solomillo à la Castellana (grilled beefsteak with strips of Serrano ham), chicken croquettes, and shellfish soup. The restaurant lies a short walk from the cathedral, in a very old building erected, the owners say, on foundations laid by the ancient Romans.

😊 Mesón Don Raimundo. Argote de Molina, 26. ☎ **95/421-29-25.** Reservations recommended. Main courses 1,500–2,500 ptas. ($12–$20); fixed-price menu 2,500 ptas. ($20). AE, DC, MC, V. Mon–Sat 12:30–5pm and 7:30pm–midnight, Sun 12:30–5pm. ANDALUSIAN.

Once a 17th-century convent, this is an attractively furnished restaurant whose entrance lies at the end of a flower-lined alleyway in the center of the Barrio de Santa Cruz. The interior contains lots of brick, terra-cotta, and carved columns, which support the beamed or arched high ceilings. Your meal might include fish stew or one of six kinds of soup (including one with clams and pine nuts), then fresh grilled king shrimp, a casserole of partridge in sherry sauce, or wild rabbit casserole. Some of the recipes were adapted from old Arab-Hispanic cookbooks. In winter the central fireplace imparts a warm glow to the antique copper and wrought-iron art objects; in summer the place is comfortably air-conditioned. Menus change weekly.

Río Grande. Calle Betis, 70. ☎ **95/427-39-56.** Reservations required. Main courses 1,800–2,600 ptas. ($14.40–$20.80); fixed-price menu 3,500 ptas. ($28). AE, DC, MC, V. Daily 1–5pm and 8pm–1am. Bus: 41 or 42. ANDALUSIAN.

This classic Sevillian restaurant is named for the Guadalquivir River, which its panoramic windows overlook. It sits against the bank of the river near Plaza de Cuba in front of the Torre del Oro. Some diners come here just for a view of the city monuments. A meal might include stuffed sweet pepper flamenca, fish-and-seafood soup seaman's style, the chef's fresh salmon, chicken-and-shellfish paella, bull tail Andalusian, and garlic-chicken Giralda. You can also have a selection of fresh shellfish that's brought in daily. Large terraces contain a snack bar, the Río Grande Pub, and a Bingo room. You can often watch sports events on the river in this pleasant (and English-speaking) spot.

INEXPENSIVE

😊 Hostería del Laurel. Plaza de los Venerables, 5. ☎ **95/422-02-95.** Reservations recommended. Main courses 750–2,500 ptas. ($6–$20). AE, DC, MC, V. Daily noon–4pm and 7:30pm–midnight. ANDALUSIAN/SPANISH.

Food on the Run

Lying directly east of the cathedral, the **Cervecería Giralda,** Calle Mateus Gago, 1 (☎ 95/422-74-35), is one of the least expensive dining spots near the cathedral, Alcázar, and Giralda Tower. Residents and tourists alike eat here. You can make a meal from the selection of tapas (appetizers), ranging from 225 to 275 ptas. ($1.80 to $2.20), or order one of the *platos combinados* (combination plates), ranging from 800 to 1,300 ptas. ($6.40 to $10.40). The place is open Monday to Saturday from 9am to midnight and on Sunday from 10am to midnight.

On the same street, the **Pizzería El Artesano,** Calle Mateus Gago, 9 (☎ 95/421-38-58), also lures in customers near the cathedral. Here the feature is an Andalusian version of pizza costing 525 to 725 ptas. ($4.20 to $5.80). It's open daily from noon to midnight.

Lying on the "opposite side" of the Guadalquivir, away from the throngs of tourists, is the Barrio de Triana. This used to be its own little village community until Seville burst its seams and absorbed it. It's still the place to go to escape the high food tariffs on the cathedral side of the river.

El Puerto, Betis, s/n (☎ 95/427-17-25), stands next door to the famed Río Grande restaurant. It has a multilevel alfresco terrace opening onto the river. You can get fresh seafood here, but the special buy is the chef's cubierto (menu of the house), costing 1,500 ptas. ($12); tapas range from 200 to 700 ptas. ($1.60 to $5.60).

At the cafeteria bar you serve yourself; inside is an inexpensive restaurant with waiter service. It's open Tuesday to Sunday; lunch is served from 1 to 4pm and dinner from 8pm to midnight. (It's closed in January.) Bus: 41 or 42.

Another way to enjoy quick meals is to eat at one of the tapas bars recommended below under "Seville After Dark." Portions, called *raciones,* are usually generous, and many tourists on the run often eat standing at the bar, making a full meal out of two orders of tapas.

Located in one of the most charming buildings on tiny, difficult-to-find Plaza de los Venerables in the labyrinthian Barrio de Santa Cruz, this hideaway restaurant has iron-barred windows stuffed with plants. Inside, amid Andalusian tiles, beamed ceilings, and more plants, you'll enjoy good regional cooking. Many diners stop for a drink and tapas at the ground-floor bar before going into one of the dining rooms. The hostería is attached to a three-star hotel.

Pizzería San Marco. Calle Mesón de Moro, 6. ☎ **95/421-43-90.** Reservations recommended. Main courses 580–1,475 ptas. ($4.65–$11.80). MC, V. Tues–Sun 1:30–4:30pm and 8:30pm–12:30am. ITALIAN.

Despite the informality implied by its name, this is actually a well-managed restaurant with sit-down service and bilingual waiters. Pizza is only one of the many items featured on the menu, and often is relegated to a secondary role, as clients usually opt for any of several kinds of pastas, salmon salads, duck in orange sauce, osso buco, chicken parmesan, and several forms of scaloppine. There's also a congenial corner for drinking, named Harry's Bar in honor of grander role models in Venice or elsewhere.

Despite the allure of the food, the real interest of the place is its setting. It's in what was originally built, more than 1,000 years ago, as an Arab bathhouse. Its interior reminds some visitors of a secularized mosque, despite the presence of a modern wing added around 1991 in anticipation of increased business from Seville's Expo celebration. The establishment is in the Barrio de Santa Cruz, on an obscure side street running into Calle Mateus Gago.

⑤ La Raza. Isabel la Católica, 2. ☎ **95/423-38-30.** Reservations recommended. Main courses 1,200–2,300 ptas. ($9.60–$18.40). AE, DC, MC, V. Daily noon–5pm and 8pm–midnight. ANDALUSIAN.

A terrace restaurant in the Parque María Luisa, La Raza is known for both its setting and its Andalusian tapas. Begin with gazpacho, then go on to one of the meat dishes, or perhaps an order of the savory paella. On Friday and Saturday there's often music to entertain guests, many of whom are American and Japanese tourists.

7 What to See & Do

Seville has a wide range of palaces, churches, cathedrals, towers, and historic hospitals. Since it would take a week or two to visit all of them, we've narrowed the sights down to the very top attractions plus a few additional sights. The only way to explore Seville is on foot, with a good map in hand—but be alert for muggers.

SUGGESTED ITINERARIES

If You Have 1 Day

Depending on the time of your arrival, visit the Alcázar and also explore the cathedral, climbing Giralda Tower for the most panoramic view of the city. Have dinner that night in one of the restaurants we recommend in the Barrio de Santa Cruz.

If You Have 2 Days

For your first day, follow our suggestions above. On the second day, take a stroll through the Barrio de Santa Cruz while it's daylight, so you can see the interesting architecture and visit typical shops selling Andalusian handcrafts. View the art collection at the Museo Provincial de Bellas Artes de Seville and stroll through the Parque María Luisa.

If You Have 3 Days

Use this day as a "mop up," exploring the attractions you missed on the first 2 days. Begin the morning by taking our walking tour of Seville. With what time remains, visit the Hospital de la Santa Caridad, Torre del Oro, and Casa de Pilatos. Try for a night of flamenco in one of the typical old quarters.

If You Have 5 Days

Spend the first 3 days as outlined above. On Day 4, travel in the environs of Seville, taking various excursions, including Itálica, $5^1/_2$ miles to the northwest, where you can see some of the most interesting Roman ruins of Spain. You'll still have time to journey to Carmona, 21 miles east of Seville, where you can explore the old town and perhaps have lunch at the parador here.

On Day 5, journey to everybody's favorite wine town, Jerez de la Frontera, 54 miles south of Seville, where you can tour the bodegas and have your fill of sherry.

THE TOP ATTRACTIONS

۞ Catedral. Plaza del Triunfo, Avenida de la Constitución. ☎ **95/421-49-71.** Admission (including a visit to the Giralda Tower) 500 ptas. ($4). Daily 11am–5pm.

The largest Gothic building in the world, and the third-largest church in Europe after St. Peter's in Rome and St. Paul's in London, this church was designed by builders with a stated goal—that "those who come after us will take us for madmen." Construction began in the late 1400s and took centuries to complete.

Built on the site of an ancient mosque, the cathedral claims to contain the remains of Columbus, with his tomb mounted on four statues.

Works of art abound, many of them architectural, such as the 15th-century stained-glass windows, the iron screens (*rejas*) closing off the chapels, the elaborate 15th-century choir stalls, and the Gothic reredos above the main altar. During Corpus Christi and the Immaculate Conception observances, altar boys with castanets dance in front of the high altar. In the Treasury are works by Goya, Murillo, and Zurbarán; here, in glass cases, a touch of the macabre shows up in the display of skulls.

After touring the dark interior, emerge into the sunlight of the Patio of Orange Trees, with its fresh citrus scents and chirping birds.

Warning: Shorts and T-shirts are definitely not allowed.

✪ **Giralda Tower.** Plaza del Triunfo. Free admission with admission to the cathedral, above. Daily 11am–5pm.

Just as Big Ben symbolizes London, La Giralda conjures up Seville—this Moorish tower, next to the cathedral, is the city's most famous monument. Erected as a minaret in the 12th century, it has seen later additions, such as 16th-century bells. To climb it is to take the walk of a lifetime. There are no steps—you ascend an endless ramp. If you make it to the top, you'll have a dazzling view of Seville. Entrance is through the cathedral.

✪ **El Alcázar.** Plaza del Triunfo. ☎ **95/422-71-63.** Admission 700 ptas. ($5.60). Tues–Sat 10:30am–5pm, Sun 10am–1pm.

This magnificent 14th-century Mudéjar palace, north of the cathedral, was built by Pedro the Cruel. It's the oldest royal residence in Europe still in use—on visits to Seville, King Juan Carlos stays here. From the Dolls' Court to the Maidens' Court through the domed Ambassadors' Room, it contains some of the finest work of Sevillian artisans. In many ways it evokes the Alhambra at Granada. Ferdinand and Isabella, who at one time lived in the Alcázar and influenced its architectural evolution, welcomed Columbus here on his return from America. On the top floor, the Oratory of the Catholic monarchs has a fine altar in polychrome tiles made by Pisano in 1504.

The well-kept gardens, filled with beautiful flowers, shrubbery, and fruit trees, are alone worth the visit.

El Parque de los Descubrimientos (Discovery Park). Isla de la Cartuja. ☎ **95/446-16-16.** "Strolling ticket" (giving access to the park and its gardens), 500 ptas. ($4); "super ticket" (giving access to the pavilions), 4,000 ptas. ($32) adults, 3,000 ptas. ($24) children. Park and gardens, June 7–Oct 12, Tues–Thurs 8pm–2am, Fri–Sat 11:30am–4am, Sun 11:30am–1am; Apr 25–June 6 and Oct 13–Dec 21, Thurs 8pm–2am, Fri–Sat 11:30am–2am, Sun 11:30am–midnight; Dec 22–Apr 24, Fri–Sun 11:30am–midnight. Pavilions, June 7–Oct 12, Tues–Sat 8pm–midnight, Sun noon–8pm; Apr 25–June 6 and Oct 13–Dec 21, Thurs 8pm–midnight, Fri–Sun noon–8pm; Dec 22–Apr 24, Fri–Sat noon–8pm, Sun 11:30am–midnight. Bus: C2 from the center of Seville.

On the 540-acre island of La Cartuja in the Guadalquivir River, site of Expo '92, the government opened a theme park in 1993. Although closed in 1996 for restoration, it's slated to be open in the summer of 1997 at which time prices and hours (stated above) might be readjusted on a slightly different schedule. Call in advance for information before heading here. Eight new bridges now join the island to Seville. The theme park itself takes up 168 acres of the site and incorporates some of the more acclaimed attractions at Expo. Among them are the Pavilion of Navigation, tracing

Seville Attractions

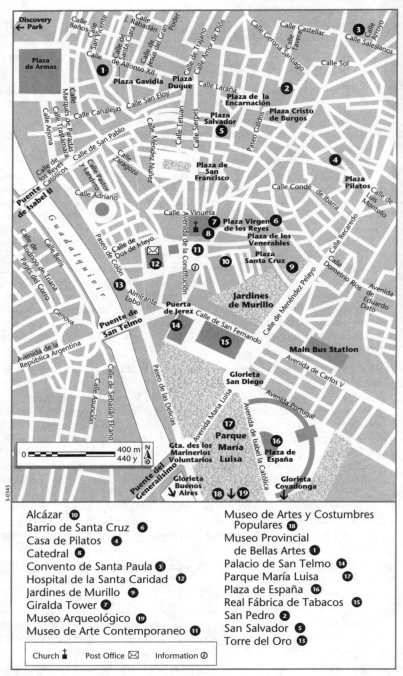

Alcázar **10**
Barrio de Santa Cruz **6**
Casa de Pilatos **4**
Catedral **8**
Convento de Santa Paula **3**
Hospital de la Santa Caridad **12**
Jardines de Murillo **9**
Giralda Tower **7**
Museo Arqueológico **19**
Museo de Arte Contemporaneo **11**

Museo de Artes y Costumbres Populares **18**
Museo Provincial de Bellas Artes **1**
Palacio de San Telmo **14**
Parque María Luisa **17**
Plaza de España **16**
Real Fábrica de Tabacos **15**
San Pedro **2**
San Salvador **5**
Torre del Oro **13**

Church ✝   Post Office ✉   Information ⓘ

259

Impressions

Seville doesn't have an ambience. It is ambience.

—James A. Michener

Seville is a pleasant city, famous for oranges and women.

—Lord Byron

the history of maritime exploration from its beginnings to the present; the Pavilion of Nature, containing flora and fauna from all over the world; and eight other pavilions, representing the autonomous regions of Spain.

The Puerto de Indias is the re-creation of a 15th-century port, with small shops and evocative taverns, along with silversmiths, cobblers, welders, and other tradespeople. Replicas of Christopher Columbus's ships in 1492, the *Pinta, Niña,* and *Santa María,* are docked here. The Children's Park has a host of entertainment, including puppet shows and water slides.

The audiovisual offerings are said to equal or top those of any theme park in the world. The computer-controlled Digital Planetarium, for example, housed in the Pavilion of the Universe, is the only one of its kind in the world—images are projected onto a 60-foot dome, taking viewers on a ride through the universe.

Buses, cable cars, a monorail, catamarans, trolley cars, and rowboats are some of the transportation available to haul visitors around. Other facilities and attractions include concerts, plays, dance clubs, two parades and a circus daily, a laser sound show with fireworks, 12 foodstalls, 15 family restaurants, seven tapas bars, and two deluxe restaurants.

Hospital de la Santa Caridad. Calle Temprado, 3. ☎ **95/422-32-22.** Admission 300 ptas. ($2.40). Mon–Sat 10am–1pm and 3:30–6pm, Sun 10:30am–12:30pm.

This 17th-century hospital is intricately linked to the legend of Miguel Manara, portrayed by Dumas and Mérimée as a scandalous Don Juan. It was once thought that he built this institution to atone for his sins, but this has been disproved. The death of Manara's beautiful young wife in 1661 caused such grief that he retired from society and entered the "Charity Brotherhood," burying corpses of the sick and diseased as well as condemned and executed criminals. Today the members of this brotherhood continue to look after the poor, the old, and invalids who have no one else to help them.

Nuns will show you through the festive orange-and-sienna courtyard. The baroque chapel contains works by the 17th-century Spanish painters Murillo and Valdés-Leál. As you're leaving the chapel, look over the exit door for the macabre picture of an archbishop being devoured by maggots.

Torre del Oro. Paseo de Cristóbal Colón. ☎ **95/422-24-19.** Admission 100 ptas. (80¢). Tues–Fri 10am–2pm, Sat–Sun 10am–1pm.

The 12-sided Tower of Gold, dating from the 13th century, overlooks the Guadalquivir River. Originally it was covered with gold tiles, but someone long ago made off with them. Recently restored, the tower has been turned into a maritime museum, the Museo Náutico, displaying drawings and engravings of the port of Seville in its golden heyday.

Casa de Pilatos. Plaza Pilatos, 1. ☎ **95/422-50-55.** Admission: Museum, 1,000 ptas. ($8); patio and gardens, 500 ptas. ($4). Museum, daily 10am–2pm and 4–6pm; patio and gardens, daily 9am–7pm.

This 16th-century Andalusian palace of the dukes of Medinaceli recaptures the splendor of the past, combining Gothic, Mudéjar, and plateresque styles in its courtyards, fountains, and salons. According to tradition, this is a reproduction of Pilate's House in Jerusalem. On display are two old carriages and the rooms filled with Greek and Roman statues. The collection of paintings includes works by Carreño, Pantoja de la Cruz, Sebastiano del Piombo, Lucas Jordán, Batalloli, Pacheco, and Goya. The palace lies about a 7-minute walk northeast of the cathedral on the northern edge of the Barrio de Santa Cruz, in a warren of labyrinthine streets whose traffic is funneled through the nearby Calle de Aguiles.

Archivo General de Indias. Avenida de la Constitución, s/n. ☎ **95/421-12-34.** Free admission. Mon–Fri 10am–1pm.

The great architect of Philip II's El Escorial outside Madrid, Juan de Herrera, was also the architect of the old Lonja (Stock Exchange), located next to the cathedral. Construction on the building lasted from 1584 to 1646. In the 17th century it was headquarters for the Academy of Seville, which was founded in part by the great Spanish artist Murillo.

In 1785, during the reign of Charles III, the building was turned over for use as a general records office for the Indies. That led to today's Archivo General de Indias, said to contain some four million antique documents, even letters exchanged between patron Queen Isabella and explorer Columbus (his detailing his discoveries and impressions). These very rare documents are locked in air-conditioned storage to keep them from disintegrating. Special permission has to be acquired before examining some of them. Many treasure hunters come here hoping to learn details of where Spanish galleons laden with gold went down off the coast of the Americas. On display in glass cases are fascinating documents in which the dreams of those early explorers come alive again.

✪ Museo Provincial de Bellas Artes de Sevilla. Plaza del Museo, 9. ☎ **95/422-18-29.** Admission 250 ptas. ($2), free for students. Tues–Sun 9am–3pm. Bus: 21, 24, 30, or 31.

This lovely old convent off Calle Alfonso XII houses one of the most important Spanish art collections. A whole gallery is devoted to two paintings by El Greco, and works by Zurbarán are exhibited; however, the devoutly religious paintings of the Seville-born Murillo are the highlights. An entire wing is given over to macabre paintings by the 17th-century artist Valdés-Leál. His painting of John the Baptist's head on a platter includes the knife—in case you didn't get "the point." The top floor, which displays modern paintings, is less interesting.

MORE ATTRACTIONS

✪ BARRIO DE SANTA CRUZ   What was once a ghetto for Spanish Jews, who were forced out of Spain in the 15th century in the wake of the Inquisition, is today the most colorful district of Seville. Near the old walls of the Alcázar, winding medieval streets with names like Vida (Life) and Muerte (Death) open onto pocket-sized plazas. Flower-filled balconies with draping bougainvillea and potted geraniums jut out over this labyrinth, shading you from the hot Andalusian summer sun. Feel free to look through numerous wrought-iron gates into patios filled with fountains and plants. In the evening it's common to see Sevillians sitting outside drinking icy sangría under the glow of lanterns.

Although the district as a whole is recommended for sightseeing, seek out in particular the **Casa de Murillo (Murillo's House),** Santa Teresa, 8 (☎ **95/421-75-35**). Bartolomé Esteban Murillo, the great Spanish painter known for his religious works, was born in Seville in 1617. He spent his last years in this house in Santa Cruz, dying in 1682. Five minor paintings of the artist are on display. The furnishings, although not owned by the artist, are period pieces. Admission is 250 ptas. ($2), and the house is open Tuesday to Saturday 10am to 2pm and 6 to 8pm.

To enter the Barrio Santa Cruz, turn right after leaving the Patio de Banderas exit of the Alcázar. Turn right again at Plaza de la Alianza, going down Calle Rodrigo Caro to Plaza de Doña Elvira. Use caution when strolling through the area, particularly at night—many robberies have occurred here.

PARQUE MARÍA LUISA   This park, dedicated to María Luisa, sister of Isabella II, was once the grounds of the Palacio de San Telmo, Avenida de Roma. Its baroque facade visible behind the deluxe Alfonso XIII Hotel, the palace today houses a seminary. The former private royal park is now open to the public.

Running south along the Guadalquivir River, the park attracts those who want to take boat rides, walk along paths bordered by flowers, jog, or go bicycling. The most romantic way to traverse it is by rented horse and carriage, but this can be expensive, depending on your negotiation with the driver.

In 1929 Seville was to host the Spanish American Exhibition, and many pavilions from other countries were erected here. The worldwide depression put a damper on the exhibition, but the pavilions still stand.

Exercise caution while walking through this park. Many muggings have been reported.

PLAZA DE ESPAÑA   The major building left from the exhibition at the Parque María Luisa (see above) is a half moon–shaped structure in Renaissance style, set on this landmark square of Seville. The architect, Anibal González, not only designed but supervised the building of this immense structure; today it's a government office building. At a canal here you can rent rowboats for excursions into the park; or you can walk across bridges spanning the canal. Set into a curved wall are alcoves, each focusing on characteristics of one of Spain's 50 provinces, as depicted in tile murals.

PLAZA DE AMÉRICA   Another landmark Sevillian square, Plaza de América represents city planning at its best: Here you can walk through gardens planted with roses, enjoying the lily ponds and the fountains and feeling the protective shade of the palms. And here you'll find a trio of elaborate buildings left over from the world exhibition that never materialized—in the center, the home of the government headquarters of Andalusia; on either side, two minor museums worth visiting only if you have time to spare.

The **Museo Arqueológico Provincial,** Plaza de América, s/n (☎ **95/423-24-01**), contains many artifacts from prehistoric times and the days of the Romans, Visigoths, and Moors. It's open Tuesday to Sunday from 10am to 2pm. Admission is 250 ptas. ($2) adults, free for students and children. Bus: 30, 31, or 34.

Also opening onto the square is the **Museo de Artes y Costumbres Populares,** Plaza de América, s/n (☎ **95/423-25-76**), displaying folkloric costumes, musical instruments, cordobán saddles, weaponry, and farm implements that document the life of the Andalusian people. It's open Tuesday to Saturday from 9:30am to 2:30pm. Admission is 250 ptas. ($2) adults, free for children and students; closed holidays.

REAL FÁBRICA DE TABACOS   When Carmen waltzed out of the tobacco factory in the first act of Bizet's opera, she made its 18th-century original in Seville world famous. The old tobacco factory was constructed between 1750 and 1766, and a hundred years later it employed 10,000 *cigarreras,* of which Carmen was one in the opera. (She rolled her cigars on her thighs.) In the 19th century these tobacco women made up the largest female work force in Spain. Many visitors arriving today, in fact, ask guides to take them to "Carmen's tobacco factory." The building, the second largest in Spain, located on Calle San Fernando near the city's landmark luxury hotel, the Alfonso XIII, is still there. But the Real Fábrica de Tabacos is now part of the Universidad de Sevilla. Look for signs of its former role, however, as reflected in the bas-reliefs of tobacco plants and Indians over the main entrances. You'll also see bas-reliefs of Columbus and Cortés. Then you can wander through the grounds for a look at student life, Sevillian style. The factory is directly south of the Alcázar gardens.

8 Especially for Kids

The greatest thrill for kids in Seville is climbing **La Giralda,** the former minaret of the Great Mosque that once stood here. The view from this 20-story bell tower is certainly worth the climb, but most kids delight in the climb itself. With some inclined ramps and some steps, the climb was originally designed to be ridden up on horseback. Little gargoyle-framed windows along the way allow you to preview the skyline of Seville.

With your family in tow, head for **Plaza de España;** you'll find rowboats as well as *pedaloes* (pedalboats) to rent. A collection of Andalusian donkey carts here also adds to the fun, and there are ducks to feed on the Isla de los Patos. If your children take to that, they'll also enjoy feeding the pigeons as well.

The tourist office (see above) will give advice on how to rent pedaloes or canoes for trips along the Guadalquivir River. Or you can go to the riverbanks near the Torre del Oro and make your own rental arrangements with **Cruceros Turísticos Torre del Oro,** Paseo Marqués de Contadero (☎ **95/421-13-96**).

Finally, to cap your family trip to Seville, take one of the horse-and-buggy rides that leave from Plaza Virgen de los Reyes on Adolfo Rodríguez Jurado, or from the Parque de María Luisa at Plaza de España. Rates are government controlled at 4,000 ptas. ($32) a ride, but prices rise during April Fair and Holy Week.

9 Organized Tours

CITY TOURS   One of the best ways to navigate your way around the labyrinth of a complicated, traffic-clogged city like Seville is to take a city tour to expose you to a historical and geographical overview. A local outfit that handles only the briefest of bus tours is **Transvías de Sevillas,** Plaza de Colón (☎ **95/490-54-09**). Tours of Seville depart every hour, on the hour, every day of the year, beginning at 10am, with the last departure scheduled for 6pm. The commentary is jaded and a bit blasé, and the overview is fairly superficial, but the cost of 1,000 ptas. ($8) per person is reasonable. Know that during the hour-long tour you'll never emerge from the bus. Reservations aren't necessary. Departures are from in front of the Transvías office, opposite the Bullring (Maestranza) on Plaza de Colón.

More appealing are the 4-hour city tours conducted twice-daily by **Visitour,** Avenida de los Descubrimientos, s/n, Isla de la Cartuja (☎ **95/415-13-47**). Morning and afternoon tours are conducted daily from 9:30am to 1:30pm and 4 to 7:30pm, and cost 4,900 ptas. ($39.20) each. Frankly, the morning tour includes more essential sights than the afternoon tour, but the combination provides a worthwhile experience whose scope you'd have a hard time matching on your own.

ANDALUSIAN EXCURSIONS   In addition to being loaded with monuments of consuming historic and cultural interest, Seville makes a worthy base for explorations of Andalusia. The best of the city's tours are offered by a company formed in 1995 from a corps of experienced travel professionals well versed in the charm and lore of the region. **Visitour,** Avenida de los Descubrimientos, s/n, Isla de la Cartuja (☎ 95/ 415-13-47). Their buses, holding between 8 and 48 passengers, offer some of the best guided tours in Andalusia, always with the option of retrieving and redepositing clients at their hotels. Reservations a day in advance are strongly recommended. Two of the company's most popular tours depart daily. A tour of Granada leaves Seville at 7am, tours all that city's major monuments and neighborhoods, and returns to Seville around 7pm. The price is 13,750 ptas. ($110). A tour of Córdoba departs from Seville at 9am, returns around 7pm, and costs 9,900 ptas. ($79.20) per person.

Two other worthy tours depart 3 or 4 days a week, depending on the season. A visit to Jerez de la Frontera and Cádiz includes a visit to the riding school at Jerez, a tour of one of the city's most interesting wine bodegas, lunch in an Andalusian village (Puerto de Santa María), and a boat ride that begins on the Guadalete River and ends in Cádiz's Atlantic harbor. The tour, departing at 9am and returning around 7pm, costs between 10,200 and 11,500 ptas. ($81.60 and $92) per person, depending on the day of the week. If at all possible, try to schedule your participation for a Thursday (or, during June and July, for Thursday or Saturday), as participants attend a riding exhibition in Jerez that's conducted only on those days.

A visit to the historic hamlet of Ronda, conducted several times a week, departs at 9am, returns at 7pm, and costs 11,750 ptas. ($94) per person.

WALKING TOUR:
The Old City

Start: At the Giralda by the cathedral.
Finish: At the Hospital de los Venerables in the Barrio de Santa Cruz.
Time: 4 hours, including rapid visits to the interiors.
Best Times: Early morning (7–11am) and late afternoon (3–7pm).
Worst Times: After dark or during the heat of midday.

Seville is so loaded with architectural and artistic treasures that this brisk overview of the central zone doesn't begin to do justice to its cultural wealth. Although this walking tour includes the city's most obvious (and spectacular) monuments, such as the Giralda and the cathedral, it also includes lesser-known churches and convents— whose elaborate decorations were paid for by gold imported from the New World during Spain's Age of Exploration. It also features promenades through the city's most desirable shopping district, and meanders through the labyrinthine alleyways of the Barrio de Santa Cruz.

Begin with a visit to the:

1. **Cathedral,** a Gothic building so enormous that even its builders recognized the folly and fanaticism of their dreams. Its crowning summit, the Giralda, one of Europe's most famous towers, was begun in the late 1100s by the Moors and raised even higher by the Catholic monarchs in the 1568. Because of the position of these connected monuments near the summit of a hill overlooking the Guadalquivir, some scholars nostalgically refer to the historic neighborhood around them as the Acropolis.

After your visit, walk to the cathedral compound's northeastern corner for a visit to the:

2. **Palacio Arzobispal (Archbishop's Palace),** a 16th-century building resting on 13th-century foundations, with a 17th-century baroque facade of great beauty. Although conceived to house the overseer of the nearby cathedral, it was sometimes pressed into service to house secular visitors. One of these was Napoléon's

Walking Tour—The Old City

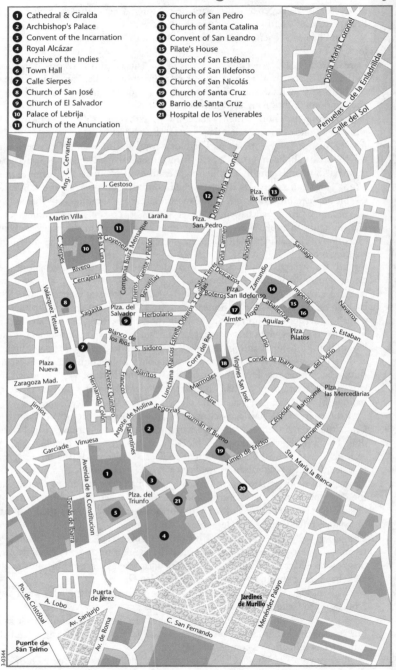

1. Cathedral & Giralda
2. Archbishop's Palace
3. Convent of the Incarnation
4. Royal Alcázar
5. Archive of the Indies
6. Town Hall
7. Calle Sierpes
8. Church of San José
9. Church of El Salvador
10. Palace of Lebrija
11. Church of the Anunciation
12. Church of San Pedro
13. Church of Santa Catalina
14. Convent of San Leandro
15. Pilate's House
16. Church of San Estéban
17. Church of San Ildefonso
18. Church of San Nicolás
19. Church of Santa Cruz
20. Barrio de Santa Cruz
21. Hospital de los Venerables

representative, Maréchal Soult, after he conquered Seville in the name of the Bonaparte family and France early in the 19th century.

From here, walk across the street, heading south, to Plaza Virgin de los Reyes, for a visit to the:

3. **Convento de la Encarnación (Convent of the Incarnation).** Its origins go back to the 1300s, shortly after the Catholic reconquest of Seville. Part of its architectural curiosity includes the widespread use of the lobed, horseshoe-shaped arches and windows traditionally used in mosques.

Exit from the church, then walk eastward across Plaza del Triunfo into the entrance of one of the most exotic palaces in Europe, the:

4. **Reales Alcázar (Royal Alcázar).** The oldest royal seat in Spain, it was begun for the Moorish caliphs in A.D. 712 as a fortress, then enlarged and embellished over the next thousand years by successive generations of Moorish and, beginning in 1248, Christian rulers. Its superimposed combination of Arab and Christian Gothic architecture creates one of the most interesting monuments in Iberia. Lavish gardens, as exotic as what you'd expect in the Old Testament, sprawl in an easterly direction in back. More than any other monument on this tour, with the exception of the cathedral, the Alcázar deserves a second visit after the end of this walking tour.

Exit from the Alcázar back onto Plaza del Triunfo. At the plaza's southwestern edge rises the imposing bulk of the:

5. **Archivo General de Indias (Archive of the Indies).** It was designed in the 1580s by Juan de Herrera, whose rectilinear austerity at El Escorial appealed to the religious fanaticism of Philip II. Built as a commodities exchange, it was abandoned for a site in Cádiz when that port replaced Seville as the most convenient debarkation point for ships coming from the New World. In 1758 it was reconfigured as the repository for the financial records and political and cultural archives of anything concerning the development of the Western Hemisphere. Its closets and storerooms contain more than four million dossiers—many bureaucratic and tedious, but sometimes of passionate interest to scholars and academics.

From here, walk half a block west to the roaring traffic of Avenida de la Constitución, then turn north, bypassing the facade of the already-visited cathedral. The avenida will end within 2 blocks at the ornate bulk of Seville's:

6. **Ayuntamiento (Town Hall).** Begun in 1527, and enlarged during the 19th century, it's the city's political showcase. For a view of its most interesting (plateresque) facade, turn right (east) when you reach it, then flank the building's eastern edge for a view of the medallions and allegorical figures that kept teams of stonemasons busy for generations. The Town Hall's northeastern facade marks the beginning of Seville's most famous and desirable shopping street:

7. **Calle Sierpes,** which stretches north from the Town Hall. The street's southern terminus, where you're standing, was once the site of a since-demolished debtor's prison where Miguel de Cervantes languished for several years, laying out the plot and characters of his innovative masterpiece *Don Quixote.*

Walk along the western edge of this famous street, turning left (west) after 2 blocks onto Calle Jovellanos for a view of the:

8. **Iglesia (Church) de San José.** Named in honor of a famous carpenter (St. Joseph, husband of the Virgin), this lavish baroque chapel functioned as the seat of the carpenter's guild after its completion in 1747.

Retrace your steps along Calle Jovellanos to Calle Sierpes, traverse its busy traffic, and continue walking due east along Calle Sagasta. Within a block, Calle Sagasta will deposit you in Plaza del Salvador, in front of the elaborate facade of the:

9. **Iglesia del Salvador (Saviour).** One of the grandest churches of Seville, preferred by many visitors to the rather chilly pomposity of the previously visited cathedral, this enormous building was begun in 1674 on the site of one of the Muslim world's holiest sites, the mosque of Ibn Addabas. Beneath the Catholic iconography you can still make out the base of the Moorish minaret (converted long ago into a Christian belfry) and the Moorish layout of the building's courtyard.

After your visit, walk 3 blocks north along Calle Cuna (a wide boulevard that Sevillanos usually refer to simply as "Cuna") for an exterior view of one of the most-envied private homes in town, the:

10. **Palacio de Lebrija or Casa de la Condesa de Lebrija,** at Calle Cuna, 18. Austere on the outside, lavish and Mudéjar on the inside, it was built in the 1400s and managed to incorporate a series of ancient mosaics, dug up from the excavations in the nearby town of Itálica, for incorporation into its floors. Although it's closed to casual visits, it's the most visible vestige of an aristocratic way of life that's rapidly fading.

From here, walk 2 short blocks east along Calle de Goyeneta for a view of the:

11. **Iglesia de la Anunciación.** Built in 1565 with profits from the New World, and associated for many centuries with both the Jesuits and the city's university, it contains a cold, rather macabre-looking crypt (Panteón de Sevillanos Ilustres) where the bodies of many of the city's governors and their families are buried.

From here, head east, passing through Plaza de la Anunciación onto Calle del Laraña Imagen for a short 2 blocks. Rising ahead of you from its position beside Plaza de San Pedro is the:

12. **Iglesia de San Pedro.** Built in the Mudéjar style in the 1300s, with some of its portals and towers added during the 1600s and 1700s, it's famous as the site where Spain's greatest painter, Velázquez, was baptized in 1599. Coffered ceilings rise above the building's main sanctuary and its eight shadowy chapels. The site is available for visits only during mass, during which visitors should remain as quiet and discreet as possible.

From Plaza de San Pedro, adjacent to the church's eastern entrance, walk east for 2 blocks along Calle del Almirante Apodaca until you reach the:

13. **Iglesia de Santa Catalina,** a 14th century Gothic-Mudéjar monument that has endured many alterations and additions during its lifespan. Most significant of these is a simple Gothic portal that was moved into its present position in 1930 from another church. Make it a point to walk around this medieval hybrid for views of horseshoe (lobed) arches that attest to the strong influence of Moorish design on its past.

After your visit, walk south for a block along Calle Carrión, whose name will change after a block to Calle Francisco Mejiás. The massive and severe-looking building that rises in about a block is the:

14. **Convento de San Leandro.** Although the building you'll see today was begun around 1580, it replaced a much older 13th-century church that was the first to be constructed in Seville after the Christian reconquest in 1248. Severe and simple, with a single barrel vault covering its single aisle, it's open only during early-morning (7am) mass and on some holy festival days.

Immediately to the southeast, opening off Plaza de Pilatos, is the grandest and most ornate palace that's open to view in Seville, the:

15. **Casa de Pilatos (Pilate's House).** One of the city's most frequently visited museums, it was built in 1521 by the marquis de Tarifa after his trip to the Holy Land where, according to legend, he was inspired by the ruined house in Jerusalem from which Pontius Pilate is said to have governed. The main entrance, modeled after

an ancient Roman triumphal arch, is fashioned from bronze, jasper, and Carrara marble, and the overall effect is one of imperial Roman grandeur.

After your visit, walk less than a block southeast for a view of the:

16. Iglesia de San Estéban. It's one of the finest examples of Mudéjar-Gothic architecture in Andalusia. Constructed during the late 1300s and early 1400s, it combines Moorish-style coffered ceilings with Gothic ribbed vaulting in ways beloved by students of the history of Spanish architecture.

From here, retrace your steps back to Plaza de Pilatos, then fork right onto Calle Caballerizas for a block until you reach Plaza de San Ildefonso. Flanking its edge rises the:

17. Iglesia de San Ildefonso. It's one of the most charming baroque churches in Seville, a colorful and graceful small-scale church filled with artistic treasures partly paid for with profits from the New World. Regrettably, it's open only during the hours of mass, during which discreet visitors can admire the interior.

From here, walk west for 2 short blocks south along Calle Virgenes till you reach the:

18. Iglesia de San Nicolás de Bari. Although the church was built in the 1700s, long after the departure of the Moors, the forest of red-marble columns that support the five aisles of its interior evoke some aspects of a mosque. The eclectic, and somewhat cluttered, aspect of its baroque interior is particularly charming.

From here, walk south for a block along Calle de Federico Rubio until you reach the soaring walls of a building usually described as the gateway to one of Seville's most colorful antique neighborhoods, the:

19. Iglesia de Santa Cruz (Holy Cross). Originally built between 1665 and 1728, and conceived as the parish church of the Barrio de Santa Cruz, which you'll visit shortly, it's prefaced with a relatively new facade that was added in 1929. This is a particularly active church, servicing the spiritual needs of a congested neighborhood, and is normally open only during the hours of mass.

At this point your tour will become less rigidly structured, and will allow you to wander through the narrow and labyrinthine alleyways of the:

20. Barrio de Santa Cruz. Before 1492, when the Jews were driven from Spain by the repressive edicts of Ferdinand and Isabella, this was the Jewish ghetto of Seville. Today it's highly desirable real estate—thick-walled houses, windowboxes studded with flowers, whose severe exteriors open onto private patios that ooze Andalusian charm. Wander at will through the neighborhood, and don't be surprised if you quickly get lost in the maze of twisting streets. Know that your final destination lies uphill (to the southwest) at a point near the cathedral (discreet signs indicate its direction). We recommend that you walk southwest along the relatively wide Calle Ximénes de Enriso, ducking into side alleyways at your whim for views of the streets that radiate out from there. At the barrio's southwestern edge, beside Plaza de los Venerables, you'll want to visit one of the barrio's greatest monuments, the:

21. Hospital de los Venerables (Hospice of the Venerable Ones). It was founded in 1675 as a retirement home for aged priests, was completed 12 years later, and is maintained today as a museum.

☕ **TAKE A BREAK**   One of the best places in this barrio to have a drink and take tapas is **Casa Román,** on Plaza de los Venerables (☎ **95/421-64-08**). This byegone-era bar has some of the finest tapas in the old quarter, and you can make your selection at a deli counter. It's also a good place to stop for a pick-me-up glass of regional wine.

From here, you're only a very short walk from the point near the cathedral where you initiated this walking tour several hot and dusty, but artistically rewarding, hours ago.

10 Outdoor Activities

From Easter until late October, you can attend a **bullfight,** as some of the best bull-fighters in Spain appear here at the Maestranza bullring, lying on Paseo de Colón (☎ **95/422-45-77**). One of the leading bullrings in Spain, the stadium attracts matadors whose fights often receive television and newspaper coverage throughout Iberia. Unless there's a special festival going on, bullfights (*corridas*) occur on Sunday. The best bullfights are staged during April Fair celebrations. Tickets tend to be pricey, and should be purchased in advance at the ticket office (*despacho de entradas*) on Calle Adriano, beside the Maestranza bullfight stadium. You'll also find many unofficial kiosks placed strategically along the main shopping street, Calle Sierpes, selling tickets. However, they charge a 20% commission for their tickets—a lot more if they think they can get it.

11 Shopping

ART GALLERIES

Rafael Ortíz. Marmolles, 12. ☎ **95/421-48-74.**

This is one of the most respected art galleries in Seville, specializing in contemporary paintings, usually from Iberian artists. Exhibitions change frequently, and because of canniness of this emporium's judgments, inventories sell out quickly. It's open Monday to Saturday from 10am to 1:30pm and 4:30 to 8:30pm.

BOOKS

Librería Vértice. San Fernando, 33. ☎ **95/421-16-54.**

Set conveniently close to Seville's university, this store stocks books in a polyglot of languages. The inventory ranges from the esoteric and professorial to Spanish romances of the soap-opera and bubblegum genre. Open Monday to Saturday from 10am to 1:30pm and 4:30 to 8:30pm.

The English Bookshop. Marqués de Nervion. ☎ **95/465-57-54.**

Smaller than many of the other book emporiums in Seville, this is the kind of place where you can find tomes on gardening, political discourse, philosophy, and pop fiction, all accumulated into one cozy place. Open Monday to Saturday from 10am to 1:45pm and 4:30 to 8:30pm.

CERAMICS

Martian. Calle Sierpes, 74. ☎ **95/421-34-13.**

Set close to the Seville Town Hall, this outfit sells a wide array of painted tiles and ceramics, the kind that invariably look better when transported away from the store and displayed in your home. The inventory includes vases, plates, cups, serving dishes, and statues, all made in or near Seville. Many of the pieces exhibit ancient geometric patterns of Andalusia. Other, floral motifs are rooted in Spanish traditions of the 18th century. Open Monday to Saturday from 10am to 1:30pm and 4:30 to 8:30pm.

El Postigo. Arfe, s/n. ☎ **95/421-39-76.**

Set in the town center near the cathedral, this shop contains one of the biggest selections in town of the ceramics for which Andalusia is famous. Some of the pieces are much, much too big to fit into your suitcase; others—especially the hand-painted tiles—make charming souvenirs that can be packed with your luggage. Open Monday to Friday from 10am to 2pm and 5 to 8pm and on Saturday from 10am to 2pm.

DEPARTMENT STORES

El Corte Inglés. Plaza del Duque, 10. ☎ **95/422-19-31.**

This is the best of the several department stores clustered in Seville's commercial center. A well-accessorized branch of a nationwide chain, it features a multilingual staff and rack after rack of every conceivable kind of merchandise for the well-stocked home, kitchen, and closet. If you're in the market for the brightly colored *feria* costumes worn by young girls during Seville's holidays, there's an impressive selection of the folkloric accessories that make Andalusia memorable. Open Monday to Saturday from 10am to 9pm.

FANS

Casa Rubio. Calle Sierpes, 56. ☎ **95/422-68-72.**

Carmen fluttered her fan and broke hearts in ways that Andalusian maidens have done with their caballeros for centuries. Casa Rubio stocks one of the city's largest supplies. They range from the austere and dramatic to some of the most florid and fanciful aids to coquetry available in Spain. Open Monday to Saturday from 10am to 1:45pm and 5 to 8pm.

FASHION

Econos. Avenida de la Constitución. ☎ **95/422-14-08.**

This is an excellent example of a small, idiosyncratic boutique loaded with fashion accessories that can be used by everyone from teenage girls to mature women. Silk scarves, costume jewelry, and an assortment of T-shirts with logos lettered in varying degrees of tastelessness—it's all here. Much of it represents the new, youthful perceptions of post-*movida* Spain. Open Monday to Friday from 10am to 2pm and 5 to 8pm and on Saturday from 10am to 2pm.

Marks & Spencer. Plaza del Duque, 6. ☎ **95/456-49-49.**

This is the Seville branch of a gigantic, upper-middle-bracket chain of clothiers based in London. As such, it caters to British expatriates and retirees ensconsed in the hills around Seville. The clothing is conservative and well made, with greater emphasis on warm-weather garb than you'd have found in equivalent branches in foggy old England. Open Monday to Saturday from 10am to 9pm.

Nicole Miller. Albareda, 16. ☎ **95/456-36-14.**

This is one of the best addresses in Seville for women who want to avoid the anonymity of El Corte Inglés, benefit from a solicitous staff, and gain access to fashion statements from Spain and the rest of Europe. Open Monday to Friday from 10am to 2pm and 5 to 8pm and on Saturday from 10am to 2pm.

Perdales. Cuna, 23. ☎ **95/421-37-09.**

This is one of the most prestigious purveyors of flamenco dresses and *feria* costumes in Seville, and as such, outfits many of the region's professional performers. Much of its merchandise is akin to *couture;* other options are less expensive and sold off the rack. Open Monday to Friday from 10am to 2pm and 5 to 8pm and on Saturday from 10am to 2pm.

Vittorio & Lucchino. Calle Sierpes, 87. ☎ **95/422-71-51.**

This outfit has made a reputation for itself as a purveyor of stylish clothing, often based on Italian models, to well-heeled women of Andalusia. If you've already exhausted the inventories of the boutiques in El Corte Inglés and not found the diaphanous and alluring garment you're looking for, this place will probably have it. Open Monday to Friday from 10am to 2pm and 5 to 8pm and on Saturday from 10am to 2pm.

GIFTS

Artesanía Textil. Calle Sierpes, 70. ☎ **95/456-28-40.**

It specializes in the nubbly and roughly textured textiles that reflect the earthiness of contemporary Spanish art. Weavings—some made of linen; others, the rough fibers of Spanish sheep—are the specialty here. Examples include place mats, tablecloths, blankets, shawls, and wall hangings. Open Monday to Friday from 10am to 2pm and 5 to 8pm and on Saturday from 10am to 2pm.

Matador. Avenida de la Constitución, 28. ☎ **95/422-62-47.**

Souvenirs of the city, T-shirts, hammered wrought-iron whatnots, and ceramics—this store carries these and about a dozen other types of unpretentious gift items you might want to display in your private space back home. Open Monday to Friday from 10am to 2pm and 5 to 8pm and on Saturday from 10am to 2pm.

Venecia. Cuna, 51. ☎ **95/422-99-94.**

The venue here is upscale, and the inventory includes lots of items you can certainly do without, but that you might not ever want to. Crystal, art objects, and fanciful accoutrements to the good life as envisioned by bourgeois Spain—it's all here. Open Monday to Friday from 10am to 2pm and 5 to 8:15pm and on Saturday from 10am to 2pm.

JEWELRY

Joyero Abrines. Calle Sierpes, 47. ☎ **95/422-84-55.**

It's the kind of place where grooms have bought engagement and wedding rings for their brides for many generations, and where generations of girlfriends have selected watches and cigarette lighters for the *hombres* of their dreams. There's another branch of this well-known store at Calle de la Asunsión, 28 (☎ 95/427-42-44). Both are open Monday to Friday from 10am to 2pm and 5 to 8:15pm and on Saturday from 10am to 2pm.

MUSIC

Virgin Megastore. Calle Sierpes, 81. ☎ **95/421-21-11.**

It's one of the few stores in Seville that deliberately rejects the Andalusian aesthetic in favor of the rock 'n' roll motif of the rest of Europe and North America. If you're looking for anything from an esoteric and obscure recording of a 19th-century zarzuela, or the punk-rock electronic vibes of an underground band in London, this place is likely to have all of that and more. It also sells computer games (they're the ones who brought Nintendo to Andalusia) and a limited roster of books. Open Monday to Friday from 10am to 2pm and on Saturday from 10am to 9pm.

RIDING GEAR

Arcab. Paseo de Cristóbal Colón, 8. ☎ **95/456-14-11.**

Few other cities in Spain identify their holidays and traditions as closely as Seville does with horseriding. If you're passionately interested in horses (or know someone who is), this place can provide an array of Andalusian-style riding costumes, harnesses, saddles, bridles, and buckles to make you and your mount feel like direct descendents of the conquistadors. Open Monday to Friday from 10am to 2pm and on Saturday from 10am to 9pm.

12 Seville After Dark

OPERA

✪ **Teatro de la Maestranza.** Núñez de Balboa. ☎ **95/422-65-73.**

It wasn't until the 1990s that Seville got its own opera house, but quickly it became one of the world's premier venues for world-class operatic performances. Naturally the focus is on works inspired by Seville itself, including Verdi's *La Forza del Destino* and Mozart's *The Marriage of Figaro.* Jazz, classical music, and even the quintessentially Spanish zarzuelas (operettas) are also performed here. The opera house can't be visited except during performances. Tickets (which vary in price, depending on the event staged) can be purchased daily from 11am to 2pm and 5 to 8pm at the box office in front of the theater.

FLAMENCO

When the moon is high in Seville and the scent of orange blossoms is in the air, it's time to wander the alleyways of the Barrio de Santa Cruz in search of the sound of castanets. Or take a taxi to be on the safe side.

El Arenal. Calle Rodo, 7. ☎ **95/421-64-92.** Cover (including the first drink) 3,700 ptas. ($29.60).

The singers clap, the guitars strum, the tension builds, and the room here feels the ancient and mysterious magic of the flamenco. It's performed here at two shows nightly, every evening at 9:30pm and 11:30pm. No food is served, but drinks are brought to the miniscule tables in a sweltering back room that's endlessly evocative of Old Andalusia.

Los Gallos. Plaza de Santa Cruz, 11. ☎ **95/421-69-81.** Cover (including the first drink) 3,000 ptas. ($24).

Negotiating through the labyrinth of narrow streets of the Barrio de Santa Cruz seems to contribute to the authenticity of reaching this intimate and high-energy flamenco club, devoted to the preservation of the venerable art form. No food is served during the shows, which begin every night at 9 and 11:30pm.

✪ **El Patio Sevillano.** Paseo de Cristóbal Colón, 11. ☎ **95/421-41-20.** Cover (including the first drink) 3,500 ptas. ($28).

In central Seville on the riverbank between two historic bridges, El Patio Sevillano is a showcase for Spanish folksong and dance, performed by exotically costumed dancers. The presentation includes a wide variety of Andalusian flamenco and songs, as well as classical pieces by such composers as de Falla, Albéniz, Granados, and Chueca. March to October, there are three shows nightly, at 7:30, 10, and 11:45pm. There are only two daily shows from November to February, beginning at 7:30 and 10pm.

DRINKS & TAPAS

La Alicantina. Plaza de El Salvador, 2. ☎ **95/422-61-22.**

What is reported to be the best seafood tapas in town are served against a typically Sevillian, glazed-tile decor. Both the bar and the sidewalk tables are always filled to overflowing. The owner serves generous portions of clams marinara, fried squid, grilled shrimp, fried codfish, and clams in béchamel sauce. Located about 5 blocks north of the cathedral, La Alicantina is open daily from 11:30am to 3:30pm and 7:30 to 11:30pm. Tapas range upward from 300 ptas. ($2.40).

Casa Román. Plaza des los Venerables. ☎ **95/421-64-08.**

Tapas are said to have originated in Andalusia, and this old-fashioned bar, incongruously named Román, looks as if it has been dishing them up since day one (actually since 1934). Definitely include this place on your tasca-hopping through the old quarter of the Barrio de Santa Cruz. At the deli counter in front you can make your selection; you might even pick up the fixings for a picnic in the Parque María Luisa. Open Monday to Friday from 9am to 3pm and 5:30pm to 12:30am and on Saturday and Sunday from 10am to 3pm and 6:30pm to 12:30am. Tapas are priced from 550 ptas. ($4.40).

El Rinconcillo. Gerona, 40. ☎ **95/422-31-83.**

El Rinconcillo has a 1930s ambience, partly because of its real age and partly because of its owners' refusal to change one iota of the decor—this has always been one of the most famous bars in Seville. Actually, it may be the oldest bar in Seville, with a history that dates back to 1670. Amid dim lighting, heavy ceiling beams, and iron-based, marble-topped tables, you can enjoy a beer or a full meal along with the rest of the easy-going clientele. The bartender will mark your tab in chalk on a well-worn wooden countertop. El Rinconcillo is especially known for its salads, omelets, hams, and selection of cheeses. Look for the art nouveau tile murals. El Rinconcillo is at the northern edge of the Barrio de Santa Cruz, near the Santa Catalina Church. It's open Thursday to Tuesday from 1pm to 2am. A complete meal will cost around 2,000 ptas. ($16).

Modesto. Cano y Cueto, 5. ☎ **95/441-68-11.**

At the northern end of Murillo Gardens, opening onto a quiet square with flowerboxes and an ornate iron railing, Modesto serves fabulous seafood tapas. The bar is air-conditioned, and you can choose your appetizers just by pointing. Upstairs there's a good-value restaurant, offering a meal for 2,000 ptas. ($16), including such dishes as fried squid, baby sole, grilled sea bass, and shrimp in garlic sauce. Modesto is open daily from 8pm to 2am. Tapas are priced from 200 ptas. ($1.60).

A SPECIAL BAR

✪ **Abades.** Abades, 1. ☎ **95/455-15-69.**

A converted mansion in the Barrio de Santa Cruz has been turned into a rendezvous that has been compared to "a living room in a luxurious movie set." One member of the Spanish press labeled it "wonderfully decadent, similar to the ambience created in a Visconti film." In the heart of the Jewish ghetto, it evokes the style of the Spanish Romantic era. The house dates from the 19th century, when it was constructed around a central courtyard with a fountain. Drinks and low-key conversations are the style here, and since its opening in 1980, visiting literati and glitterati have continually put in their appearances. Young men and women in jeans also patronize the place, enjoying the comfort of the sofas and wicker armchairs.

The ingredients of a special drink called *aqua de Sevilla* are a secret, but we suspect sparkling white wine, pineapple juice, and eggs (the whites and yolks mixed in separately, of course). Classical music is played in the background. Take a taxi to get here at night, as it might not be safe to wander late along the narrow streets of the barrio. In summer, it's open daily from 9pm to 4am; in winter, daily from 8pm to 2:30am.

13 Easy Excursions

CARMONA

21 miles (34km) E of Seville

An easy hour-long bus trip from the main terminal in Seville, Carmona is an ancient city dating from Neolithic times. It grew in power and prestige under the Moors, establishing ties with Castile in 1252.

Surrounded by fortified walls, Carmona has three Moorish fortresses—one a parador and, the other two, the **Alcázar de la Puerta de Córdoba** and **Alcázar de la Puerta de Sevilla.** The top attraction is the **Seville Gate,** with its double Moorish arch, opposite St. Peter's Church. Note, too, the **Córdoba Gate** on Calle Santa María de Gracia, which was attached to the ancient Roman walls in the 17th century.

The town itself is a virtual national landmark, filled with narrow streets, whitewashed walls, and Renaissance mansions. **Plaza de San Fernando** is the most important square, with many elegant 17th-century houses. The most important church is dedicated to **Santa María** and stands on Calle Martín López. You enter a Moorish ablutionary patio before exploring the interior with its 15th-century white vaulting.

A **Roman necropolis (necrópolis Romana) and amphitheater** at Jorge Bonsor contain the remains of a thousand families who lived in and around Carmona 2,000 years ago. Of the two important tombs, the Elephant Vault consists of three dining rooms and a kitchen. The other, the Servilia Tomb, was the size of a nobleman's villa. On site is a **Museo Arqueológico,** displaying artifacts found at the site. It's open April to October, Tuesday to Saturday from 9am to 2pm and on Sunday from 10am to 2pm; off-season, Tuesday to Friday from 10am to 2pm and 4 to 6pm and on Saturday and Sunday from 10am to 2pm. Admission is 225 ptas. ($1.80). If you're driving to Carmona, exit from Seville's eastern periphery onto the N-V superhighway, following the signs to the airport, then to Carmona on the road to Madrid. The Carmona turnoff is clearly marked.

WHERE TO STAY & DINE

✪ **Casa de Carmona.** Plaza de Lasso, 1, 41410 Carmona (Sevilla). ☎ **95/414-33-00,** or 212/686-9213 for reservations in the U.S. Fax 95/414-37-52. 12 rms, 18 suites. A/C MINIBAR TV TEL. 22,000 ptas. ($176) double; 26,000 ptas. ($208) suite. AE, MC, V. Rates increase 30% or so during the Feria de Sevilla and Easter week (Semana Santa). Free parking.

One of the most elegant and intimate hotels in Andalusia, this plush hideaway was originally built as the home of the Lasso family during the 1500s. Several years ago, a team of entrepreneurs added the many features required for a luxury hotel, all the while retaining the marble columns, massive masonry, and graceful proportions of the building's original construction. Set at the edge of the village, the hotel offers an outdoor swimming pool with a flowering terrace, an inner courtyard covered by a canvas awning to guard against the midsummer heat, and a small exercise room. The most visible public room still maintains vestiges of its original function as a library. Each bedroom is a cozy enclave of opulent furnishings, with a distinct decor theme inspired by ancient Rome, medieval Andalusia, or Renaissance Spain.

On the premises is a restaurant whose tables are set up outdoors. Its culinary inspiration derives from modern interpretations of Andalusian and international cuisine, with meals served daily from 1 to 4pm and from 9 to 11:30pm and priced from around 4,000 ptas. ($32) each.

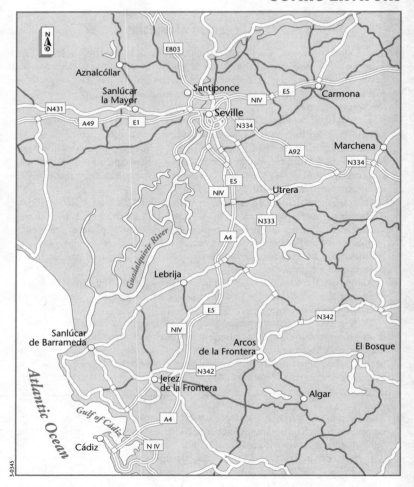

ITÁLICA

5¹/₂ miles (9km) NW of Seville

Lovers of Roman history will flock to Itálica (☎ **95/599-73-76**), the ruins of an ancient city northwest of Seville on the major road to Lisbon, near the small town of Santiponce.

After the battle of Ilipa, Publius Cornelius Scipio Africanus founded Itálica in 206 B.C. Two of the most famous of Roman emperors, Trajan and Hadrian, were born here. Indeed, master builder Hadrian was to have a major influence on his hometown. In his reign the **amphitheater,** the ruins of which can be seen today, was among the largest in the Roman Empire. Lead pipes that carried water from the Guadalquivir River still remain. A small **museum** displays some of the Roman statuary found here, although the finest pieces have been shipped to Seville. Many mosaics, depicting beasts, gods, and birds, are on exhibit, and others are constantly being discovered. The ruins, including a Roman theater, can be explored for 250 ptas. ($2).

The Legacy of Al-Andalus

The Moors who once occupied Andalusia—notably Seville, Granada, and Córdoba—left more than architectural treasures, including the Giralda tower at Seville, the great mosque at Córdoba, or the Alahambra at Granada. Their intellectual and cultural legacy still influence modern life, not only in Spain, but in all of the Western world.

The Arab princesses, the sultans, and their harems are long gone, and can only be enjoyed today in the tales of Washington Irving, but their legend lives on. The Moors (an ethnic mixture of Berbers, Hispano-Romans, and Arabs which made up Andalusia's Muslim population) occupied southern Spain for eight centuries and turned it into a seat of learning. It was a time of soaring achievements in philosophy, medicine, and music.

Of course, the debate still rages over whether this "occupation" was good for Andalusia (or, as the Moors called it, Al-Andalus). Certainly, when the Catholic monarchs, Ferdinand and Isabella, took over and began to persecute the Jewish population as well as the Moors who remained, such an act of racism and anti-Semitism did little to further intellectual activity, agricultural production, or architectural achievement.

Along with the importation of the eggplant and the almond came the Arabian steed, but also breakthroughs in academia, including astronomy and a new and different view of Aristotle.

Such intellectual giants emerged as Maiminides—the El Hakim in Sir Walter Scott's *Talisman*. It's said that Columbus evolved his theories about a new route to the East after hours and hours spent studying the charts of Al-Idrisi, a geographer of the Middle Ages who drew up a world map as early as 1154. Long before its use by the age of explorers in Portugal, Arabs were using the compass as a navigational

The site is open April to September, Tuesday to Saturday from 9am to 6:30pm and on Sunday from 9am to 3pm; October to March, Tuesday to Saturday from 9am to 5:30pm and on Sunday from 10am to 4pm.

If you're driving, exit from the northwest periphery of Seville, following the signs for highway E-803 in the direction of Zafra and Lisbon. But if you don't have a car, take the bus marked CALLE DE SANTIPONCE leaving from Calle Marqués de Parada near the railway station in Seville. Buses depart every hour for the 30-minute trip.

JEREZ DE LA FRONTERA
54 miles (87km) S of Seville

The charming little Andalusian town of Jerez made a name for itself in England with the thousands of casks of golden sherry it shipped there over the centuries. Though its origins date back nearly 3,000 years, Jerez is nonetheless a modern, progressive town with wide boulevards (as well as an interesting old quarter). Busloads of visitors pour in every year to get free drinks at one of the bodegas where wine is aged and bottled.

The town is pronounced both *Her*-ez and *Her*-eth, in Andalusian and Castilian, respectively. The French and the Moors called it various names, including Heres and Scheris, which the English corrupted to Sherry.

aid. Even such astronomical breakthroughs occurred as charting the positions of the planets.

Córdoba's scholars strove to outdistance Baghdad as a center for sciences and the arts, attracting in time Abd al-Rahman II, who introduced the fifth string to the Arab lute, which later led to the development of the six-string guitar.

Abd al-Rahman II even ordained the way food was to be eaten at mealtimes, a legacy that lives to this day. Before, everyone ran around helping themselves to whatever was offered. He devised a method where courses were served in a regimented order, ending with dessert, fruit, and nuts. Many of the old recipes from the Arab cupboard, such as lamb cooked with honey, have been rediscovered by Andalusian chefs.

Arab poetry may also have inspired the first ballads sung by European troubadours, which was to have an enormous impact on later Western literature. Arab numerals, of course, replaced the more awkward Roman system, and Arabs pioneered the science of algebra. Ibn Muadh of Jaén wrote the first European treatise on trigonometry.

Many Spanish words today owe their origins to the Arabic language, including the words *alcázar* for fortress, *arroz* for rice, *naranja* for orange, and *limón* for lemon. The Moors brought an irrigation system to Andalusia, which increased crop production; many of today's systems follow those 1,000-year-old channels. Paper first arrived in Europe through Córdoba.

Though the fanatical Isabel la Católica may have thrown a fit at such a "heretical" idea, it was really a trio of peoples who shaped modern Spain as a nation: the Jews, the Christians, and most definitely the Arabs. The Arabs and the Jews may have been run out of the country during the Middle Ages, but their influence lingers on.

ESSENTIALS

GETTING THERE   By Plane   Iberia and Aviaco offer flights to Jerez Monday to Friday from Barcelona and Zaragoza, as well as daily flights from Madrid. The airport lies about 7 miles (11km) northeast of the city center (follow the signs to Seville). There's an Iberia ticketing and information office located on Plaza de Aluries.

By Train   Trains from Madrid arrive daily. On the TALGO the trip takes 4½ hours. The **railway station** in Jerez lies at Plaza de la Estación (☎ 956/ 34-23-19), at the eastern end of Calle Medina.

By Bus   Bus connections are more frequent than train connections, and the location of the bus terminal is also more convenient. You'll find it on Calle Cartuja, at the corner of Calle Madre de Díos, a 12-minute walk east of the Alcázar. Seven buses a day arrive from Seville (1½ hours). Phone 956/34-10-63 for more information.

By Car   Jerez lies on the highway connecting Seville with Cádiz, Algeciras, Gibraltar, and the ferryboat landing for Tangier, Morocco. There's also an overland road connecting Jerez with Granada and Málaga.

VISITOR INFORMATION   The **tourist information office** is on Calle Larga (☎ 956/33-11-50); to reach it from the bus terminals, take Calle Medina to Calle Honda and continue along as the road turns to the right. The English-speaking staff can provide directions, transportation suggestions, open hours, and so on for any bodega you might want to visit. You'll also be given a map pinpointing the location of various bodegas. Open April to October, Monday to Friday from 8am to 3pm and 5 to 8pm and on Saturday from 10am to 1:30pm; November to March, Monday to Friday from 8am to 3pm and 5 to 7pm and on Saturday from 10am to 2pm.

WHAT TO SEE & DO

✪ TOURING THE BODEGAS   Jerez is not surrounded by vineyards, as you might expect. The vineyards lie to the north and west of Jerez, in the "Sherry Triangle" among the towns of Jerez, Sanlúcar de Barrameda, and El Puerto de Santa María (the latter two on the coast). This is where the best-quality soil is found; it contains an average of 60% chalk, which is ideal for the cultivation of grapes used in sherry production, principally the white Palomino de Jerez. The ideal time to visit is September. However, visitors can count on the finest in hospitality all year round, since Jerez is widely known for the warm welcome it bestows.

There must be more than a hundred bodegas in and around Jerez, where you can not only see how sherries are made, bottled, and aged, but also get free samples. Among the most famous brands are Sandeman, Pedro Domecq, and González Byass, the maker of Tío Pepe.

On a typical visit to a bodega, you'll be shown through several buildings in which sherry and brandy are manufactured. In one building you'll see grapes being pressed and sorted; in another, being bottled; in a third, thousands of large oak casks. Then it's on to an attractive bar where various sherries—amber, dark gold, cream, red, sweet, and velvety—can be sampled. If either is offered, try the very dry La Ina sherry or the Fundador brandy, one of the most popular in the world.

Warning: These drinks are more potent than you might expect.

Most bodegas are open Monday to Friday only, from 10:30am to 1:30pm. Regrettably, many of them are closed in August; many do reopen by the third week of August to prepare for the wine festival in early September.

Of the dozens of bodegas you can visit, the most popular are listed below. Some of them charge an admission fee and require a reservation.

A favorite among British visitors is **Harveys of Bristol,** Calle Arcos, 57 (☎ 959/48-34-00), which doesn't require a reservation. An English-speaking guide leads a 2-hour tour year round, except for the first 3 weeks of August. You should visit Monday to Friday from 7am to 3pm, paying an admission of 300 ptas. ($2.40).

You'll definitely want to visit **Williams & Humbert Limited,** Nuño de Cañas, 1 (☎ 956/33-31-00), which offers tours at noon and 1:30pm Monday to Friday, charging 300 ptas. ($2.40). Their premium brands include the world-famous Dry Sack Medium Sherry, Canasta Cream, Fino Pando, and Manzanilla Alegría, in addition to Gran Duque de Alba Gran Reserva Brandy. It's wise to reserve in advance.

Another famous name is **González Byass,** Manuel María González, 12, (☎ 956/34-00-00); admission is 375 ptas. ($3), and reservations are required. Tours depart at 10am, 11am, noon, and 1pm Monday to Friday. Equally famous is **Pedro Domecq,** Calle San Ildefonso, 3 (☎ 956/15-15-00), requiring a reservation and charging no admission. Tours depart Monday to Friday at 10am, 11am, and noon.

THE DANCING HORSES OF JEREZ   A rival of sorts to Vienna's famous Spanish Riding School is the **Escuela Andaluza del Arte Ecuestre (Andalusian School of Equestrian Art),** Avenida Duque de Abrantes, 11 (☎ 956/31-11-11). In fact, the long, hard schooling that brings horse and rider into perfect harmony originated in this province. The Viennese school was started with Hispano-Arab horses sent from this region, the same steeds you can see today in Jerez. Every Thursday at noon, crowds come to admire the Dancing Horses of Jerez as they perform in a show that includes local folklore. For reservations call 956/60-99-54. Admission is 2,400 ptas. ($19.20) for adults and 975 ptas. ($7.80) for children. Bus: 18.

A NEARBY ATTRACTION

Since many people go to Jerez specifically to visit a bodega, August or weekend closings can be very disappointing. If this happens to you, make a trip to the nearby village of **Lebrija,** about halfway between Jerez and Seville, $8^1/_2$ miles (14km) west of the main highway. A good spot to get a glimpse of rural Spain, Lebrija is a local winemaking center where some very fine sherries originate. At one small bodega, that of Juan García, you're courteously escorted around by the owner. There are several other bodegas in Lebrija, and the local citizens will gladly point them out to you. It's all very casual—lacking the rigidity and formality attached to the bodegas of Jerez.

WHERE TO DINE

El Bosque. Alcalde Álvaro Domecq, 26. ☎ **956/18-08-80.** Reservations required. Main courses 1,800–2,600 ptas. ($14.40–$20.80); fixed-price menus 4,500–9,500 ptas. ($36–$76). AE, DC, MC, V. Mon–Sat 1:30–5pm and 8:30pm–1am. SPANISH/INTERNATIONAL.

Lying less than a mile northeast of the city center, the city's most elegant restaurant was established just after World War II. A favorite of the sherry-producing aristocracy, it retains a strong emphasis on bullfighting memorabilia, which make up most of the decoration.

Order the excellent rabo de toro (bull's-tail stew) if you're truly going native. You might begin with a soothing Andalusian gazpacho, then try one of the fried fish dishes such as hake Seville style. Rice with king prawns and baby shrimp omelets are deservedly popular dishes. Occasionally, Laguna duck in honey with chestnuts and pears is a feature. The desserts are usually good, including the pistachio ice cream.

⑤ Gaitán. Calle Gaitán, 3. ☎ **956/34-58-59.** Reservations recommended. Main courses 950–2,400 ptas. ($7.60–$19.20). AE, DC, MC, V. Mon–Sat 1–4:30pm and 8:30–11:30pm, Sun 1–4:30pm. ANDALUSIAN.

This small restaurant near the Puerta Santa María is owned by Juan Hurtado, who has won acclaim for the food served here. Surrounded by walls displaying celebrity photographs, you can enjoy such Andalusian dishes as garlic soup, various stews, duck à la Sevillana, and fried seafood. One special dish is lamb cooked with honey, based on a recipe so ancient it goes back to the Muslim occupation of Spain. For dessert, the almond tart is a favorite.

Restaurante Tendido 6. Calle Circo, 10. ☎ **956/34-48-35.** Reservations required. Main courses 400–2,000 ptas. ($3.20–$16). AE, DC, MC, V. Mon–Sat noon–4pm and 8–11:30pm. SPANISH.

This combination restaurant and tapas bar has loyal clients who come from many walks of life. The chef creates a dignified regional cuisine that includes grilled rump steak, fish soup, and a wide array of Spanish dishes, including Basque and Castilian. There's nothing really exciting here, but the long-tested recipes are filled with flavor and the place is a good value. The Tendido is on the south side of Plaza de Toros.

Appendix

A Basic Phrases & Vocabulary

English	Spanish	Pronunciation
Hello	**Buenos días**	*bway*-noss *dee*-ahss
How are you?	**¿Como está usted?**	koh-moh ess-*tah* oo-*steth*
Very well	**Muy bien**	mwee byen
Thank you	**Gracias**	*gra*-thee-ahss
Good-bye	**Adiós**	ad-*dyohss*
Please	**Por favor**	pohr fah-*bohr*
Yes	**Sí**	see
No	**No**	noh
Excuse me	**Pardóneme**	pahr-*doh*-neh-may
Give me . . .	**Deme . . .**	*day*-may . . .
Where is . . . ?	**¿Donde está . . . ?**	*dohn*-day ess-*tah*. . . ?
the station	**la estación**	la ess-tah-*thyohn*
a hotel	**un hotel**	oon oh-*tel*
a restaurant	**un restaurante**	oon res-tow-*rahn*-tay
the toilet	**el servicio**	el ser-*vee*-the-o
To the right	**A la derecha**	ah lah day-*ray*-chuh
To the left	**A la izquierda**	ah lah eeth-*kyehr*-duh
Straight ahead	**Adelante**	ah-day-*lahn*-tay
I would like . . .	**Quiero . . .**	*kyehr*-oh . . .
to eat	**comer**	ko-*mayr*
a room	**una habitación**	*oo*-nah ah-bee-tah-*hyon*
the check	**la cuenta**	la *kwen*-tah
How much?	**¿Cuánto?**	*kwahn*-toh
When?	**¿Cuándo?**	*kwan*-doh
Yesterday	**Ayer**	ah-*yeyr*
Today	**Hoy**	oy
Tomorrow	**Mañana**	mah-*nyah*-nah
Breakfast	**Desayuno**	deh-sai-*yoo*-noh
Lunch	**Comida**	ko-*mee*-dah
Dinner	**Cena**	*thay*-nah

NUMBERS

1	**uno** (*oo*-noh)	3	**tres** (trayss)
2	**dos** (dose)	4	**cuatro** (*kwah*-troh)

5	**cinco** (*theen*-koh)	17	**dezassete** (dehz-ai-*saih*-teh)
6	**seis** (*sayss*)	18	**dieciocho** (*dyeth-ee-oh*-choh)
7	**sieti** (*syeh*-tay)	19	**diecinueve** (dyeth-ee-*nyway*-bay)
8	**ocho** (*oh*-choh)	20	**veinte** (*bayn*-tey)
9	**nueve** (*nway*-bay)	30	**treinta** (*trayn*-tah)
10	**diez** (dyeth)	40	**cuarenta** (kwah-*ren*-tah)
11	**once** (*ohn*-thay)	50	**cincuenta** (theen-*kwhen*-tah)
12	**doce** (*doh*-thay)	60	**sesenta** (say-*sen*-tah)
13	**trece** (*tray*-thay)	70	**setenta** (say-*ten*-tah)
14	**catorce** (kah-*tor*-thay)	80	**ochenta** (oh-*chayn*-tah)
15	**quince** (*keen*-thay)	90	**noventa** (noh-*ben*-tah)
16	**dieciséis**(dyeth-ee-*sayss*)	100	**cien/ciento** (thyen/ *thyen*-toe)

B Menu Savvy

alliolo   sauce made from garlic and olive oil

arroz amb feseola i naps   rice with beans and turnips

arroz con costra   rice dish of chicken, rabbit, sausages, black pudding, chickpeas, spices, and pork meatballs—everything "hidden" under a layer of beaten egg crust

arroz empedrado   rice cooked with tomatoes and cod and a top layer of white beans

bacalao al ajo arriero   cod-and-garlic dish named after Leonese mule drivers

bacalao al pil-pil   cod with garlic and chile peppers

bacalao a la vizcaina   cod with dried peppers and onion

bajoques farcides   peppers stuffed with rice, pork, tomatoes, and spices

butifarra   Catalonian sausage made with blood, spices, and eggs

caldereta   stew or a stew pot

caldereta extremeña   kid or goat stew

caldillo de perro   "dog soup," made with onions, fresh fish, and orange juice

caldo gallego   soup made with cabbage, potatoes, beans, and various meat flavorings

caseolada   potato-and-vegetable stew with bacon and ribs

chanfaina salmantina   rice, giblets, lamb sweetbreads, and pieces of *chorizo*

chilindrón   sauce made from tomatoes, peppers, garlic, and *chorizo*

chorizo   spicy pork sausage

cochifrito navarro   small pieces of fried lamb

cocido de pelotas   stew of minced meat wrapped in cabbage leaves and cooked with poultry, bacon, chickpeas, potatoes, and spices

cocido español   Spanish stew

cocido madrileña   chickpea stew of Madrid, with potatoes, cabbage, turnips, beef, marrow, bacon, *chorizo,* and black pudding

empanada   crusted pie of Galicia, with a variety of fillings

escudella   Catalán version of chickpea stew

fabada   white-bean stew of Asturias

habas a la catalana   stew of broad beans, herbs, and spices

Judías blancas   haricot beans

Judías negras   runner beans

lacón con grelos   salted ham with turnip tops

magras con tomate   slices of slightly fried ham dipped in tomato sauce

mar y cielo   "sea and heaven," made with sausages, rabbit, shrimp, and fish

merluza a la gallega   Galician hake with onion, potatoes, and herbs

merluza a la sidra   hake cooked with cider
morcilla   black sausage akin to black pudding
paella alicantina   rice dish made with chicken and rabbit
pato a la naranja   duck with orange, an old Valencian dish
pericana   cod, olive oil, dry peppers, and garlic
picada   sauce made from nuts, parsley, garlic, saffron, and cinnamon
pilota   ball made of meat, parsley, breadcrumbs, and eggs
pinchito   small kebab
pisto manchego   vegetable stew from La Mancha
pollo a la chilindrón   chicken cooked in a tomato, onion, and pepper sauce
romesco   Mediterranean sauce, with olive oil, red pepper, bread, garlic, and maybe
cognac
salsa verde   green sauce to accompany fish
samfaina   sauce made from tomatoes, eggplant, onions, and zucchini
sangría   drink made with fruit, brandy, and wine
sofrito   sauce made from peppers, onions, garlic, tomatoes, and olive oil
sopa de ajo castellana   garlic soup with ham, bread, eggs, and spices
sopa castellanas   bread, broth, ham, and sometimes a poached egg and garlic
tapas   small dishes or appetizers served with drinks at a tavern
tortilla de patatas   Spanish omelet with potatoes
trucha a la navarra   trout fried with a piece of ham
turrón   almond paste
zarzuela   fish stew

Index

Madrid

FROMMER'S COMPLETE TRAVEL GUIDES

(Comprehensive guides to destinations around the world, with selections in all price ranges—from deluxe to budget)

Acapulco/Ixtapa/Zihuatenjo
Alaska
Amsterdam
Arizona
Atlanta
Australia
Austria
Bahamas
Bangkok
Barcelona, Madrid & Seville
Belgium, Holland & Luxembourg
Berlin
Bermuda
Boston
Budapest & the Best of Hungary
California
Canada
Cancún, Cozumel & the Yucatán
Caribbean
Caribbean Cruises & Ports of Call
Caribbean Ports of Call
Carolinas & Georgia
Chicago
Colorado
Costa Rica
Denver, Boulder & Colorado Springs
Dublin
England

Florida
France
Germany
Greece
Hawaii
Hong Kong
Honolulu/Waikiki/Oahu
Ireland
Italy
Jamaica & Barbados
Japan
Las Vegas
London
Los Angeles
Maryland & Delaware
Maui
Mexico
Mexico City
Miami & the Keys
Montana & Wyoming
Montréal & Québec City
Munich & the Bavarian Alps
Nashville & Memphis
Nepal
New England
New Mexico
New Orleans
New York City
Northern New England
Nova Scotia, New Brunswick & Prince Edward Island

Paris
Philadelphia & the Amish Country
Portugal
Prague & the Best of the Czech Republic
Puerto Rico
Puerto Vallarta, Manzanillo & Guadalajara
Rome
San Antonio & Austin
San Diego
San Francisco
Santa Fe, Taos & Albuquerque
Scandinavia
Scotland
Seattle & Portland
South Pacific
Spain
Switzerland
Thailand
Tokyo
Toronto
U.S.A.
Utah
Vancouver & Victoria
Vienna
Virgin Islands
Virginia
Walt Disney World & Orlando
Washington, D.C.
Washington & Oregon

FROMMER'S FRUGAL TRAVELER'S GUIDES

(The grown-up guides to budget travel, offering dream vacations at down-to-earth prices)

Australia from $45 a Day
Berlin from $50 a Day
California from $60 a Day
Caribbean from $60 a Day
Costa Rica & Belize from $35 a Day
Eastern Europe from $30 a Day

England from $50 a Day
Europe from $50 a Day
Florida from $50 a Day
Greece from $45 a Day
Hawaii from $60 a Day
India from $40 a Day
Ireland from $45 a Day
Italy from $50 a Day

Israel from $45 a Day
London from $60 a Day
Mexico from $35 a Day
New York from $70 a Day
New Zealand from $45 a Day
Paris from $60 a Day
Washington, D.C. from $50 a Day

FROMMER'S PORTABLE GUIDES

(Pocket-size guides for travelers who want everything in a nutshell)

Charleston & Savannah   Las Vegas   Washington, D.C.   New Orleans   San Francisco

FROMMER'S FAMILY GUIDES

(The complete guides for successful family vacations)

California with Kids	New England with Kids	San Francisco with Kids
Los Angeles with Kids	New York City with Kids	Washington, D.C. with Kids

FROMMER'S AMERICA ON WHEELS

(Everything you need for a successful road trip, including full-color road maps and ratings for every hotel)

California & Nevada	Midwest & the Great	Northwest & the	Southwest
Florida	Lake States	Great Plains States	Texas & the South-
Mid-Atlantic	New York & the New	Southeast	Central States
	England States		

FROMMER'S WALKING TOURS

(Memorable neighborhood strolls through the world's great cities)

Berlin	Montréal & Québec City	Spain's Favorite Cities
Chicago	New York	Tokyo
England's Favorite Cities	Paris	Venice
London	San Francisco	Washington, D.C.

SPECIAL-INTEREST TITLES

Arthur Frommer's Branson!
Arthur Frommer's New World of Travel
The Civil War Trust's Official Guide to the
　Civil War Discovery Trail
Frommer's America's 100 Best-Loved State
　Parks
Frommer's Caribbean Hideaways
Frommer's Complete Hostel Vacation Guide to
　England, Scotland & Wales
Frommer's Food Lover's Companion to France
Frommer's Food Lover's Companion to Italy
Frommer's Great European Driving Tours

Frommer's National Park Guide
Outside Magazine's Adventure Guide to New
　England
Outside Magazine's Adventure Guide to
　Northern California
Places Rated Almanac
Retirement Places Rated
USA Sports Traveler's and TV Viewer's
　Golf Tournament Guide
USA Sports Minor League Baseball Book
USA Today Golf Atlas
Wonderful Weekends from NYC

FROMMER'S IRREVERENT GUIDES

(Wickedly honest guides for sophisticated travelers)

Amsterdam	Manhattan	Paris	U.S. Virgin Islands
Chicago	Miami	San Francisco	Walt Disney World
London	New Orleans	Santa Fe	Washington, D.C.

UNOFFICIAL GUIDES

(Get the unbiased truth from these candid, value-conscious guides)

Atlanta	Euro Disneyland	Mini-Mickey
Branson, Missouri	The Great Smoky & Blue	Skiing in the West
Chicago	Ridge Mountains	Walt Disney World
Cruises	Las Vegas	Walt Disney World Companion
Disneyland	Miami & the Keys	Washington, D.C.

BAEDEKER

(With four-color photographs and a free pull-out map)

Amsterdam	Florence	London	Scotland
Athens	Florida	Mexico	Singapore
Austria	Germany	New York	South Africa
Bali	Great Britain	Paris	Spain
Belgium	Greece	Portugal	Switzerland
Budapest	Greek Islands	Prague	Thailand
California	Hawaii	Provence	Tokyo
Canada	Hong Kong	Rome	Turkish Coast
Caribbean	Ireland	San Francisco	Tuscany
China	Israel	St. Petersburg	Venice
Copenhagen	Italy	Scandinavia	Vienna
Crete	Lisbon		

FROMMER'S BY NIGHT GUIDES

(The series for those who know that life begins after dark)

Amsterdam	London	Miami	Paris
Chicago	Los Angeles	New Orleans	San Francisco
Las Vegas	Manhattan		

FROMMER'S BEST BEACH VACATIONS

(The top places to sun, stroll, shop, stay, play, party, and swim, with ratings for each beach)

California	Hawaii	New England
Carolinas & Georgia	Mid-Atlantic (from New	
Florida	York to Washington, D.C.)	

FROMMER'S BED & BREAKFAST GUIDES

(Selective guides with four-color photos and full descriptions of the best inns in each region)

California	Great American Cities	New England	The Rockies
Caribbean	Hawaii	Pacific Northwest	Southwest

FROMMER'S DRIVING TOURS

(Four-color photos and detailed maps outlining spectacular scenic driving routes)

Australia	France	Italy	Spain
Austria	Germany	Scandinavia	Switzerland
Britain	Ireland	Scotland	U.S.A.
Florida			

FROMMER'S BORN TO SHOP

(The ultimate guides for travelers who love to shop)

France	Hong Kong	Mexico
Great Britain	London	New York

TRAVEL & LEISURE GUIDES

(Sophisticated pocket-size guides for discriminating travelers)

Amsterdam	Hong Kong	New York	San Francisco
Boston	London	Paris	Washington, D.C.